W9-ADV-830

THE POLITICS OF KOREAN NATIONALISM

PUBLISHED UNDER THE AUSPICES OF
The Center for Japanese Studies
UNIVERSITY OF CALIFORNIA, BERKELEY

CHONG-SIK LEE

THE POLITICS OF KOREAN NATIONALISM

1965
BERKELEY AND LOS ANGELES

UNIVERSITY OF CALIFORNIA PRESS

University of California Press
Berkeley and Los Angeles, California
Cambridge University Press
London, England

Second Printing, 1965
Library of Congress Catalog Card Number 63-19029
Printed in the United States of America

To Robert A. Scalapino

Preface

THE NATIONALISM of the new independent countries is one of the most important forces in the world today. The twentieth century has been an era of national revolutions, and the events of this era are likely to have a prolonged impact upon those of the future.

Awareness of the significance of this sociopolitical force has led many scholars to explore the development of nationalism and nationalist movements. Increased knowledge of the factors involved in these developments, of the pattern of behavior exhibited by the nationalists, and of the reaction of particular groups toward certain external forces and influences should contribute greatly toward an understanding both of the particular nations concerned and also of politics and human behavior in general.

It was with this assumption that I undertook this study of the nationalist movement in Korea. There are two major dimensions to the work. Essentially it is an account of the struggles of the Koreans against an alien regime to regain their independence. (The word "regain" is used because Korea, although for centuries a vassal kingdom under imperial China, was for all practical purposes independent until the latter part of the nineteenth century.) But it attempts also to discover uniformities and recurring patterns that might contribute to the understanding of political movements in general.

There are five parts. Part I examines the Yi dynasty in Korea (1392–1910), particularly the latter half. Certain social, political, and intellectual aspects of the old society are analyzed in an attempt to determine their consequences. This part provides a view of the background against which the early mass movements were carried out. The traditions of old Korea were important determinants of both the values and the behavior of the nationalists.

Part II deals with the changes that culminated in the Japanese annexation in 1910. It begins with the Tonghak rebellion of 1894–1895, which precipitated the first Sino-Japanese war and made manifest the weaknesses of the old regime. Also examined are the origins of the Sino-Japanese war, the repercussions of the war upon the Korean government, the attempts by progressives to regenerate Korean society and prevent the downfall of the kingdom, and the process through which Korea lost her sovereignty.

After Japan gained dominion over Korea, the Japanese governors-general ruled the country with great severity until the "March First movement" took place in 1919. Part III examines Japanese rule in this period and its consequences. It also examines the March First movement, which was an explosion of pent-up emotions against alien, authoritarian rule and at the same time a manifestation of growing nationalism in Korea.

The events of 1919 precipitated a revival of nationalist activity by Koreans residing abroad. Many nationalists made efforts at establishing a government-in-exile and attempted to unify the movement. Many others in various parts of the world continued their stubborn struggles against the Japanese. Part IV deals with the activities of the nationalists abroad until the liberaton of their homeland in 1945.

Despite the movements abroad, Japanese control over Korea never wavered. It was obvious to all that Japanese rule could not be terminated by the Koreans alone and that the Japanese would not voluntarily withdraw. But the Koreans within the country carried on various nationalistic movements, striving to maintain national consciousness among the people, and, indeed, there were some incidents of mass demonstrations. Part V deals with the activities of nationalists within Korea against the background of Japanese rule. A short chapter of conclusions follows Part V.

Although the treatment is chronological, except insofar as events in Parts IV and V were concurrent, I have attempted, at what seemed appropriate points in the narrative, to single out the major problems and distinctive characteristics. For example, special attention has been paid to the question of values and ideology. The interaction and conflict of conservatism, progressive liberalism, and radicalism are noted. Particularly after 1920, communism became significant; this development is studied in detail. The nationalist movement is also studied as a political movement, with particular focus upon the roles of the elite and the masses. Especially in Part IV, where the movement in exile is examined, prominent attention is given to the problem of factionalism, its causes and consequences.

It is necessary to discuss some of the terms used. "Nationalism" is used as the word was defined by the Royal Institute of International Affairs: "a consciousness, on the part of individuals or groups, of membership in a nation, or a desire to forward the strength, liberty, or prosperity of a nation . . ." This definition is applicable to both the earlier nationalists and the later nationalists abroad who strove to regain Korean independence, as well as to those within Korea who followed the gradualist approach and sought to strengthen the Korean nation. "Nation" is used to denote an aggregate of individuals united by political ties, and ties of race, religion, language, or tradition. Although these definitions may not be precise, they serve here because Korea has had a long history as a distinctive political unit. "Nationalist" is applied to persons and groups who aspired and worked to foster and achieve nationalism.

One term presents special problems in assigning it a definition and category. It is the term "Communist." Although it is relatively easy to define and identify a nationalist, to categorize those persons involved in Communist activities is a much more complex task. Difficulty arises because, although the Communists of Korea espoused international communism and were dedicated to the cause of establishing a Communist society, they also advocated the liberation of the homeland. There is further complication because many Koreans became Communists as a result, at least in part, of nationalist aspirations. Many of those who later became adamant Communists joined the Communist camp in the belief that the goal of Korean independence would thereby be best served.

It is very difficult, however, to determine precisely whether a certain Communist was dedicated more to communism or to nationalism. Those persons and groups who participated to a significant extent in the nationalist movement, Communist-oriented or not, are included in this study. I have excluded those whose activities were addressed primarily to Communist ends, or have dealt with them summarily.

A final word concerning my general attitude and the limitations of the work is necessary. Since the subject is complex and the data are vast, I am obliged to be both humble and tentative. Although all known available materials were scrutinized and every opportunity was utilized to question the persons involved in the movement, I cannot overlook the possibility that some errors have crept into the factual account. The same qualification would also apply to my interpretations of data. Further, every historian and social scientist would no doubt recognize that one's predispositions and sympathies are very difficult to surmount, no matter how objective and scientific one may strive to be. I am cognizant of the possibility of prejudice and have made every effort to support my assertions with reliable data. But I cannot lay claim to being totally immune to prejudices.

One apologetic note toward my compatriots, the Koreans, must be offered. Alexis de Tocqueville wrote in the Preface to *The Old Regime and the French Revolution* many years ago:

> I have not shrunk from wounding the feelings of individuals and classes [nor from] affronting certain opinions and ancient loyalties, laudable though these may be. In so doing I have often felt regret but never any qualms of conscience, and I can only hope that those who may be inclined to take offense at anything in this book will realize that its author has aimed at complete honesty and impartiality.

I share the feelings of Tocqueville and offer his statement as the expression of my own.

I AM INDEBTED to many persons and institutions for making the writing and publication of this book possible. I owe a primary debt to Professor Robert A. Scalapino, at whose suggestion I undertook the study. He is responsible for making many of the documentary sources for this book in Japan and Korea accessible to me and securing many other documents of importance for the University of California Library. He has read the manuscript at various stages and offered invaluable criticism. Professor Paw-key Sohn was very generous with his time and his private documentary collections. I have been fortunate to receive his guidance on various aspects of Korean history. I also owe a special debt to Mr. Key P. Yang of the Library of Congress, whose advice and assistance was far beyond the call of duty. I am grateful to Professors Michael C. Rogers, Paul Seabury, and Henry W. Ehrmann, for reading the manuscript at an earlier stage and offering advice. I had the benefit of Professor Edward W. Wagner's reading of the first chapter of the final draft.

Mrs. Margaret Uridge and Mrs. Jeannot Nyles of the Interlibrary Borrowing Service of the University of California were very generous in their assistance. My thanks go also to Miss Elizabeth Huff and her staff at the East Asiatic Library and Mrs. Anne Reed and her staff of the Newspaper Division, both of the University of California, Berkeley, for unfailing help. I was generously assisted by librarians at the Hoover Institution on War, Revolution, and Peace, the Harvard-Yenching Institute Library, and the East Asiatic Library of Columbia University. I am indebted to Mr. Chin Ha Choy, the president of the Korean National Association in Los Angeles, for authorizing me to use the files of *Shinhan Minbo*. I wish to thank Mr. Kingsley Lyu, then of the Library of Congress, for showing me his unpublished manuscript.

I am grateful to the Committees on Research at the University of California, Berkeley, and at Dartmouth College, which came to my aid with grants at critical points in the preparation of the manuscript. I am also indebted to the Center for Japanese Studies, Institute of International Relations, University of California, Berkeley, for their support in the publication of this book.

My vote of thanks also goes to four of my senior colleagues at Dartmouth, Professors Henry W. Ehrmann, Gene M. Lyons, Wing-tsit Chan, and Colin Campbell, whose encouragement and assistance were most appreciated. I should also like to acknowledge my debts for moral support and sympathy of Mrs. Dee Scalapino, to my wife, Myung Sook Lee, and to many friends. My final note of profound gratitude goes to my editor, Jesse M. Phillips, whose wisdom and patience made this a much better book than it would otherwise have been. Of course, I am alone responsible for the content.

I should like to add that this book is based on my doctoral dissertation, "Korean Nationalist Movement, 1905–1945," submitted to the University of California, Berkeley, in 1961. For reasons of space and readability, I had to reduce much of the information contained therein. To those few who wish to explore some of the events covered in this book in more detail, I recommend a reading of appropriate sections of the dissertation.

With few exceptions, I have followed the customary rule of presenting Oriental names with the family name first. I have generally followed the McCune-Reichauer system of transliteration of Korean words.

Hanover, New Hampshire C-S. L.
April, 1963

Contents

I

Dynastic Korea

1

Legacy of the Past

THE "PAST" is a relative term. Legend puts the founding of Korea at some four thousand years ago. At least two thousand of these years can be traced by documents. Since our interest lies in understanding the motives and behavior of the Korean nationalists of recent times, we can confine our study of the past to the aspects of life which were fundamental to political behavior, and it will be sufficient for our purpose to note some of the legacies of the Yi dynasty, which came into power in 1392 and lasted until 1910. This is possible because the Yi dynasty espoused one dogma, and this dogma synthesized the traits that had been handed on from the earlier past and developed new ones.

Yi Korea was governed by the strict application of Confucian precepts. As early as the Three Kingdoms period in China (A.D. 221–265), Confucianism had been transmitted from its homeland into Korea, but it did not flourish until the early part of the Yi period, when it rapidly gained strength because the founder of the dynasty used it to counter the influence of Buddhism, which had been espoused by the preceding Koryŏ dynasty. Through official patronage Confucianism came eventually to dominate every aspect of life in Korea. It molded the thought patterns of the people—the national character

—as well as the cultural, political, social, and economic patterns of the nation. It is not an over-statement to describe the Yi Korea as a Confucian dynasty.

The early Yi period, up to the reign of Sŏngjong (1469–1494), witnessed much progress in government administration, science, agriculture, and military preparedness, and during the reign of Sejong (1418–1450) remarkable technological advances were made, particularly in astronomy, printing, and climatology, in some respects surpassing the contemporary achievements in Europe. Even the Confucianism of the early period was not yet the metaphysical and abstract doctrine of Chu Hsi (1130–1200) that monopolized the later period. Emphasis was placed, rather, on practical methods that would be of help in governing. But what finally became anchored in Korea was the orthodoxy of Chu Hsi. By the time of the purges of literati, during the reign of Yŏnsangun (1494–1506), the followers of this doctrine had entrenched themselves around the royal court and academies and were dominant in intellectual and political affairs.[1]

In metaphysical and abstract characteristics the teachings of Chu Hsi are analogous to those of Plato. The main stress is on the principle, or nature, of phenomena—the Platonic essence. Every phenomenon, according to Chu Hsi, had its principle (*li*), and the highest activity anyone could undertake was that of searching constantly for the objective principle and cultivating himself so that he might transcend the phenomenal world and enter the world of pure and perfect ideas. A few paragraphs from Chu's writings will illustrate this:

> Confucius spoke of "the conquest of self and return to propriety." The Doctrine of the Mean says: "Advance toward equilibrium and harmony"; or again: "Prize the virtuous nature and pursue the path of inquiry and study." The Great Learning speaks of "the exemplification of illustrious virtue." And the Book of History says: "The mind of the body is unstable; the mind of the spirit is but small. Be discriminating; be undivided, that you may sincerely hold fast to the mean." The teachings of the sage, whether they be a thousand or ten thousand words, are only that man should preserve Heavenly Principle (*T'ien li*) and extinguish human desire (*jen yu*).
>
> Man's nature is originally clear, but it is like a pearl immersed in impure water, where its luster cannot be seen. Being removed from the dirty water, however, it becomes lustrous of itself as before. If each person could himself realize that it is human desire that causes this obscuring, this would

bring enlightenment (*ming*). It is only on this point alone that all one's efforts must be concentrated.

At the same time, however, one should pursue the "investigation of things." Today investigate one thing, and tomorrow investigate another. Then, just as when mobile troops storm a besieged city or capture a fortified spot, human desire will automatically be dissolved away.[2]

It was this abstract, metaphysical, and intuitional philosophy that governed the Korean kingdom. Confucianism, as Chu Hsi had expounded it, became not only the guide and tool for the conduct of government, but also the ruling principle of social and familial life. The result was the development of a closed society characterized by rigidity, blandness, and stagnation. Chu Hsi-ism, as it can be called, was a high philosophy, virtuous in its aspiration. Its success, however, revealed its weaknesses. Beneath the surface forms of virtue and propriety seethed intense competitiveness, and outbreaks of ferocity were not lacking. Especially in the late seventeenth and early eighteenth century any actual or alleged deviation from the principles of Chu Hsi was persecuted. The penalty could be loss of position, honor, and even life, and such persecution was used by rival elite factions for grasping political power rather than for the settlement of disputes over theory.[3]

According to MacIver, social stratification is a universal phenomenon.[4] If this generalization is true of ancient and medieval Europe, it is even more so in the case of Asia; but between the social orders of Europe and Asia a clear distinction can be made in the factors determining status. Whereas social rank in Europe was determined largely by wealth, the single most important factor in Asia, particularly in the northeast, was learning. In China, as Weber has remarked, social rank was determined "more by qualification for office than by wealth." [5] In Korea, as also in Japan, the Chinese system was the model for the sociopolitical structure—a hierarchy of scholars, farmers, artisans, and merchants. But different environments and other influences produced some departures from the model. One most noticeable feature in Japan was that the uppermost class came to be not the scholar-officials, but the warriors. Korea adhered more closely to the model, but its society was caste-ridden.

In China there was a substantial degree of social mobility. Although a bureaucratic gentry formed the upper stratum, "a plebeian could also acquire a knowledge of writing," and, if he did this successfully, "he shared the prestige of any other scholar. . . . Even in the feudal period the stratum of literati was not hereditary or exclusive." [6] In Korea, as in China, the civil service examination was the principal way open for anyone to ascend in social status, but no Korean was allowed to take the examination unless he were born in an upper-class family, and commoners and members of the lowly class were altogether excluded.[7]

It was not only immobility that characterized the social system in Korea. There, as in Japan, the classes were demarked with detailed, rigid stratification. Each class and subclass was bound by minute restrictions, enforced by aristocrats, which defined the mode of life even to the particulars of clothing, food, and habitation. In Korea the hierarchical divisions, as recognized by most historians, were the yangban, the professionals, the commoners, and the lowly or the pariahs.

Thus at the top was the yangban ("two ranks," or "two groups") class. The name was originally used in the Koryŏ dynasty to indicate collectively the *tongban* ("East group"), who were the civil officers, and the *sŏban* ("West group"), who were the military. Since social status was of a hereditary nature, the term "yangban" came to denote the nobility in general. Among the yangbans the highest status was held by sons of legitimate marriages; next were sons by concubines. Even among the yangbans only the sons of legitimate marriages were allowed to take the highest grades of examinations. Sons of concubines were restricted to those for professional or technical posts.

Except for the qualification by descent for taking the examinations, marked resemblances can be seen in the Chinese and Korean literati. In both countries they sought government service not only as a source of income, but as their normal field of activity. "Constitutionally—and this was the theory of the Confucians—the emperor [of China, and likewise the king of Korea,] could rule *only* by using certified literati as officials; 'Classically' he could rule only by using orthodox Confucian officials"; and only those adept in Confucian principles and traditions could be considered "competent for correctly ordering the internal administration and the charismatically correct life conduct of the prince, ritually and politically." [8] In Korea, under these age-old principles, yangbans educated in Confucianism monopolized the government positions; education was a privilege enjoyed mostly, if not solely, by the yangban and professional classes.[9]

All the grades of the civil service examinations except those for the professional class (one level lower than the yangbans) were, like the examinations in China, "intended as tests in penmanship, in style, in mastery of classic writings, and finally . . . in conformity with the prescribed mental outlook." [10] The successful examinees—that is, the ones appointed to offices—were provided with prebends befitting their rank and accorded corresponding social prestige and honor.[11] But whereas in China the movement in the stratum of literati and gentry was both upward and downward, depending on the ability a man displayed in the examinations, a yangban's failure or nonappointment did not deprive him of his social status. Regardless of intellectual capacity, the yangbans held to the notion that the only possible role for them was that of cultivating themselves in order to transcend the phenomenal world and attain self-perfection and thus be prepared to be of service to the king.

Because a man was born a yangban, any profession other than government service was a disgrace for him and his family. Consequently most of the yangbans, owing to the disproportion between the numbers competing in the examinations and the positions open to those who passed, were idle, living parasitically on the more successful members of their families.[12] The eventual result of this exclusive and hereditary system was that a significant element of Korean society lived in idleness and worse:

> Even if they were in poverty, they would rather die of hunger than work to earn the necessities. They also live by means of robbery, fraud and extortion. The largest number of them are addicted to gambling, drunkenness and debauchery.[13]

Of course, not all the yangbans fell into this depth of degradation, but there seem to have been few exceptions in the latter part of the Yi dynasty. An extreme dogma intent on producing a nation of saints had created practically the opposite.

The yangbans were beyond anyone's control. In theory Korea was ruled under an absolute monarchial system. The king was to be the benefactor of all and the keeper of justice; he was to see to it that the laws were strictly obeyed and that justice was rendered to all his subjects, whom he was to protect from the exactions of high officials. This theory was generally practiced during the first hundred years of the Yi dynasty and intermittently afterward by some of the capable kings. But in many instances the king died and left infant heirs or no direct successors. The authority for choosing a new sovereign then fell to the court officials and the royal relatives, who engaged in struggles to enthrone a king favorable to their interests or to install a regent who was of their own family. Said a foreign observer in the late nineteenth century:

> Usually the throne is occupied by do-nothings, by corrupt natures who are rotten with debauchery, old before their time, besotted and utterly incapable. . . . The great aristocratic families, profiting by several successive regencies and by occupation of the throne by two or three insignificant sovereigns, have absorbed nearly complete authority. Koreans are beginning to repeat that the king sees nothing, knows nothing, and can do nothing.[14]

The competition between rival groups at the court was fierce. In order to sustain, prolong, or perpetuate a hard-won position in the government, many of the unscrupulous scholar-politicians resorted to murder to get rid of their enemies, and in order to forestall revenge by relatives of the victims they arranged to exterminate these potential enemies as well. Continuous factional struggles narrowed the concern of most of the officials to the interest of family, clan, or, at most, faction. Thus the welfare of the country was generally neglected.[15]

During the last three hundred years of the Yi dynasty many an able statesman was removed or killed in the intrigues, plots, and purges that drove all the factions to extremes. Some efforts to eliminate factionalism were made in the reigns of Yŏngjo (1724–1776) and Chŏngjo (1776–1800), but in vain. The reforms attempted by progressive scholars and politicians were inevitably linked with the factional controversies by jealous opponents and, consequently, totally impeded.[16]

There remains an important distinction within the yangban class to be noted. Despite a laudable history of military victories in the Three Kingdoms and Koryŏ periods, the military profession was looked upon as degraded by the Yi dynasty. The scholars repeated the saying that "men of letters must be prepared in armaments," but men of noble birth shunned military life as something ignoble.

During this long period of isolation and almost unbroken peace, opportunities for attaining distinction in warfare were practically nonexistent, and it was natural that the yangbans should turn to what were regarded as nobler pursuits. Impelled by a passion to ascend to the status of a Confucian princely man, which entailed the mastery of philosophy and literature, they left the military life for persons of the lower classes. Although most of the yangbans were unemployed, nothing but the best satisfied their hearts.

Military officers except the ones in the central government were subordinate to provincial and local magistrates. There were camps throughout the country, and no regular troops in them. A few professional officers and their assistants operated the camps, but the troops were recruited from the lowest classes and were ordinarily engaged in farm work or occupations of their own. Twice a year, roll calls were made and some training was provided. The condition of the troops has been described by the scholar Chŏng Yak-yong (1762–1836):

> The so-called troops of the time are all from the slave and lowly classes. Even the underage and old ones are joined in columns to fill the muster. Their hats are just like broken gourd shells, and they are clad in rags. . . . Men are hired as occasions arise to fill the day's training.[17]

There was a virtual absence of military preparedness.

The second stratum of Korean society was the small class of the professionals and clerks. The term "middle people" (*Chung-in*) was applied to the professionals because they lived in the central part of Seoul, the capital of the kingdom. Although men of this class were given an education similar to that of the yangbans, they were trained to serve the government as accountants, interpreters, meteorologists, surveyors, judicial officers, copyists, and the like, and, regardless of ability, were restricted to taking examinations that were mainly of a professional character; their knowledge of the classics was not to be examined to the fullest extent. Their role in the affairs of the government was to act according to the instructions of their yangban superiors.

The professional class, besides being probably the smallest, was more nearly closed than any other. Most of the functions performed by the middle people were necessary only for the central government.

Further, the primary qualification for this group was the possession of professional knowledge, the acquisition of which was by no means an easy task. As in the case of the technical professions of some other societies, special knowledge was transmitted from one generation to the next without allowing the secrets of technique to become known to outsiders. Many of the positions held by members of this class were in effect hereditary, despite the examination system.

Another category of persons usually included in the second stratum was that of the clerks and lower military officers. Far below the yangbans in status and prestige, they were still part of the official apparatus and hence were above the commoners. The clerks were originally recruited by the government to perform compulsory duties among the lower classes, but the actual power of the government, particularly at the local level, was gradually shifted into their hands. This despised yet powerful class was equivalent to the Yamen runners in China.

While governors and high officials in provincial and prefectural governments were centrally appointed and were transferred from time to time, the clerks were recruited from among the residents in each area and usually inherited their positions from one generation to the next. On many occasions, therefore, the clerks were in a more advantageous situation than the yangban officials and handled government affairs as they saw fit. As yangban morality slackened after the beginning of factional struggles, the clerks began to tyrannize over the common people. If officials were not already corrupt upon arrival at a new post, the local clerks corrupted them through intrigues and inducements. According to Chŏng Yak-yong:

> The people cultivate the soil for a living, but the clerks exploit the people as their profession. They exploit their prey by skinning and hammering the people, reaping their harvest from the labor and grain of the people. This became their habit, and they now do it as a matter of course. Without restraining the clerks, no one can govern the people.[18]

The commoners were the third stratum. These were the people who engaged in farming, commerce, and trades and who supplied the financial and other needs of the yangban-dominated government. Along with the lowly class, they constituted the ruled elements of the society, the two higher classes being the rulers. The relationship of rulers and ruled could easily be justified not only in terms of actual power, but by Confucian precept. For it was Mencius who said:

> Some labor with their minds, and some labor with their strength. Those who labor with their minds govern others; those who labor with their strength are governed by others. Those who are governed by others support them; those who govern others are supported by them.[19]

Under this philosophical justification the distinction between rulers and ruled was rigidly maintained. The only way to break it was by insurrection. There were, indeed, numerous revolts during the five centuries of the Yi dynasty, but none of these succeeded. The majority of the populace were indifferent to the system of government so long as they were able to get their livelihood in the accustomed way. The political and social structure of Korea was never seriously jeopardized at least internally until the late nineteenth century.

The most numerous and important group within the commoners class was, of course, that of the farmers. Korea, like the neighboring countries, has been predominantly agricultural. The system of land-ownership, however, differed from that of China, where both public and private fields were recognized. The Yi dynasty recognized no private ownership of land. The official doctrine was that the dynasty owned the entire domain and that the farmers tilled the land as a privilege. Some of the fortunate yangbans who were appointed to official posts were allotted territories from which they were to collect tenant fees, and the farmers who tilled such lands were reduced to perpetual tenancy, paying rent to shifting landlords and at the same time being subject to a land tax payable directly to the government.

Farmers also tilled lands not assigned to officials. The central government and the local governments reserved some lands, the income from which was to be used for official purposes. These farmers paid rents directly to government agencies responsible for land management. Also some reserved lands were tilled by slaves attached to government agencies. This system of land management and finance seems to have worked well in the early part of the Yi dynasty; later it broke down. Eventually more than one official—that is, landlord—was assigned to one piece of land, and all these officials exacted rent. In the end the yangban landlords burdened the tenants to the point of forcing many to abandon their age-old right of cultivation and become farm slaves. In addition, farmers were subject to frauds and other abuses by the yangban families and the local clerks.

Since each village was practically self-sufficient, commercial activities in Korea were very limited. The merchant class was small, and its role in society was minimal. Because of the Confucian notion that commerce was a profession of meanness, the social status of the merchants was below that of the farmers: the farmers toiled in honesty and faithfulness, but the merchants extracted their profits through deceit and intrigue—at least, were believed to do so—and were not to be respected.

Owing to the government policy of isolation the only spheres of activity open to the merchants were those of purveying to the government and circulating the small amounts of surplus commodities between communities. Purveying was carried on by resident merchants in Seoul and the other large cities. Surplus products were handled by guilds of lesser merchants who transported merchandise on their backs from one local fair to another. By necessity the purveyors identified their interest with that of the regime; the others also sought some governmental protection. In contrast to the merchants of the West, who formed the basis of the modern middle class and were the forerunners of liberalism, those of Korea tied their lot to the conservative regime and wholeheartedly supported the reactionary policies of the government.

Little need be said about the fourth and lowest stratum. The lowly class consisted of family slaves, government slaves, slaughterers, butchers, sorcerers, and convicts. Being the most despised of all, the slaughterers formed a class of their own, lower than that of the rest. Not being allowed to live in the villages, they had their communities outside. The slave class was composed of those who were born to slave mothers, of persons who sold themselves or were sold by their parents, and of abandoned children who were found and raised. Numerically and socially the slave class was of little significance; it greatly decreased in the late nineteenth century.

Such, in general, was the social system in Korea before the downfall of the dynasty and the capitulation to Japan. Within this compartmentalized structure and under a highly dogmatic ideology, the Korean court carried out a seclusion policy exceeding in rigidity that of China.[20] After the devastating invasions by the Japanese (1592–1597) and the Manchus (1627 and 1636), Korea was a hermit kingdom until 1876, when Japan forced the opening of the ports. The sole channels of communication with the outside world during this period were provided by the annual tribute missions sent to China and occasional contacts with Japan. This channel did, indeed, introduce some new thoughts by way of the Catholic priests in Peking as early as 1601. It is reported that Yi Ik, a progressive scholar of the reign of Yŏngjo, read most of the Western writings that were available in Chinese translations and wrote on many scientific subjects.[21] But the new knowledge was regarded by the ruling class as not only unnecessary, but highly undesirable: the best possible model of a good government, the essence of government, had been provided by the golden age of Yao and Shun in ancient China, and all the shortcomings in Korean practice were owing only to the inability of the rulers to persevere in the ways of the ancient kings. Justification for rejecting the new knowledge was easily found in Confucianism, for Catholicism and the other Western ideas that were introduced into China by missionary priests attacked its very foundation, the Five Relationships. The declaration issued on the occasion of the first persecution of the Catholics in Korea, in 1801, stated in part:

> For human beings there is a code of human relationships, and for the nation there is a culture. The paganism of today disregards father, disregards prince, destroys human relations, betrays the culture, and degrades one to the level of a barbarous creature.[22]

In view of the internal condition of Yi Korea, it is not surprising that the country, when necessity forced modernization upon it, had great difficulty in achieving reforms. The success of Japan in this respect is often attributed to the activities of the disgruntled samurai class and the rising power of the merchants. Japanese society had, however, accumulated enough wealth under the feudal system to enable a modern government to operate efficiently, once it was established. The leaders of new Japan also found a strong symbol of national unity in the conservative institution of the emperor. Also the Japanese tradition of adapting the new from outside was favorable. Unfortunately for Korea, no such factors were present when the country was coerced to enter international society in 1876.

Dogmatic and formalistic adherence to Chu Hsi-ism and Confucianism was such that even the Tsung-li Yamen in Peking (1861–1901) experienced strain in handling Korean relationships. While the leaders in Japan immediately recognized points of inferiority to the West and took steps to learn from the enemy, the Korean elites blindly worshiped their own philosophy and polity and made no attempts at adaptation. Nothing but the final capitulation would make them realize how grave a mistake had been committed. The country was impoverished and the government was corrupt, but the educated class in general viewed the situation with complacency because it allowed them superior status and power without their offering anything in return.

Hostile relationships between classes, more specifically between the two divisions of the rulers and the ruled, impeded the growth of nationalism in Korea. Until the distinction between the yangbans and the rest of the population could be diminished, it would be impossible to unite all under one symbol. Because Korean royalty had been deeply involved in government affairs and at the head of a corrupt regime, the king failed to become the center for national cohesion as did the Japanese emperor. Modern nationalism in Korea was to begin as a movement against the regime rather than in defense of it.

Perhaps we can single out the following as the most noticeable characteristics of Korean elitedom in the late Yi period: (1) formalistic and ritualistic following of a dogma even when the philosophy from which it derived was not actually practiced, (2) attachment of more importance to familial and personal relationships than to impersonal and institutional relationships, (3) factionalism, and (4) provincialism.

The first point need not be elaborated. Our discussion of the Confucian policy and its eventual corruption is testimony. The second and third points can be viewed together. The emphasis placed on familial and personal relationships was the basic cause of factionalism. Perhaps during comparative prosperity, when the family was sufficiently provided for, national harmony could exist. But when because of extreme poverty people were forced to choose between one or the other, the ultimate choice rested in the relationship of the family rather than in the larger confines of the society or the state. Factional alliances were, of course, not limited to the family or the clan. In order to enhance one's own influence and power, or that of one's family, the sphere of activity had to be enlarged. But, for the most part, intimate connections could not go beyond a small group, the faction. Alliance would be based upon either personal affinity or affinity of interest. In the struggle for power all others would be regarded as enemies or, at best, neutrals.

We have not heretofore touched on the fourth point. Provincialism was owing mainly to the official discrimination imposed upon the inhabitants of the northern territory in governmental employment. Although the founder of the Yi dynasty was from the north, his successors began to look upon that area with suspicion.[23] In combination with the ambitious politicians of central and southern Korea, who wished to monopolize the affairs of government, the royal court adopted stringent discrimination against the north. Later, when the factional struggles became extreme, the politicians of the southwest were also largely excluded. The withholding of government positions led to loss of elite prestige in these areas, which in turn led to general contempt for the ruling class.

Dallet's church history, based on the reports of Catholic missionaries and published in 1874, sets forth some of the differences between the provinces and can be taken to reflect the opinions of Koreans of the period:

Those of the two northern provinces, particularly of Pyongan, [the other being Hamgyong,] are stronger, more savage and more violent than the other Koreans. There are very few nobles among them, and consequently very few dignitaries. It is thought that they are the secret enemies of the dynasty, and so the government, while it humors them, watches over them closely and always dreads an insurrection on their part which would be extremely difficult to overcome. The people of Hwanghae [in the central part] have the reputation of being narrow and limited, and they are accused of great avarice and of bad faith. The populace of Kyonggi, or province of the capital, is flighty, inconstant and given to luxurious living and pleasure. It is this populace which has set the tone for the whole country, and it is particularly to it that what we have said [about] the Koreans' ambition, rapacity, prodigality and ostentation applies. Dignitaries, nobles and scholars are numerous there. The people of Chungchong [to the south of the capital] resemble those of Kyonggi in all points, and share their vices and good qualities to a lesser degree. In the [southern] province of Cholla few nobles are encountered. The inhabitants are regarded by the other

Koreans as coarse, hypocritical, and rascally, seeking only their own interest and always ready to commit the most odious treason if they can profit from it. The [southeastern] province of Kyongsang has a character apart. Habits are much more simple, morals less corrupt, and the old customs more faithfully preserved. There is little luxury and few foolish expenditures, thus the tiny heritages are handed down in the same family from father to son year after year. Literary study flourishes there more than elsewhere, and often young persons are found who devote the evening and part of the night to reading after working in the fields all day long. Women of rank are not shut in as strictly as in other provinces, but go out during the day accompanied by a slave, and need fear no insult nor any lack of respect. . . . The nobles, who are quite numerous in this province, belong to the Nam-in party [or Southern faction], and since the most recent revolutions [they] have no longer any part in dignities and public offices.[24]

Unfortunately the attitudes thus described survived the political changes in later generations and contributed greatly to the factional tensions and disruptions among the nationalists.

This was the background from which the nationalist movement emerged, the traditional Korea that capitulated to the Japanese in 1910. After the opening of the ports in 1876 Korea underwent some internal changes. Some of the changes were advanced by educated reformers. The more extensive and violent changes, however, came from the lower classes, who rose in revolt against the existing social and political structure and were not concerned with reforms in any modern sense.

In China the Taiping rebellion of 1850–1864 was the forerunner of subsequent revolutions. The Tonghak movement or rebellion of 1894–1895 was similarly a harbinger of revolution in Korea. But the collapse of the Yi dynasty forestalled further revolutionary action, and instead of this there came the nationalist movement.

II

Demise of the Korean Kingdom

2

The Tonghak Rebellion

THE YEARS between 1876 and 1905 are probably the most important period in the history of modern Korea. In 1876 Japan forced the opening of the ports of the "hermit kingdom." Within a few years, encouraged to do so by her ancient suzerain, China, Korea concluded treaties with various Western countries. An opportunity to join the ranks of modern nations was provided; or so it seemed. Korea lacked the necessary foundations for making a transformation of her institutions within the time that was available. The opportunity passed, and in 1905 Korean independence was submerged when Japan took over the foreign relations of the kingdom and imposed a so-called protectorate.

Although the government failed to modernize during this period of thirty years, and the protectorate of 1905 was followed by annexation to Japan in 1910, Korea did undergo almost revolutionary changes in the meanwhile, socially, politically, and economically. Because of ingrained ultraconservatism, the process was necessarily slow. Yet in the early part of the twentieth century a modern Korean nation was coming into being.

The Tonghak rebellion of 1894–1895 was both a symptom and a cause of change. In terms of the wide area of territory covered and the number of persons involved, this was a rebellion unprecedented in Korean history. It was a mass movement of the oppressed segments of the populace in nearly every part of the kingdom, a movement against the existing philosophical and intellectual mentality of the society, and a movement against corruption in the social system and in the government. Above all, it was a movement to exalt the national identity of the Koreans vis-à-vis the Japanese and other outsiders.

This is not to say that the Tonghak rebellion was a full-fledged nationalist movement aimed at the construction of a modern nation. It had its primitive aspects and other weaknesses. In the end it was subdued, with some assistance from foreign powers, by the Korean government. But it left a significant impress, and, though this was not the object of its leaders, it quickened the modernization that was beginning to develop in Korea.

In its characteristics the Tonghak rebellion was not unique in recent Far Eastern history. The Taiping rebellion of 1850–1864 and the Boxer incident of 1900 in China, for instance, can be seen to have striking resemblances to it. This is not surprising, since conditions in the two countries were similar in many ways. Analogous Tonghak and Taiping elements were: the characteristics of the founders and leaders; the use of religion as the doctrinal basis of the movements; elaborate organizations; armed attacks upon the government; and nationalistic ideals. The most marked trait shared by the Tonghaks and the Boxers was xenophobia, although the Tonghaks did not physically attack foreigners and did not have government support as the Boxers did.

Tonghak as a religion had its beginning in 1860. The founder, Ch'oe Che-u, like Hung Hsiu-ch'üan of the Taiping movement, was a son of a defeated scholar—one who was discriminated against by the government. The factional struggles in eighteenth-century Korea, and even more the "in-law politics" (*sedo chŏngch'i*) of the nineteenth century, had alienated many rural literati from politics, and especially those in the southern provinces found themselves excluded from the government. The literati families in this area, except those with large landholdings, lived in destitution. Ch'oe came from such a deprived family. He attempted to enter the civil service on several occasions, but, like Hung Hsiu-ch'üan, lacked official support and consequently was unable to pass any of the examinations.

Ch'oe Che-u was proud of his lineage, which is said to have been traced back to the famous minister of Silla, Ch'oe Ch'i-won. He lamented the deplorable fate of his family, blamed his inability to advance in the world on his impiousness, and called himself an unfortunate man.[1] Again like Hung, Ch'oe was thus a politically frustrated and economically insolvent man with an ambitious personality. His concerns extended from his own family to the country as a whole, and he was particularly disturbed by the rise of Catholicism in Korea. Retiring to a remote mountain for a period of soul searching, he received what he regarded as a revelation from God.

Both Hung in China and Ch'oe in Korea based their religions upon their visions, but the precepts they adopted were quite dissimilar. Whereas Taiping precepts were born of a distorted Christianity, those of Tonghak formed a well-constructed syncretism based upon the four religious or philosophical ideas then known in Korea—Confucianism, Buddhism, Taoism, and Catholicism—and intermixed with the native shamanism. Ch'oe called his teaching *Tonghak* ("the Eastern Learning"), as opposed to Catholicism, then known as *Sŏhak* ("the Western Learning"). Absorbing major principles from varied sources, he arrived at a religion of his own:

> The Heavenly fortune is in a cyclical motion. In antiquity there was a period when ignorant people were unaware of the Heavenly benefits. This was followed by an era of obedience to the will of Heaven through the intercession of sages. The modern world has been a period of disobedience of man to the Heavenly principles, but a World of New Creation will soon come, in which man and God will communicate directly. All who believe in the Lord of Heaven, represented on earth by Ch'oe Che-u, and strive for virtue will become fairies (*sŏnin*) on earth. The old world will be destroyed by an invasion of the Westerners against which no arms may prevail. Only Tonghak will be able to annihilate the enemy through the use of incantation and magic. In the World of New Creation those who have been rich and noble will become poor and lowly, and those who have been poor and lowly will become rich and noble.[2]

In addition, a system of rules or commandments was established. Obedience to these was prerequisite for becoming a fairy—an immortal being—on earth and enjoying the benefits of the World of New Creation.[3]

The promise of a prosperous and equalitarian new world to be realized in the very near future, coupled with the magic power of healing preached by the Tonghaks, attracted a multitude of followers in Kyongsang Province, where Ch'oe introduced his religion, and the reciting of Tonghak incantations soon became a common phenomenon.[4] But as the new doctrine began to sweep Kyongsang the attention of the government was drawn to it, and since the term *Ch'ŏnju* ("Lord of Heaven") was used in the incantations and precepts, the Tonghak religion was accused of being a heretical teaching similar to Catholicism. Ch'oe Che-u was consequently arrested, and in 1864 he was executed for the crime of confusing the people.

After the martyrdom of the founder, leadership fell upon Ch'oe Sihyŏng and missionary activities were carried on, attended by all the difficulties of a persecuted religion, in Kyongsang, Cholla, and Chungchong provinces. From a firm base in the south the teaching of Tonghak gradually spread northward. By the time the first gathering of the group was held, in 1893, it had spread over the entire Korean peninsula.

Tonghak obviously had many attractions. Unlike Christianity and Buddhism, which promise rewards after death, it offered immediate, everlasting rewards during one's lifetime. The repugnant social and political system of the present, it promised, would soon fall and be replaced by one in which the fate of the people would be transformed. For these bountiful benefits nothing more than the observance of a few rituals and prohibitions (e.g., avoidance of evil deeds, greed, and adultery) was demanded.

In essence, Tonghak was a revolutionary religion, and it contained a seed of nationalism or, more specifically, national consciousness. The belief that foreign invasion could be overcome only by Tonghak magic cannot be regarded simply as xenophobic. Rather, nationalistic sentiment and xenophobia were mingled too subtly for clear distinction, and both attitudes were products of the contemporary situation. Korea in the 1860's was still a hermit kingdom, and the many attempts by foreigners to open its ports had been met by the opposition of an obstinate government. "Repel the barbarians" was a slogan adopted by the government, though whether a determined invasion could have been repelled is highly questionable. When British and French troops occupied Peking, rumors that the barbarians were also intent on attacking Korea created panic in the government as well as among the populace.

In this connection the name of the new religion presents an interesting case for exploration. The term *tong* ("east") was a common expression among the Koreans and Chinese to denote Korea and was based on the country's being to the east of China, the Middle Kingdom situated in the center of the world. Ch'oe Che-u used the term in this sense: "I was born in the East and received [the teachings] in the East. The *do* ('way') is *Ch'ŏndo* ('the Heavenly Way'), but the *hak* ('learning') is *tonghak*." He added, however, a new meaning to *tong*, according to at least one scholar. Ishii Toshio, who has carefully analyzed the development of Tonghak thought, singles out Ch'oe's next sentences as signifying the emergence of a Korean and an Asian nationalism: ". . . the world is divided into East and West. How could one say that West is East and that East is West?" [5] This division of the world into two parts and the designation of Korea as the eastern part may be regarded as commonplace, but in Ishii's interpretation the "East" represented here is not identical with the traditional concept. Chinese prestige was fast declining in Korea at this time because of the inability of the Middle Kingdom to keep the barbarians out. When Ch'oe saw the world as divided into two parts and referred to Korea as the East, he omitted China from the concept, Ishii asserts, and his idea of Tonghak can be taken to imply the destruction of Chunghua-ism—the belief in the supremacy of the Middle Kingdom. The outlook in which China was the center of the world and the ruler over all the surrounding states was replaced with a new outlook which regarded Asia as part of a larger world and gave Asian nationalism a beginning. With Chinese superiority eliminated there would be no alternative for Korea except to become both politically and philosophically independent. Ishii concludes, therefore, that Tonghak was a nationalistic concept stimulated by new thoughts derived from Western civilization and that its antialienism or exclusivism was a reaction against the encroachment of Western powers. He also distinguishes the xenophobia of the Tonghak leaders from that of the governing class. Xenophobia at the governmental level arose from and sought to preserve medievalistic Chunghua-ism. Among the Tonghaks it was based on nationalistic thought and, as such, filled the gap between the new outlook of Catholicism, which demanded the opening of the country, and the fixed attitudes of old Korea.[6]

It seems clear that the religious teachings of Tonghak contained potent political ideas, making the spread of the doctrine a social movement of grave importance. To be sure, these ideas bore no resemblance to the revolutionary ideas of nineteenth-century liberalism in the West. As a revolutionary doctrine Tonghak was totally inadequate. It predicted the downfall of the existing political and social structure, but the people were not to be directly responsible for the change. No human rights were expounded, and at first no exhortation was made to encourage the rise of the people. The existing structure was to be destroyed by foreigners, and only after this were the Tonghaks to build a new world of their own. One might see in this expectation a version of the idea of a two-stage revolution; it obviously explains the hesitation of Ch'oe Si-hyŏng, the successor of the founder, to lead the armed uprising of his followers later on. Whatever its defects in revolutionary theory, the Tonghak doctrine served adequately to turn the minds of the people against the government.

A rare case of the description of personal experience with the new religion is found in the autobiography of Kim Ku, an important nationalist leader after 1919 and one who was a member of Tonghak in his youth: [7]

> It was rumored at that time that O Ŭng-sŏn, who lived in Kaetgol, about twenty *ri* south of my village, and Ch'oe Hyŏn, who lived in the next village, had been learning Tonghak principles. . . . It was said that in going in and out of houses they did not use doors; they appeared or disappeared instantaneously; they could walk in the sky and go to visit Ch'oe To-myŏng, the leader in Chungchong Province, within a night. I began to have curiosity about Tonghak and decided to visit them.
>
> As instructed by others, I did not eat any odorous foods, and I bathed clean and wore new clothing to go to see them. I heard that one would not be received otherwise. . . . As I approached Mr. O's house, I could hear people reading something aloud. It was different from the tone of chanting Buddhist sutras or other poems and sounded rather like singing songs in harmony. When I called at the house, a young and handsome man of the yangban class appeared, wearing a gentleman's hat. As I politely bowed, he politely bowed back. I was very much impressed and. after telling him my name and address, said, "Even if I were a mature man with a proper hat, a gentleman of yangban birth would not bow to me. Now, seeing that I am only a boy of the commoners' class, you are treating me overcourteously." He smiled and said that he was a follower of Tonghak and that in the teachings of the founder there was no discrimination according to wealth or birth, and hence all were to be treated equally. When I told him the purpose of my visit, he politely explained to me the history and major principles of the religion. . . . The principles were that the wicked people of the last era of the world should renew themselves and lead new lives in order to become a new people. By doing so they would be able to serve the true king in the future in constructing a new nation in Kerong Mountain.

I was overjoyed to hear his teachings. . . . Since I had previously determined to become a man of good heart . . . it was very important for me to have God within me and act according to the way of Heaven. Also, for a man who was of the commoners' class and filled with indignation, the equalitarianism preached by Tonghak was extremely precious. Also the prediction [that] the Yi dynasty was coming to an end was well received by me, because I had been disappointed by the corruption in the government. I was filled with a desire to join Tonghak and asked the procedure for entering. I was told that I should bring one *mal* (30 lb.) of rice, three dozen sheets of window paper, and one pair of candles. I looked through *Tonggyŏng taejŏn, P'alpy'ŏn kasa,* and *Kungwŏlga* [8] there and returned home.

After joining Tonghak I studied diligently and strove to propagate the teachings. . . . At this time there were few yangbans joining, and most of those entering were of the lower classes. Within a few months I obtained several hundred followers. My name was widely known in the district. Many came to ask me about the teachings, and rumors were circulated about me. . . . Some said that they saw Kim Ch'ang-ŏm [9] walking in the air more than two meters above the ground. With these rumors becoming widespread, I gained several thousand followers within a year.

Kim's experience makes it clear that the teachings of Tonghak were not simply religious, but were political and social also, being consciously aimed at the lower and the oppressed classes, as is evident in the kinds of appeals used. From the standpoint of religion or philosophy, Ch'oe Che-u lacked originality, and Tonghak can hardly be regarded as a significant contribution in those realms. Its importance lies in the fact that this pseudo religion served as a channel for the organization of oppressed members of society who wished to destroy the sociopolitical structure in which they found themselves.

Between 1892 and 1894 the Tonghak movement can be divided into two phases. In the first, during 1892 and 1893, activities were largely confined to mass demonstrations seeking an end to official persecution. In the second, from February to November of 1894, the Tonghaks were joined by disgruntled masses and engaged in armed revolt against the government forces, displaying all the traits of revolutionaries. Even in the first phase of peaceful demonstrations and petitionings, however, they never confined their activities to seeking religious freedom alone.

It was a common practice during the Yi dynasty for heirs, relatives, and friends of those convicted for crimes to petition the royal court to redress the grievances. By custom, petitioners presented their cause to the king while he was proceeding through the streets, or they dashed into the palace and sounded the drum. The leader of the petitioners would be arrested for creating a disturbance, but his petition would be read and the necessary adjustment made, at the royal discretion, to redress the grievance. If the petitioners won their case through the petition, then the heirs and others connected with the accused's crime would be restored to their former status although the accused might already have been executed. In the same manner, petitions were also submitted to local governors.

Departing from the traditional procedure, the Tonghaks in submitting their petitions and requesting the mercy of king or governor mobilized their forces on each occasion, expressing a threatening attitude. The first and more superficial purpose was to remove from the founder the label of heretic and follower of the Western learning. But it was obvious that the removal was desired not only for the sake of the founder's memory, but for securing legal sanction which would permit the Tonghaks to preach without being persecuted. This second purpose was the more urgent. Officials and members of the ruling class were using the pretext of suppressing the heretical religion to enrich themselves by arresting, sometimes murdering, the Tonghak followers and plundering their property. Both officials and unemployed yangbans were engaged in this task. The results of the petitioning were almost negligible. In March, 1893, about forty leaders of Tonghak prostrated themselves before the royal palace, submitted their petition, and remained near the palace for three days, but were not granted their wish, the removal of the charge of heresy, and, although the government gave a promise of better treatment, persecution was continued and there were further reports of atrocities. Some of the Tonghak leaders then advocated outright attack upon the government, in opposition to the view of Ch'oe Si-hyŏng, the successor of the founder. Finding no legal means for altering the situation, Ch'oe called for a gathering of local leaders from all over Korea at Po-ŭn, in Chungchong Province.[10]

By May, 1893, leaders and followers numbering more than twenty thousand were assembled at Po-ŭn. Stone walls were built around the headquarters, and banners were flown. The most conspicuous banner was one bearing the inscription "Reject Japan and Repel the Foreigners." This slogan had already appeared during the petitioning before the palace in Seoul. Later it was used by the Tonghaks throughout their rebellion.

When a high official was sent from the central government to disperse the gathering, the leaders persisted in the assertion that, despite their patriotic desire to reject the Japanese and repel the foreigners and thereby do a service to the country, local officials were treating them as brigands and continuing to persecute them: if they disbanded now, they would certainly still be regarded as brigands and it would be impossible for them to live in peace. They requested, therefore, that their case be laid before the king, so that they might return peacefully to their ordinary occupations. After twenty days of unarmed demonstrations they dispersed when news came of the dispatch of Royal Guards from Seoul and the official from the central government gave them a promise of leniency.[11]

On April 26, during the gathering at Po-ŭn, the Tonghak leaders posted a proclamation at the provincial government building which clearly and even eloquently set forth their intentions: [12]

There are three difficulties in human affairs. The first is the difficulty of a subject. He must establish his integrity, be loyal to the utmost, and die for the nation. The second is the difficulty of a son. He must do his best to fulfill the duties of filial piety and serve his parent with his own life. The third is the difficulty of a wife. She must be chaste, emulate the *Yŏl* (a woman who prefers to die rather than remarry), and follow her husband even to death.

It is man's nature to be born and to die. It is the order of the time which will determine whether there will be troubles. If one is born at a time of no troubles, but of happiness and peace, it is a pleasure to follow the way of loyalty and filial piety. But when one is born at a time of troubles and difficulties, it is difficult to die for loyalty and filial piety. Those who are fortunate to be born and do not perform their duties have the inclination to kill. Those unwilling to die for their duties cannot establish the bonds of a subject or a son. Those happy to die for their duties can develop the honor of loyalty and filial piety.

Today, the foreign brigands are confidently scheming to start a war. When one earnestly looks at the national capital, it is full of nests of barbarians. We are not able to refrain from thinking of the grievance of Imjin (the Japanese invasion under Hideyoshi in 1592) or the shame of Pyŏngin (the attack by French warships in 1866). Even at present the country is filled with reminders of barbarous atrocities that were committed. The ancestral temples throughout the nation have had the grief of receiving offerings of millet during the past five hundred years. Nevertheless the principles of righteousness, decorum, wisdom, filial piety, brotherliness, loyalty, and trust are still maintained.

The Japanese brigands still have a warlike heart and contain within themselves an intention for mischief. Poison is set forth everywhere, and danger is constant. But all seems as though quiet; hence it is said to be peaceful.

Today's condition, however, is little different from being on a pile of firewood.

Although we are stupid people of the field, we till the lands of the king according to the laws established by the king before him, thereby supporting our parents. Although the difference between the nobility and the lowly people among the subjects is extreme, why should there be a difference in their performance of the duties of loyalty and filial piety?

The wish to be loyal to the nation is the humble feeling of the masses, but there is no way to reach His Majesty. We presume to think that we do not compare in family honor and virtue in holding state positions in prudence of movement as well as in the sincerity of our loyalty and patriotism. But there is an old saying: "When a mansion is leaning over, it is difficult to support it with a single block; when there is a big wave, a single reed cannot resist it." We are several ten-thousands. We are all sworn to combine our strength till death. By completely destroying the Japanese and the foreigners we wish to repay the grace of the king. We humbly beg you, Sir, to cooperate with us in the same spirit, and mobilize and select warriors with loyalty and integrity, so that we may jointly support the desire of the nation. We entreat you with our utmost.

This proclamation, which is also a petition, abandons the theme of redressing the grievance committed against the founder. In substance it is an expression of xenophobia, stressing the wrongs done and the dangers threatened by Japan. The Po-ŭn demonstrations thus mark a turning point in the Tonghak movement, the shift from predominantly religious to predominantly political concerns.

The second and final phase of the movement, the violent struggle against the government, began in February, 1894, with an uprising in Kobu Prefecture, of Cholla Province. Conditions in Cholla were no different from those in the neighboring provinces except that possibly the officials were somewhat more corrupt. Peasant revolts had occurred previously in this region.[13] Blame for the 1894 uprising was put on two prefectural governors. Among the misdeeds of one of them, Cho Pyŏng-gap, were the following:

He permitted the people to cultivate virgin land without taxation, according to the national law, but invariably reversed his decision in the harvest seasons and extorted taxes. He collected refined rice as tax and submitted coarse grain to the national government, profiting from the difference. Although an old irrigation dam was in good condition, he ordered a new dam to be constructed and paid no wages for the labor. When the dam was finished, he increased the already burdensome tax on the use of water. Despite a custom that grain collected as water tax was to be used to pay for further irrigation works, he pocketed all the income from it.[14]

After petitions to Cho were tried twice and found futile, a revolt broke out on February 15, 1894. It was led by Chŏn Pong-jun, who had headed the local residents in their petitionings and been the leader of the local Tonghak group.[15] A mob of more than a thousand attacked the prefectural offices, punished the officials, destroyed the new dam, distributed the grain collected as water tax, and raided the arms depot. Another mob, numbering several thousand, rose in nearby Mujang under another leader and attacked the government offices, taking government property and distributing it.[16] The rioters, having accomplished their object of destroying the Kobu dam and driving out covetous officials, disbanded.

The government in Seoul promptly arrested Cho Pyŏng-gap and removed the provincial governor from office, and sent Kim Ch'ang-sŏk, magistrate of Changhŭng, to investigate. Kim Ch'ang-sŏk blindly resorted to harsh punishment of the rioters—Tonghaks and others. Some Tonghak members and their families were executed, and their homes were destroyed. This provoked another revolt, which grew to be a national movement. In the latter part of April[17] the former Tonghak leader at Kobu, Chŏn Pong-jun, gathered several thousand followers at a mountain headquarters, Paeksan.[18] On May 11 his forces, at Hwangt'ohyŏn, defeated troops sent by the provincial governor. On May 13 they invaded Mujang, a center of Tonghak activity, where many members had been arrested. The rebels broke open the prison and took revenge on the town officials by murdering most of them and setting fire to their houses.

While the rebels were at Mujang, May 13–16, Chŏn Pong-jun issued a proclamation explaining the purpose of the revolt. In its phrasing and much of its substance this proclamation resembled the one posted at Po-ŭn. It begins with Confucian references to the relationships of prince and subjects, father and son, and exempts the king from faults:

> Our present king is virtuous, filial, compassionate, and loving. He is also divinely intelligent and consecratedly wise. If the officials were also wise and virtuous in assisting the king and seconding the brilliant one, we would have attained the days of Yao-Shun and the rule of Wên-ching.[19]

It then goes well beyond the Po-ŭn essay and pointedly attacks the oppressive and corrupt practices of the officials and asserts the need for protecting the nation and appeasing the people. Although allegiance to the king is professed, the rebels are self-appointed as the protectors of the nation and executors of justice:

> We cannot sit and see the nation facing extinction. Everyone of the same mind has deliberated on the eternal principle [of human relationships] and now raises the banner of righteousness in order to serve the public, defend the nation, and pacify the people. . . . Although today's scenes may seem alarming, do not be frightened. Let everyone continue to engage in his profession. Let us all celebrate the days of transformed peace, all be enriched by divine (imperial) kindness. All will be fortunate indeed.

The Confucian tenor of the argument was, besides being customary, probably intended to appeal to the traditional outlook of both the educated classes and the common people. By clear implication, Confucian principles were evoked as justification for overturning the government. We can conclude that the object of the rebels was the total overthrow not of the dynasty, but of the socio-political structure in which it was embedded. Yet, since the king himself was powerless, what the Tonghaks intended was not far from revolution.

While Chŏn's predominantly Tonghak group was having success in its revolt, mobs rose violently in the three provinces south of Seoul. They attacked government facilities, freed prisoners and slaves, destroyed yangban houses, and bound, whipped, and otherwise humiliated the yangbans.[20] The mobs also plundered grain from government storehouses and seized arms at arsenals. Yangbans and other well-to-do persons banded together for defense, but were no match for the mobs and the rebels. On many occasions the rebels defeated government forces. Chŏnju, the capital of Cholla Province, fell to them, but Royal Guards dispatched from Seoul succeeded in driving them from the city. Thus before the end of May the rebels were routed and scattered, except for a few leaders and followers, and the first armed revolt of the Tonghaks was ended.[21] Chinese troops arrived at Asan Bay on June 8, and no doubt this news further weakened the morale of the rebels.

As will be noted in the next chapter, the government at Seoul requested the assistance of the Chinese in suppressing the Tonghaks. This action gave the Japanese an excuse for sending in their troops, and the Sino-Japanese war broke out on the Korean peninsula in June of 1894. The Japanese won a decisive victory over the Chinese forces, but by a series of blunders, particularly the murder of Queen

Min, in October, and the introduction of radical reform programs, soon deeply antagonized the people of Korea.

Chŏn Pong-jun, the Tonghak leader of the rebels, immediately recognized the opportunity that would be afforded by a surge of anti-Japanese sentiment and during late June and July again assembled several thousand followers, reoccupying Chŏnju without resistance.[22] The Tonghaks then prepared for a northern march to repel the Japanese. Chŏn's plan for action was opposed by the more pacific supreme leader of the Tonghaks, Ch'oe Si-hyŏng, but external and internal pressures eventually forced him to accept Chŏn's policy.[23]

In September the Tonghaks marched north. At several places they proved to be superior to the government forces, but when they attempted to take Kongju, the capital of Chungchong Province, they were defeated by well-trained and well-equipped Japanese troops.[24] Government and Japanese troops together are reported to have killed about 36,000 rebels during January and February, 1895, in the Kangjin area.[25] This was a crippling blow to the Tonghaks.

In the meantime other uprisings occurred in the north. Local Tonghak leaders banded their followers together, enlisted other men from the generally disgruntled populace, and attacked cities held by government forces and the Japanese. An American missionary who spent seven months with the rebels in Hwanghae Province vividly recorded the developments in that area:

> It was reported that any one who spoke anything against the Tong Hak must have his top knot cut off. Fabulous reports were given of their numbers in *other* places. They then after trying in vain to get the people in a body to join their ranks, started for the different magistracies. Magistrates were seized, books burned, guns, ammunition, spears, and banners plundered.
>
> To the ordinary Korean such power so quickly acquired seemed to substantiate their reports of magical power. Little persuasion or threatening was now needed to swell the ranks. Thousands joined in a day, several who attended our Christian meeting in the morning were on the warpath in the evening. Great were the promises and bright the prospects of the initiated. They struck a very effective chord in the Korean's heart.
>
> No sickness would enter the house; crops would never fail; debts would not be paid nor taxes; in the battle the bullets of the enemy would be changed to water. It gave an opportunity also to pay off an old score with an enemy.[26]

But the mob, induced to join by superstition and rumor, could not withstand the Japanese troops. As soon as it was proved that the magic attributed to the teachings of Tonghak did not work, the

Tonghak forces fell apart despite the restraint of any leader. Chŏn Pong-jun's second attempt thus ended in failure. In December he was betrayed by one of his followers and arrested by the government.[27] The organized revolt of the Tonghaks was over. Although Tonghak groups engaged in local revolts during the succeeding years, they were unable to carry the offensive into larger areas.

The Tonghak followers dispersed, and it was only after the beginning of the Russo-Japanese War in 1904 that they were mobilized again, this time as a pro-Japanese political group, Ilchinhoe. In 1906, Son Pyŏng-hi, who had been in exile in Japan since 1900, returned to Korea and revived the Tonghaks as a religious body under the new designation of Ch'ŏndogyo ("Teaching of the Way of Heaven"). At the same time he expelled some sixty leaders of Ilchinhoe from Ch'ŏndogyo, eliminating with them the pro-Japanese political tone from his group.

As to why the rebellion of 1893–1894 was abortive, we may point to weak organization and to the undisciplined state of the rebels, their lack of training, and their being ill equipped. But the government army, except for the Royal Guards, was not much better. The ordinary troops probably would not have been able to control the rebels. The loyalty of most of them was doubtful; certainly they were not dedicated enough to risk their lives in a last-ditch fight. Only when Japanese troops were brought in was pacification assured. We must, therefore, conclude that the failure of the rebellion was owing more to the presence of alien soldiers than to the chaotic situation within the Tonghak ranks, and we should remember that the last phase of the rebellion was actually provoked by the Japanese intervention.

The precepts of Tonghak, as we have noted, were addressed to a primitive society, and so were the devices used to attract new comrades in arms. Unfounded rumors and assurances of magic power were given more prominence than any other appeals, and probably these were the most potent. Failure of the magic brought swift disintegration, but nothing else could have attracted the masses. For although all the peasants were tyrannized, and all shared the sense of indignation against the government, the course of combat showed that few were willing to risk their lives, no matter how miserable, for an improved future. Suppression and misery were not new; complacency had dominated the attitude of their fathers and the generations before them. Revolution was an adventure, but the masses were not adventurous either by habit or by sentiment. Only if there were an extraordinary stimulus, in this case happiness without sacrifice, could they have been aroused.

The Tonghaks' failure suggests the difficulty that would be encountered later by the nationalist leaders, particularly the reformers. The upper classes of the old society were staunchly opposed to any change; the masses were ignorant and complacent. Where would one solicit help and support for a reformist cause? An accelerated program of modern education would have been necessary. But education requires time if it is to bring a profound change of outlook.

The immediate effects of the rebellion were deleterious. The country was torn by warfare, and great numbers of persons were killed on both sides. Normal farm activities were interrupted, not only because large areas became battlefields, but also because many farmers participated in the rebellion. Orderly administration of the country hardly existed before; such as it was, it was now further disturbed. The gravest immediate effect, however, was in the international sphere, owing to the excuse given the Japanese government to put its troops into Korea—the first step toward continental expansion.

In a long view, the rebellion had some eventually favorable effects. It provided political education on a gigantic scale. Even though the majority or most of the rebels were moved by blind faith in the magic power of the leaders, they came to be aware of their own potentialities. From mere desperation under an oppressive government, they came to have hope in the future, at the same time identifying themselves as their own masters, as had not been so in earlier uprisings, none of which spread so far or had comparable success. The yangban class suffered a blow from which it has never fully recovered.

Nationalism by definition presupposes social harmony, and the breakdown of rigid social distinctions can conduce to the growth of nationalism. The Japanese ascendancy, for its part, both increased the need and provided the occasion for the Korean people to rally round a new unifying symbol. Nationalism, slowly emerging, became this symbol.

3

The First Sino-Japanese War and the Genesis of Korean Nationalism

CHINA HAD BEEN the recognized suzerain of Korea for several centuries, an undisputed superior, though the relationship was more cultural than it was military or economic. In the latter part of the nineteenth century, when Korea became a center of international rivalries and the traditional position was threatened by other powers, the Peking government began to take a more active interest. After the mutiny of 1882 in Seoul, Yüan Shih-kai was sent in as "resident regent" to supervise the Korean government.[1]

Japan also had an active interest, as is evident from her role in breaking the isolation policy of Korea in 1876. Japanese merchants were doing business there by 1880, and many of them prospered, but this economic penetration was overshadowed by Chinese competition. In 1884 the Japanese Minister in Korea gave assistance to an attempted *coup d'état* by Korean progressives. When this failed, Japanese influence suffered a decline.[2] Meanwhile several Western powers—the United States, Great Britain, Germany, France, Italy, and Russia—took the opportunity of the loosening of the isolation policy to conclude treaty relationships with Korea. With the exception of Russia, they restricted their activities largely to the economic sphere and served as restraining forces in the conflict of interest between China and Japan.

In the monarchial government of Korea, control had been shifting between the Taewongun—the father of the king and regent of Korea—and the Min clan headed by the queen. After the Chinese abducted the regent to Tientsin in 1882 because of his implication in the mutiny, the Min clan held control under Chinese protection.[3] Although both China and Japan withdrew their troops in compliance with the Tientsin treaty of 1885, Chinese superiority was maintained.

There is no doubt that the Japanese themselves were chiefly responsible for the weakening of their position, and their leaders were never to be satisfied until it should be reversed. Conquest of Korea had been an open issue within Japan since 1873,[4] although both ability and opportunity for such a venture were lacking.

But the balance of power in the Far East did change significantly during the two decades after the opening of the Korean ports. In Japan the new regime vigorously carried out reforms: finance was stabilized, industry was expanded, and modern military practice was adopted. China, long the dominant power, had been torn by foreign wars and internal rebellion.[5] Intelligence reports were circulating within the Japanese military staff that China's capability was no longer to be feared; so far as the military leaders were concerned, the moment for Japan to seize hegemony over the Far East and begin continental expansion had arrived.

The opportunity desired by the Japanese expansionists was very conveniently given by the Tonghak rebellion, which, spreading over Korea, finally moved the government to seek help from China—although some officials expressed apprehension. Upon receiving the request, transmitted through Yüan Shih-kai, Li Hung-chang in Peking immediately granted it and, complying with the terms of the Tientsin treaty, informed the Japanese government. About 4,000 Chinese troops arrived at Asan Bay on June 8, 1894.[6]

Before the Chinese government made known its decision on June 3, Japanese officials in Korea and leaders in Japan were well advanced in their schemes. The Japanese acting minister in Korea, Sugimura Fukashi (Shun), for example, encouraged the Chinese to send troops into Korea and at the same time requested his government to send its troops to maintain the balance. On June 1 Yüan Shih-kai sent a cablegram to Li Hung-chang about the attitude of the Japanese: the translator at the Japanese legation, Yüan reported, had informed him that the prolonged disturbance by the Tonghak rebels had caused great commercial loss and other anxieties. "The Koreans certainly could not terminate the rebellion—so why did not China suppress it quickly? Our (Japanese) government would not have any objection." [7] Two days later Yüan sent another cable message to Li:

> Sugimura of the Japanese legation came to see me to convey the idea that China is expected to suppress the rebellion quickly on behalf of Korea, and he asked whether China will promise to do so or not . . . Sugimura is my old friend and his conversation emphasized [the plight of] Japanese businessmen in Korea. It seems to me he has no other intention.[8]

Meanwhile Sugimura reported to his superiors that the sending of the Chinese troops was a further step toward consolidation of the Chinese position and suggested that his government also send troops.[9] On June 2 the Japanese cabinet immediately agreed upon the necessity for such action.[10]

According to Ōtori Keisuke, the Japanese minister to Korea, there were differing opinions as to the mission of the troops. Conflict between the cabinet and the military leaders, the central problem for many a Japanese cabinet before 1945, was already manifest. Thus a biography of Ōtori states:

> The opinion of the government was divided into two groups. Count Itō (then premier), who was in charge of political affairs, seemed to have tried to avoid conflict with the Chinese by adhering to pacifism to the end. On the other hand Lieutenant General Kawakami (Sōroku), who was only an assistant chief of staff but in actuality was the head of the army, . . . wanted to take the opportunity to place Korea under our protection in order to contribute to the growth of the empire. Therefore, although the cabinet regarded the motive of sending troops as a means to maintain the balance of power, the general staff saw it as an opportunity to start the war.[11]

The military view has been described by Hayashi Tadasu, then vice-minister of foreign affairs. On the same day that the cabinet decided to send troops into Korea, Foreign Minister Mutsu Munemitsu, Hayashi, and Lieutenant General Kawakami met at Mutsu's residence and discussed the problem:

In the incidents at Seoul in 1882 and 1884 the Chinese forestalled us and we ended in failures. We must forestall the Chinese this time and recover from the losses on previous occasions. It is said that the Chinese forces now in Asan, Korea, number 5,000. If they hear of our marching into Seoul, the Chinese troops, being accustomed to victories, will surely come to attack our troops. If we destroy them there, 20,000 to 30,000 troops would be sent by Li Hung-chang out of 40,000 troops under him. We then may send as many troops to meet them in Pyongyang. After winning the battle in Pyongyang, we may conclude a peace treaty and place Korea under our influence.[12]

When Mutsu, the leader of the expansionist group, expressed doubt whether Premier Itō would consent to sending a force of 7,000 troops, Kawakami answered, "Let us present it as a brigade. Since the premier knows that a brigade is composed of 2,000 troops, he will probably not disapprove. But if we send a mixed brigade, it will have seven to eight thousand troops." [13]

An Imperial headquarters (*daihonei*) was established in Tokyo on June 5. According to Professor Tabohashi, the authority on Sino-Japanese relations of this period, the headquarters was established in order to transfer the power of decision from the cabinet to the Military Department, the purpose of this transfer being to facilitate the opening of the war.[14] Six warships, carrying 431 marines, were immediately dispatched to Chemulpo (the present Inchon), and the marines were in Seoul on June 10. Army troops began to arrive at Inchon on June 12.

The situation in Korea by this time was almost back to normal and did not warrant the presence of so many troops for the maintenance of order. This fact, however, was not to deter the Japanese military staff from carrying out its preëstablished designs. Some of the documents exchanged within the Japanese hierarchy reveal the process through which the design was executed. For instance, the commander of the squadron at Inchon, Lieutenant General Itō of the Japanese Navy, wrote to a friend in the Navy Department:

. . . conditions in this place and in Seoul are very quiet and there has not been the slightest incident, nor have I heard of any. It is rumored that the Chinese troops in Asan are to return to China in the near future and that they are now awaiting their orders and ships. Our reconnaissance reports the same . . .[15]

Shrewd Li Hung-chang, well aware of the adverse situation China confronted, was not to spare any means to pacify the Japanese.

Ōtori, returning to Seoul on June 10, sent similar reports to the Foreign Minister:

The condition in Seoul is calm. There is no change in the condition of rebels. Until further reports by telegram are sent, please hold the dispatch of the rest of the troops. . . . It is feared that under the present situation in Seoul there is no justification to send in numerous troops.[16]

These reports were presumably hidden from Premier Itō.

Although negotiations were carried out between Ōtori and Yüan Shih-kai for withdrawing the troops of both countries and agreement had almost been reached,[17] and Ōtori on June 16 again reported the situation as peaceful, the policy of the Japanese military leaders was not to be changed.[18] To the pro-war faction, as well as to the Foreign Minister, it was important that the Army troops should march into Seoul rather than wait at Inchon. For their having dispatched a disproportionate force to Korea without the full knowledge of the cabinet, the burden of starting a war fell upon Mutsu and Kawakami. The Foreign Minister therefore in a telegram on June 13 had already ordered Ōtori to find any possible pretext:

In accordance with your opinion, the General Staff Office ordered Ōshima (commander of the mixed brigade) to station the troops in Inchon. What is your reason for preventing the advancement of the troops into Seoul? As you know, it has been fully anticipated that this action would cause the Chinese and the Koreans to have some apprehensions. If the troops of Ōshima are stationed in Inchon for long, perhaps the opportunity to advance to Seoul will be lost. If nothing is done and the troops advance nowhere and if they are finally to return to Japan without accomplishing anything, it will not only be unsightly, but will not be good policy. Unless there are especially grave obstacles, it would be preferable to advance the troops into Seoul without delay.[19]

Not content with this message, he sent another immediately afterward, ordering that the task of subjugating the Tonghak rebels be used as the excuse for advancing the troops into Seoul:

Although it will be necessary to station a small part of the troops in Inchon . . . it will be advisable to advance the main forces of Ōshima's unit into Seoul despite some diplomatic controversy. Since the quick restoration of peace is most desirable, it will be permissible to offer the subjugation of the insurgents by the Japanese troops in the event the Chinese troops do not advance from Asan. Regarding future policy toward Korea, the Japanese government may inevitably have to use force. This minister is in the process of negotiating with Count Itō.[20]

These orders seem to have surprised Ōtori, who had been negotiating for evacuation of the troops. In his reply he questioned the intentions of the foreign minister:

The insurgents are defeated in Cholla Province, and the Chinese troops are not sent into Seoul. In these circumstances it is not only unnecessary to send numerous troops into Seoul in order to protect the legation and the residents, but would provoke the Chinese and the Russians as well as others to send in their troops. . . . Unless the present situation changes and we are placed in danger, no good reason can be found to advance four thousand troops into Seoul. I believe this kind of action by the Japanese government would endanger our diplomatic relationship.[21]

It was then that the idea of reforming the Korean government and removing the obnoxious Min clan was proposed. Sugimura Fukashi, the secretary of the Japanese legation, who had disagreed with Ōtori on evacuation of the troops, sent a memorandum to Mutsu urging his government to use the occasion to extend Japanese power, carry out a revolution against the existing Korean government, and enforce reforms. The memorandum, sent from Inchon on June 13 without Ōtori's knowledge, said:

1. Through our action on this occasion we must suppress the pretensions of the Chinese in Korea, reduce the power and influence of the Chinese over Korea in the future, and secretly increase our power. In order to achieve this purpose we must not withdraw the troops, but make the other side propose the evacuation of the troops and also let them carry out their proposals.

2. Arouse a revolution within Korea, remove the Min clan, and advance the opposition party or the neutrals to the government. The power of Min Yong-jun [22] has been waning during the past few days, and also the return of the Taewongun into the royal court [23] has opened opportunities. If we . . . advance the troops into Seoul, this purpose will be attained almost with certainty. Therefore it is necessary that the troops not be evacuated until the revolution is completed. I believe that if the Min party should be removed and the opposition party or the neutrals advanced to the government it will be of advantage to Korea in the future and, consequently, to our advantage.

3. When matters are settled, we must attain agreement with the Chinese government and advise the Korean government to carry out internal reforms under the allegation that the Korean government has not been able to subdue the insurgents and hence has disturbed the neighboring nations. The treaty of Tientsin states that the governments of China and Japan may advise the Korean government, invite foreign instructors, and train the troops. According to these provisions, the area of advice may be extended.[24]

It is not clear whether Mutsu received this memorandum before the cabinet meeting on June 14, but the cabinet did then decide upon reform in Korea. The Foreign Minister therefore proposed to the Chinese government a joint carrying-out of reforms in Korea; [25] at the same time he ordered Ōtori to station the Japanese troops in Seoul upon whatever excuse might be available.[26]

The Chinese minister to Japan, Wang Fêng-ch'ou, delivered on June 21 the anticipated reply of Li Hung-chang rejecting the proposals. The Japanese government thereupon, on June 22, declared its intention to carry out the reforms alone and, on June 23, ordered that the troops at Inchon should march into Seoul and that those on ships should be landed.[27] On June 27 Foreign Secretary Katō Masuo arrived in Seoul with the instructions of Foreign Minister Mutsu to Ōtori that "War is inevitable under the present situation. So that the blame may not be placed upon us, produce an excuse to open the war through whatever means may be necessary." [28]

On June 28 Mutsu sent detailed instructions to Ōtori regarding reform proposals to be placed before the Korean court.[29] On the same day Ōtori presented the famous five points of reforms.[30]

Li Hung-chang, at the seat of power in China, suspecting the Japanese intention, desperately tried to resolve the Korean situation without a war; the Russian and British ministers to China, Count A. P. Cassini and Sir Nicholas Occoner, were called in to mediate a withdrawal of the troops of both China and Japan; but all was in vain. On July 13 Mutsu notified Ōtori that "the most urgent task at this time is to promote a conflict between China and Japan. [You are instructed] to employ whatever methods may be necessary. I shall take all the responsibility, and hence you need not reflect upon the consequences." [31] On July 19 the Imperial headquarters instructed Major General Ōshima to attack the Chinese troops in Korea at his discretion.[32]

Acting upon the Foreign Minister's orders, Ōtori began maneuvers to accomplish what was desired. On July 10 he laid before three commissioners appointed by the Korean government another detailed plan for reform. This consisted of twenty-seven articles, with the proviso that seven [33] must be carried out within ten days and the Japanese Minister be notified of the decision within three days.[34] Obviously the execution of the plan was physically impossible. The

Korean government therefore refused to accept it, arguing that it was clearly an interference with internal affairs, and instead made a counterdemand that the Japanese withdraw their troops.[35]

Ōtori, now intent upon provoking conflict in Korea, went on to demand that the government repair the telecommunication lines between Seoul and Pusan immediately and construct quarters for 1,000 soldiers.[36] On July 20 he further demanded of the Korean government that the Chinese troops be withdrawn immediately: because Korea was an independent nation, the Chinese were not justified in sending their troops "to protect a tributary state." [37] When the baffled Korean government replied on July 22 that it was in the process of negotiating with the Chinese for withdrawal of their troops, the Japanese minister presented the argument that the reply was unsatisfactory and that, to carry out a treaty provision [38] and protect the independence of Korea, Japan might resort to military force.[39]

As is clear from Sugimura's memorandum of June 13, the first step for the Japanese to take with regard to domestic politics in Korea was to remove the dominant Min clan. On July 23, two days before the opening of the conflict with the Chinese troops, a Japanese regiment surrounded and attacked the royal palace, repelling or disarming the royal guards and other Korean troops in Seoul. The Taewongun, a strong opponent of the Min clan and father of the king, was induced to take over the government [40] and the members of the Min clan were either dismissed or sent into exile.[41] The Taewongun was in no sense pro-Japanese, but because he was the only influential figure capable of replacing the Min clan he was chosen as a lesser evil.

The events of the Sino-Japanese War of 1894–1895 need not be retold here. The Japanese engaged the Chinese fleet in the first modern sea battle on June 25 and subsequently defeated the crumbling Chinese forces at sea and on land. The Chinese regent, Yüan Shih-kai, fled to China in the early stages of the war, and the Japanese consolidated their position in Korea. The cabinet was reorganized under Japanese hegemony and staffed with pro-Japanese and neutral members. Various governmental reforms were initiated under Japanese supervision; most of the proposed social reforms were not effected.[42]

If all the reforms had been realized, Korea would have been modernized to a substantial degree. But the radical nature of the program and the fact that Japanese military power was behind it provoked the Korean people to regard reform as undesirable. The successive cabinets between 1894 and 1896 were regarded by the Korean elite as puppets of the Japanese; consequently the programs of these cabinets were held in disfavor. Furthermore, there were conflicts between the Taewongun, who continued to be anti-Japanese, and the pro-Japanese cabinets. Hence Ōtori, still minister to Korea, was unable to get results. In October, 1895, he was replaced by the former Minister of Home Affairs, Inoue Kaoru, who was able to wield more influence in the Korean court. Immediately after his arrival, Inoue removed the ex-regent from power, placed the monarchy and the queen under his control, brought back pro-Japanese Korean progressives from exile,[43] and attempted to reinforce measures for reform.

The triumph of the Japanese was temporary. Serious pressures from abroad and a series of blunders in Korea soon brought about a loss of their prestige and predominance. The decline was precipitated by Japan's inability to repel the pressure exerted by Russia, Germany, and France against the terms of the Treaty of Shimonoseki (April 17, 1895). Japan had acquired from China the Liaotung Peninsula, Formosa, and the Pescadores, in addition to indemnity, and, by the terms of a new commercial treaty signed the next year at Peking, was also accorded extraterritoriality and given most-favored-nation status.

Intervening in China's favor, the tripartite powers forced the relinquishment of the Liaotung Peninsula. In December, 1895, Japan announced that the territory would be restored. This concession toward the tripartite powers, especially toward Russia, was regarded in Korea as a sign of weakness. The disgruntled royal court, including the king, the queen, and the Min clan, therefore began to carry out designs to end Japanese power in Korea. The court encouraged a closer relationship with the Russian chargé d'affaires in Seoul and strove to take control from the pro-Japanese cabinet. Upon the discovery of the plot of Pak Yŏng-hyo, the pro-Japanese Minister of Home Affairs, to stage a palace revolt in collaboration with Korean military officers trained under Japanese advisers, some of the pro-

Japanese elements fled the country and most of the Japanese advisers were forced to leave.[44] Inoue at this time was replaced as minister to Korea by an Army lieutenant general, Miura Gorō.[45]

Considering the delicate international situation of Korea, Miura, a stereotype of the simple-minded soldier, was a bad choice for this all-important position. What was needed was a seasoned diplomat, not a bully-like samurai. Miura's blunders finally caused Japan to withdraw from Korea. The assassination of Queen Min is a case in point.

The character of Miura and of his actions is clearly depicted in the statement of preliminary inquiry issued January 20, 1896, by the Hiroshima local court which tried him and his followers on the charge of complicity in the murder of the queen:[46]

> . . . Miura Goro assumed his official duties as His Imperial Majesty's Envoy Extraordinary and Minister Plenipotentiary at Seoul on the last of September, the 28th year of Meiji (1895). According to his observations, things in Korea were tending in a wrong direction. The Court was daily growing more and more arbitrary, and attempting wanton interference with the conduct of State affairs. Disorder and confusion were in this way introduced into the system of administration that had just been reorganized under the guidance and advice of the Imperial Government. The Court went so far in turning its back upon Japan that a project was mooted for disbanding the Kunreitai (*kunrentai*) troops, drilled by Japanese officers, and punishing their officers. Moreover, a report came to the knowledge of the said Miura that the Court had under contemplation a scheme for usurping all political power by degrading some and killing others of the Cabinet Ministers suspected of devotion to the cause of progress and independence.
>
> Under these circumstances, he was greatly perturbed, inasmuch as he thought that the attitude assumed by the Court not only showed remarkable ingratitude towards this country [Japan], which had spent labour and money for the sake of Korea, but was also calculated to thwart the work of internal reform and jeopardize the independence of the Kingdom. The accused felt it to be of urgent importance to apply an effective remedy to this state of affairs, so as on the one hand to secure the independence of the Korean Kingdom, and on the other, to maintain the prestige of this Empire in that country. While thoughts like these agitated his mind, he was secretly approached by the Tai Won-kun (Taewongun) with a request for assistance, the Prince being indignant at the untoward turn that events were taking and having determined to undertake the reform of the Court and thus discharge his duty of advising the King.
>
> The accused then held at the Legation a conference with Sugimura Fukashi

and Okamoto Ryunosuke, on the 3rd of October last. The decision arrived at on that occasion was that assistance should be rendered to the Tai Won-kun's entry into the Palace by making use of the Kunrentai who, being halted by the Court, felt themselves in danger, and of the young men who deeply lamented the course of events, and also by causing the Japanese troops stationed in Seoul to offer their support to the enterprise. It was further resolved that this opportunity should be availed of for taking the life of the Queen, who exercised overwhelming influence in the Court. . . . Miura Goro and others decided to carry out the concerted plan by the middle of the month.

On October 7, 1895, according to the same statement, An Kyŏng-su, the Korean Minister of War, visited the Japanese legation. Referring to the projected disbanding of the *hullyŏndae* (*kunrentai,* Japanese-trained troops), he asked Miura's views on the subject. The Japanese minister decided that the moment for reversing the unfavorable direction of events had arrived and that no more delay should be made:

Miura Goro and Sugimura Fakashi consequently determined to carry out the plot on the night of that very day. . . . Miuro Goro further issued instructions to [the] Commander of the Japanese Battalion in Seoul, ordering him to facilitate the Tai Won-kun's entry into the palace by directing the disposition of the Kunrentai troops, and by calling out the Imperial force for their support. Miura also summoned [two of his followers] and requested them to collect their friends, meeting Okamoto at Yongsan, and act as the Tai Won-kun's bodyguard on the occasion of His Highness's entrance into the Palace.

Miura told them that on the success of the enterprise depended the eradication of the evils that had done so much michief to the Kingdom for the past twenty years, and instigated them to dispatch the Queen when they entered the Palace. [Okamoto] assembled the whole party outside the front gate of the Prince's residence and declared that on entering the Palace the "fox" should be dealt with according as exigency might require, the obvious purport of this declaration being to instigate his followers to murder Her Majesty the Queen. . . . About dawn, the whole party entered the Palace through the Kwang-hwa Gate, and at once proceeded to the inner-chamber.

Accounts of the atrocities committed by the Japanese *sōshi* ("strong men") within the palace in the early morning of October 8 appear in a few different versions, disagreeing in details but unanimous in substance. The report prepared by the Korean Higher Court in 1896 by order of the pro-Russian Minister of Justice Yi Pŏm-jin is probably the most accurate.[47] It states that the Japanese soldiers, entering from the Kwanghwa Gate, surrounded the building occupied by the king and queen. Under protection of the troops, thirty or more *sōshi* rushed in with drawn swords and searched the private rooms. They seized the palace women, dragged them about by the hair, and beat them to make them divulge the whereabouts of the queen. An American who was connected with the royal guard was also asked similar questions and threatened. The *sōshi* finally found the queen hiding in a side room and cut her down with their swords. Her body was then wrapped up with a silk quilt and taken to a grove of trees not far distant; wood was piled around, kerosene was poured on, and all was set on fire.

Afterward the cabinet attempted to maintain a fiction that the queen had fled. Foreign delegates in Seoul, however, particularly the American, Dr. Horace Allen, and the Russian, Karl Waeber, as well as the Koreans, pressed for investigation. The Japanese press also strongly suspected the involvement of the *sōshi* and urged that the situation be clarified.[48] Inoue Kaoru was sent to investigate, and Miura was shortly replaced as minister by Komura Jutarō, who had been the chief of the Bureau of Political Affairs in the Foreign Ministry. Miura and his followers were recalled to Japan and subsequently arrested and tried, but were released for lack of evidence. On December 1 the Korean government formally announced the death of the queen.[49]

Amid the confusion of rumors and suppositions, the masses seem at first to have shown indifference:

> Rumors were constantly flying about but the Korean people seemed to be impervious to any impression one way or the other. When interrogated they said it was a quarrel of the aristocracy, some of whom were getting killed and many others were fleeing—it did not concern the people.[50]

But this did not last long after the facts became known. On November 28 a group of loyalists attempted to attack the cabinet members. Im Ch'oe-su, who had angrily resigned from the post of chamberlain, was approached by Yi Chae-sun, the Minister of the Royal Household, with a secret message from the king urging elimination of the traitorous cabinet.[51] He then conferred with several military officials and made contact with two commanders of the royal guards. Im

Ch'oe-su gathered together more than thirty associates and mobilized about two hundred troops from royal guard companies for an attack on the palace. But the two commanders, who had promised to open the gates, betrayed the plan, and guards on duty repulsed the attack.[52] Those involved in the plot were arrested. Im Ch'oe-su and another leader were sentenced to death; some others were exiled.[53] The sentences were particularly harsh because the cabinet had been attacked.[54] Yi Se-jin, one of the loyalists, escaped arrest and went to a province south of Seoul where he rose in arms in collaboration with the prefectural governor, but their group was suppressed by government forces.[55]

Although the assassination of the queen did not evoke any large-scale revolt, the news of it traveled afar, and indignation against the Japanese became deeply implanted in the Korean people. Kim Ku, an important nationalist leader of a later period, provides us with interesting illustration. Traveling in Manchuria in 1895 and 1896,[56] he heard a rumor that a man by the name of Kim Ri-ŏn, with the support of the Chinese local officials, was organizing an army to oppose the Japanese. On going to Shantaokou, Liaoning Province, to ascertain the facts, he found that Kim Ri-ŏn had been mobilizing a sizable armed force of hunters in Cho'san, Kanggae, and the Pyŏkdong area across the Yalu River in Korea, as well as within Manchuria. The reason given for the contemplated revolt was vengeance for the murder of the "national mother." The group distributed inflammatory manifestoes and in January, 1896, mounted an attack by more than three hundred men on the city of Kanggae, where they were quickly repelled by government troops.[57]

After this defeat Kim Ku took upon himself the task of revenge. Early in 1896 he met a strange man at a ferry station between Seoul and Anak—a Japanese in disguise. Since the man was traveling under a Korean name and was secretly carrying a Japanese sword, Kim Ku concluded that he must have had a part in the assassination of the queen, or in any event was a person harmful for Korea. Determined to revenge the national grievance, Kim attacked the Japanese and killed him.[58]

Kim Ku at this time was only a man of the commoners' class, and except for his passionate character and extraordinary courage there is no reason for us not to see him as an embodiment of the sentiment of the general public. From scattered incidents such as these, however, we can surmise that the murder of the queen did contribute greatly to anti-Japanese feeling, which in turn was one of the major elements which aroused Korean nationalist sentiment. It should be remembered, too, that the Tonghaks had been agitating in various parts of Korea with anti-Japanese slogans.

If the Japanese had not been implicated, the event might not have had much significance. When the officials and the common people were ordered to cover their hats with white as a sign of mourning for the queen, there were complaints among the population and the decree was not faithfully observed. People murmured, "What benefit did she grant me so that I should whiten my hat for the second time?" [59] In this respect the indifference of the masses at the time of the assassination may have been appropriate. But the Japanese were implicated, and the angry attempts to destroy the pro-Japanese cabinet indicate how significant, for Korean nationalism, the event was. Still, the masses might have let it pass without much more disturbance if the cabinet had taken care not to provoke them. Instead, uneasily aware of their insecurity and blinded by determination to reform the country according to the Japanese plan, the cabinet pushed the reform program to extremes and infuriated the populace.

Japanese-backed reforms had been under way since July, 1894. In large part these did not directly affect the public. For instance, the program for allowing official employment of able persons regardless of family origin could not change the existing social structure: the lower classes had not in the past had the opportunity for appropriate education, and they could not qualify for government positions; further, because of the problem of unemployment even among the yangbans, there could be no openings for persons from below. Reform in the governmental structure was therefore a least concern of the masses. The decisions of the cabinet to eliminate social distinctions, repeal the prohibition of early marriages, permit widows to remarry, etc., were regarded by the public, particularly the gentry with Confucian education, as the impositions of a foreign government and were generally ignored. But there could not be indifference to the last measure of reform ordered by the cabinet—the cutting-off of the topknot which had been worn for centuries as the sign of a mature man.

Under the Confucian precept that the body had been received from one's parents and that, consequently, the beginning of filial piety was not to inflict any damage upon it, a man was expected not even to trim his hair, which instead was to be tied in a knot atop his head. Although in ordinary times not all the people may have been aware of this ethical justification for the topknot, it was inevitable that Confucian anthority for the style should be invoked when the change was proposed. To the iconoclastic cabinet, however, removal of the awkward topknot meant an expression of progress.

On November 1, 1895, a royal proclamation let it be known that the king had had his topknot cut off and that his subjects ought to follow his example in order to contribute to the great task of modernizing Korea. On the same day the Acting Minister of Home Affairs issued a statement that cutting the hair short was beneficial to sanitation and convenient at work, and that the king, "desiring to produce a nation of wealth and strength," had set an example for the people by having his own hair cut first. "All the people of Great Korea," it was decreed, "must follow this holy desire." Immediately, policemen were sent to the streets and into each household to cut off topknots. Except for those who hid themselves, almost every man in Seoul "suffered the disgrace," and wailing was heard everywhere. "The people all over the domain were hurt by the murder of the queen and were enraged by the order of the cabinet to cut the topknots." [60] To an American observer it seemed that "the whole Korean people were worked up to a white heat against Japan, comparable only with the feelings elicited by the invasion of 1592." [61] Nevertheless the cabinet did not withdraw the decree. Special officials were sent out to expedite the reform. Roadblocks were set up at city gates, with the result that travelers avoided the major cities. Kim Ku tells that the people zealously recited the phrase, "I would rather become a devil underneath the ground without a head, than remain a man and cut my hair." [62]

The extraordinary pressures applied by some officials did not help the situation. Confucian scholars in various areas began to organize their followers, who soon rose in revolt. At least three provincial governors were killed, and many prefectural chiefs and lower officers. At least one newly appointed governor did not dare to proceed to his post.[63]

Such an uprising finally provided an occasion for the downfall of the cabinet and with it the Japanese power in Korea. Early in 1896, when rebels in Chunchon, Kangwon Province, became powerful and killed the provincial governor, a detachment from the royal guard was sent to subjugate them. But this in effect left Seoul unguarded.[64] Whether or not there were political connections between the rebels and the pro-Russian plotters then hiding in the Russian legation, the end result was the same: on the pretext of providing protection approximately a hundred and fifty Russian sailors were brought to Seoul from Inchon on February 9 and on the next day the king secretly fled with his son, the crown prince, to the legation, where he established headquarters until February of 1897. The so-called escape of the king from his own palace was a decisive blow to the cabinet and other pro-Japanese elements and to the Japanese. In effect it ended the period of supremacy Japan had achieved in Korea through victory in the war with China. Although the king lacked power of his own —for he did not command any troops primarily loyal to himself— he was still a symbol of power, and whoever could get his support could act in the king's name and thus hold mastery over the government. Unfortunately for Korea this king was irresolute, and his followers were not adept at governing or especially interested in the betterment of the country. Some of the pro-Japanese cabinet members seem to have been dedicated to the cause of reform, but the obstacles in their path were too formidable for surmounting. Other progressive elements were alienated from the masses because of the association of the Japanese with reform; had they been able to identify themselves with such groups as the Tonghaks, the future of Korea would have been quite different.

A few explanations given for the event of February 10, 1896, may be of help in understanding the situation in Korea. According to Japanese diplomatic sources, the king was told that the ex-regent (his father) and Kim Hong-jip (the premier) intended to remove him from the throne and replace him with Yi Chun-yong, his nephew, and also that the Japanese were secretly assisting this intrigue.[65] According to the secretary of the American legation, Dr. Allen, when the king asked him whether it would be wise to seek help from Russia, he endorsed the proposal and brought the Russian minister to the house of a Korean officer entrusted with the royal plans.[66]

Hwang Hyŏn presents a more detailed story. The king disliked the restrictions imposed on him by the government and, in order to eliminate the premier, decided to seek Russian aid through Yi Pŏm-jin and others who had been hiding in the Russian legation since August, 1895. Yi's group had bribed the Russians by promising that they could change the situation and would lead Korea to serve Russia's interests. The Russian minister was pleased with the scheme and therefore brought in the sailors from Inchon on the pretext of protecting the legation. Yi's group further used forty thousand pieces of silver to bribe court attendants to report to the king the intentions of the ex-regent and the premier and persuade him to flee from the palace. Startled and suspicious, the king had no choice but to make his escape. Yi Pŏm-jin's group hired two ordinary women's chairs to disguise the royal persons and successfully transported them to the Russian legation.[67] Whether or not we accept this narrative as fact, we can surmise that the king was distressed by the murder of his consort and likely to be pleased by an action that might rid the country of the Japanese.

Such is the record of the first modern attempt of the Japanese at ascendancy in Korea. In a larger context, this was their first modern attempt at expansion onto the continent. And the Japanese military leaders had in some respects succeeded in their mission. They drove the Chinese from Korea and proved to the world that Japan was capable of becoming a modern power. The victory of 1895 greatly exalted the Japanese position, externally and also internally—for the Japanese oligarchy reaped the incidental benefit of quieting the harsh opposition of the new political parties within Japan. But a dear price had to be paid. The insistence upon obtaining Liaotung[68] eventually cost the Japanese not only the Liaotung Peninsula, but also their paramount position in Korea.

The failure of the Japanese to retain power in Korea may be attributed to lack of military strength—the primary means they employed—or to lack of flexible diplomatic tactics which could be combined with military strength. But this was still the age of Spencer and Darwin: the Japanese put the failure to lack of military strength, the most convenient interpretation for the expansionists, and concentrated their national energy upon building a stronger military force. The tripartite intervention and the subsequent loss of Korea stimulated nationalism in Japan, the direction of which was to be determined by the policy of further nationalistic aggression.[69]

The failure also intensified the hostility of the Koreans, who now not only hated the Japanese but regarded them with contempt.[70] Nor did other elements than the military fare any better in gaining respect. Inoue, while he was minister to Korea, informed the Japanese cabinet on July 2, 1895, that

> Since last year, sundry kinds of Japanese have followed one another into Korea and attempted to carry out various schemes. On every possible occasion these Japanese cited the obligation of implanting independence into Korea; and, taking advantage of the victory of the Japanese army, they lodged all kinds of problems and orders upon the Koreans. Hence the Korean officials and the people were greatly annoyed, and in the end they came to be afraid of the Japanese. Also in the recent period, various Japanese have been ravaging the Korean business world . . .[71]

There is no doubt that anti-Japanese sentiment brought Koreans of the various classes closer to each other than they had been at any time in the preceding three hundred years. The people found a common enemy—a new symbol to rally around. Since animosities between classes were reduced and a new common symbol was provided, we may conclude that modern Korean nationalism was in the process of emerging. It is significant that none of the leaders retained any allegiance to China, the former suzerain.

The two symbols which aroused the greatest excitement were the assassinated queen and the topknots, and these were conservative or reactionary symbols. The queen was, certainly, a woman of extraordinarily strong character. She had been in the center of the turmoil of Korean politics for nearly two decades, struggling fiercely against her father-in-law, the Taewongun. If her assassins had not been Japanese, probably the murder would not have aroused popular feeling. She was part of the despotic monarchical system and was involved in intrigues and mischief. Her concern was, for the most part, not the welfare of the Korean people, but the enhancement of her own and her clan's power.[72]

The topknot was a no less conservative symbol. If the radical cabinet and its more radical Japanese advisers had not ordered the cutting of the topknot, the style might have gradually disappeared as Western ideas and customs were introduced into Korea. But when the topknot was selected by the pro-Japanese cabinet as a target for elimination, it became a symbol to be defended even at the expense of many lives. Retention of the topknot came to be identified not only with the preservation of age-old native custom and habit, but also with the national identity itself.

Thus the two symbols show clearly the conservative or reactionary character of early modern Korean nationalism. We can also determine the nature of the movement by examining the characteristics and motives of the leaders. Yangbans and lower-class persons alike participated in the uprisings: but the entire leadership came from the elite of the old society, and these men were, inevitably, trained and indoctrinated in the Confucian principles.[73] The masses who shared their sentiments rallied under them to oppose the policy of the government in power. The victims of the uprisings, i.e., the local governors and officials, were no less conservative or reactionary, but that could not protect them from the "Righteous Armies."

In the heat of resentment against the pro-Japanese government and the Japanese, the populace rallied to the call of the leaders, but when their initial zeal and sense of mission was removed through the lapse of time and by military defeats, the inarticulate elements of the Righteous Armies began to manifest their true identity:

> In the initial period of forced trimming of topknots, the entire nation was enraged and hence the Righteous Armies rose everywhere. But as time went by, their initial spirit vanished. Encountering the royal forces from the capital, they were miserably defeated, suffering a great number of casualties. Moreover, the number of those who were stirred to action by righteousness was very small. Those lured by the possibility of fame inaugurated the revolts and those who relished mischief followed them. When these pretenders formed a large group, they were collectively called a Righteous brigade. Half of them were even from the remnants of the Tonghaks who turned their faces to join the revolts. There were some who committed outrageous crimes not any different from those of the mad bandits. . . . Some of the leaders killed local officials, fearing reprisals . . .[74]

It would, therefore, be incorrect to assume that a true sense of national solidarity then existed among the participants in the movement or in the Korean populace as a whole. But when we consider the environment in which the uprisings took place, we can conclude that, except perhaps for the Tonghaks, the Righteous Armies were the first movement on a mass scale for Korean identity, rejecting both China and Japan. In this sense, the period of the Tonghaks and the Righteous Armies saw the beginning of modern Korean nationalism, even though the symbols involved and the attitudes of the participants were of a dubious nature and the activities were of a negative character, lacking constructive plans.

The events of the three years 1894–1896 provided the Korean leaders with some lessons which, unfortunately, they did not take. They could very well have realized that the time had come for reforming the country and strengthening its economic and military capability. But the fact that the Japanese had yielded to Russian ascendancy largely prevented the elite from realizing the necessity of reform. They seem to have believed that Korean independence could somehow be maintained by skillful manipulation of foreign interests. Something like the old relationship with China seems to have been contemplated, and the old mode of thinking remained dominant.

Of the action of Yi Pŏm-jin in facilitating the escape of the king to the Russian legation, Hwang Hyŏn states that it was not motivated by loyalty to the king or by patriotism; and "neither was it because he favored the Russians more than the Japanese. It was merely to win the power."[75] Foreign powers were regarded as tools for use in internal political battles.

Further, Japan's use of the pretext of reform as a tool for her advancement in Korea made reform repugnant to the ruling elite, already conservative as a result of centuries of indulgence in a static or classical mode of thinking. Regardless of other contingencies, it would have been easy for the elite to believe that the pro-Japanese cabinet had been destroyed by the strength of orthodox conservative leaders who were opposed to reform. This fruit of victory was not to be discarded. Korea was to remain conservative. The Russian diplomats on whom the king and the new cabinet relied were not inclined toward advising any change from a conservative, class-bound society. Advocating reform in Korea would have been tantamount to opposing the institutions of Russia itself! The other foreign power in Korea, the United States, was not interested in becoming a guardian of the crumbling kingdom.

Whether the country was ready for reform under indigenous

leadership and whether the nationalism of the succeeding years was enlightened and strong enough to sustain the independence can be considered more adequately when we have examined the developments in Korea after 1896.

4

The Reformist Movement

THROUGH skillful manipulation of domestic and international situations, the politicians who had taken refuge in the Russian legation ascended to power. On their part, the luring of the king to the legation was a superb move. They were afraid for their lives if they should openly challenge the pro-Japanese cabinet, and since the king still held nominal power, their interests could best be served by establishing him in the legation, where diplomatic immunity and the Russian sailors protected them.

Thus the fate of Korea was entrusted to the pro-Russian politicians. These men ruled from 1896 to 1905, the most crucial years in Korean history. Conscientious and efficient use of this decade would have changed the future of the country and might even have changed considerably the history of the Far East and the world. The new, pro-Russian cabinet, however, was not capable of achieving the possibilities of the situation. By the end of the period Japan had regained control, and the annexation of Korea followed in 1910.

The last years of the Yi dynasty were in several ways important for nationalist movements. (1) Some attempts were made by a small number of young intellectuals to reform Korea in order to forestall the downfall of the kingdom; their efforts were the beginning of the reformist-nationalist movement. (2) The militaristic territorial-nationalist movement, which continued up to 1945, expanded during this period. (3) As the Korean kingdom collapsed, the hitherto apolitical and apathetic masses were aroused, and their sense of nationalism was increased. In this chapter we shall examine the years between 1896 and 1898, focusing our attention on the reformist-nationalist movement of the Independence Club.

The king and the crown prince came to the Russian legation in the early hours of February 11, 1896. Later that morning the royal court, now located in the legation, began to function again. The first order of business was to establish a new cabinet.[1] Except that the members took a pro-Russian line of policy, i.e., listened to the Russian Minister instead of the Japanese Minister, and were more conservative, or reactionary, than those whom they replaced, there was little substantial difference between the new cabinet and the old.

Having lost the queen, who had actually been the intelligence and the guiding force behind the throne, the king accepted whatever suggestions were given by the Russian Minister and by a group of ill-chosen confidants.[2] Concerned mainly with plans for bestowing the highest honors possible upon his late consort, he delayed the official funeral until he had made himself emperor.[3] The queen was posthumously named Myŏngsŏng ("Bright Achievement") in January, 1897. In October of that year, eight months after the king's return to a newly constructed palace, a pompous ceremony was held to signify his accession to the title of emperor, the kingdom being renamed Taehan Cheguk ("Great Han Empire") and the deceased queen thereby becoming the Empress Myŏngsŏng. The ceremony cost nearly 100,000 *won*. In November an elaborate national funeral was observed for the empress, straining the treasury to the limit.[4]

While the emperor was preoccupied with ceremonies, he leaned heavily on the Russian Minister for guidance in governmental affairs. Japanese advisers and military instructors were replaced by Russian; Russian weapons were purchased; a school for teaching the Russian language was established; the railroad between Seoul and Wonsan was connected with the Siberian line; and Russians were granted concessions for mining and lumbering. As the Russian involvement increased, other foreign powers demanded equal shares in the development or exploitation of Korea. During the next few years Americans obtained concessions for gold mining and for railroad construction between Seoul and Inchon, British and German interests obtained concessions for gold mining, and a French company operated the railroad line from Seoul to Uiju.

Japan had suffered a loss in the game of power politics, but was by no means completely ousted. The failure in Korea brought about some political struggles in the Japanese Diet, after which an agreement was reached between the government and the Liberal party (*Jiyūtō*) for creating six additional army divisions and starting a new armament program.[5] Russia had to be countered militarily sooner or later. Preparations for another major war were begun immediately after the loss of the spoils of the war with China. Having experienced the impossibility of handling Korean affairs singlehandedly, however, the Japanese government decided to "solve the (immediate) situation through negotiation with Russia." [6] Thus on May 14, 1896, while the Korean king was still ruling from the Russian legation, representatives of Russia (Karl Waeber) and Japan (Komura Jutarō) signed a memorandum agreeing that "The two Representatives will always aim at recommending his Majesty (the king of Korea) to appoint liberal and moderate men as Ministers, and to show clemency to his subjects." [7] By the Lobanoff-Yamagata protocol, signed in Moscow on June 9, 1896, the two governments further agreed to "lend by mutual accord their assistance to Korea." [8] Thus in the delicate balance of power between Russia and Japan there was an opportunity for the Korean government to pursue progressive policies. But the king and the cabinet decided that the only sane policy was to lean on the stronger power, which at this time seemed to be Russia. Efforts by Sŏ Chae-p'il (Philip Jaisohn) and members of the Independence Club to alter the government policy, to be discussed shortly, were all in vain.

The excessive reliance upon Russia accelerated the demise of the Korean kingdom (or empire). From the moment when the king entered the legation, the control of governmental affairs was shifted from the cabinet to one individual, Kim Hong-yuk. A man of lowly origin from Tanch'ŏn in Hamgyong Province, adjacent to Russia, Kim Hong-yuk had learned to speak Russian and had served as an interpreter at the legation for several years.[9] Although the Russian Minister did not interfere in the matter of the appointment of officials, the interpreter always invoked his name:

> The king held [Kim Hong-yuk] more and more dearly. At this time the king was relying on the Russian Minister, and there was no word of his that he would not follow. It is difficult to translate the Russian language, and

only Hong-yuk was able to do so. Because of this he came to have licentious desires and to practice deceit. . . . If Hong-yuk told the king that the Russian Minister wished someone to be appointed to a certain position, the king let it be done. Many ministers and high-ranking officials were appointed from his own clan.[10]

Chŏng Kyo provides some specific examples:

Nam Chŏng-ch'ŏl was appointed Minister of Home Affairs. At this time many major and minor officials were appointed through Kim Hong-yuk who used the pretext of the Russian Minister. Kim Chung-hwan was made head of the Bureau of Local Affairs [and] Yi Ch'ung-gu was made Minister of Police Affairs—all through Hong-yuk's false submission to the king that the Russian Minister Waeber wished so. About half of the officials were appointed this way. . . . Nam Chŏng-ch'ŏl sent his concubine [to Kim Hong-yuk], let her commit adultery with him, and obtained the ministerial post.[11]

Besides securing the appointment of others, for various rewards, the nearly illiterate Kim Hong-yuk had himself appointed Vice-Minister of Education and later mayor of Seoul. His influence extended to all official posts. Until 1898, when he was dismissed from the mayorship and sent into exile, he was a virtual tyrant over Korea.[12]

It would be difficult to exaggerate the harmful effect of this kind of corruption, which was made worse by the monarch's unconcern. Some conscientious scholars submitted memorials desperately warning of the doom facing the country, but he was more interested in the proposals of persons who brought him money and goods in exchange for special privileges.[13]

The central government being so chaotic, local administration could hardly fare better. Prefectural governorships were sold openly.[14] As the officials became increasingly oppressive, the people suffered more and more. Revolts were frequent occurrences; bandits flourished everywhere; and some of the Tonghak leaders revived their movement.[15]

It was during this turmoil that Sŏ Chae-p'il (Philip Jaisohn) launched the reform movement associated with the Independence Club. This movement began early in 1896 and lasted nearly two years. Unique in Korean history, it was akin to the movements led by Wang K'ang-nien and Liang Ch'i-ch'ao in China; and just as neither Wang nor Liang was able to bring about governmental reform in China, so Sŏ Chae-p'il's efforts ended in a failure. Probably what was needed was a Sun Yat-sen, but Korea did not produce a revolutionary leader of this kind in time to prevent the downfall of the nation.[16]

Sŏ Chae-p'il was of noble birth and belonged to the generation of young Koreans who came into contact with Western ideas in the 1870's.[17] In 1884 he joined Kim Ok-kyun in the impetuous *émeute* against the Min clan. When this failed, the participants were obliged to go into exile. Sŏ Chae-p'il eventually reached the United States, became an American citizen, Anglicized his name to "Philip Jaisohn," married an American woman, and obtained a degree in medicine from George Washington University.[18]

After more than a decade of a difficult yet successful life in the United States, Jaisohn was fully saturated with democratic ideals. Although he intended to stay in his adopted country and his immediate concern was with establishing himself there, late in 1895 he was stirred by meeting a comrade of his youth and learning of the recent changes in Korea and the opportunities for reform that, at the time, seemed to be opening.[19] Jaisohn and his wife arrived in Seoul in January, 1896.

One of Jaisohn's hopes was to establish a democracy, which he thought could be realized through education. "The main purpose of my return," he wrote, "was to teach the people and to cultivate leadership." He also wished to "expel the pro-Chinese forces [and] establish a completely independent Korea." [20] Soon after his return he was offered the post of Foreign Minister in the pro-Japanese cabinet. This he declined, saying that he had no political ambitions and did not like the attitude of the Japanese Minister in Korea, Komura Jutarō; he did, however, accept a nominal post as an adviser to the Privy Council.[21] The first task he undertook was to destroy the Yŏngŭnmun, the gate on the west side of Seoul where Korean kings traditionally received delegates from the suzerain. Another gate was erected on the same site and completed in November, 1896, and was designated as the Tongnipmun, or "Independence Arch." Jaisohn hoped that the change in this symbolic structure would influence the people toward a more independent outlook.[22]

The task which most occupied Jaisohn during his two years' stay in Korea, however, was the publication of a newspaper, *The Inde-*

pendent (*Tongnip Shinmun*). Money for the venture was solicited from Yu Kil-jun, the pro-Japanese Minister of Home Affairs. Although Yu had to flee to Japan after the king's escape to the Russian legation, he arranged beforehand that the new cabinet should provide 5,000 *won* for Jaisohn's newspaper. Printing machinery was imported from Japan, and the first issue appeared on April 7, 1896, in Korean and English.[23] Only 300 copies of the Korean edition were printed at first; the number was soon increased to 500 and later reached 3,000 copies.[24]

Although Jaisohn was careful not to offend the king, his methods and arguments were very radical in the Korean context. First of all, he decided that not a single Chinese character was to be used in his newspaper and thus by advocating the sole use of the Korean ŏnmun —the alphabet of phonetic symbols invented by King Sejong in 1443 —started a literary revolution similar to that inaugurated in China by the Peking University group two decades later. This bold innovation had a lasting impact, although later generations have modified Jaisohn's policy and intermixed the Chinese characters and Korean symbols. We cannot be quite certain, however, that it helped Jaisohn's efforts for governmental reform. The yangban class had long been contemptuous of ŏnmun and had not been trained in reading materials in the Korean script, the use of which had been left to women and persons of the lower classes. Jaisohn's radical use of ŏnmun probably alienated most of the elite, whom he needed especially to reach.

His arguments were no less radical. As early as the fourth issue of the paper (April 14, 1896), an editorial expounded the necessity for the popular election of officials up to the provincial level. Since no one was trained in political science in Korea, Jaisohn pointed out, no one was capable of governing the people. The only thing to be hoped for was the placing of honest men in government positions. But when the selection of officials was made by only one man, mistakes in selection were likely to be frequent. It was for this reason, Jaisohn asserted, that people abroad elected their own officials. If the Korean people should choose theirs, the king could not be blamed for the mistakes: therefore the provincial and prefectural governors ought to be elected by the local people. Jaisohn further asserted that government officials were not only subjects of the king, but also servants of the people. This apparent effort not to provoke the king weakened Jaisohn's arguments, which were challenging enough to antagonize the ruling class and yet not forceful enough to arouse and consolidate the disgruntled elements of the populace. Officials might be infuriated by the notion that they were servants of the people; to oppressed people in the rural areas it was simply and totally alien.

In general, Jaisohn's editorials were addressed to moral education and to awakening the people to the new knowledge of the West. He constantly chastised moral corruption and called for reform. In essence, he held that if everyone became virtuous and diligent the country would become prosperous. Jaisohn's arguments had a strong Puritan tenor, and his role, therefore, was not much different from that of the Christian missionaries who began to move into Korea in 1885.[25]

As the rapid increase in sales would indicate, the newspaper drew some response, at least from residents of Seoul. The British geographer Isabella Bird Bishop wrote, commenting on *The Independent:*

> Only those who have formed some idea of the besotted ignorance of the Korean concerning current events in his own country, and of the credulity which makes him the victim of every rumor set afloat in the capital, can appreciate the significance of this step and its probable effect in enlightening the people, and in creating a public opinion which shall sit in judgment on regal and official misdeeds. It is already fulfilling an important function in unearthing abuses and dragging them into daylight, and is creating a desire for rational education and reasonable reform, and is becoming something of a terror to evil-doers. . . . The sight of newsboys passing through the streets with bundles of a newspaper in En-mun [ŏnmun] under their arms, and of men reading them in their shops, is among the novelties of 1897.[26]

In addition to his newspaper work, Jaisohn organized a political party to disseminate democratic ideals. This party, the Independence Club (*Tongnip Hyŏphoe*), was founded on July 2, 1896, in Seoul. A building where kings in the past had entertained Chinese delegates, Mohwagwan ("China Adoration Hall"), was renamed the "Hall of Independence" and used by the club. The original membership, approximately thirty persons, included high-ranking government officials and civilians.[27] Jaisohn, being an American citizen, served unofficially as an adviser.

At first the club's activities were confined to weekly meetings, which often included debates by the members on issues likely to propagate liberal thoughts. Jaisohn wrote afterward that the meetings had a humorous aspect in that none of the group had any training in parliamentary procedure or public speaking, and such topics as "Is it right to have one's hair cut?" and "Is it necessary to have street lights?" were debated. When the members ran out of topics, they played chess or engaged in other social activities.[28] Debates on politics and administration were kept to a minimum during the first year because of the sensitivity of the governmental officials who were members. Those who had no connection with the government and advocated political discussions and criticism were countered by the "moderate group" of the officials.[29] In November, 1897, the *Korean Repository* noted that "the club is essentially an educational and social institution and stands aloof from politics." [30]

But as Russia's power in Korea became evident and her demands for concessions increased, the younger nongovernmental members of the club became insistent upon political activity, particularly when the Russian minister, Alexis Spayer, gained a lease of Deer Island (Chŏlyŏng-do) in Pusan harbor from the Acting Minister of Foreign Affairs, Min Chong-muk. Numbering hundreds by that time—February, 1898—they held public meetings and drafted a letter to Min vigorously attacking the lease as a first step toward Korea's becoming a protectorate as had happened in Indochina. The *Independent* echoed this sentiment and criticized the government in pointed language.[31]

The exposure of the incident by the club and its newpaper made it clear that the decision to lease the island was that of the Acting Minister alone and lacked the approval of the cabinet; Min had, in fact, been appointed temporarily because the Minister of Foreign Affairs, Yi To-jae, declined to take part in the negotiations. Min was dismissed, but for only one day. Spayer put pressure upon the king by threatening to withdraw the Russian advisers; the interpreter, Kim Hong-yuk, joined in and succeeded in having Min installed as Minister of Foreign Affairs.[32]

When the Independence Club actively delved into the political sphere, most of the moderates (those with government positions) withdrew from membership. Led by Yun Ch'i-ho, who had returned from a tour of study in the United States, the younger group continued their radical activities. Street meetings continued, some anti-Russian handbills were posted, and memorials were submitted. The tone of the arguments at the public meetings and in the letters, already pungent, now became more so. Finally, on March 7, indignant over the anti-Russian feelings that were mounting among the population in Seoul,[33] Spayer submitted an ultimatum accusing the government of ingratitude and demanding that a decision be made within twenty-four hours as to whether further Russian assistance was needed. He also obtained immediate audience with the emperor and stipulated that unless a number of anti-Russian officials were eliminated and the hostile demonstrations were suppressed his government would withdraw its financial adviser and all its military instructors, numbering about sixty.[34]

The ultimatum was, of course, welcomed by the Independence Club. Earlier, according to Chŏng Kyo, who was then secretary of the club, Jaisohn secretly instructed him to hold a mass meeting to urge that the government dismiss the Russian financial adviser and the military instructors.[35] On March 9 or 10, at a meeting attended by 8,000 persons, the members unanimously decided to submit a letter to the government demanding the dismissal.[36] Since the population in Seoul, at least this part of it, was manifesting anti-Russian sentiment, the government yielded.

The haughty and self-righteous attitude of Spayer could not favorably have impressed the Korean court, and if the Japanese accounts are accurate, the dismissal of the Russians had the Japanese blessing also.[37] In any event, the financial adviser and the military instructors left in a few days, and Spayer had himself transferred to Brazil. The Russo-Korean Bank, established in Seoul less than a month before, was closed. Russian dominance thus collapsed, mainly because of Spayer's errors of judgment. Already, however, the center of Russian interest was shifting to Manchuria, relaxing the pressure upon Korea.

This outcome was a victory for the Independence Club and for Jaisohn himself, but it had adverse consequences for them. The government, still dominated by conservatives and increasingly angered by the activities of the club and the pointed criticism published in *The Independent,* used the incident as grounds for dropping Jaisohn from his post as adviser to the Privy Council. The government also let it be known to the American consul general that Jaisohn's removal from Korea was desired.

Although in 1896 the government had been willing to accept Jaisohn in Korea and had even financed the newspaper, a clash was inevitable. Jaisohn's editorial arguments were highly respectful of the monarch, and his criticisms of officials were somewhat less harsh than he would have liked, but the conservatives found no consolation in these facts. Also, he was regarded as arrogant.[38] It is possible that his American citizenship was a sore point.[39] Further, his followers' pleas for an independent foreign policy, basically an antiforeign policy, offended both the Russians and the Japanese. The Russian ambassador in the United States is said to have tried to persuade President Theodore Roosevelt to recall Jaisohn from Korea; an American employed by the Japanese government wrote an article ridiculing his work, calling him an idiot and a Don Quixote; finally, a telegram was sent from the United States falsely stating that his mother-in-law was seriously ill. Under multiple pressures Jaisohn and his wife left Korea in May, 1898.[40]

Jaisohn's career as a reformer and educator of Korea was thus short and turbulent, but his followers continued their activities until the government ordered the disbanding of the Independence Club late in 1898. In fact, during the few months of its existence that remained, the club increased its influence. For a while it seemed that Korea was on the way to becoming a constitutional monarchy. The Independence Club constantly exposed the wrongs of government officials, prevented foreign agents from taking advantage of the country's weakness, and forced the government to listen to public opinion. For instance, in July, 1898, when the government secretly brought in thirty foreigners from Shanghai to be employed as royal guards, opposition from the club was such that the men were sent back.[41]

In early October of the same year the club carried out a massive demonstration against corruption and inefficiency among the cabinet members by holding public meetings in front of the government buildings, mobilizing nearly ten thousand residents of Seoul. The demonstrators stayed there for three consecutive days, and the cabinet finally resigned en masse.[42] The club was able to hold an interview with the new government which led to an agreement to establish a working "privy council" where public opinion would be reflected.

Furthermore, on October 29 the club mobilized several thousand persons in the main business street of Seoul and held a "Joint Conference of the Government Officials and the People" (*Kwanmin Kongdonghoe*). Although the meeting was initiated by the club, student groups and many other organizations took part, and some cabinet ministers attended under pressure. The conference came to agreement upon six articles which were subsequently sanctioned by the emperor and published in the government gazette. Had these articles been faithfully executed, many mistakes of the past might have been corrected. The six articles proposed:

1. That both officials and people shall determine not to rely on any foreign aid but to do their best to strengthen and uphold the Imperial prerogatives.
2. That all documents pertaining to foreign loans, the hiring of foreign soldiers, to grant concessions, etc., in short, every document drawn up between the Korean government and a foreigner shall be signed and stamped by all the Ministers of State and the President of the Privy Council.
3. That important offenders shall be punished only after they have been given a public trial and an ample opportunity to defend themselves.
4. That to His Majesty shall belong the power of appointing his ministers, but that in case the majority of the Cabinet disapproves a man, he shall not be appointed.
5. That all sources of revenue and methods of raising taxes shall be placed under the control of the Finance Department, no other department or officer or a private corporation being allowed to interfere therewith, and that the annual estimates and balance shall be made public.
6. That the existing laws and regulations shall be enforced without fear or favor.[43]

The Independence Club was triumphant and vigorous. By a royal order of November 3, the club was to elect twenty-five members or half the membership of the Privy Council on November 5. But enemies of the club succeeded in discrediting it before dawn of that day.

According to Chŏng Kyo, the plot against the club was masterminded by Cho Pyŏng-sik, the incumbent Second Minister of the State Council, who had earlier been dismissed from his post because of the club's opposition. If Chŏng's account is correct, Cho produced an anonymous letter alleging that the club intended to proclaim a republic on November 5 and elect Pak Chŏng-yang, the incumbent premier, as president; the vice-presidency and key cabinet appointments were to be filled by club officers. On the basis of this letter the arrest of the leaders of the club was ordered early on the morning of November 5. Seventeen were arrested, and documents of the club were confiscated.[44] Within a few hours an imperial order disbanding the club was issued.

Popular support was too impressive to keep the leaders in jail for long. A multitude soon gathered before the government buildings and again remained for several days, and merchants closed their shops in protest. When attempts to persuade the demonstrators to leave were unsuccessful, the use of arms was considered. Foreign Minister Min Chong-muk asked the opinions of the British and American representatives in Korea—all of whom were appalled at the notion.[45] Unable to resist public and diplomatic opinion, Cho Pyŏng-sik and Min Chong-muk resigned from their posts and released the club leaders.

Subsequent developments leading to the collapse of the movement have been described by Yun Ch'i-ho, the club president:

> Naturally enough the Independents demanded the punishment of those who had played the nasty trick. The people held meetings in front of the Palace. But since the wretched plot against the Independents had been concocted and carried out by some of the most influential so-called courtiers, the redress was not granted. The government decided to solve the problem in a way worthy of Korean statesmanship. A band of hoodlums was organized into a Peddlers' Guild; and, on the morning of November 21, the braves "cleaned out" the people's meeting by brutal force, injuring a number of people who had been asking for nothing but justice. The people of the city took side with the Independents, and fights ensued between them and the loyal peddlers, backed by the powers that be. Riots took place. In order to protect certain worthies from justice, the government came near plunging the whole city into ruin and anarchy.
>
> On the twenty-sixth of November, His Majesty, in the presence of the representatives of the treaty Powers, of the soldiers and of the officials, most graciously and solemnly promised to the people:
>
> 1. That the peddlers should be dispersed.
> 2. That the persons who manufactured the fabrications against the Independents should be punished.
> 3. That the Independence Club should be re-established.
> 4. That the Six Articles should be gradually enforced.[46]

The eventual downfall of the club was not solely blamed upon the government. Even to the club president, the movement was becoming too wild and radical:

> It is true that none of the Imperial promises had yet been fulfilled; but the people should have been patient. *But the run of uninterrupted success blinded some of the hot-headed youths, and the popular meetings had gone beyond the more or less wise control of the Independence Club.* The meetings, restarted on the 6th of December against sober advice, became careless and impudent. On the 16th of December the Privy Council recommended the recall of Pak

Yonghio [from Japan]. The popular meeting had the imprudence to endorse the action of the Privy Council. The more conservative part of the people revolted against the very mention of the name. When suspicion went abroad that the popular agitations had been started in the interest of Pak, the meetings lost the sympathy of the people. The government seized this opportunity and ventured to use violence in dispensing a handful of men who tried to keep up the fruitless demonstrations.

The government promised most solemnly that all past misconducts would be pardoned and that no arrest of those who had been prominent in the People's Meeting should be made. Those promises have been kept in the shape of arresting the former Independents on fictitious information, such as planning to make Pak Yonghio the King of Korea, etc.!!! [47]

Such, in brief substance, is the history of the only progressive movement in Korea under the old regime. The entire movement was addressed to maintaining, while modernizing and strengthening, the Korean kingdom, in this sense it was the first of the reformist-nationalist type. Although the numbers of persons reported to have been present at the mass meetings may have been exaggerated, there is no doubt that the strength of the Independents was considerable. Jaisohn reported that the club had at least 2,000 members at the end of 1898,[48] and there is little reason to doubt his statement. Considering that the movement lasted only about two years, this small fraction in a population of eighteen to twenty millions is nevertheless an indication of vitality. And although some of the members were not sincere believers in progress, these and other conservatives like them nevertheless did pay homage to the ideas of the Independence Club.

Enlightenment—which actually meant the imitation of Western customs and manners—was very much in vogue and probably was one of the reasons why the government tolerated the Independents as long as it did. Another factor favorable to the progressives arose from the Japanese victory over China in 1895, after which the Korean Court abrogated all political and cultural obligations to its traditional suzerain, and from the tripartite intervention, after which the Japanese overlordship was also removed. Since Korean independence had been so frequently discussed in power politics—everything that Japan and Russia did in Korea was in the name of Korean independence—the notion of independence was in the air. That the king should declare himself emperor testifies to it. Under the Confucian conception of international order, only the head of the Middle Kingdom was entitled to be emperor, and no ruler in a country within the sphere of Chinese control would have been so presumptuous as to use the title.

Thus the notions of enlightenment and independence were popular, at least superficially, among some of the Korean people. Overestimation of progressive sentiment was, however, one of the crucial errors made by the Independents. The Christian mission schools had just been opened, and these schools had only a few hundred students.[49] Contacts with the West since 1876, though considerable, were mostly limited to small coteries in the capital. Korea was not ready for progressive reforms originating at the grass-roots level.

As in Japan, positive and successful reform was possible only from the top. The Korean government, like the Chinese, made a few concessions and promises to the advocates of reform, but grudgingly and only under pressure. Every opportunity to eliminate the source of the pressure was sought by the ruling elite. Indeed, the progressives in Korea were suppressed at the first opportunity that became available.

The experience of modern Asia indicates that a major reform and rejuvenation of a reactionary society and government is possible only through the effective use of violence, through revolution, which means the complete replacement of rulers by a new element. No halfway measure has yet succeeded in Asia. (Thailand might be an exception to this generalization.) Reform by pressure presupposes an organized and influential group with at least a rudimentary progressive consciousness such as normally arises from education. When most members of the educated class remain reactionary or conservative in outlook, progressive leaders are forced to educate a new group, and when the need is urgent, education may take too long. Jaisohn chose this long and precarious road. Revolution was not on the agenda of the Independence Club.

The Independents became active soon after the defeat of the Tonghaks, but sought no connection with them. Since the Tonghaks were numerous throughout Korea and the Independence Club had many branches in the provinces, connections could easily have been made. Had the Independents provided intellectual leadership and the Tonghaks the strength of their numbers, a revolution or at least a stronger pressure group could have been produced. Perhaps the fear of involving the Japanese military power forestalled the thought of an alliance, or, more significantly, the religious and social differences between the two groups. Most of the leaders of the Independence Club, including Jaisohn and Yun Ch'i-ho, were Christian converts and of Yanghan origin. It is most likely that an alliance with the Tonghaks was unacceptable to them because of their nonpragmatic idealism: the newly acquired and hence zealous conviction that right makes might. Alliance with such a subversive and heathenish group would have seemed sinister and ungentlemanly. Born out of idealism, the progressive movement died from lack of realistic political experience. The task of governing Korea was left to self-righteous and often corrupt conservatives who fancied that their rule might be perpetuated through the manipulation of international rivalries.

5

Demise of the Korean Kingdom

AFTER THE PROGRESSIVES were crushed at the end of 1898, politics in Korea returned to the normal, traditional behavior. Corruption, self-aggrandizement, and inefficiency were dominant within the government, as before. Meanwhile, Russia, Japan, Britain, Germany, and the United States were engaged in a Far Eastern power struggle centered in the issue of "cutting the China melon." Only Russia and Japan were actively involved in Korea, where the Japanese government wished to obtain a free hand in exchange for recognizing Russian predominance in Manchuria. Russia was unwilling to negotiate on those terms, and a compromise was reached in 1898 which slightly favored the Japanese position in Korea.[1] Tension between the two increased, particularly after the Boxer uprising in 1900, when the Russian attempt to occupy Manchuria was opposed by the Japanese as a threat to their hegemony in Korea. The tsar's adamant desire to occupy Manchuria and northern Korea finally led to the shelling of his warships at Port Arthur by the Japanese on February 10, 1904, and the surprising defeat of Russia in the ensuing war. Japan, whose statesmen in 1900 had been skeptical of their position in world politics, then cast off her inferiority complex and emerged as a confident giant, her position as a world power firmly established by the signing of the Treaty of Portsmouth on September 5, 1905.

It can be stated without exaggeration that the tsar's insistent expansionist policy in the Far East was decisive for recent world history. Had he accepted the sane advice of his ministers and averted the disastrous war with Japan,[2] revolution within his country could have been averted or delayed, and Japan would not have gained the overconfidence which eventually led to the disaster of the 1940's. Had the balance of power been maintained in the Far East for a longer time, the fate of Korea might have been different. But with Russia eliminated, Japan was free to move into Korea and, having fought two wars over the country, saw no need for further hesitation.

Soon after the opening of the war with Russia, Japan began a series of negotiations with Korea. By the protocol of February 23, 1904, Korea pledged to place full confidence in Japan and to follow the advice of Japan with regard to improvements in administration. Japan in turn promised to "ensure the safety and repose of the Imperial House of Korea" and also to guarantee the independence and territorial integrity of the Korean Empire. Japan was, further, allowed to "occupy when the circumstances require such places as may be necessary from strategic points of view." [3]

On May 19, when the Japanese Army had marched into Manchuria and Japanese strength had been sufficiently displayed, the Korean government was made to sever diplomatic relations with Russia. On August 22 an agreement concerning financial and diplomatic advisers for Korea was signed.

Although only financial and diplomatic advisers were stipulated, the Japanese recommended advisers on police affairs, the Imperial household, and defense, and these were soon in office. With the exception of one pro-Japanese American, Durham Stevens,[4] who became diplomatic adviser, all were former Japanese officials. Although these newcomers were termed advisers, the agreement required that "all matters . . . shall be dealt with after [their] counsel has been taken." This was the beginning of the "rule by advisers," which lasted for three years, when it was replaced by the "rule by vice-ministers."

Although the advisers wielded great power, the arrangement proved to be unsatisfactory. According to Hayashi Gonsuke, the Japanese

Minister in Korea, the three chief advisers constantly complained of inadequate power, for

> it was natural that the Japanese opinion was not effectively communicated. The source of the obstacle was not in the [Korean] government. The cabinet ministers at this time did not have any real power. The point at which the Japanese opinion was bottlenecked was the royal court. The center of this was the monarch.[5]

Hayashi, "determined that it was about time to handle the situation on a full scale," went to Tokyo in the autumn of 1905 and conferred with Foreign Minister Komura Jutarō. When they explained to Premier Katsura Tarō the difficulties faced in Korea, Katsura suggested that the country should be made a protectorate. Itō Hirobumi, a leading statesman and former premier, was selected to undertake negotiations toward accomplishing what Katsura had suggested.[6]

On November 9 Marquis Itō, accompanied by an impressive retinue, arrived in Seoul. On November 16 the Korean government was given the draft of a convention providing for the control of its foreign relations by Japan. By this convention, the Ministry of Foreign Affairs and the legations abroad would be eliminated, and within Korea a Japanese regent-general would be stationed in lieu of the minister; the Japanese consuls at the seaports would be replaced by residents. Since diplomatic negotiations—or what the Japanese preferred to call, with some justification, foreign intrigues—had been the only means of survival for the Korean government in the past decade, the Japanese took this means of removing the root of their troubles in Korea.

The events surrounding the convention of 1905, while not of great importance in the over-all history of the Far East, were of major significance for the nationalist movement in Korea. Heated, suicidal revolts arose for some time after the signing of the convention, and many of the national heroes and traitors of modern Korean history emerged during this period. Even the Korean emperor gained some luster for resisting the treaty—although unsuccessfully—and for eventually seeking the help of foreign powers meeting at The Hague in 1907, a maneuver which cost him the crown.

According to Professor Ladd, who accompanied Itō and later published a strongly pro-Japanese account of the trip,[7] Emperor Kojong repeatedly refused to consent to the convention despite the marquis' intimation that he "could not predict what the result would be if His

Majesty refused [and] feared that it might be less acceptable than what he now proposed." The emperor then expressed a desire to confer with his ministers and ascertain also "the intention of the people at large." While agreeing that the ministers should be consulted, Itō did not see any constitutional ground for consulting the people at large and remarked that "if such action should lead to popular ferment and excitement and possibly public disturbances . . . the responsibility would rest with His Majesty."[8] Probably the emperor wished to find out public opinion from such a privy council as the Independence Club had demanded, but he had himself crushed the progressive movement just a few years before, as the marquis was well aware.

Failing to obtain the consent of the emperor, Itō turned to the cabinet. His action is reported by Ladd:

> On the 17th of November, at 11 A.M., all of the Korean Ministers went to the Japanese Legation, lunched there, and conferred with Mr. Hayashi until 3 o'clock, when they adjourned to the Palace and held a meeting in the Emperor's presence. Their decision was, finally, to refuse to agree to the Convention in the form in which it had been proposed. Marquis Itō was taking dinner with General Hasegawa,[9] when, at 7:30, he received a message from Mr. Hayashi conveying this intelligence and a request to come to the Palace. Accordingly, at 8 o'clock, he went to the Palace in company with General Hasegawa, the latter's aide, and the three or four mounted gendarmes, who accompanied Marquis Itō wherever he went. *There were no other Japanese guards or soldiers in attendance, and none in the immediate vicinity of the Palace.*[10]

The final, colorless drama took place within the palace. Contrary to Ladd's statement that no Japanese troops were in the vicinity, Hayashi's and the contemporary Korean accounts indicate that the convention was signed under coercion. According to the *Hwangsŏng Shinmun* ("Imperial Capital News"), Japanese troops surrounded the building where the cabinet was holding its meeting.[11] Marquis Itō and General Hasegawa went into the meeting and urged the cabinet to consent to the Japanese proposals. Premier Han Kyu-sŏl and two other ministers were not to be intimidated, but Foreign Minister Pak Che-sun suggested that if some changes were made regarding the treatment of the Imperial house the convention might be accepted. Itō immediately made a few changes in the wording; five ministers then signed the document. The premier, however, rose from the meeting and requested an audience with the emperor. The Japanese seized the opportunity to confine him in a side room, with Japanese gendarmes guarding him. When Itō again attempted to persuade him to sign and asserted that this was the command of the emperor, Han retorted that the dynasty was more important than the emperor. Itō then ruled that five out of eight cabinet members was a majority. The state seal having been brought to the meeting, the convention was sealed immediately.[12] Thus on November 17, 1905, Korea became a protectorate of Japan.

Hayashi's account reveals the careful planning of the Japanese. He had previously told Itō:

> One more arrangement is to ask General Hasegawa to send a sentry. The ministers will gather as arranged. Since this is a very important matter for Korea, of course, the ministers will dislike it. If they are to go to the palace after the meeting at the legation, they might escape on the way. In order to prevent this, we must send gendarmes or other troops. Of course, they will be called escorts. . . .
>
> Another thing is the State seal. It seems that the seal is taken care of very carefully and even the Minister of the Royal Household does not have it. There is a special officer to keep it. I must send a man at early morning to the foreign ministry to watch for that officer. I asked another thing of General Hasegawa. This actually does not matter either way, but if the treaty is signed one or two ministers might commit suicide. I do not care, but I arranged it so that this would not happen.[13]

If the entire cabinet had refused to sign, the marquis probably would have formed a more submissive new cabinet and obtained what he wanted anyway. The five ministers who took the pragmatic choice of staying in power, and who afterward provided more active support for the Japanese than was necessary, were branded "the five traitors," never to be forgiven by more patriotic Koreans. The ministers were Pak Che-sun (foreign affairs), Yi Wan-Yong (education), Yi Kŭn-t'aek (war), Yi Chi-yong (home affairs), and Kwon Chung-hyŏn (agriculture, commerce, and industry). They became the objects of many attempts at assassination.

Because of precautionary measures taken by the Japanese troops, no major disturbance ensued in Seoul:

> All the Japanese troops in the district had been for days parading the streets and open places fronting the Imperial residence. The field-guns were out, and the men were fully armed. They marched, counter-marched, stormed, made

feint attacks, occupied the gates, put their guns in position, and did everything, short of actual violence, that they could to demonstrate to the Koreans that they were able to enforce their demands.[14]

But the Korean people as a whole were in a sullen mood. There was not much they could do in the face of naked power, but their hatred against Japan mounted. While the ministers were still in the process of signing, the residence of Foreign Minister Pak Che-sun was set on fire.[15] In the following few days the *Hwangsŏng Shinmun* and the *Taehan Maeil Shinbo* ("Great Korean Daily News") reported details of the circumstances of the signing of the convention, defying the Japanese censors already active in Korea, and accused the Japanese of unfaithfulness and the ministers of disloyalty. A number of former ministers prostrated themselves before the royal court and submitted memorials requesting annulment of the treaty. Some former high officials committed suicide and left memorials and letters which were published in the newspapers.[16]

In further demonstrations of sentiment, shops and schools were closed in Seoul and the first attempts were made to assassinate the ministers who signed the convention. Japanese gendarmes retaliated by arresting the newspaper publishers and other intractable elements, but the public was not easily made submissive.

Nor was resentment confined to the capital: elders of the yangban class constantly spread the news that the protectorate had been imposed through coercion. These Confucian leaders started the long series of armed revolts by groups known as the Righteous Armies.

The first such revolt was led by Ch'oe Ik-hyŏn, who had been a provincial governor and held other high office. On numerous occasions Ch'oe had submitted memorials to the emperor admonishing sloth and corruption in the government and warning of Japanese intrigues. Further—for he was widely respected as a Confucian scholar—he had sent letters on the same topics to his followers throughout Korea. The Japanese therefore called him a disturber of the peace and urged the Korean government to expel him.[17] When the protectorate was established, Ch'oe submitted two memorials to the throne, denouncing the five traitors, and also sent a long letter to the Japanese authorities indicating "sixteen wrongs." Although closely watched by Japanese troops, he managed to gather eighty Confucian followers in May, 1906. These were joined soon by others. This group occupied several towns, and Ch'oe's force swelled to several hundred. But the rebellion was quickly put down by Japanese and Korean government troops. Ch'oe was captured and was exiled to Tsushima, where he died in December of the same year.[18]

Of course, untrained rebels with outmoded weapons could not stand against troops of a modern army fit to defeat Russia. But common sense was not being considered, and the effect of Ch'oe's venture was immeasurable. When his body was brought to Pusan, wailing multitudes came to the pier and thousands of people followed his coffin to the north, the number of mourners increasing in snowball fashion, so that the procession moved less than three miles a day. Fearing mob action, the Japanese Army first attempted to disperse the crowds and then abandoned hope of doing so. An automobile was finally called for faster transportation, but still it took ten days to move Choe's body the seventy-five miles to his burial place. Street wailing was observed everywhere in the country.[19]

Although in 1906 public sentiment was strongly behind the patriots and hence strongly anti-Japanese, the activities of the Righteous Armies in that year were small in scale. The Japanese recorded only three groups of insurgents: that of Ch'oe (approximately 450 followers), another under the former cabinet minister Min Chong-sik (approximately 500), and one under Shin Tol-sŏk (approximately 1,000). The Korean casualties reported were 82 killed and 145 captured; the Japanese, three policemen killed and one soldier wounded. Captured arms included 717 guns, 71 daggers, and 574 spears.[20] Full-scale revolts did not take place until the summer of 1907, after the emperor had been forced to abdicate.

Like the majority of the Korean people, the emperor was deeply displeased by the convention Marquis Itō and Minister Hayashi had succeeded in concluding with his country. The Japanese statesmen had analyzed the situation correctly: the conduct of foreign relations was the single most important power of the emperor. With Korea practically defenseless before the Japanese Army, the only course open to him—besides quietly submitting—was to seek help from outside. He probably realized the futility of it, but this was not to stop him from trying.

On or about October 20, 1905, a few weeks before the arrival of

Itō, Emperor Kojong had dispatched a letter to President Theodore Roosevelt seeking American assistance against the impending threat. The message was entrusted to Homer Hulbert, an American teacher in Korea who was Jaisohn's friend as well as a confidant of the emperor. Hulbert reached Washington on November 15 and sought an interview with Secretary of State Elihu Root, who was too busy to see him. Horace Allen, the former American Minister, had earlier advised his government not to invoke the treaty of 1882 between Korea and the United States, and E. V. Morgan, the new minister, had sent a cable to Washington concerning Hulbert's intentions.[21] Finally, on November 21, four days after the signing of the convention, Hulbert delivered the letter to Secretary Root and received nothing more than a polite acknowledgment.[22]

The emperor's letter in substance pointed to the treaty of 1882 and the friendly relationship between the two countries, and requested aid to prevent the Japanese encroachment. The letter became known in Korea and created a sensation after the newspaper *Taehan Maeil Shinbo* published a copy on February 1, 1906. Itō Hirobumi, by then the regent-general, reproached the emperor through the Minister of the Royal Household; the emperor asserted complete innocence in the matter.

Another attempt to enlist foreign support was made at The Hague in 1907. The idea of presenting the case of Korea before the Second International Peace Conference was conceived by Yi Chun, prosecutor at the Supreme Court, and Yi Sang-sŏl, a former cabinet officer. The two eventually succeeded in reaching the emperor and gaining his consent to sending an emissary to The Hague. With Yi Wi-jong, the son of the Korean minister to St. Petersburg, who acted as interpreter, they arrived at The Hague in June, bearing official letters from Emperor Kojong to Nicholas II and to the peace conference. In submitting Korea's case the emissaries argued that because the protectorate convention was signed under coercion it was null and void, that Japan was a violator of international law, and that Korean independence ought to be restored by the intervention of the powers assembled at the conference.[23]

The emissaries were admitted through the good offices of the Russian representative, but were forced to withdraw when the Japanese representative argued that Korea had relegated all diplomatic rights to Japan and therefore could not have a separate delegation.[24] Yi Chun committed suicide at The Hague.

Although this mission failed, the repercussions were great. The Korean attempt "surprised the world. The more surprised was the Japanese government, and it was a bolt from the blue to Regent-General Itō, who was directly responsible for Korea." [25] Enraged and humiliated, Itō ordered an immediate investigation to establish the connection between the mission and the emperor. In July, when a chest of documents containing a draft of the letter to Nicholas II was discovered in a church in Seoul, Itō notified the emperor that his action was not only a violation of the convention, but also a hostile act that would justify Japan's declaring war against Korea. In a telegram to Premier Saionji in Tokyo he stated: ". . . this kind of event happens because the protectorate convention transferred the power only over diplomacy. In order to prevent further nuisance, Japan must control the internal administration of Korea as well." [26]

The Japanese were in possession of full control over Korea. The only obstacle to their exercise of it was the emperor, who was powerless and yet continued his mischievous attempts. Now, however, they had enough excuses to remove him from the throne, and they easily accomplished this without having to take direct action. In May, 1907, the cabinet of Premier Yi Wan-yong had been staffed with mostly pro-Japanese politicians. On July 16 the cabinet requested that the emperor abdicate in favor of his son. When he refused and sought the advice of Itō, the regent-general stated that the matter was outside his responsibility. On July 19 the cabinet met again, and the Minister of Agriculture, Song Pyŏng-jun,[27] denounced the emperor for having lost the trust of the people, countered the will of Heaven, and disgraced the Divine position.[28] Thereupon Kojong consented to yield the throne to his son.

Having successfully removed the obstinate monarch from the seat of power, the Japanese made rapid progress in legalizing the *de facto* status. On July 25 was signed the "Convention Concerning the Administration of Korea," under which it became a breach of agreement not to abide by the recommendations of the regent-general. On August 1 the Korean Army was disbanded, and on August 8 various Japanese were appointed vice-ministers. On July 12, 1909, judicial powers were transferred to the Japanese courts. On June 21, 1910, police powers were transferred. On August 22, 1910, Korea was annexed to Japan.[29]

Large-scale movements against the Japanese had their beginning around the time of the abdication. On the evening of July 18, 1907, while the cabinet was trying to persuade the emperor to abdicate, people gathered in large numbers in the streets of Seoul, spontaneously formed a "people's meeting" in the fashion of the Independence Club meetings, and deliberated on the dangers faced by the nation. Demonstrations continued into the next afternoon, when scores of Korean troops joined the crowd and fought with Japanese policemen; a few persons were killed.[30] On July 20, when the emperor relegated his power to his son, a mob set fire to the residence of the premier. The next day more buildings in Seoul and several Japanese residences in Inchon were set on fire.[31] During this time, in various parts of Korea crowds gathered, newspaper articles accusing the Japanese and the "five traitors" were read aloud, heated speeches were delivered, Japanese buildings and facilities were stoned, and inflammatory leaflets were distributed. In general, peace and order gave way to riotous feelings which could not be controlled.[32] These manifestations of popular resentment were paving the way for armed revolts.

The first large-scale military uprisings occurred when the Korean Army was disbanded on August 1. The army at this time numbered about 6,000 men. The officers were Japanese-trained. In the entire country there were fourteen battalions, including the Imperial Guards in Seoul. Each unit had a number of Japanese officers as training instructors, but these so-called advisers were virtually the commanders of the units. In addition, Japanese troops were stationed in many strategic areas.[33]

The decision to disband the army was reached by the Japanese authorities and the Korean Minister of Defense on July 31. Korean officers were summoned the next morning and given the imperial decree. The officers were to return to the camps, bring their troops unarmed to the training ground near the palace, and perform a ceremony of disbanding, after which sums of money would be distributed to the soldiers according to their rank. Japanese units were dispatched to the camps to collect arms.

The orderly process of disbanding was, however, disrupted by the suicide of Pak Sŏng-hwan, commander of a battalion of the Imperial Guards in Seoul. Along with other officers, Pak received the order to bring his troops to Hullyŏnwon—the training ground—for disbanding, but upon returning to his battalion he killed himself. When Japanese troops came to take over the camp, Pak's men fired upon them. Another battalion of the guards joined Pak's unit against the Japanese and a fierce skirmish broke out. After a few hours the Japanese troops occupied the camps of both battalions. Approximately a hundred Korean soldiers were killed and five hundred captured; the Japanese casualties numbered about thirty killed or wounded.[34]

Similar resistance was offered by Korean units at Wonju, Kangwon Province, and on Kanghwa Island. The battalion commander at Wonju led his troops against a Japanese company stationed in the same city; a Korean platoon on Kanghwa was joined by civilians in resisting a Japanese unit sent to disarm them. The Japanese did not succeed in subduing the Koreans in these two areas.[35]

Militarily, the results of these actions could not have been very gratifying to the Korean troops, but the effect upon the people was immeasurable. The Korean people, bitterly resentful of the political inroads by the Japanese, were powerless and disorganized. The rebellion did not change the situation materially, but it did provide an impetus and an example, as the continuous activities of the Righteous Armies after August, 1907, indicate.

The Japanese blamed the discharged troops for spreading "dangerous thoughts," [36] and obviously these men, who had been drawn into the army from different provinces, were able to spread the news of rebellions to wide areas and in an extremely convincing manner. They also contributed materially to the forces of the rebels. Because of the low social status of soldiers in this period, they could hardly enter any stable occupation, and the most logical choice for them was to join the Righteous Armies, where they would hold prominent positions.

The Japanese garrison army which undertook the task of subjugating the rebels compiled some statistics regarding them. From these statistics which are set forth in table 1, and bearing in mind that no figures on such an unorganized movement can be accurate, we can comprehend at least the scale of the rebel actions.

TABLE 1

(*a*) COLLISIONS BETWEEN JAPANESE FORCES AND KOREAN INSURGENTS, 1907–1911

Period	Times	Number of Insurgents
1907 (Aug.–Dec.)	323	44,116
1908	1,451	69,832
1909	898	25,763
1910	147	1,891
1911 (Jan.–June)	33	216
Total	2,852	141,815

(*b*) DAMAGES SUFFERED BY KOREAN INSURGENTS

Period	Killed	Wounded	Captured	Total	Captured Weapons		
					Guns	Daggers	Spears
1907 (Aug. to Dec.)	3,627	1,492	139	5,258	1,235	7	
1908	11,562	1,719	1,417	14,698	5,081	85	59
1909	2,374	435	329	3,138	1,392	245	18
1910	125	54	48	227	116	20	1
1911	9	6	61	76	10	1	
Total	17,697	3,706	1,994	23,397	7,834	358	78

SOURCE: Headquarters, Japanese Garrison Army in Korea, *Bōto tōbatsushi* [Record of Subjugation of Insurgents] (Seoul, 1913), Appendix, tables 2–3.

It is clear from the numbers involved, the casualties, and the arms captured that the Righteous Armies were not negligible bands. The record of major combats available to us also indicates that action was not confined to any particular province or region.[37] The appalling number of casualties indicates both the resolution of the Koreans and, by the disproportionate ratio of the killed to the wounded, the ruthlessness of the Japanese.

Referring to the character of the rebels, the Japanese garrison army report states that

Although it seems that there are some differences in the kinds of rioters, their true purpose is either in fame or benefit. The followers are generally ignorant wanderers joined only for the purpose of obtaining their means of livelihood, or because of intimidations. They have joined the movement just temporarily and they are not concerned with the nation. . . . It is for this reason that even the strong groups strive to avoid our forces after one or two encounters, and whenever the situation is disadvantageous, they disguise themselves as common people and then rise again as bandits even though they claim to be the Righteous Army and profess their patriotism and their loyalty to the king.[38]

This view seems to be much prejudiced. The assertion that the rebels avoided major encounters for selfish reasons is, of course, illogical. The Righteous Armies were resorting to guerrilla tactics, the most appropriate choice. That the rebels were totally unconcerned with the national situation may have been true of some of them, but the perils they risked would seem to prove that they did not rebel simply to win fame or benefit.

The same report attempts to classify the participants and list their motives, finding among the rebels:

Soldiers dissatisfied with the disbanding of the army
Confucian scholars or yangbans instigated the people
Men with political ambition who joined the rebellion just in case it should succeed
Bandits prevalent in the old regime who used the situation to legitimatize their activities
Those influenced by Christianity who were manipulated by missionaries seeking to enlarge their own power and advantages [39]

These generally derogatory observations were considerably modified by General Akashi Motojirō, who became commander of the Japanese gendarmerie in Korea in 1907 and in a report dated December, 1908, warned against the tendency to label the rebels as mere bandits:

. . . among the rebels there are Confucian scholars, former troops, vagabonds, those merely in despair, bandits, pirates and others. All these are mixed and [their composition is] very complicated, as the confessions of the surrendered testify.[40]

It was inevitable that all elements of Korean society would be represented, including the lawless; but whatever the social strata of the rebels and whatever their sideline motives, the quotient of patriotism was very high. Further, the Japanese seem to have failed to record that ruthless suppression and indiscriminate shooting and burning produced more candidates for the Righteous Armies. F. A. McKenzie, who traveled the countryside to observe the rebels in action, found that

> What struck me most about this form of punishment, however, was not the suffering of the villagers so much as the futility of the proceedings, from the Japanese point of view. In place of pacifying a people, they were turning hundreds of quiet families into rebels. During the next few days I was to see at least one town and many scores of villages treated as this one. To what end? The villagers were certainly not the people fighting the Japanese. All they wanted to do was to look quietly after their own affairs. Japan professed a desire to conciliate Korea and to win the affection and support of her people. In one province at least the policy of houseburning had reduced a prosperous community to ruin, increased the rebel forces, and sown a crop of bitter hatred, which it would take generations to root out.[41]

Although the Japanese reports do not state why it should be so, they do sometimes note where the sympathy of the Korean villagers lay:

> . . . the rebels have considerable sympathy from the people, depending upon the area. There are Korean officers within my unit who clearly affirm this fact. In some areas [people are] submissive to the rebels because of their power. Therefore, there are still many difficulties in carrying out intelligence work; the situation has not changed from ancient times. Prisoners or the surrendered confess that town chiefs or village chiefs know the rebels personally [but] do not yet have the courage to report this to the authorities . . . In short, the ignorant people and village officials are still deceived and intimidated by the rebels, and they lack earnestness toward the authorities.[42]

Whether the people's sympathy should be attributed to ignorance or patriotism may be dismissed as a matter of opinion. The support given to the Righteous Armies, however, is evidence of a significant change: the people's apathy toward political events was lessening. Atrocities committed by the Japanese troops, as indicated by McKenzie, brought political questions to the doorsteps of the villagers, who consequently could no longer regard politics as none of their business.

Japanese references to rebels in this period and nationalists in the succeeding years are usually preceded by such qualifications as "ignorant" or "unaware of the world situation." But even the Japanese military officers were forced to pay respect to some of the insurgent leaders. We find an instance in the biography of General Akashi. Hŏ Wi, a "general" of the Righteous Armies, led a group of about 500 rebels in Kangwon Province from April to December, 1908.[43] He had been head secretary to the emperor and also served as chief justice. Captured, Hŏ stated:

Our attempt to facilitate the reconstruction of Korea is not merely for the Koreans alone. It is based on the peace of the Far East. If Japan swallows Korea, China will certainly have animosities against Japan. If the relationship between Japan and China is not harmonious, how can there be peace in the Far East. Only if Japan protects Korea with earnestness and only if Japan supports China with sincerity, can Japan maintain eternal peace in the Far East as the leader of the area. My desire for reconstruction of Korea is based on the world situation and for eternal peace of the Far East rather than purely for Japan or for Korea . . .[44]

He was taken to Seoul and interrogated by General Akashi, who admired his patriotism and loyalty to the emperor, agreed with his policies for the peace in the Far East, and petitioned the regent-general to spare his life.[45] Hŏ, however, was executed.

Despite the ardent patriotism of Hŏ Wi and many others like him, high and low, the powerful Japanese Army was able to put an end to the Korean resistance. The Korean people in 1910 became subjects of the Japanese emperor.

The revolts and armed uprisings after 1894 suggest that the Koreans were acquiring national consciousness, which until then had been largely restricted to the upper class, while the masses were apathetic or, at best, apolitical.

National consciousness appeared among the lower classes in a crude and primitive fashion during the Tonghak rebellion; but probably it would be an exaggeration to regard this as a phase of nationalism, although in the Tonghaks' xenophobic attitude we can discern traces of national consciousness, particularly toward the last. Undeniably, the rebellion helped destroy old class boundaries and directed popular attention to the encroachments of the Japanese.

Succeeding events revealed that national consciousness was growing among Koreans of all classes. Even if some, or many, of the post-1905 rebels were mere bandits, they acted in the name of patriotism to legitimatize their activities, and this meant that patriotism—or nationalism—was becoming popular. The fact remains, however, that the Korean nationalist movement up to 1910 was still in the category of "traditional nationalism" and its leaders were intent on maintaining the *status quo.* Their loyalty was to the existing political forms, the emperor, and rule by the literati class. Yet at the same time there were evidences—as in the case of the Independence Club—of "modern nationalism."[46] After 1905 a number of small groups were organized, such as the *Taehan Chaganghoe* ("Great Korean Self-Strengthening Association"),[47] which strove to maintain independence by reforming Korea and strengthening her foundations. But none of these organizations could remain for long.

Modern Korean nationalism, as will be seen, was a product of the post-annexation era. It grew in a new political environment under varying stimuli.

III

The March First Movement

6

Japanese Rule: The First Phase

As IS EVIDENT in previous chapters, Japanese army leaders were chiefly responsible for and instrumental in formulating and executing Japanese policies affecting Korea. The final process of annexation was entrusted to General Terauchi Masatake, whom even Japanese politicians had accused of being dictatorial.

Up to March 1, 1919, when the people rose in the mass demonstrations that have become known as the March First movement, Korea was ruled in military fashion by the Japanese government-general. Although many sugar-coated proclamations "for the prosperity and welfare of the Korean people" were issued by the Japanese government before the annexation, these proved to be no more than a facade for conquest. The official term for the annexation, *Nikkan heigō* [1] ("amalgamation of Japan and Korea"), would have meant providing at least a semblance of rights for the Koreans, but even by Japanese historians Terauchi's rule has generally been described as *budan-seiji* ("military dictatorial government").

If we take official pronouncements as a guide, Japanese policies in Korea and Formosa were close to the "identity" and "paternalism" of French colonial policies before World War II. But Japanese practice in Korea was much akin to that of the Russian Empire in

Poland during the nineteenth century. The reason for the similarity is not hard to find.

The principal aide to Governor-General Terauchi up to 1914 was Lieutenant General Akashi Motojirō, who had studied the colonial policies of Russia while he was military attaché in St. Petersburg between 1902 and 1904.[2] Terauchi, an army general and Minister of the Army at the time of his appointment to the governor-generalship, was no expert in colonial administration. It is reasonable to assume that Akashi played a major role in shaping his policies in Korea.

Akashi came to Korea in 1907 as commander of the Japanese gendarmerie. After carrying out for a year the not too difficult mission of subjugating insurgent Koreans, he was appointed director of the police affairs for the regency-general. The success of the Japanese government in annexing and maintaining its rule over Korea, and the accompanying "unscrupulous and brutal oppressions," are in great part attributed to this "authoritarian despot." [3]

Governor-General Terauchi arrived in Korea in July, 1910, to begin his rule in the new territory. With the assistance of Akashi, he introduced oppressive measures into politics, industry, communications, and other phases of life, to the extent that the "entire Korean peninsula was turned into a military camp" and his "extreme military dictatorship gave the impression that Korea had returned to the medieval authoritarian regime." [4]

On August 25, three days after the signing of the treaty of annexation, all political organizations were ordered to be dissolved within a week. All meetings, debates, and speeches were prohibited, regardless of their nature.[5]

Any news item not satisfactory to the government was suppressed, and any publisher who was not discreet enough to heed the order was immediately suspended from further publication; also many newspapers published in Japan were prohibited from being imported into Korea.[6] The *Taehan Maeil Shinbo,* which had been able to print anti-Japanese propaganda up to this time because its co-publisher was a British subject, was purchased in a forced sale and turned into a pro-Japanese organ, the *Maeil Shinbo* ("Daily News"). The five other Korean newspapers in Seoul were closed down by government order immediately after the annexation.[7]

Most Japanese newspapers in Korea met the same fate, accepting the government's suggestion that they cease publication. An English-language newspaper, the *Seoul Press*, was published under government sponsorship.[8]

Before annexation there were one or two newspapers in most of the cities, but all the Korean publishers were ordered to close their shops, and finally only one Japanese newspaper was allowed in each city. These and any remaining periodicals were forbidden to report matters related to politics.[9] The Tokyo *Nichi Nichi* commented editorially on October 2, 1910:

> It is not that there are no newspapers in Korea, but that there is no freedom of speech (*genron*). The frequency of suppression of newspapers in Korea has increased in the recent period around the Korean annexation. There were many newspapers published in Japan which were not allowed to be sent into Korea. We do not wish to raise the matters of the past, since we presume that this was necessary because of special circumstances surrounding the annexation. What we are concerned about is . . . after the annexation. We accept the government policy that freedom of speech is harmful in ruling newly attached people. We must, however, oppose the government when it prohibits all comments and advice which are originated through good intentions . . .[10]

The suppressive attitude of General Akashi was also reflected in the police ordinance prohibiting the possession of arms by Koreans —both firearms and such potential weapons as swords and knives. Even professional hunters were not allowed to possess hunting knives. In order to execute these extreme policies, by the notorious Decree No. 10 (Dec. 16, 1910) the government-general permitted the local chiefs of police to render summary judgments in cases of crimes punishable by up to three months in jail.

Objections to the dictatorship of the government-general were voiced not only by Koreans. Representative Ōishi Masami, for example, declared in the Japanese Diet in March, 1911:

> I object to the grant of the right to rule by decree to the Korean governor-general. At present, Governor-General Terauchi is abusing the right. He has promulgated a decree on newspapers to suppress freedom of speech, issued a decree on corporations to restrict enterprise, tied down the freedom of the people, and persecuted newspapers and business to an extreme. To grant the right to govern by decree to such an unconstitutional governor-general is extremely dangerous. The menace felt by the people because of the dictatorial government is very severe, and I object to this absolutely.[11]

Objections were of no avail. Until he left Korea in June, 1916, Terauchi exercised his dictatorial policy without mercy.[12] The biographer of Akashi quotes the statement of an unidentified Japanese writer:

> There was neither negligence nor remissness. Newspapers were checked one by one; controls on companies were exercised to an extreme, unsatisfactory companies being destroyed one after another. Reporters and writers were at their wit's end, gasping. If one grumbled, he would be arrested. It was just unbearable. I felt as if I were in hell.[13]

General Hasegawa, the commander of the Japanese Army in Korea before the annexation, replaced Terauchi as governor-general in October, 1916, but did not change his oppressive policies. "I do not know much about politics," said Hasegawa; "all I intend to do is to follow the way established by Terauchi." [14] He did so until he was replaced in 1919 by Admiral Saitō after the March First movement began.

The suppressive policy of Terauchi and Akashi can be accurately described as hysterical. By 1911 the activities of the Righteous Armies were coming to an end, the army and gendarmerie had killed thousands of Korean rebels, and order was restored, but the Koreans were still far from convinced that the presence of the Japanese was desirable and necessary for Korea's future. Terauchi and Akashi seem to have decided that this conviction could be implanted through fear. They decided, therefore, to arrest the most vocal elements in the northern provinces and show them what the Japanese were capable of doing. These provinces were chosen because Christianity was strong in the north, and also because the New People's Association (*Shinminhoe*), a secret organization established by An Ch'ang-ho, Yi Kap, Yi Tong-hwi and others in 1908 to promote industry and advance educational standards, was influential there.[15]

Determined to make a display that would eliminate all anti-Japanese thoughts at once, the governor-general and his aide caused a charge to be fabricated against 123 Korean Christian leaders in the north. The charge was that they had attempted to assassinate Terauchi around December 27–28, 1911, while he was going to Shinuiju to celebrate the construction of the bridge across the Yalu River. Approximately 700 Koreans were arrested, from among whom the 123 were selected. For more than a year Japanese gendarmes and policemen subjected the victims to tortures too grim to be described. Confessions were wanted, but were difficult to obtain. Despite eloquent evidence presented against the charges, the Japanese court sentenced 105 of the Koreans to terms of five to ten years in prison, acquitting the rest.[16]

Yi Chong-guk, a Korean employed by the Japanese government, investigated the reaction of the people and reported that the incident was regarded as a great "demonstration of policy" and that it "increased the discontent of the Korean people to the extreme and enhanced the spirit to resist the Japanese government." [17] It should be added that the 123 who were tortured later took active parts in the March First movement and the nationalist movement abroad. This, then, in extreme form, was the political aspect of Japanese policy in Korea.

The discontent of the people was not merely political. Most Koreans were farmers.[18] Economically, the farmers suffered more severely than any others from the annexation and the subsequent radical change from an archaic system of landownership to a modern one.

From the unification of Korea by the Silla dynasty, in the seventh century, down to the time of the annexation in 1910, the official doctrine was that the land was the property of the sovereign. Government at all levels was supported by the income from land taxes, generally paid in produce. Instead of salaries public officials received the right to collect land taxes from the farmers, the size of an official's collecting area depending upon his rank in the government. Aside from some private slaves and a small minority of farmers who had acquired special rights by cultivating virgin lands, the farmers of Korea were in effect tenants on very long terms—from one generation to the next. So long as they paid the tax and complied with the demands of various officials and imposters, they held established rights to the land they tilled. Ownership was never an issue, since neither landlords nor farmers legally or theoretically owned the land.[19]

Modern government and administration obviously could not operate within this equivocal system. Landownership had to be fixed for taxation as well as for conforming to the modern—or capitalistic—form of economy. Therefore a gigantic land survey was begun in 1910 and completed in 1918. In deciding who should own the land and have rights to it in the modern sense, the Japanese government-general had two alternatives. Ownership could be given either to the farmers, who had tilled the land for generations, or to those who had the right to collect the land taxes. The latter alternative was taken, through a decree that those who had a proper claim to land must register it within a specified period in order to legalize their ownership.[20]

The result was that local gentry registered their claims at will, often extending them over the common property of a village or clan and even over the lands of small independent farmers who had rightful claims under the old system. Uneducated farmers who had no conception of ownership in the modern sense and no knowledge of how to overcome red tape became members of an "unpropertied proletariat" and had to continue their existence as land tenants in a truly modern meaning. If no one claimed a property, it automatically came under government ownership.[21]

By the end of 1914 landlord families representing a little less than 2 per cent of the population on farms held roughly half of the total cultivated area. About 22 per cent were families farming their own land. Of the remainder of the population on farms, about 41 per cent were families who worked as tenants but owned some land and about 35 per cent were tenant families with no land of their own.[22]

Thus within a few years about 76 per cent of the farm population became tenants, partly or wholly, in the modern sense, deprived of their old, near-hereditary rights to the land and attached to it only by short-term contracts. They were required to pay fees to the landlords as before, but with a new burden created by the change from a predominantly barter to a predominantly money economy. The government-general imposed taxes payable in currency, and although the taxes were imposed on the owners of land, wherever there were tenants the burden fell upon them. It should be added that many landlords suffered impounding of their land for tax delinquency.[23] Some farmers left Korea and emigrated to Manchuria, where conditions were more tolerable.

Meanwhile Japanese immigration into Korea increased year by

year, as did the extent of Japanese landholdings. The immigrants had the blessing of their home government and of the newly created Colonial Industrial Bank (*Shokusan Ginkō*), which was willing to lend money to the newcomers. At the end of 1905 there were only 42,460 Japanese in Korea. This figure was quadrupled by the end of 1910, when it reached 171,543. At the end of 1918 the number was 336,812.[24] Japanese landholdings at the end of 1910 were about 87,000 *chōbu*[25] and by 1923 had reached 335,099 *chōbu*.[26] Although a small number of Koreans did become rich landowners, the rise of Japanese landlords was more obvious. It was natural for the generally poverty-stricken Korean farmers to blame much of their misery upon the newcomers, practically all of whom were prosperous, or seemed to be so.

To Korean political and economic discontent there was added resentment of the behavior of Japanese residents. Koreans, particularly members of the elite, were proud of their ancient traditions, culture, and observance of Confucian propriety; in their view the Japanese civilization was somewhat inferior to their own. Although their country had deteriorated economically and politically, they prized the quality of their culture. The Japanese, in general, despised the peculiarities of Korean civilization. Further, despite the official status of Korea as a part of Japan, most of the Japanese regarded the annexation as a conquest and displayed the arrogance of conquerors. The Koreans saw them as such and regarded their rule as a transitional one to which no complete submission was justified.[27]

Interrogating Korean demonstrators in 1919, the Japanese gendarmerie noted the following complaints:[28]

There is discrimination between Korean and Japanese officials
The Japanese despise Koreans
The Japanese tend to strike Korean people, regardless of cause
Lower officials, both Japanese and Korean, are arrogant to the people
There is no special treatment of the yangbans and literati
Government employment opportunity is limited to an extreme degree
No Korean holds an important position in government
Only Koreans are whipped (in legal cases)
Various administrative processes are complicated
Laws are too frequently issued and do not suit the standard of the people
The encouragement of industry is mostly against the will of the people, and the methods used are coercive

The burden of taxation is too heavy [and] is no lighter than that of the despotic government of the old Korea
There is too heavy a load of forced labor
As the Japanese increase in Korea, land and other properties are going into their hands
Some teachers of country schools are losing their jobs

The accumulation of complaints such as these led to the explosion of March 1, 1919. For instead of the officially proclaimed policy of the "equal grace of the emperor," Koreans endured the discriminations that many colonial populations have experienced.

The Japanese government did, however, espouse the principle of equality among all Koreans. In 1910 the traditional class distinctions were legally abolished. It is not to be denied that this policy brought about a benefit to the future Korea—a social revolution of grandiose scale—but the government-general alienated an important segment of the population in the process. Through the policy of egalitarianism the yangbans, whose sole profession was government employment, were deprived of their ancient monopoly, but there was a grave mistake in the Japanese assumption that the ancient tradition of respect could be eliminated by decree. The former yangbans continued to be held in esteem, being practically the only educated and propertied class. Thus the Japanese government, i.e., the governors-general, estranged high as well as low classes in Korea and consequently had to rely upon military power for success.

The significance of this mistake was manifested in the March First movement, whose leaders made use of the sudden death, in January, 1919, of the old emperor. In keeping with the tradition of filial piety, many of his former subjects came to the capital to mourn his death. Thus when the uprising began in Seoul, mourners returning to rural areas carried the news home and served as catalysts for the spread of the movement. The important fact in this connection is that most of those who came to mourn were former yangbans. Members of other classes would have had neither financial means to travel nor reverence enough for the former ruler to wish to make the journey.

Living conditions under the harsh rule of Terauchi probably were not much worse than they would have been if the Yi dynasty had lasted on. But this, if they reflected on it, could be no consolation to the Korean people, who were completely aware that the new regime was a foreign imposition. So, in the first place, the majority were not satisfied with the annexation. In the second place, they were fast awakening. Even before the annexation, the reform movement of some elite groups was having effects upon the populace, and Western thought was spreading rapidly by way of the new school system and Christianity.

After 1896 the Korean government established a number of elementary schools, high schools, foreign-language schools, and normal schools in which instruction was no longer confined to the Chinese classics and there was an endeavor to emulate Western educational curriculums.[29] Private schools were also established, both by Korean leaders and by foreign missionaries,[30] and by 1910 there were about 2,000 of these institutions, with approximately 200,000 students.[31] In that year Terauchi notified his subordinates that "In some of the private schools the desire for independence is propagated and opposition to the Empire is encouraged; hence, extreme care must be taken to control them." [32] A scene in the Taesōng school in Pyongyang, established in 1907 by the nationalist leader An Ch'ang-ho, has been described by Yi Kwang-su in his novel *Mujōng*. It illustrates the point made by Terauchi:

> Finally the principal came up to the dais. There was applause. . . . The principal looked at the audience with solemn posture and started his speech. "People," he said, "the minds of your ancestors were never so dulled as yours, neither were they so lazy or phlegmatic. The spirit of your ancestors who built the fortress of Pyongyang was grandiose, and the ideals of our ancestors who built Ŭlmildae and Pubyŏknu (major observation towers) were great . . . You must destroy the crumbling fortress of Pyongyang and Ŭlmildae, sweep them into the Taedong River, and build a new fortress and new Ŭlmildae with fresh spirit and fresh ideals.[33]

Many of the private schools, including the Taesōng school, were abolished by the government-general for obvious reasons.

After the annexation the Japanese government continued the establishing of schools. By the end of 1918 the number was 1,251, with 133,407 students.[34] Here the objective was to educate loyal subjects for the Japanese emperor, but an unintended by-product was the enlightenment of students and the Korean people as to their misery.

After the annexation, also, young Koreans had more opportunities to study in Japan.[35] As is often the case with colonial students, many of these young persons became ardent advocates of nationalism for their mother country.[36] A report in 1916 stated that there were seven Korean student organizations in Japan (five in Tokyo, one in Kyoto, and one in Osaka) which professed to "engage in fraternal activities, in the cultivation of mind and body, or in scholastic activities"; but, the report asserted, "they all engage in political discussions or discussion of current events. Some of them even discuss the overthrow of the status quo or overthrow of oppression." [37] Out of 212 blacklisted Koreans in Japan (*yō shisatsu-sha*) in 1920, 151 were students.[38]

Japan in this period was experiencing a surge of liberalism unprecedented in her history. Korean students were affected by this liberal current and also found some sympathizers and supporters of their aspirations among the Japanese. They were particularly influenced by Professor Yoshino Sakuzō, of Tokyo University. A prolific writer and orator, and a leader in the liberal movement in Japan, Yoshino encouraged the Korean students through personal contacts and writings.[39] Under Yoshino's auspices some Tokyo University students organized the New Men's Society (*Shinjinkai*) under the platform of "liberation of humanity" and "rational reform of Japan," and held meetings to discuss liberalism and current issues.[40] Most of the members were in favor of Korean independence.[41] Yoshino wrote on liberal topics for a Christian periodical, *Shinjin* ("New People"), and for one of the most popular magazines in Japan, *Chūō Kōron* ("Central Review"). In 1918, he and Fukuda Tokuzō, an economist, organized the Dawn Society (*Reimeikai*) and conducted meetings to promote the liberal cause.

The Korean students in Japan had access to foreign newspapers, newspapers published by anti-Japanese Koreans in Hawaii and the United States,[42] and anti-Japanese history books written by Koreans in China,[43] and themselves contributed to anti-Japanese publications abroad [44] and published magazines attacking the annexation.[45] Since laws on publication and security control were much looser in Japan than in Korea, these activities were often carried on openly.

Some political statements made by Korean students have been preserved by the Japanese police. Yi Kwang-su, later a prolific writer and an important leader in the nationalist movement, told a meeting of the Student Fraternal Association at the Korean Y.M.C.A. in Tokyo on January 22, 1916:

> Anyone who wishes to live must fight. . . . We must live, but there is a great obstacle in our future. It is the migration of the Japanese into Korea which I am speaking about. The Japanese are continuously migrating into Korea and taking all the profits [while] our people are leaving their homeland and moving to foreign lands. Is this not miserable? The Japanese authorities do not pay any attention to this problem, nor do they provide freedom and power to our people. And yet they say that their policy is a good one. How can we simply watch this . . . ? [46]

Chang Tŏk-su, also a nationalist leader in later years, addressed a similar meeting on April 28:

> Under the present conditions in our society, people will ridicule a man who carries out a great enterprise for the nation, sacrificing his life. People ridicule him as a man who resorts to violence. But, friends, if someone harms our parents, wives, or children through violence, or disgraces them, are we supposed to disregard it coolly? As long as we are born men, are we not to attempt to defend them against violence or to attempt to avenge them? This is a right we receive from heaven.[47]

Song Chin-u, a leader of the March First movement, had declared at a conference at the Y.M.C.A. on April 9, 1915:

> I believe that the present situation will be destroyed in the near future, and an opportunity for our young people to manifest their true pure and noble value will soon arise. Therefore, we must prepare ourselves to carry out the responsibility. Four powers are necessary to destroy the present situation. One is public opinion; the second is oratory stimulus; the third is writing; and the fourth is actual execution of plans . . .[48]

Many statements of a similar nature could be cited, all expounding on injustice and the need for students to take the leadership in bringing about changes in Korea.

Chinese students in Japan at this time were ideologically oriented more to the left.[49] One explanation for the "lack of ideological content" among the Koreans would be that the Chinese students were essentially fighting against indigenous reactionary forces and needed some new ideological tools, whereas the Korean students blamed all evils on the Japanese and centered their attention on patriotism.[50]

The March First movement, when it came, was a manifestation

of the failure of Japanese colonial policy. Whether the Japanese interest was in Korea alone or in the entire Far East—Korea serving as a step to further expansion in Manchuria and China—whatever the motive was, the necessity which the government-general faced after the annexation was to pacify the Koreans and integrate Korea with Japan. Or, putting it differently, what was needed was the establishment of legitimate authority by the use of subtle methods to cultivate a union between the two societies. The militant, dictatorial, and discriminatory policies of the government-general from 1910 to 1919, and in later periods as well, could not be regarded by the Korean populace as legitimate. To accept the propaganda and become a Japanese subject was generally regarded as treason, at least in the early period of Japanese rule.

What was minimally necessary, we may say in retrospect, was to create a condition in which the Koreans would be inwardly divided in their thought. Up to 1919 the Japanese had failed to do even this.

7

The March First Movement

On January 8, 1918, President Wilson set forth his Fourteen Points, in which the doctrine of self-determination was enunciated. Wilson could hardly have anticipated the extent to which the people of many countries would be stirred by his statement, or have foreseen the effect in Korea. What he did was to stir up hope.

The Korean people were in despair during the first decade of Japanese occupation. Their future as an independent people seemed doomed. They had seen the futility of suicidal resistance to the Japanese Army. But their discontent remained, and they longed for a miracle that might lift their burden.

After the World War broke out in 1914, many Koreans were speculating on the future of international affairs. Early in 1915 a number of nationalist leaders in China and Manchuria organized themselves into the Korean Revolutionary Corps (*Koryŏ Hyŏng-myŏng-dan*), led by Pak Ŭn-sik and Yi Tong-hwi. They believed that the war would soon end in favor of Germany. Since Japan had aided the Allies and had offended the Chinese through the Twenty-one Demands, the Koreans reasoned that Germany and China would join to attack Japan. Korea then could take the side of Germany and China, provide some assistance in the warfare, and be able to obtain independence when Japan was defeated. Of course, the anticipated war did not break out, and some of the agents sent into Korea by the Revolutionary Corps were arrested.

Another group highly interested in world developments was in Japan. Pak I-gyu, Shin Ik-hi,[1] Song Chin-u, and several other students met in Tokyo sometime in 1916. Song is reported to have said:

> If China and Japan open fire against each other, Britain and Russia will be too busy to do anything in the Far East because of their involvement in Europe. Since the United States has great sympathy toward China, she may assist China. A small island nation like Japan could not counter China.[2]

Pak I-gyu is reported to have said:

> The result of a war between Japan and China is obvious. We must [on this occasion] obtain the influence of the United States through the Christian church. If we declare the revival of Korea, there must be some reaction from the United States and China. We hope for the earliest breakup of diplomatic relations between Japan and China.[3]

In short, Koreans abroad, specifically the educated who had access to the news, were keenly observing the turn of events. They were hoping for some development favorable to their plans for Korea and were, naturally, overjoyed when Wilson took his stand for self-determination.

The first group to respond to the opportunity for action which the Fourteen Points seemed to present were the Korean nationalists in the United States. Including those in Hawaii, they numbered about 6,000 and had already been organized in the Korean National Association (*Taehanin Kungminhoe*) and had carried out various nationalistic activities under its auspices. As early as 1905 those in Hawaii had sent Yun Pyŏng-gu (the Rev. P. K. Yoon) and Syngman Rhee to the Portsmouth conference to appeal for President Roosevelt's mediation in favor of Korea.[4] The Korean National Association provided financial support to Yi Chae-myŏng, who went to Seoul in 1907 to assassinate Yi Wan-yong, a pro-Japanese cabinet member. It also collected funds to support the court defense of Chang In-hwan and Chŏn Myŏng-un, the assassins of Durham Stevens, the pro-Japanese American who was adviser to the old Korean government in 1905–1908. Pak Yong-man, one of its leaders in Hawaii, organized military schools for Koreans in Nebraska between 1910 and 1912 and in Hawaii between 1914 and 1916. The association also maintained branches in Manchuria and Siberia from 1911 to 1915.[5]

Immediately after Wilson's proclamation was released, the officers and some members of the Korean National Association met in San Francisco. They decided that a petition should be sent to the peace conference when the war was over and that an appeal should be made to Wilson to recognize Korean independence. Delegates were selected, and eventually, in December, 1918, Syngman Rhee and Chŏng Han-gyŏng (Henry Chung) set out for Paris by way of Washington, D.C.[6]

Despite their preparations, the delegates were unable to attend the peace conference because they could not get passports. In Washington the Department of State explained that they were subjects of Japan and must therefore obtain passports from Japanese authorities. They then requested passports as declarants, but "they had made no declaration of a desire to become American citizens" and, furthermore, "under the laws they could not." They then asked for permits to depart from the United States, "but it was declared that such permits would be useless, as they could not serve, in the absence of passports, to obtain entrance for them to another country." [7]

As a last resort the delegates sent a petition to the President. On this the New York *Times* for March 17, 1919, commented as follows:

President Wilson has been asked by the Korean National Association to initiate action at the Peace Conference looking to independence for Korea, with the country to be guided by a mandatory until such time as the League of Nations shall decide that it is "fit for full self-government."

The copy of the letter to the President was made public here today by Syngman Rhee, who, with Henry Chung, is an authorized delegate of the association in the United States.[8]

The Korean nationalists in China, acting independently of the group in the United States, were successful in sending a delegate to the peace conference. A small group had been organized in Shanghai as the New Korea Youth Association (*Shinhan Ch'ŏngnyŏndang*) in June–July, 1918, under the leadership of Yŏ Un-hyŏng (Woon Hyung Lyuh) and Chang Tŏk-su. One of their leaders, Yŏ Un-hyŏng, attended a reception given by the Shanghai diplomatic corps and the Pan Pacific Conference for Charles Crane, who presented himself as an unofficial representative of President Wilson. Yŏ was inspired by Crane's speech on the principle of self-determination and was later encouraged by Crane to believe that the principle applied to Korea. Two copies of a petition for Korean independence were prepared in the name of the association, one copy being addressed to President Wilson, the other to the peace conference. Wilson's copy was handed to Crane and the other entrusted to Millard, publisher of the *Millard Review*, who was then in Shanghai and was going on to Paris.[9] At the same time Kim Kyu-sik, an American-educated Korean youth, was called from Peking and dispatched to the peace conference, where he carried out extensive propaganda activities for Korea.[10]

A third group to respond to Wilson's pronouncement were Korean students in Japan. News of the armistice further stimulated them, so that by January, 1919, they were debating the problems of independence in radical terms and asserting that one must sacrifice one's life for the cause. At an oratorial meeting at the Y.M.C.A. on January 6 they decided that, since their compatriots abroad were already conducting an independence movement, they also should become active. They appointed a committee of ten to prepare a program. After debating late into the night about methods, the committee agreed that a declaration of independence should be sent as a petition to the Japanese government, members of the Diet, and foreign diplomats.[11]

The author of the declaration, Yi Kwang-su, who had an important part in the entire independence movement, gives an interesting account of the planning stage of the students' program. He tells that on hearing of the news of the armistice in Peking, he returned to Tokyo by way of Seoul, arriving in December, 1918:

> It was the winter vacation. I started to select people. I talked to everyone who seemed to be trustworthy. Finally I decided on Ch'oe P'al-yong. He was studying political science at Waseda [University], but was not a close friend of mine. He was a big, manly type. . . . After talking at a drinking place for the workers, we finally discovered that we held the same opinions. So I gave him the draft of the declaration of independence and the petition to be submitted to the Japanese Diet. I also gave him 300 yen for printing expenses.[12]

Yi was involved in sending one of the student leaders, Song Kebaek, to Seoul. This turned out to be one of the important factors in promoting the uprisings within Korea. Yi had previously consulted Hyŏn Sang-yun in Seoul about a movement in Korea while he was on the way to Tokyo:

> We discussed on the telephone that an independence movement must be carried out at this time. The reason that I called Mr. Hyŏn is that he was my trusting friend, but he also had a close student-teacher relationship with Ch'oe Rin. I told him of the armistice news, which could be better obtained in Peking than in Korea. My idea was to influence Ch'oe through Hyŏn; then Ch'oe could influence Son Pyŏng-hi, so that the Ch'ŏndogyo could start an independence movement.[13]

Song Ke-baek was sent from Tokyo to Korea with a copy of the declaration and the message that the students in Tokyo intended to declare independence on February 8 and that a simultaneous movement in Korea ought to be encouraged. Yi advised Song to get in touch with Hyŏn Sang-yun at the Chungang High School in Seoul.[14]

After the meeting of January 6, the committee reported the next afternoon and the afternoon following to audiences of about 200 students at the Y.M.C.A. and received the approval of all present. Each time there were inflammatory speeches and some of the leaders were arrested. The remaining committee members and the two newly elected ones continued secretly to advance the movement, establishing the Korean Youth Independence Corps (*Chosŏn Ch'ŏngnyŏn Tongnipdan*) and drafting a "Petition for a Call of the National Congress," a declaration of independence, and a resolution. The petition was written in Japanese; the declaration and the resolution were prepared in Korean, Japanese, and English. Korean and Japanese versions of the declaration were mimeographed at night (600 copies of each) at the home of Kim Hi-sul in Tokyo.

After the police detected that the students were collecting independence funds and producing documents, some students were investigated on February 6. The group became alarmed and on the morning of February 8 sent copies of the printed materials to Japanese cabinet members, members of the Diet, and the Korean Government-General and to the various newspapers, magazines, and scholars. That afternoon about 200 students congregated at the Y.M.C.A. under the pretext of electing officers for a student association. The declaration and the resolution were placed on the platform, and methods for promoting the independence movement were announced. When the participants became vehement and the situation became confused, the police ordered them to disperse. When they did not obey, 27 were arrested, including ten members of the committee. Nine were sentenced to seven to nine months in prison.[15]

News of nationalist activities abroad provided a spark for the leaders in Korea. Hyŏn Sang-yun has indicated the connections between the movement abroad and the uprisings in Korea:

> In order to carry out the movement within Korea, it was determined that the most effective way would be to persuade Ch'ŏndogyo. I was a graduate of Posŏng Middle School, and since the school was operated by Ch'ŏndogyo, I visited Ch'oe Rin, who had been the principal of the school. I advised Ch'oe Rin that Ch'ŏndogyo must be brought into the movement. After the first meeting on the subject, I and Mr. Song Chin-u visited Ch'oe Rin almost every night. At first Mr. Ch'oe was hesitant. . . . But as the situation within and without the country became more urgent, he agreed on the movement. At this time we obtained the news that Syngman Rhee and Kim Kyu-sik were planning to attend the Paris peace conference. Yŏ Un-hyŏng, Chang Tŏk-su, and Sŏnu Hyŏk and others in Shanghai sent Sŏnu Hyŏk into Pyongan Province and secretly instigated the Christians in the area. Yŏ Un-hong returned from the United States and told us that the Koreans in America were also planning to carry out a movement.[16]

While the leaders of Ch'ŏndogyo were contemplating an independence movement, Song Ke-Baek arrived from Japan with a draft of the declaration which was to be read in Tokyo on February 8. The declaration encouraged Ch'oe Nam-sŏn, an important publisher and historian, to join the movement; it was also used to secure the approval of Son Pyŏng-hi, the supreme leader of Ch'ŏndogyo, who is reported to have said: "At a time when young students are carrying out this kind of righteous action, we cannot just sit and watch." [17] It was decided thereupon that a movement for independence would be carried out on a national scale in coöperation with other religious groups, Ch'ŏndogyo providing 200,000 yen to meet the expenses.

Hyŏn comments, further, on the situation of the Christians at this time:

> Christians in Seoul and other localities had already felt the need of an independence movement, and they were holding frequent meetings in secret. They were in a very excited condition. In Seoul, Pastor Ham T'ae-yŏng, Yi Kapsŏng, and others were secretly conferring on a scheme. . . . Pastors Kil

Sŏn-ju, of Pyongyang, and Yang Sun-baek, of Sunchon, were meeting to discuss the movement. This is why the Christian leaders immediately agreed to the proposal of Ch'ŏndogyo when this was advanced through Yi Sŭng-hun.[18]

The report of the Japanese gendarmerie headquarters, to which we shall refer frequently, attributes great importance to the part played by Korean Christians. An American missionary, Shannon McCune, says the report,

> went to the United States on October 1, 1918, for four months on the excuse that his mother was ill. . . . McCune and [President] Wilson seemed to have had some negotiation and understanding about the future of Korea, [and] officers of Christian churches in Sunchon knew about it and their ambition began to rise. McCune began to have frequent correspondence with Yang Sun-baek, Chu Hyŏn-Ch'ŭk, Hong Song-il, etc. . . . McCune returned to Sunchon on February 1, 1919, and there was frequent traffic by the three, in addition to Kim Chi-ŭng, to McCune's residence. All plans for the movement seem to have materialized there. McCune told the first three that "there is no doubt that Korea will become independent according to the principle of President Wilson. But I cannot publicly assist the movement. If the Koreans themselves demonstrate to foreign countries that they cannot bear the oppression of Japan, the long-cherished wish may be attained at the peace conference." This was the secret viewpoint of the "mystical president."
>
> Most of the Christians had a strong determination and high spirit to attain independence according to the principle of self-determination, and their independence movement had a force that could not be countered.[19]

Interest in the doctrine of self-determination also became widespread among the younger generation and the students in Korea. They began to pay special attention to such newspapers and magazines as were available.[20] Especially after the students in Tokyo carried out their independence demonstration, those in Korea were highly aroused. The government noticed that exchanges of letters between students in Japan and Korea became more frequent, and many students returning from Japan sought out students who were leaders.[21]

Although nationalist influence from abroad was considerable, it reached only the educated part of the public. News of nationalist activities abroad was suppressed in Korea by the government, and the masses were largely kept ignorant of these events. But the sudden death of the old former emperor, on January 22, 1919, affected the whole populace.

The government-general announced the cause of the emperor's death as cerebral anemia, but various rumors spread that he had killed himself or been poisoned. It was rumored that "because he sent emissaries to The Hague, he was poisoned," or "because he declined to sign an oath that he did not want the independence, he was poisoned." Another rumor had it that the emperor committed suicide because he was unhappy over the forced marriage of the prince to a Japanese girl. In any event, Japan was blamed for his death, and anti-Japanese feeling flared high.[22]

The official funeral was set for March 3. During the intervening weeks people began to congregate in public under the pretext of mourning for the emperor, and great numbers from the provinces streamed into Seoul, amounting to an influx of about 200,000 by the time of the funeral.[23]

Although the government-general chose not to treat the deceased as the head of the state, people began to wear the traditional white hats. But the Japanese gendarmerie correctly observed that

> Most of those who showed the sign of mourning did not have any true sentiment for the Yi dynasty or for the emperor. It was rather to express their anti-Japanese feeling which they felt every day and to express their complaints against the present government. . . . Especially, the wearing of white hats gradually increased the malignant feelings of the public and undeniably expressed anti-Japanese thoughts and sorrow at the national ruin. This became more obvious when it was noticed that although only about half of the people wore white hats at the time of the funeral almost everyone wore them after the uprisings.[24]

Immediately, plans to utilize the opportunity afforded by the death of the emperor were drawn up by the nationalist leaders—Ch'oe Rin, Ch'oe Nam-sŏn, Song Chin-u, and Hyŏn Sang-yun—and in the course of several meetings the following program was agreed upon:

Solicit comrades and execute nationwide demonstrations for independence
Issue the declaration of independence
Submit memorandums to the Japanese government, to the two legislative houses, and to the government-general
Send a message to the American President asking for assistance toward independence
Send messages to the foreign representatives at the Peace Conference asking for assistance toward independence
Ch'oe Nam-sŏn to draft the declaration, memoranda and the messages
Issue the documents in the name of representatives of the Korean people
Select representatives from among members of Ch'ŏndogyo, Christians, and renowned figures of the defunct Korean government [25]

Negotiations with Christians were fruitful. An elder, Yi Sŭng-hun, who had been sentenced to ten years in prison at the time of the so-called attempt to assassinate Terauchi and been released, agreed to the plan of the Ch'ŏndogyo leaders. Going to Sunchon, Chongju, and Pyongyang, he brought into the movement several Korean pastors of the Presbyterian and Methodist churches. On returning to Seoul in the middle of February Yi discovered that some difficulties had arisen over a separate movement contemplated by Christians who proposed that members of their churches should unite to submit a petition for independence to the Japanese government. The danger of creating two separate movements, however, was soon averted. The basic difference between the two groups was that the Ch'ŏndogyo leaders planned to carry out a nationwide demonstration for independence, whereas the Christian leaders planned a movement merely to submit a petition requesting independence. At a conference in Seoul on February 22 the Christian leaders accepted the Ch'ŏndogyo plan and soon afterward sent pastors into the provinces to enroll more participants; one of the pastors, Hyŏn Sun, was sent to Shanghai to collect news on the peace conference and facilitate the exchange of information.[26]

Im Kyu was selected to submit the memorandums to the Japanese government. He translated Ch'oe's drafts into Japanese, was given papers signed (or sealed) by the group's representatives, and set off for Tokyo on February 27. An Se-sik, who was made responsible for submitting messages to foreign and other agencies in Japan, traveled to Tokyo at the same time. The petitions to the American President and the delegates at the peace conference were taken by Kim Chi-hwan to Manchuria and sent on to Hyŏn Sun in Shanghai through the Chinese mail.[27]

Another detail of the preparations for the uprisings was the propaganda organ. A Korean newspaper, *Tongnip Shinmun* ("Independence News"), was planned. On the eve of the uprisings Yi Chong-rin wrote copy for the newspaper, and the first edition was run off at the Ch'ŏndogyo printing house at dawn on March 1.[28]

During February certain Buddhist leaders agreed to take part in the movement, and groups of students in Seoul from Yŏnhi College, Posŏng Law and Commercial School, and Kyŏngsŏng Medical College were added also.[29]

By the latter part of February various component groups in the movement agreed that:

Since there will be several hundred thousand people in Seoul to observe the national funeral of the late emperor, this opportunity must be used

Since the police vigilance might be severe on the day of the funeral, the movement must be started two days ahead, on March 1

At 2:00 P.M., March 1, the Declaration will be read at Pagoda Park in Seoul, and in other areas "Tongnip manse" ("Long live independence") will be simultaneously shouted out at the same designated hour, and demonstrations will be carried out throughout the nation

The declaration and other documents will be drafted and printed by Ch'ŏndogyo and will be distributed by both (Ch'ŏndogyo and Christian) groups

The memorandums to the Japanese legislature will be submitted by Ch'ŏndogyo, and the message to the United States President and the delegates at the peace conference will be delivered by the Christians

Signatories of letters and documents will be from both groups, and since some Buddhists wish to join in a few of them will be added [30]

The drafts of the declaration and other statements made by Ch'oe Nam-sŏn were completed and approved on February 26.[31] By midnight of the next day 21,000 copies of the declaration were printed and sorted for distribution.[32]

The last conference of the signers of the declaration was held on February 28 at Son Pyŏng-hi's house. Pagoda Park had been chosen for the reading of the declaration, but since there would be masses of students and other persons at the park, it was felt some disturbance might interfere. Therefore, the location was changed to a restaurant, Myŏng-wŏl-gwan. It was also decided that the memorandum to the government-general should be submitted by Yi Kap-sŏng. It was agreed further that after the declaration of independence was read all the nationalist leaders would maintain the dignity of patriots by remaining at the place and calmly submitting to arrest.[33]

At this time the printed copies of the declaration of independence were carried by members of Ch'ŏndogyo and the Christian churches into the provinces.[34] Along with the copies were sent notices that the declaration would be read in Seoul at 2:00 P.M. on March 1, and, that, if possible, in each locality copies of the declaration should be distributed and "Tongnip manse" be cried out at the same hour. "If 'manse' is shouted throughout Korea," the notice added, "Korea will assuredly become independent." [35]

Thus the preparations were completed. One crucial factor in a movement of this kind, operating under a dictatorial government, especially when the police are known for their ability in detective work, is the observance of complete secrecy. Although the movement was planned on a national scale and required the work of many persons from the planning stage to the eventual distribution of the printed declaration, no definite information on the planned uprising seems to have been obtained by the police. On March 1 the governor-general and his cabinet were inspecting Hullyŏnwon, where the funeral was scheduled to be held, when the report of the uprisings reached them. According to a Japanese author, they "turned pale and dashed in their cars to the Government-General Building." [36]

The March First movement was touched off at dawn by the posting of copies of a manifesto issued in the name of the "National Congress" (*Kungmin Taehoe*) along the main street of Seoul. The manifesto asserted that the emperor had been assassinated by poisoning, and it appealed to the conscience of the Korean people to revenge his death and that of the murdered queen. It also stated that many small nations were obtaining their independence through the principle of national self-determination advocated by President Wilson; that the opportunity for Korean independence had arrived; and that Koreans abroad were engaged in appealing for independence at the peace conference and therefore the people at home must support the endeavor through mass demonstrations. Because of the rumors that had been circulating since the death of the emperor, the people were in an anticipatory mood and already constituted a mob waiting for a leader. The news of the manifesto spread quickly and attained a maximum effect.[37]

The following is the full text: [38]

How miserable are our 20,000,000 compatriots. Do you know the reason for the sudden demise of His Majesty the Emperor? He has been always healthy and there was no news of his illness. But he has suddenly expired at midnight in his sleeping chamber. Would this be ordinary? As we advocated the national independence in the Paris Peace Conference, the cunning Japanese produced a certificate stating that "The Korean people are happy with Japanese rule and do not wish to separate from the Japanese," in order to cover the eyes and ears of the world. Yi Wan-yong signed it as the representative of the nobility; Kim Yun-sik signed it as the representative of the scholars; Yun T'aek-yong signed it as the representative of the royal relatives; Cho Chung-ŭng and Song Pyŏng-jun signed it as social representatives; Shin Hŭng-u signed it as the representative of educational and religious fields. It was then submitted to His Majesty for his royal seal—the worst crime possible. His Majesty was most enraged and reprimanded them. They did not know what to do, and fearing other incidents in the future, they finally decided to assassinate His Majesty. Yun Tŏk-yong and Han Sang-hak, two traitors, were made to serve His Majesty's dinner, and poison was secretly added to his food at night through the two waiting women.

The Royal Body was immediately torn by agony and soon the Emperor took his last breath. There is no way to describe the pain and agony in our hearts. The two women were also put to death by poison, immediately, so that the intrigue might not be leaked out. The hands of the brigands are becoming more obvious, and cruelty is running to extremes. We have not yet revenged the humiliation of the past (the murder of the queen). And yet another calamity is brought upon us. Ask the blue sky who is incurring these misfortunes. If our people still exist, how could we neglect to cleanse these humiliations? Since the American President proclaimed the Fourteen Points, the voice of national self-determination has swept the world, and twelve nations, including Poland, Ireland, and Czechoslovakia, have obtained independence. How could we, the people of the great Korean nation, miss this opportunity? Our compatriots abroad are utilizing this opportunity to appeal for the recovery of national sovereignty, but the compatriots within our country are still unmoved. Support is not very strong, and opinions are not decided. Think, our compatriots! Now is the great opportunity to reform the world and recover us the ruined nation. If the entire nation rises in unity, we may recover our lost national rights and save the already ruined nation.

Also, in order to revenge the mortal foe of His Majesty and Her Highness, our 20,000,000 compatriots, arise!

January, thirteenth year of Yung-hi (1919).
Kungmin Taehoe. (*Seal*)

Leaflets of similar nature were posted.[39] For example:

Oh, our compatriots:
The opportunity to take revenge against the enemy of the Royal Emperor and recover the national sovereignty has come. Rise in unanimity and help carry out the great deed.
January, thirteenth year of Yung-hi.
Kungmin Taehoe. (*Seal*)

After the manifesto and leaflets were found by the police, during the morning the Christian schools in the West Gate area and the Central Y.M.C.A. were surrounded and searched. Officers and clerks of these institutions were arrested, and their homes were also searched. No indication was found that the uprisings were scheduled for the afternoon.[40]

At 2:00 P.M. twenty-nine of the thirty-three signatories of the declaration met at the restaurant as planned. The memorandum to the government-general was delivered by a student, and the police were notified of the event. Yi Chong-il placed about a hundred copies of the declaration on the table for inspection. The reading of the document was omitted. Han Yong-un, a Buddhist monk, stood up and delivered a speech which was regarded as the announcement of the declaration. All arose and cried "manse" three times. As they were about to raise toasts, policemen hurried into the room and arrested them.[41]

At Pagoda Park and the vicinity people had begun to congregate from noon onward. The crowd was estimated to be between four and five thousand, including many students. At two o'clock a young man mounted a platform in the center of the park. "The people who had been rumbling with noise became calm as still water, and all the attention was centered on the youth. He brought out a sheet of printed paper. The people became more tense." In this situation the young man read aloud the declaration of independence. On finishing the reading, he declared that "Since our country became independent from this day, we must cry out 'Tongnip manse,' " and led the shouting. The people echoed the cry and displayed the Korean flag, and soon afterward students entrusted with the printed declaration distributed 1,500 copies throughout Seoul.[42]

Presently the cry of "manse" was echoing from one end of the city to the other. The streets were filled with people frenzied with shouting. The crowd met the vehicle carrying the twenty-nine leaders to the police station and surrounded it, applauding and crying "manse." The leaders returned the cry and handed out copies of the declaration. As the leaders disappeared into the police station, the crowd separated into three groups and began peaceful demonstrations. One group advanced to Tŏksu-gung, the former palace, where the casket of the deceased king was placed and his close relatives were mourning. The demonstrators gathered in the compound and cried "manse" three times, after which they marched to the streets. The second group went first to the United States consulate and then to the French. Speeches were delivered and the "manse" was shouted. The third and largest group set out for the Government-General Building. Although it was the intention of the leaders to conduct a demonstration of a peaceful nature, and their instructions were closely observed, an incident of violence occurred when the third group approached Honmachi, the Japanese residence area. The Japanese residents had noticed the throng and requested that police be sent. At the entrance to the area, police and gendarmes appeared and ordered the crowd to disperse. When the order was not obeyed, they decided to seal off the street. Some persons in the crowd began to shout that the police and gendarmes were waiting for darkness to massacre them all. The demonstrators panicked and started to seek ways to escape. Japanese residents who had been watching the scene then joined the police in striking the Koreans with fists, feet, and sticks. Thus, although the leaders intended to demonstrate peacefully against the government, the incident at Honmachi led the movement into a racial struggle against all the Japanese.[43]

On the same day demonstrations of a similar nature were carried out in other Korean cities. On the second day demonstrations were continued in some areas and begun in new ones. The demonstrations in Seoul were suspended on the second day because it was the eve of the emperor's funeral and also was Sunday, which was observed as a day of rest by the Christians. On the third day the demonstrations in Seoul were resumed. As the vigilance of the Japanese police, gendarmes, and troops increased, the demonstrators shifted their activities to after dark. Instead of marching in the streets they set up bonfires on the hillsides, occasionally with people gathered round and shouting "manse" in unison.

Something of the scale of the demonstrations is shown by the official estimate of the government-general that there were one million participants.[44] A Korean source puts the number at more than two million.[45] For the period from March 1 to April 30, 1919, the statistics of the Japanese gendarmerie show 848 incidents (332 with violence, 516 without), 357 incidents prevented, a tally of 587,641 persons involved, and arrests of 26,713 persons.[46]

As for casualties, the same report lists Korean casualties as 553 killed and 1,409 injured, and the Japanese as 9 killed and 186 injured (including, of civilians, 1 killed and 30 injured).[47] Statistics from nationalist sources, for the longer period from March 1, 1919, to March 1, 1920, show as many as 7,645 Koreans killed and 45,562 injured.[48]

From all the available and highly divergent accountings it is evident that the movement was conducted on a large scale and was met by severe suppressive measures. Its diminishment or suppression is shown in government-general's tally of the number of persons arrested by months, from 12,522 in March to 455 in December, 1919.[49] The same report is interestingly revealing of the geographical distribution, religious affiliation, educational level, age level, and occupation of those arrested (see Table 2).

TABLE 2

(*a*) NUMBER OF ARRESTED, BY PROVINCE OR REGION

Province or region	Male	Female
Kyonggi	3,349	141
(City of Seoul—1,337 men, 128 women)		
North Chungchong	578	. . .
South Chungchong	681	6
North Kyongsang	2,103	22
South Kyongsang	2,377	72
North Cholla	622	17
South Cholla	785	6
Hwanghae	2,495	85
North Pyongan	1,180	26
South Pyongan	1,541	46
Kangwon	1,156	6
North Hamgyong	633	26
South Hamgyong	1,383	5
Siberia and Manchuria	171	6
Total	19,054	471

(*b*) RELIGIOUS AFFILIATION OF THE ARRESTED

Denomination	Male	Female	Total
Ch'ŏndogyo	2,268	15	2,283
Shich'ŏngyo	14	. . .	14
Buddhist	220	. . .	220
Confucianist	346	. . .	346
Methodist	518	42	560
Presbyterian	2,254	232	2,486
Congregational	7	. . .	7
Other Protestants	286	34	320
Catholics	54	1	55
Other religions	21	. . .	21
No religious affiliation	9,255	49	9,304
Unknown	3,809	98	3,907
Total	19,054	471	19,525

TABLE 2 (*Continued*)

(*c*) Educational Level of the Arrested

Education	Male	Female	Total
High school or above	81	1	82
Middle school	697	77	774
Elementary school	2,846	156	3,002
Classic country-school	3,751	3	3,754
Can read and write	1,220	46	1,266
No education	6,031	94	6,125
Unknown	4,428	94	4,522
Total	19,054	471	19,525

(*d*) Age Level of the Arrested

Age, in years	Male	Female	Total
Under 18	980	97	1,077
19–20	1,403	100	1,503
21–25	3,880	114	3,994
26–30	3,272	38	3,310
31–40	4,479	46	4,525
41–50	2,492	28	2,520
51–60	1,407	27	1,434
61–70	541	6	547
Above 70	87	2	89
Unknown	513	13	526
Total	19,054	471	19,525

(*e*) Occupation of the Arrested

Occupation	Male	Female	Total
Middle-school teachers:			
Public schools	2	. . .	2
Private schools	58	22	80
Primary-school teachers:			
Public schools	23	2	25
Private schools	272	40	312
College students:			
Public schools	73	. . .	73
Private schools	58	4	62

Occupation	Male	Female	Total
Middle-school students:			
Public schools	363	13	376
Private schools	555	52	607
Primary-school students:			
Public schools	360	12	372
Private schools	373	73	446
Heads of local governments (*myŏn* and *ri*)	51	. . .	51
Myŏn office clerks	153	. . .	153
Government or corporation employees	137	4	141
Medical doctors	81	. . .	81
Clerical service	25	. . .	25
Monks (Buddhist)	120	. . .	120
Christian workers:			
Ministers	54	. . .	54
Evangelists and teachers	114	13	127
Elders	61	2	63
Ch'ŏndogyo workers:			
Heads of districts	26	. . .	26
Evangelists and teachers	58	1	59
Other officers	38	2	40
Farmers	10,823	41	10,864
Fishermen	50	. . .	50
Mineworkers and mine operators	17	. . .	17
Stoneworkers	11	. . .	11
Metalworkers	60	. . .	60
Machine and tool makers	40	1	41
Weavers, dyers	31	. . .	31
Paper producers	12	. . .	12
Leather and rubber workers	54	. . .	54
Wood and bamboo workers	10	. . .	10
Public service	383	73	456
Food-products workers	55	2	57
Clothing workers, costume makers	87	6	93
Construction, civil engineering	15	. . .	15
Printing, photography	30	. . .	30
Barbers	63	. . .	63
Industry	61	. . .	61
Grain merchants	193	. . .	193
Drug merchants	73	. . .	73
Sundry-goods merchants	498	1	499
Brokers	41	. . .	41

TABLE 2 (*Continued*)

(*e*) OCCUPATION OF THE ARRESTED (*Continued*)

Occupation	Male	Female	Total
Second-hand merchants	35	...	35
Warehouse operators	60	...	60
Inn and restaurant operators	233	4	237
Businessmen and women	475	3	478
Transportation business	8	...	8
Servants, daily hire, etc.	739	5	744
General laborers	254	...	254
Unemployed	1,053	75	1,128
Unknown	535	20	555
Total	19,054	471	19,525

SOURCE: Korean Government-General, Governor's Office, *Chōsen no dokuritsu shisō oyobi undō* [The Korean Independence Thought and Movement] (Seoul, 1924), pp. 98–106.

It is not a matter of great importance for our purpose to determine whether the number of participants was one or two million. As the preceding lists testify, people in every province and in every grouping of religion, education, age, and occupation were involved in the uprisings, leaving no doubt that the movement was truly national.

The intent of the leaders can be understood by reading the declaration of independence. In brief, this document asserts the following seven points:[50]

Korea is an independent nation
Korea is suffering under an alien oppression
Every Korean has a moral duty to bring about independence
The merging of Japan and Korea is altogether harmful
The independence of Korea will be for the good of Japan, Korea, and China
A new age of justice has come
Koreans must display their desire and ability to maintain independence

Except for the first paragraph, it is hardly a declaration at all and is, instead, an exhortation to the people to rise so that their desire for independence may be known to the world. It is also designed to support the petitions to the Japanese government for the granting of independence.

On the other hand, the declaration is not based simply on abstract doctrines. It presents rational reasons for the request for independence, one of them being the good of Japan and China as well as Korea. It also appeals to the spirit of a new age of justice, obviously referring to the principle of self-determination. It is in essence addressed at once to the Korean people, the Japanese government, and the other foreign powers and for the specific purpose of urging the Japanese to grant independence, rather than for the Koreans to obtain it through violent revolution.

There were two major reasons for the pacifistic character of the declaration and the movement. One was the fact that a violent militaristic effort was not possible; as one of the leaders stated in court, the people could not be asked to fight with bare fists. The other reason was the important role of the Christian leaders, who would not have joined the movement if it had not been pacifistic. The intentions and expectations of the leaders were accurately summed up long afterward by one of them, Hyŏn Sang-yun, in 1946:

> At this time we did not believe that the Korean independence would be immediately realized . . . because World War I had not been extended into Korea and also because Japan was on the side of the Allies. But we seriously felt that we must express the desires of the people before the world, as a beginning stage of the independence movement.[51]

The local leaders, according to the gendarmerie report, could be classed by their belief as:

> Those who believed that Korean independence might be attained through the assistance of the United States at the Peace Conference.
> Those who believed that Korean independence might be attained through the Declaration of Independence.
> Those who believed that there must be a great disturbance in order that the voice of independence might be heard abroad.
> Those who did not expect complete independence, but believed the disturbance to be a foundation for later independence.
> Those who believed that the disturbance in Korea might bring some results, because there were rice riots in Japan.[52]

As to the motives of the ordinary followers of the movement, the report presented the following analysis of participants in Kangwon Province:

By instigation of Christians and Ch'ŏndogyo members—the greatest number
After seeing other areas carrying out the movement—a great number
Followed others as an obligation—a small number
Owing to dissatisfaction and complaints in ordinary times—some
Misunderstood that Korea was already independent and followed others as a celebration—extremely few
Private resentment against Japanese—extremely few [53]

Discounting the official bias, we can accept this attribution as generally representative.

Among the factors which intensified and to some extent prolonged the movement the most noticeable were the support of organized religious groups, the support of students, the support of merchants, and effective propaganda.

Religious groups alone had an effective machinery of communication on a national scale, since all political organizations had been dissolved at the beginning of Japanese rule. Industry in Korea was still in its infancy, so that there was no organized labor force, and there was virtually no organization of the farmers. Thus the only possible organizations on a national scale were of a religious nature. Among these Ch'ŏndogyo and the Protestant Christian churches mobilized almost their entire memberships and utilized all their facilities for the movement.

Next to the religious groups, students took the most conspicuous part. In the early stages of the movement, only the students of middle-school level and higher were involved, but pupils in elementary schools participated later. Japanese government statistics indicate that out of 1,251 schools in Korea, including elementary schools, 203 schools took part in the movement; out of a student population of 133,557 there were 11,133 who took part, mostly from the middle schools and above.[54] Immediately after the movement began, most schools closed for several weeks. Those in Seoul were not reopened until June.[55] The school closings, caused either by student or teacher strikes, contributed to what might be called, from the Japanese viewpoint, a subversive atmosphere. Since merchants in many areas also went on strike, almost all the visible activities in the country stopped, making the presence of the Japanese security forces more conspicuous and completing the picture of a country in protest.

Merchant strikes had a tradition of their own from the period of the old Korea. It was the practice during the Yi regime for merchants to close their shops simultaneously in order to express dissatisfaction with the government, and, however reluctantly, the government in the earlier period acknowledged such demonstrations and to some extent altered its policies. Thus again, on March 9, 1919, merchants in Seoul resorted to this passive form of resistance. All the Korean shops in Seoul, regardless of size, were closed and trade was discontinued. Soon the merchants in Inchon and Kaesong shut down their businesses.

The Japanese government detested merchant strikes for reasons somewhat different from those of the Yi regime. The earlier government could not tolerate the strikes for financial reasons, needing the tax revenues from Chong-no, the main street in Seoul, which was the center of financial activity. The Japanese feared the effect upon public opinion, since the strikes gave an atmosphere of disquiet to the whole city and encouraged the Korean public to believe that the government was powerless against the stoppage of trade.[56] When the strikes had continued for three or four weeks, the police headquarters called in sixty influential merchants in Seoul and issued a grave warning; also, a hundred infantrymen were sent to supervise the reopening of the shops. Normal business was resumed about the middle of April.[57] Strikes also occurred among conductors and drivers of street cars, workers in factories (e.g., the Tō-a Tobacco Company), and even among policemen of Korean nationality.

The Japanese police had the additional task of suppressing the secret publications that were distributed and posted—not to mention the wall scribblings. According to the gendarmerie,

> The distribution of subversive documents was the greatest harmful element leading toward the disturbance of the minds of the educated elements. The contents of the documents were items which would cause them to burn with indignation, [and] some were reprints of anti-Japanese papers published abroad. There was none which did not induce resentment toward the authorities and the Japanese. If the distributors and publishers were arrested, others took their places to continue publication. If these were arrested, others again took their places, and there was no end.[58]

No end, that is to say, while the movement was actively progressing. In order to suppress the publications, traffic at night was restricted; unscheduled searches were made in inns, restaurants, and homes; and suspected persons were interrogated and their possessions examined.[59]

Rumors spread during the period of the demonstrations contributed to the intensification and prolongation of the unrest. Because there was little or no means of verification, especially among the uneducated, the rumors were often believed to be true. Some of those prevalent were: that President Wilson was to come to Korea by airplane to assist Korean independence; that scores of United States battleships had been dispatched to Korea; that American troops had already landed at Inchon; that the peace conference had recognized the independence of Korea.[60]

Along with nationalist propaganda and rumors we can class, for its effects, based on actual events, the action of the government-general in trying to suppress the demonstrations and uproot the causes—i.e., arrest or remove all persons implicated in the demonstrations—for the Japanese police and military personnel resorted to forms of cruelty quite in the tradition of the nine years of absolute rule by the Terauchi government. An anonymous Western writer who witnessed the demonstrations and the measures taken against them wrote on March 21, 1919, that

> Beating and torture are the cardinal principles of police methods in Korea. When making arrests, usually the victim is cuffed and kicked by several policemen. . . . Instances are not infrequent where Japanese in civilian clothes have arrested demonstrators in the presence of the police and have treated them shamefully. . . . From released prisoners stories of cruelty and torture are now pouring out. One student was asked to tell who the leaders were, and his finger nails were pushed back from the skin to assist his memory. Another prisoner had his finger tips burned for the same purpose. Still another was put in an upright press, which operated with a screw from the back. When the screw is turned, the four sides contract, and while the pressure becomes stronger, the questioning is carried on—a way of squeezing out information.[61]

It is certain that most of the arrested suffered at least some flogging. Multitudes of those not arrested also suffered beating and flogging by police, gendarmes and troops.

Atrocities on a large scale were committed in scattered areas. For instance, several whole villages were burned. The *Japanese Advertiser*, published in Tokyo, described many such incidents during 1919. The June 6 issue of this newspaper carried the following account:

> With the permission of the Governor-General Hasegawa, members of the Relief Society are busily distributing daily necessities to the Korean people outdoors. . . . The relief materials are distributed in various villages and

towns, including Cheam, Suchon, Hwasuri, approximately twenty-one miles west of Suwon. . . . These towns are burned either totally or partially. The greatest distance between the towns is twenty miles. . . . The soldiers had to travel long distances to set fire to these villages. . . . The total number of houses burned in this area is 317; those without homes are approximately 1,600; killed are 39. One Japanese policeman was stoned to death in Kentari. The reason that he was stoned was that he fired into a crowd which was shouting "manse" and killed one of the demonstrators. The mob dashed to him and killed him. This town is approximately 14 miles from where the Japanese troops committed the greatest atrocities.[62]

The Japanese explanation was that

From the middle of March to the end, there were frequent disturbances in Suwon. . . . The mob set fire and destroyed the government buildings and the Japanese residents' houses. In Hwasu and Sakang, the mob killed policemen, and a policeman in Hwasu was exposed to great cruelty upon his death. . . . Therefore the Police Department of Kyonggi Province organized a special investigation team composed of gendarmes and policemen and carried out an investigation of the suspects in the area between April 2 and 15, arresting 803. Since some of them resisted arrest, ten were killed and nineteen wounded. In order to achieve the maximum effect, the team worked at night; there were accidental fires and deliberate setting of fires to facilitate the escape of criminals. In sixty-four villages, 276 houses were burned. Although the truth is as stated above, the head of the police department and others in charge were submitted to administrative disciplinary action because of their neglect of care at the time of arrests.[63]

We need not comment on this explanation beyond noting that although cruelty may not have been the official policy, the atrocities were tacitly approved by the higher echelons of the army. Small-scale brutality existed almost everywhere in Korea, as many witnesses—both Western and Korean—testify. No doubt, the suppression of a national movement necessitates the use of some force. Nonetheless, the Japanese approach to the problem was extreme, and the continuing demonstrations by the Korean people indicate that their reaction was vehement.

If the purpose of the March First movement was to obtain independence, it was clearly a failure. The Japanese government suppressed the movement, and foreign governments, including that of the United States, showed no interest, at least not officially. The Japanese government was not in the least inclined to part with Korea voluntarily. But the intention of the leaders to let the world know of the desires of the Korean people and of their discontent under Japanese rule succeeded. Through the efforts of the nationalists abroad, the case of Korea was made known and was given wide publicity. Associations supporting Korea were organized in the United States and Great Britain, much to the discomfort of the Japanese government; and, as we have seen, the Japanese public became aware of the failure of the government's policy. The governor-general was replaced and the so-called era of *bunka-seiji* ("culture polity") was inaugurated. Government restrictions on the press and political activities were relaxed, and the Koreans were given considerable freedom.

Since the movement did not attempt the forcible overthrow of the Japanese regime, it cannot be called a revolution. But some of the subsequent changes were revolutionary in character. The new administration permitted many activities which the preceding governors-general would not have tolerated. The price paid by the Koreans may have been too high. Nevertheless, the Japanese government would not have reëxamined its policy, nor have conceded so much, without the March First movement. But the true significance of the movement can be found only if we place it in a historical perspective.

The characteristics manifested by the March First movement were no longer those of the Tonghaks of 1894–1895 or the Righteous Armies of 1895–1912. It was truly national, in the sense that every element of the society was represented.

Since students took leading roles in the demonstrations and also spread to the villages to propagandize, it was a movement not only of the older generations, but of the new generations as well. (One third of the arrested were under twenty-five years of age.) The strenuous effort to Japanize Korea through education had brought about its countereffect. Christianity also stimulated nationalism, despite the pacifism associated with it. The gendarmerie report observed that

> Students and Christians who have had contact with foreign ideas and performed the central role in the recent disturbance may not be able to remove the deeply imbedded desire for independence. It will be impossible to anticipate that these will be assimilated to become good, loyal subjects of the Japanese emperor.[64]

A further matter of social and, indeed, historical significance was the active participation of women—students and others—whereas in the long history of Korea women had been kept in an inferior position and their appearing in public had been regarded as improper.

Another factor to be noted is the reliance of the leaders not upon the traditional ideas of Confucianism, as in the case of the Tonghaks, but upon the principle of self-determination received from the West. This reflects a profound change in Korean society, culture, and patterns of thinking. The Japanese government contributed toward this change, but one must not neglect the efforts of the reformers who since the late nineteenth century had striven to bring new ideas into Korea: in this sense the March First movement can be related to the beginnings of the era of modern nationalism.

The attempted *coup d'état* in 1884 by a handful of progressives was premature. A decade later the old government paid some lip service to reforms, which were generally thwarted by the tradition of conservatism and the strength of reactionary elements. But the masses were not sitting idly by to suffer the consequences of corruption and ruin of the government, as was poignantly revealed in the Tonghak movement.

Philip Jaisohn's attempt to reform Korea during 1896–1898 also ended in failure, but Jaisohn was able to solicit more supporters than the progressives of 1884, and his Independence Club was strong enough to pressure the cabinet to announce in public its promise to ameliorate the situation. Although Jaisohn's ideals were not realized in 1896, when he was forced to leave Korea, they were not uprooted.[65] After 1897 vernacular newspapers emerged in Korea and professed new thoughts.

At about the same time there was, inspired by foreign missionaries and by books imported from Japan, the surge of desire for the "new education." After 1906 educational associations emerged in almost every province, and private schools were established one after another, all with the intention of enlightening the younger generation and instilling nationalistic ideals. New kinds of novels, modeled upon the Western style, emerged after 1905 and were intent on the same purpose. Although the drive for education, particularly in its nationalistic content, was drastically curtailed by the government-general after 1910, the political content in novels, poems, songs, and other writings still persisted, and the "new literary movement up to 1919 was political rather than purely literary." [66] Since the writings of this period were in the Korean vernacular, the audience was not limited as in the past to one particular class.

It is safe to conclude that in 1919 Korean nationalism was on a steady road of progress, and that the March First movement was not merely an outburst of accumulated indignation and idealism.

IV

The Exiled Movement

8

The Korean Provisional Government

THE WAVE of demonstrations that began in Seoul on March 1, 1919, spread rapidly over Korea and eventually into the Korean communities in Manchuria and southeastern Siberia. News of the movement soon reached the Korean nationalists abroad. Yi Kwang-su had already been dispatched by Korean students in Japan to Shanghai to report their declaration of independence to the world, and Hyŏn Sun was sent there by the leaders in Seoul for liaison purposes. The most cosmopolitan city of the Far East, Shanghai was a strategic center of communication for the nationalists, and there was the further advantage that the people of China and the Chinese press were generally sympathetic to movements for independence. Of Koreans living abroad, about 600,000 were in southeastern Manchuria, 200,000 in the Maritime Province of Siberia, and 6,000 in the United States and Hawaii, and nationalists were active in all these areas.[1] There was, however, no single organization to bind them together, and in terms of location, the United States and Hawaii were too far away from Korea to become the center of the nationalist movement, Manchuria and Siberia too remote from the channels of international communication. Shanghai had qualifications that were lacking elsewhere, although there were only about 400 Koreans in the city in the early part of 1919. The number increased to about 700 by autumn.

When news of the March First demonstrations reached Shanghai, Yi Kwang-su and Hyŏn Sun collaborated with the New Korean Young Men's Association (*Shinhan Ch'ŏngnyŏn-dang*), led by Yŏ Un-hyŏng and Chang Tŏk-su, in setting up an office in the French Concession for disseminating reports on the movement to Chinese and foreign newspapers.[2] Other leaders soon arrived from Japan, the United States, Siberia, and Korea, and meetings were held for discussing the possibility of establishing a permanent organization for the independence movement.

The majority advocated the forming of a provisional government, holding that a government was needed in order to obtain public support at home and abroad and to prepare for the event of Korea's actually attaining independence. A minority, preferring a party organization, argued that the proposed government lacked sovereignty, territory, and sufficient numbers of people and would probably, for these reasons, fail.[3]

While the question was being debated, Yi Kwang-su dispatched Yi Pong-su to Seoul to ascertain the intentions of the leaders of the March First movement. Yi Pong-su found them to be without definite leanings either way.[4] By the time he was back in Shanghai, the pressure for the provisional government had become so strong that the minority was ready to yield, and on the night of his return, which was about two weeks after the beginning of the discussions, the Korean Provisional Government was created.[5] The next day, April 10, the following officers were elected:[6]

Premier	Syngman Rhee (Yi Sŭng-man)
Minister of Home Affairs	An Ch'ang-ho (Chang Ho Ahn)
Minister of Foreign Affairs	Kim Kyu-sik (Kiusic Kimm)
Minister of Justice	Yi Shi-yŏng
Minister of Finance	Ch'oe Chae-hyŏng
Minister of Military Affairs	Yi Tong-hwi
Minister of Transportation	Mun Ch'ang-bŏm

The meeting also decided to form a provisional legislative assembly composed of representatives of the eight provinces of Korea and the groups in Siberia, China, and the United States.[7] At later meetings assembly members to represent the various areas were selected from among the Koreans present in Shanghai at the time.

None of those elected to ministerial positions were present except Yi Shi-yŏng, the Minister of Justice, who had served as a judge in the old Korean government.[8] Syngman Rhee, was in the United States, engaged in propaganda activities. An Ch'ang-ho, like Rhee a famous progressive leader of the late nineteenth century, was en route to Shanghai from California, where he headed the Korean National Association. Kim Kyu-sik, a graduate of Roanoke College (Virginia), was in Paris, having been sent to the peace conference by the New Korea Young Men's Association of Shanghai. Ch'oe Chae-hyŏng, who was in Siberia organizing the Korean nationalist military group, was killed in combat with the Japanese in May, 1920, and never reached Shanghai. Yi Tong-hwi and Mun Ch'ang-bŏm were in the border area of Manchuria and Siberia, also organizing military groups.[9] The intention behind the election of persons not present in Shanghai was obviously to select the most renowned figures among the Koreans abroad and thus endow the organization with legitimacy.

In the absence of most of the elected officials, committees were created for each ministry.[10] Otherwise the only interim activities on which the participants agreed was the proclamation of the Korean Provisional Government and the continuation of propaganda work at the Paris peace conference. Accordingly, on April 13 the establishment of the government was announced and credentials as ambassador plenipotentiary were sent to Kim Kyu-sik in Paris.[11]

On May 25 An Ch'ang-ho arrived. He adhered to his basic philosophy of strengthening the nation before attempting any radical action, however, and refused to accept a position of leadership. It was, he said later, in response to a request from the nationalists for help in uniting Koreans everywhere that he left California and came to Shanghai as a delegate of the Korean National Association in the United States, and his inclinations were not toward the immediate establishment of a government. He agreed with the minority that it would be better to organize a Korean independence party.[12] Although the advocates of a government stressed the fortunate opportunity for independence, An believed that the principle of national self-determination was not likely to be applied to Korea and emphasized the fact that the Korean people were still powerless to oppose the Japanese rule.[13]

The persistence of the younger leaders, combined with his own desire to unite all the nationalist leaders, however, brought An into the organization.[14] He stipulated that efforts be made to assemble the leaders from Korea and elsewhere and that the government structure be subject to overhaul when most of them had arrived.[15]

But the task of assembling even the elected ministers was difficult. Rhee regarded his propaganda activity in the United States as more important and stayed on in the United States until late in 1920. Two of the ministers, Ch'oe and Mun, never came to Shanghai. Since all of them were widely scattered, the expense involved in traveling was a problem in itself, and, like An Ch'ang-ho, not all of them favored the establishment of a government. On the other hand, the desire to establish a government in Siberia was quite strong among the nationalists there, as Yi Tong-hwi was able to point out when he arrived in September, 1919.

Upon An's accepting office, the Provisional Government began to have an active life. In the absence of Syngman Rhee, An presided as acting premier. Funds were obtained for opening government offices,[16] leaders were called in to Shanghai, the *Tongnip Shinmun* ("Independence News") was published as the governmental organ, and future plans were deliberated. On August 5, the committee system in the ministries was abolished. Since most of the ministers were still absent, younger leaders served as vice-ministers to conduct necessary business.

In August the number of officers present was deemed sufficient to present a reorganizational plan to the Provisional Legislative Assembly. On August 28 the executive department, headed by An Ch'ang-ho, submitted the following plan:[17]

> That the premier system of government be reorganized into a presidential government and Syngman Rhee be elected the President.
>
> That the six ministries be reorganized into seven ministries and one bureau with the following portfolios:
>
> Premier, Yi Tong-hwi; Home Minister, Yi Tong-nyŏng; Foreign Minister, Pak Yong-man; Defense Minister, No (Ro) Paek-rin; Finance Minister, Yi Shi-yŏng; Minister of Justice, Shin Kyu-sik; Minister of Education, Kim Kyu-sik; Minister of Transportation, Mun Ch'ang-bŏm; Director of the Bureau of Labor, An Ch'ang-ho.

The proposed reorganization derived from An's desire to maintain unity.[18] Yet it was also related, crucially, to the fact that a group drawn from the various provinces, meeting secretly in Seoul on April 23, had adopted a provisional constitution and prepared a draft of governmental organization naming Rhee as *chipjŏnggwan ch'ongjae* ("chief executive"), Yi Tong-hwi as premier, and An Ch'ang-ho as head of the Bureau of Labor. Article Six of the Seoul constitution stated that "this basic law shall be effective until the official National Assembly has convened and proclaimed the constitution." [19] In presenting the plan for reorganization, An stated that

> The main point [is] to reorganize the government as closely as possible to the system adopted by the Seoul government. . . . The organization of two governments, one in Shanghai and the other in Seoul, was proclaimed simultaneously . . . This made people suspect that two governments were established for our people. It became essential for us to proclaim to the world that there is only one government. In order to do so, it is the proper course to sacrifice the system of the Shanghai government and recognize the Seoul government.[20]

A further cause for reorganization in Shanghai was the fact that after the action of the Seoul group Rhee used the title of president in letters to foreign governments in reporting the establishment of the provisional government in Seoul and omitted mentioning that he had been elected premier by the government in Shanghai. On August 25, three days before submitting the plan, An had sent the following cablegram to Rhee:

> The provisional government (in Shanghai) has a premier system, and the Seoul government has a chief executive. Since neither government uses the presidential designation, you are not a president. At present you must use the title of chief executive to represent the government. If you act as president without amending the constitution, you are violating the constitution and opposing the principle of unity. Please do not act as president.

Rhee, from Washington, D.C., replied on August 26:

> In order to obtain recognition of the provisional government, I used the title of president to communicate with other governments. I announced the conditions in Korea under the presidential designation. Therefore I cannot alter it now. If the news of conflict among ourselves is known to the world, it will create a great obstacle to the independence movement. If so, the responsibility will rest with you.[21]

When the reorganization plan was presented on August 28, there was opposition to it as giving too much weight to the government proclaimed in Seoul and disregarding the work that was carried on in Shanghai. Some argued that undue honor was given to Syngman Rhee and Yi Tong-hwi. Some, mentioning a rumor that Rhee was the primary cause of the reorganization, requested an inquiry. Some objected to the fact that An Ch'ang-ho was given the insignificant position of Director of the Labor Bureau and requested that the bureau be made a ministry. An Ch'ang-ho declared that the rumor was false and threatened to resign from the government if the Labor Bureau were made a ministry. The reorganization plan was, nevertheless, regarded as unacceptable by most members of the Provisional Legislative Assembly because of the personnel changes it proposed.

An Ch'ang-ho spent several days persuading each opposed member,[22] and on September 6 the reorganization plan was adopted. Immediately the assembly elected An Ch'ang-ho acting president, on the grounds that neither Syngman Rhee, the president, nor Yi Tong-hwi, the premier, was in Shanghai. The cabinet maintained that this election was unconstitutional and decided that it should, as a body, act on behalf of the president until Rhee took office. With Yi Tong-hwi's arrival on September 18, however, the problem of leadership was eliminated. The governmental structure finally agreed upon by the Legislative Assembly thus instituted a presidential government, with a cabinet under the president and responsible to the legislative branch.

The problem of how to treat the old Korean royalty had also divided the Assembly. The original Shanghai constitution stated that the Republic of Korea should extend benevolent treatment to the former imperial house. At the meeting on September 3 it was moved that the provision for special consideration be eliminated. The opposition argued that the multitudes who mourned the death of the emperor indicated the sentiment of the people and that retaining the provision would be favorable for the independence movement.[23] On September 5 the motion was defeated by a vote of nine to ten—a vote revelatory of the backgrounds of the opposing members and their basic conservatism. In April the restoration of the old imperial government had been proposed by a few, and the provision for special treatment of the imperial house had been inserted by the advocates of a republic to placate this minority.[24] That equality of all the people and a representative system of government were advocated by both the Seoul and the Shanghai groups is evidence that all the leaders were progressive enough to advocate liberal ideals; but, very naturally, many of them still had nostalgic feelings toward the old regime. This seemingly paradoxical attitude was typical of not among a few of the leaders only, but of the Korean nationalists on all levels.

Another divisive tendency can be discerned. The leaders differed in the strategies they emphasized for achieving the ultimate goal of independence, and in this respect there were three groups, by no means mutually exclusive. One group relied heavily on propaganda. As in the March First movement, most of the nationalists were at one time or another dedicated to the policy of drawing the attention of foreign powers to the situation of the Korean people. The Provisional Government as a whole actively supported the efforts of Kim Kyu-sik at Paris and of Syngman Rhee and Philip Jaisohn in the United States, and these three men can be regarded as the leaders of the propagandist group. Rhee's conviction of the primacy of what he termed "diplomatic" work was, however, excessive. According to his semiofficial biographer, "Rhee's philosophy as to how to wage the fight was set forth in a long report which he sent to the provisional government on July 5, 1919," in which he urged that "efforts must more or less for the time being be concentrated on the United States," and insisted that effectiveness would result from concentration.[25] This conviction explains his alleged monopoly of funds for his activities in the United States and his reluctance to visit Shanghai.

A second group consisted of those who advocated immediate military action against Japan. Examples of these were the nationalists in Manchuria and the Maritime Province of Siberia and, within the Provisional Government, Premier Yi Tong-hwi. As early as 1910 Yi Tong-hwi led a radical group which advocated mounting an attack on the Japanese by consolidating the financial and human resources of the Koreans in Chientao and the Maritime Province.[26] The sentiment of the military group was well displayed in a proposal to the Legislative Assembly in March, 1920, for transferring the Ministry of Military Affairs to Manchuria, organizing and training "at least ten to twenty infantry regiments" there, and having "at least ten regiments in readiness for combat before the end of the year." [27]

The third group, under the leadership of An Ch'ang-ho, were gradualists, favoring long-range preparation for independence without excluding the possibility of having to wage war for it. A statement made by An expresses their opinion:

Japan, which is ruling the Korean people, is one of the three strongest nations in the world, and in order for the weak Korean people to drive out the Japanese and gain independence from them, great efforts are necessary. I do not think that this can be attained at all in my lifetime. Therefore, in a long span of time, the Korean people must cultivate economic and organizational power which will become the elements of strength.[28]

The advocates of immediate military action were the most radical and impatient. In their opinion, the longer the offensive was put off, the more difficult would it be to defeat the Japanese. But actually victory was not expected. The militarists urged that an attempt be made in order that the duties of the nationalists toward their country should be performed.

The problem of differing policy emphases plagued the Provisional Government from its inception and eventually became one of the reasons for its breaking up. In the meanwhile An Ch'ang-ho mediated the differences. He objected to the reckless militarist policy, but saw that the only way to preserve the government was by everyone's taking a middle road; and indeed a compromise was reached among the leaders of the Provisional Government early in 1920. In a New Year's speech An summed up the immediate objectives on which all could agree: uniting the Korean people under the Provisional Government; preparing the people and the government militarily and otherwise; continuing propaganda activities to win the sympathies of foreign powers.[29] The consensus, however, lasted hardly a year. An Ch'ang-ho and Yi Tong-hwi both resigned in 1921, and by that time the Shanghai government had undergone much stress and change. Although the organizational structure and the name were maintained, with a few years of interruptions, until 1945, the Provisional Government after 1921 cannot be treated as identical with that of the earlier period. From 1919 to 1921, however, the majority of Korean nationalists abroad were indeed united in the Provisional Government, and this was the only period during which most of the leaders attempted to work together.

Of the objectives emphasized by An Ch'ang-ho, the first was obviously the most important: the uniting of all Koreans under the Provisional Government. A remarkable effort toward accomplishing this was begun soon after he joined the government and accepted the leadership. On July 10, 1919, Cabinet Order No. 1 was issued, instituting a *yŏnt'ongje*, or "united communication system," under the Ministry of Transportation. Each province and prefecture within Korea was to have officers in charge of communications with Shanghai. The functions of these persons included:

Dissemination of laws, orders, and other instructions issued by the Provisional Government
Preparation and encouragement of demonstrations
In the event a war for independence started abroad, mobilization and transportation of soldiers and other necessary personnel and [securing of] materials
Mobilization of agents to collect funds for the government
Collection and transmission of funds for the government
Sale of government bonds when issued
Communication of information

The *yŏnt'ongje* officers were also entrusted with rendering reports every five days covering any of the following:

The names and addresses of those killed while engaged in the independence movement [and] the situation at the time of death
The same concerning the wounded
The same information concerning those executed or arrested by the enemy
The names, addresses, ages, and a summary of the activities of those who planned independence movements and accomplished significant results
The names, addresses, and ages of those who made patriotic donations, and the amount contributed
The names, addresses, and ages of those with military experience
Public opinion on the independence movement
Security measures of the enemy and the means to evade them
Other relevant information

Each office in the communication system was also ordered to organize groups in its area to carry out demonstrations at designated times and places.[30]

After the March First movement was begun in Korea, the security measures of the Japanese government were tightened. Even if the communication system were established temporarily, its lasting for any long period was hardly to be expected. The officers would have to be well known and respected by the people in their areas, be prepared to suffer the consequences of discovery by the Japanese police, and be able to work in secret, escape detection, and, if arrested, keep the secrets of the government. Considering the efficiency and cruelty of the Japanese police, persons equal to all these demands would be few. Many of the significant leaders in Korea were already under arrest in connection with the March First movement, and the Provisional Government had to obtain its communications men among those left over.

Despite these difficulties the system was put into operation. The leaders had some hope that the principle of national self-determination could be realized, and were anxious to keep the Korean people informed of the world situation and of the policies of the Provisional Government so that they would be prepared to respond to the call of that government if a proper opportunity should arise. The communication system in its own way symbolizes the situation of the Korean nationalists at the time. They did not see a bright future, but they clung to a thread of hope.

Agents were sent to Korea, and suitable persons were appointed as communications officers. The Ministry of Transportation set up an office at Antung, Manchuria, to serve as a liaison point for the branches in Korea. This task was notably aided by an Irishman, George L. Shaw, who had an ocean transport and trade business in Antung. Because of Shaw's extraterritorial status, the Koreans were able to use his office with safety until July, 1921, when he was arrested and evicted. A vertical line of communication was used in order to prevent mass arrests of participants.[31]

Through this system reports were sent to Shanghai, agents were dispatched to propagandize for the independence movement and inform the people of the international situation, patriotic donations were collected, and bonds of the provisional government were sold. It worked moderately well for nearly two years.[32] But during the same time Japanese security measures were tightened further. By the end of 1921 the entire system had been destroyed.

Efforts to unite Korean residents outside Korea were from the beginning less successful. Cabinet Order No. 2, issued March 16, 1920, called for the establishment of Korean Residents Associations as intermediaries between the people and the Provisional Government, but no new organization was achieved. Korean residents in the United States and Hawaii, as well as those in Shanghai, had already formed comparable organizations, and these continued to support the Provisional Government. Elsewhere the order was ineffective.

Much attention was directed to Manchuria and Siberia. Although Korean residents across the Pacific were giving indispensable aid to the Provisional Government by sending money, those in Manchuria and Siberia were greater in number and were the only ones capable of military action. United support in that area would have provided additional funds and a strong foundation for the contemplated Provisional Government Army.

But the Koreans in Manchuria and Siberia were enrolled in a dozen diverse groups. The Korean People's Association (*Hanjokhoe*), under Yi T'ak in West Chientao, and North Chientao Great Korean National Association (*Puk Kando Taehan Kungminhoe*), under Ku Ch'un-sŏn, were primarily self-governing organizations.[33] Others, such as the group under Sŏ Il in North Chientao, were primarily military. In all, there were about 3,000 to 4,000 Korean fighters equipped in varying degrees and enrolled in various groups. Most of the organizations had friendly relationships with the local Chinese authorities, and some had connections with the Soviet government in Siberia.[34]

To further the unification of the Korean people, it was necessary for the Provisional Government to bring these groups under its control. As delegates to them, the government appointed An T'ae-guk and Paek Yŏng-ip. An was assigned to North Chientao, which was

> not only the area in which the greatest number of Koreans were residing, but also the area where factional struggle was the harshest. Except for the Hawaiian Islands, the North Chientao area was the most difficult place to achieve unity.[35]

Yet unity might have been achieved there had not An T'ae-guk died. "All the leaders were unanimous in the opinion that only one person could bring about harmony in the North Chientao area. That person was An T'ae-guk." [36] An, one of the leaders of the New People's Society (*Shinminhoe*) within Korea and one of those sentenced to prison for the so-called attempt to assassinate Governor-General Terauchi, was very dynamic and had the ability to harmonize differences.[37] Unfortunately for the Provisional Government, he fell ill before leaving Shanghai and died February 5, 1920. An Ch'ang-ho is reported to have wept over this severe loss to the nationalist movement.[38]

Efforts for unification were continued, however, and delegates were dispatched to Manchuria and Siberia, but, except among a few small groups in West Chientao, in vain. A letter from North Chientao describes the situation confronting the Provisional Government there:

The organizations established in this area after March, 1919, to engage in the independence movement are about twelve. All of them advocate the prosperity of Korea and the destruction of Japan. But each strives to attain a superior position through its own activities and does not wish to obey your government.[39]

First of all, military groups were self-sufficient and independent. Each group was clustered round its leaders, and uniting under the Provisional Government would have meant taking orders from outsiders who had nothing to contribute directly to their activities and were, instead, relying on them for income.

Secondly, the military groups were largely composed of die-hard nationalists interested mainly in attacks on the Japanese across the Tumen River. Many of these men had been members of the Righteous Armies. They occasionally penetrated into the Japanese-occupied homeland and often succeeded in their missions. But the only way they knew to express their patriotism was by killing as many Japanese and Japanese collaborators as possible. They were not willing to share their restricted income with such a group as the Provisional Government, which had been created without their prior consent and whose claim to represent the Korean nation they did not accept.

Last, the basic requirement for leadership of any of these groups was renown, which in this period still meant that their leaders had to be men who had held significant positions in the old Korean government. Therefore most of the military groups were led by members of the old elite, deeply loyal to the dynasty and the old social and political structure. The reformist leaders at Shanghai were westernized intellectuals, military by neither inclination or training.

All that the Provisional Government could offer was the advantage of being united. To enlist the leaders of the military groups, the Provisional Government needed to muster substantial foreign aid, making it practical and advantageous for them to come under its direction. Winning foreign support, thus, was intricately connected with the problem of uniting the nationalists abroad. This was a vicious circle which the leaders of the Provisional Government failed to break.

According to An Ch'ang-ho's New Year's speech in 1920, the so-called diplomatic propaganda of the Provisional Government was to win allies in the event of a war for independence. Rhee, however, regarded military activities as absurd and dangerous: guerrilla raids by Korean nationalists merely incensed the Japanese and provided them with more excuses for suppression in Korea; the only way to win independence was by appealing to the conscience of the Western powers. Beliefs similar to Rhee's, but less extreme, were held by the Provisional Government's agent at the Paris peace conference. The relations of Premier Yi Tong-hwi with the Soviet Union, on the other hand, were intended to promote military action.

Kim Kyu-sik had been sent to Paris in January, 1919, by the New Korea Young Men's Association. When the Provisional Government was organized, in April, he was elected Minister of Foreign Affairs; upon the reorganization of the government in September he became Minister of Education. The financing of his work at the peace conference, begun by the Association, was continued by the Provisional Government.[40] He was in Paris until late August, when he was appointed chairman of the Korean Commission in Washington, D.C.

On May 12, 1919, Kim Kyu-sik submitted the "Petition of the Korean People and Nation for Liberation from Japan and for the Reconstitution of Korea as an Independent State" and the "Claims of the Korean People and Nation" [41] to the peace conference, but the Korean issue was not formally considered. Kim's attempts to speak at the conference were unsuccessful, owing to the participation of Japan as one of the victors in the war.[42] While he was in Paris, Kim established the Bureau d'Information Coréen to transmit news about the uprisings in Korea and to propagate the Korean cause. The Bureau sent news circulars to newspapers in France and published pamphlets for general distribution.[43] Obstructed in his attempts to influence the official delegates, Kim found, nevertheless, a significant number of foreign sympathizers on the periphery of the conference.[44]

When Kim arrived in Washington in September, 1919,[45] the chief Korean organizations in the United States devoted to propaganda activities and having connections with the Provisional Government in Shanghai were the Korean Commission (in Washington), the Korean Information Bureau (in Philadelphia), and the Korean National Association (in San Francisco and Honolulu).

The beginning of full propaganda activities on behalf of independence by the Korean nationalists in the United States had been made at the First Korean Congress, April 14–16, 1919, in Philadelphia. Philip Jaisohn was chairman of the meeting, Syngman Rhee was an active participant, and many who later were members of the Korean Commission had important roles. Like the Provisional Government, the First Congress was triggered by the March First movement. On March 27 Hyŏn Sun in Shanghai sent news of the movement by cablegram to Syngman Rhee, who was then in Washington as a representative of the Korean National Association and was attempting to obtain a passport in order to attend the peace conference. As news of the demonstrations was spread, Korean nationalists in the Washington area decided that a three-day congress should be held. Philip Jaisohn in his capacity as chairman released a statement to the press explaining that

> We called the Korean Congress because we want America to realize that Korea is a victim of Japan. Korea's wrongs have been insidiously covered up by Japan, and we believe that America will champion the cause of Korea as she has that of other oppressed peoples, once she knows the facts.[46]

Invitations were sent to Koreans in the United States, Hawaii, and Mexico. About seventy Koreans, including a number of students, responded to the call.[47]

The object of the First Korean Congress was, as Jaisohn stated, publicity for the cause of Korea. Probably the title given the gathering was aimed toward the American public, especially the people of Philadelphia, the seat of the first American Congress. On the last day of the congress the participants, headed by a platoon of mounted reserves and a band, and each bearing the Korean and American flags, paraded to Independence Hall, where Syngman Rhee read the Korean declaration of independence.

To maximize the sympathies of the American public, Korean speakers at the congress eulogized American history and institutions. Most of the speeches were delivered in English and were printed and distributed to the public. An "Appeal to America" reminded the American people that they also had fought for liberty and democracy. "Our cause," the Korean appeal asserted, "is a just one before the Laws of God and Man. Our aim is freedom from militaristic autocracy; our object is democracy for Asia; our hope is universal Christianity." A resolution unanimously adopted by the congress was entitled "Aims and Aspirations of the Koreans." Its ten items, in brief, enunciated:

Belief in government which derives its power from the governed
The intention to model an independent Korean government after that of the United States so far as was consistent with the education of the masses, who with improved education would be allowed increasing participation in the government
The intention to allow universal suffrage at local and provincial levels
The intention to place executive responsibility in a president, vice president, and cabinet, who would be responsible to the national legislature
Belief in freedom of religion
Belief in free commerce with all nations
Belief in education of the people as more important than any other function of government
Belief in modern sanitary practices to protect the health of the people
Belief in freedom of speech and the press
Belief in liberty of action so long as there is no conflict with the rights of others and the laws and interests of the nation

The resolution, with its obvious reflection of the influence of American democratic principles, is, it is interesting to note, similar to the resolutions drafted in Seoul and Shanghai and was prepared when details of the program formulated in Seoul were not yet known.[48]

The relationship of the congress to the provisional government—or governments—of Korea was obscure. When a question was presented from the floor that someone should inform the congress as to the identity and the status of the Provisional Government, the information at hand consisted solely of a cablegram sent by Hyŏn Sun in Shanghai to the Korean National Association in San Francisco and received on April 4. This message stated that a provisional government had been formed by Korean nationalists in the Far East with headquarters in an unnamed Manchurian city.[49] Further uncertainty was caused by the announcement in Seoul, in April, of a provisional government which would be organized by "elected officials" who were then residing abroad. Philip Jaisohn's summary statement on the status of the provisional government is typical of the justifications of the provisional government put forth by nationalist leaders.

It does not make any difference [Jaisohn declared] whether the President of the Provisional Korean Government is in prison or whether he is in France;

> he may be in America; that does not make any difference . . . It does not make the government non-existent, because it is not generally known where it is located. It is the will of the people that makes the government, and it does not make any difference whether the President is in jail or where he is. . . . If you read the history of this country when the Revolutionary War broke out, you will recall that the Government was not established in any one place, they were forced to move around. . . . They had a capital in Yorktown, and then came to Philadelphia. That does not make the government illegal. As somebody has well expressed it in Korean, "The new provisional government of Korea is a personification of the will of the people of Korea . . ." There is a will manifested by these Korean revolutionists and they should be the governors of Korea. Now we want to recognize them. Whether or not we believe in the cause that these Koreans are fighting for today, that is the question that is before us, and the question as to where they are located will be developed in good time.[50]

Uncertainty about the two provisional governments was unavoidable at this time, and the later disputes between the two can be seen as having roots in the impossibility of bringing them together in the beginning. The government that the congress supported was actually the one proclaimed in Seoul, not the one being organized in Shanghai.

The Korean Information Bureau was created by the congress on the last day on the urgent advice of Philip Jaisohn who believed that most Americans did not take the Korean independence movement seriously and that this attitude had been brought about by Japanese cleverness: through publicity agents the Japanese had led them into thinking that Koreans were weak and spineless, that they had no common sense and could not help themselves, and that they needed nurses and guardians. Jaisohn insisted that the principles and ideals that the Koreans advocated so ardently were the same as those of the American people, and that as soon as the Americans were informed of the Korean cause their hearts would be opened. The congress and also the Korean National Association in San Francisco agreed that a permanent information agency should be set up and that Jaisohn should head it.[51]

Shortly after the congress adjourned, the Bureau published the *Proceedings of the First Korean Congress* and various pamphlets reporting Japanese atrocities and the cause of Korean independence. A monthly magazine, the *Korea Review,* was started and was issued regularly from April, 1919, until 1922. The Bureau also carried out an active campaign to enlist American sympathizers in the League of the Friends of Korea.[52]

By executive order of Rhee as president, the Korean Commission was created in the autumn of 1919.[53] The first chairman was Kim Kyu-sik, recently arrived from France.[54] The Commission between 1919 and 1921 addressed itself chiefly to influencing the United States government, particularly members of Congress.[55]

Earlier, the Korean problem had received notice in the United States Senate on June 30, 1919, when Senator Selden P. Spencer, of Missouri, introduced a resolution requesting that the Secretary of State inform the Senate whether the situation in Korea indicated the necessity of the United States exerting its offices on behalf of that country under the treaty of May 22, 1882, and again on July 15 when Senator George W. Norris, of Nebraska, discussed the problem on the Senate floor in connection with ratification of the Versailles Treaty.[56] The Commission's "Briefs for Korea," which summed up the claims and charges of the Korean nationalists against Japan, was read into the *Congressional Record* by Senator Spencer on September 19.[57] A resolution expressing the sympathy of the United States Senate with the aspirations of the Korean people for a government of their own choice was introduced by Senator James D. Phelan, of California, on October 1, and Representative William E. Mason, of Illinois, introduced an identical resolution in the House of Representatives on October 24, but neither resolution was reported out of the Committees on Foreign Relations and Foreign Affairs.[58] On October 13 Senator Norris defended the cause of Korea before the Senate in an eloquent speech which covered fourteen pages of the *Congressional Record*.[59] These actions no doubt encouraged the nationalists and served to spread interest in the cause of Korea, but it became obvious that no dramatic move was to be expected from the Congress.[60]

Among the publications sponsored by the Korean Commission were *Korea's Fight for Freedom*, by Frederick A. McKenzie,[61] and *The Case of Korea*, by a member of the Commission, Henry Chung.[62] The effect of these books in the United States is not known, but McKenzie's was widely distributed in England and given sympathetic reviews by many newspapers. From this book came the establishment of the League of the Friends of Korea in the United Kingdom, on October

26, 1920, at a meeting in the House of Commons, presided over by Sir Robert Newman.[63]

Earl K. Hwang, a representative of the Korean Commission, was thus introduced at the first meeting of the League by F. A. McKenzie:

> He came to Europe as a soldier in the American army during the war, and after the armistice, hearing of the great needs of his people, induced the American authorities to give him his discharge in France and since then has worked mainly in Paris for Korea . . . His services have been of the most varied kind and of the utmost value. He has kept the cause of Korea before the diplomatists of Europe. He edits a monthly magazine in French on Korea. He looks after the interests of his fellow Koreans of all classes who come to Europe.[64]

The magazine referred to was *La Corée Libre*.[65] It was similar in the content and form to the *Korea Review* published by the Korean Information Bureau in the United States.

From the preceding account it should be clear that the Koreans overseas, especially those in the United States and Hawaii, were as vigorous as their counterparts in Korea and China in seeking to obtain or recover Korean independence. Tremendous energy and a huge sum of money given by Koreans and sympathizers were poured into propaganda activities in an effort to gain the backing of the Western powers.[66] Philip Jaisohn devoted the entire period of two years to these activities and eventually went bankrupt,[67] and many other nationalists also gave their full time.

To some extent the nationalists were rewarded. Distinguished legislators in the United States, Great Britain, and France spoke openly against the Japanese occupation in Korea, so that at least the desire of the Korean people was made known to the world. Of course, abrupt changes in policy could not be expected. The governments just mentioned had close relationships with Japan; so far as their policy makers were concerned, the Korean nationalists were a nuisance and providing active assistance to the cause of Korean independence was out of question. Even so, the Japanese government acutely felt the strain of the situation. In July, 1919, Premier Hara Takashi informed Governor-General Hasegawa that the disturbance in Korea had become a target of criticism in the United States and that the March First movement had brought disadvantage to Japan in many respects.[68] About the same time, the American ambassador in Tokyo told Army Minister Tanaka Giichi that he had received appeals from all directions regarding the wretched conditions in Korea and that reform in Korea would be most welcome to the United States.[69] A great part of the credit for such pressures must be given to the overseas nationalists.

Whereas the response of governments in the West was covert when favorable and mostly indifferent in outward expression, the emerging Soviet Union was openly receptive to the Korean appeal for aid and was, indeed, the only country with which the Korean Provisional Government can be said to have had a relationship close to what is meant by "diplomacy." China was still in the confusion of revolutionary struggles. Although the Korean leaders established some contacts with the revolutionary regime in Canton, there was no active support from any of the various governments in China.[70]

Contacts with the Bolsheviks existed as early as June, 1918. Korean nationalists in large numbers were operating in the Maritime Province of Siberia and in southeastern Manchuria near the Siberian border. These groups needed weapons for their anti-Japanese forays; the Bolsheviks, who were fighting the White Russians, Czechs, and Japanese, needed allies. Some of the Korean nationalists, lured by the military and financial aid of the Bolsheviks, organized Communist parties in Siberia and Manchuria. Yi Tong-hwi, the future premier of the Provisional Government, organized the Korean People's Socialist party (*Hanin Sahoedang*) in June, 1918, at Khabarovsk. In April, 1919, this group changed its name to the Koryŏ Communist party (*Koryŏ Kongsandang*).[71]

It was natural that Yi Tong-hwi should turn to the Russians when he came to occupy the central position in the Provisional Government. Although his colleagues continually reported on their extensive propaganda activities in the West, none of the Western governments were showing any positive intention of giving the active support that Yi wanted in order to build a great army under the Provisional Government.

Since the Russian Revolution [Yi stated], the Bolsheviks are gradually coming to Siberia and Mongolia. I have been in the Siberia area for a long time and I know a good many Russians. I hope to win coöperation from them. . . . To bring the matter [of the independence movement] before the League of Nations is one way, but even if we fail, we must continue our efforts . . . Although we have some relations with the southern Chinese group [of Sun Yat-sen], we cannot anticipate any great assistance. It is the same with France and England. The United States did not even join the League. To join with the Russian Bolsheviks is therefore the only short cut.[72]

In October, 1919, major leaders of the Provisional Government —An Ch'ang-ho, Yi Tong-hwi, Yi Tong-nyŏng, Yi Shi-yŏng, Shin Kyu-sik, and Yŏ Un-hyŏng—met and decided to send a three-member mission to Russia. The men selected were Yŏ Un-hyŏng, An Kŏng-gŭn, and Han Hyŏng-gwŏn.[73] The original plan was to call An Kŏng-gŭn from Siberia and then send the three to Moscow in January as delegates of the Provisional Government. Contrary to the original decision, however, Han Hyŏng-gwŏn was sent without the others. This change of plan was made by Yi Tong-hwi in consultation with Kim Rip, a personal follower who was the chief secretary to the cabinet, but his motive is not known.[74]

One of the objects of the mission was to establish an understanding that the Soviet Russian government would furnish aid to the Korean residents in Siberia, estimated to number between 40,000 and 50,000.[75] But Premier Yi's decision to send only one commissioner, along with subsequent developments, would seem to indicate that he was primarily interested in financial assistance.

Han Hyŏng-gwŏn left Shanghai about May, 1920, with Ko Ch'ang-il as an interpreter.[76] Why his departure was delayed is not known, nor is information on the negotiations available, but it is clear that the Russian government was cordial. Han received a promise of two million rubles and was given an initial payment of 600,000 rubles. He made two trips to transport the money, part of which went to Kim Rip, who appeared in Shanghai in December, 1920, with 400,000 rubles. The Russian funds might have greatly assisted the Provisional Government; but the government was by then in turmoil, and Premier Yi withheld them.

At this time Syngman Rhee visited the Provisional Government, arriving in Shanghai on December 8, 1920.

President Rhee, to use the title he insisted upon, had been the head of the government for nearly two years. During that time he had delegated authority and kept aloof from internal discords, devoting his attention to propagandizing in Washington. It may be suspected that he had absented himself not only because of his conviction that he could thus best serve the nationalist cause, but also from a temperamental inclination. Rhee's reputation as a political figure of the 1890's and as a scholar who had earned a doctoral degree at an eminent university in the United States [77] had created a mystical reverence for him which he may have been loathe to risk losing in direct dealings with his supporters. As early as March, 1920, however, the Provisional Legislative Assembly had passed a resolution urging his visit.[78] The time had come when he could defer it no longer.

Even before Rhee reached Shanghai, the Provisional Government was in decline. Initial enthusiasm had faded; the response of the League of Nations and the foreign powers had been nil; the communication lines with Korea had been broken by the Japanese; the army on which so many nationalists set their hopes had not been and could not be assembled; and the government lacked adequate financial resources. Once Rhee was present, all the problems of the government were laid upon him, in particular the immediately pressing problems of finance and factionalism. He could not provide the charismatic leadership that was needed and expected; nor did he bring the panacea for the government's ills. Soon his record was under sharp attack.

Beginning early in January, 1921, cabinet meetings were held for the purposes of examining the past conduct of the government and setting up new policies in the presence of the president. Factional disruption came into the open on January 24 when Yi Tong-hwi offered to resign the premiership. Yi stated, and others echoed his opinion, that Rhee and Henry Chung, in Washington, had committed a diplomatic blunder and diluted the spirit of Korean independence by submitting a petition to President Wilson that Korea be placed under a League of Nations mandate. Although Yi had additional reasons for breaking with the Shanghai government, the matter of the petition was crucial and became the central point of attack by those opposed to Rhee's leadership.

Rhee replied that the petition was intended to stimulate propaganda, not to hinder Korean independence, and as an issue was already outdated. Adverse criticism of the petition, he asserted, was really directed against himself. To proposals of allowing the premier to have full authority in his absence, and of substituting a cabinet council in the place of a single chief executive in the future, Rhee's answer was that his remaining in Washington had been unavoidable owing to the importance of his work in the United States, that the cabinet council was contradictory to the principles of the Seoul government and therefore inadmissible, and that these issues, like the controversy over the petition, were really no longer pertinent.[79]

The disagreement between Rhee and a majority of the cabinet members brought about a mass resignation. On January 26, resignations were submitted by Yi Tong-hwi, An Ch'ang-ho, and Kim Kyu-sik, among others.[80] The reasons given by the resigning cabinet members were as follows:

1. The Provisional Legislative Assembly invited the provisional president to the seat of government because of confusion in the political picture and the divided nature of public opinion. Under these circumstances, the position of the government was unsteady. Responsibility lay in President Rhee's confused policies. The cabinet members attempted to ameliorate the situation by co-operating with the President, and we regret that no favorable result was obtained.

2. In paying respect to the spirit of the Seoul government, which has been emphasized by Syngman Rhee, we have attempted to improve the administrative structure without changing the membership of the cabinet. By doing so, we hoped to correct the faults of the past and recapture the divided public opinion. Syngman Rhee, however, refused to admit the errors of the past, and he did not provide alternate policies. Disregarding public opinion, he merely insisted upon following his temporary decisions . . . Since the will of the majority was not followed and no policy for improvement was adopted, nothing but conflict has resulted.

3. We submitted our resignations because correcting the confused state of the government would only cause a great struggle . . . and if we were to maintain the *status quo*, this, in effect would be an act of assisting the dubious policies of Syngman Rhee. We decided, therefore, that it better satisfied our consciences to support the Provisional Government as common people than to retain our public offices.[81]

Subsequent statements issued in 1921 by various groups in China, Manchuria, and the United States indicated that the opponents of the Provisional Government desired the elimination of Rhee. On April 19 a proclamation criticizing Rhee, Henry Chung, and An Ch'ang-ho was issued by a group of fifty-four Korean nationalist and national-Communist leaders in North China who had stayed apart from the government. This group declared that the petition submitted by Rhee and Chung was a betrayal of the people equal to the traitorous actions of Yi Wan-Yong and Song Pyŏng-jun, the signers of the protectorate and annexation treaties. An Ch'ang-ho was accused of withholding knowledge of the petition while he was head of the Korean National Association and pushing Rhee into the presidency. The proclamation also asserted that when Kim Kyu-sik was in Europe people ridiculed him by asking, "Why did the Koreans elect as President Syngman Rhee, who petitioned to place Korea under the mandate system even while they were carrying out an independence movement?" Those who supported Rhee were denounced for not impeaching him.[82]

On April 20 the Chŏng-Ku-dan, another group in China, issued a statement attacking the Provisional Government as unrepresentative.[83] On April 24 a so-called Military Unification Conference (*Kunsa T'ong-il Hoe-i*), held in Peking by Pak Yong-man and representatives from groups in Manchuria, Siberia, and Hawaii that were not affiliated with the Shanghai government, sent a letter to the Provisional Legislative Assembly demanding that it dissolve within three days.[84] On May 26 a number of leaders in Manchuria who had previously supported the Provisional Government sent a resolution to the government urging reform and announcing that the representatives for West Chientao would be recalled if their advice were not heeded.[85]

Despite the several resignations, Syngman Rhee retained the support of some members of the Provisional Government. On March 5 Cho Wan-gu, Yun Ki-sŏp, and forty-three others announced their determination to stand by the Provisional Government and its president. These followers organized the Mutual Assistance Society (*Hyŏpsŏnghoe*) to help continue the existing government.[86] Shin Kyu-sik, the Minister of Justice, took a second office as premier and Yi Shi-yŏng, Yi Tong-nyŏng, and No Paek-rin became cabinet members. Syngman Rhee returned to the United States in June, 1921. Before leaving he informed the Legislative Assembly that many cabinet members had resigned unexpectedly, causing much of his time to be devoted to reorganization of the government, and requested the coöperation of the members of the Assembly in carrying out the duties of the government.[87]

Thus the Shanghai government broke under multiple pressures.

The responsibility of Rhee was no doubt great. He not only failed to bring about an improvement, but contributed considerably to the disruption. Shin Hŭng-u (Hugh Heung-woo Cynn), a long-time friend of Rhee and his prison mate in the 1890's, later commented that

> Rhee went to Shanghai in 1920 and collided with many Koreans there. Some unpleasant situations developed, and Rhee returned to America with some disagreeable feelings. Responsibility for this situation lies on both sides, but I thought his lack of the sense of compromise was a main cause.[88]

In his friend's opinion, Rhee's greatest faults were stubbornness and the inability to compromise. Shin also stated that Rhee became "angry without any reserve if anyone opposed his beliefs." Recalling their experiences in prison, Shin said he had once moved to another cell in the prison after a harsh argument.[89] If this was the case with a close friend, whose friendship began in childhood and lasted until their maturity, no doubt Rhee's personality played a role in the breakup of the Provisional Government.

But it will be foolish to blame one man for the disruption of the government. Environmental factors lowered the morale of the Korean nationalists. Paek Ch'ŏl, a contemporary literary critic, has said that the failure of the March First movement within Korea "meant the bankruptcy of the nation," and that "because of the failure of this movement, an era of despair and pessimism dawned upon the entire people." [90] To a great degree the nationalists regarded the Provisional Government as a continuation of the March First movement. It was inevitable that they should fall into a state of mind like that of their compatriots within Korea.

Divergent beliefs as to the correct policies for the nationalist movement existed from the beginning of the Provisional Government. Although the differences were alleviated temporarily under the skillful guidance of An Ch'ang-ho, disappointments renewed them. To such a man as Yi Tong-hwi, there was no alternative to active warfare. Although Yi seemed to yield to the diplomatic approach, his solution was war and the diplomacy was useful merely to win allies for the warfare. It was natural that he should decide to send only one delegate to Moscow, instead of the contemplated mission, since his purpose was to get military or financial assistance, and that Yi's group should withhold the money they obtained—all efforts were to be concentrated upon winning further help from Moscow. Yi seems to have reasoned that success could be achieved, or at least assisted, by propagating the cause of communism. Yi's military policy and his leaning toward Russia thus directed him and his followers to the Communist movement.

After coming to Shanghai, Yi established the Koryŏ Communist party (*Koryŏ Kongsandang*) in May, 1920, and drew some influential nationalist leaders into it. The money obtained in Moscow, which had been intended for the use of the Provisional Government, was diverted by Yi Tong-hwi and his associates to further Communist activities.[91] From that time the problems of communism constantly plagued the Korean nationalist movement, not only abroad but within Korea as well.

Some leaders of the Provisional Government, such as An Ch'ang-ho and Yŏ Un-hyŏng, regarded the establishing of the government as a mistake. Although An did his best to enhance the influence of the government while he was in the position of leadership, it was inevitable that he should become discouraged and withdraw.[92] He wanted to cultivate the national strength through a long period of time rather than resort to reckless or radical actions. Facing strong opposition from the other nationalists in Shanghai, An could find no reason to stay in the Provisional Government.

One of the most disruptive factors was financial difficulty. Had there been ample funds, differences in policy lines could easily have been modified, or diverse policies could have been pursued simultaneously. But the treasury of the Provisional Government was not blessed with ideal conditions. Of the income from patriotic donations, poll taxes, and government bonds, a large part was allocated for propaganda activities in the United States and France. The Moscow funds never reached the government's treasury.

The straits of the Provisional Government intensified the normal factional struggles. Factionalism is almost an ever present fashion in the Far East, where political allegiance depends so often on kinship relations or other personal ties, and groups are usually of the leader-follower type. Large groups, be they labor unions, trade associations, or political parties, are conglomerations of these sociopolitical atoms.

When the going is difficult, latent factional conflict among the subgroups emerges on the surface and endangers the existence of the larger body.

In an exile movement the problem of factionalism is much more intense than in a political environment within a sovereign state. Exiled revolutionaries are likely to be dedicated yet embittered men. Often their hopes are shaken by repeated failures. Determined to serve what they deem to be the call of their country, each leader-follower group within the movement advocates a different policy which it considers to have the best probability of success. Unity under this condition is impossible.

The divergent policies advocated by the leaders of the Provisional Government have already been noted. Difference in policies was not only derived from their personality differences, but also from the different processes of acculturation that they had undergone after their departure from Korea. Most of the Korean nationalist leaders left Korea between the years 1905 and 1910, some going to the United States, some to Siberia, some to China. Consciously or unconsciously, they acquired different sets of beliefs, values, and ways of thinking. They were Americanized, Russianized, or Sinocized, all in varying extent. Although still Korean at heart, they were no longer the stereotype Korean in their behavior and thinking, if there ever was such. Thus it was impossible for a charismatic leader to emerge and unite them.

The factionalism of the nationalists was further complicated by their antecedent parochialism or provincialism. They were not able to eradicate traits of the past. Personal and local ties often played a more important role than impersonal issues or policies. The Provisional Government had its *Kiho* faction (of Seoul and the vicinity), a *Sŏbuk* faction (of northwestern Korea), and a *Samnam* faction (of the three southern provinces), more often than not vying with one another.

The Provisional Government epitomizes the general condition of the Korean nationalists during this period and later. The nationalists in this period, whether they were affiliated with the Provisional Government or not, were dedicated patriots. At the same time, they were wishful idealists. When the hope for help from the West failed and their strength waned, they fell into dejection and disappointment, and their frustrated emotions were directed against each other. They were unanimously in agreement in their opposition to Japan, but they were no longer able to agree on who represented the true and legitimate interests of the Korean people.

The disruption of the Provisional Government was, however, only the beginning of internal conflicts among the Korean nationalists.

9

The Period of Disillusionment

EVERY EXILED MOVEMENT has periods of slump. The exiled revolutionaries fall from time to time into despair, anguish, and melancholy. Some revolutionaries fall from the ranks and submit to their enemies who are the recognized authorities over their homeland. Some others, lured by various temptations, turn completely round and work for their former enemies against their former comrades. The most dedicated remain in the revolutionary camp, but they cannot help being restless. When activities against the enemy accomplish no result, the revolutionaries reflect upon their past record and criticize others within their ranks for failing the cause of their people.

This situation is most likely to develop when affairs within the homeland are tranquil and the enemy is firmly in control. Revolutionary activities can operate best when there are disturbances and general disorder. As Crane Brinton demonstrated in his *Anatomy of Revolution,* a revolution cannot succeed unless the society in which it takes place meets certain prerequisites of disorder.[1] The comparatively peaceful and orderly years between 1921 and 1930 in Korea were the worst period of slump for the Korean nationalists abroad.

Internationally this was the period of pacification when the League of Nations was at its zenith. Japan was still enjoying the fruits of victory in the World War, and her power and authority in Korea were never effectively challenged. The Korean people, who had risen against the Japanese in 1919, simmered down after their frustrations were released. Disorders there were, both in Japan and Korea, but not beyond the control of the security forces. Furthermore, some of the reforms introduced by the Japanese government in Korea after 1919 considerably reduced the tension there.

Despite these unfavorable conditions and the disruption of the Provisional Government in 1921, the majority of the Korean nationalists abroad did not abandon their hopes. To be sure, there were many deserters. Some lost faith in a movement based abroad and returned to Korea, where moderate radical activity was still possible. Some remained abroad, but chose not to participate in any of the organized movements. Still there was the majority whose only concern was for reviving the independence movement.

The work of the dedicated nationalists in this period was carried on in three areas. In Manchuria the militarist nationalists were active in small bands of guerrilla units until 1931, when the Japanese conquered and pacified the whole region.[2] In China proper the nationalists were active mainly in efforts to reunite the movement: they had little success. In the United States the Washington Disarmament Conference of 1921 offered a ray of hope for a time. The nationalists in these three areas maintained some connections, as we shall see. There was also a nationalist movement within Korea, but of a nature quite different from the movement abroad; it will be treated in a separate chapter.

In Manchuria and Siberia, considering the adverse environment and the lack of substantial assistance from foreign powers, the resistance of Korean militarists to the Japanese was remarkable. Initially some factors were favorable to them. Although the attitude of the regional government in Mukden under Chang Tso-lin was ambivalent and after 1925 was pro-Japanese, the local and ordinary people were generally sympathetic.

Sporadic attacks against the Japanese were made earlier around the eastern Yalu and Tumen rivers, but most of the military groups were formed after the demonstrations of March 1, 1919. Japanese agents asserted in June, 1919, that a Korean military academy had been set up by Yi Tong-hwi in the Manchurian town of Mishan, near the Russian border.[3] Several military groups sprang up in southeastern Manchuria, numbering from a few hundred to more than a thousand men. They were usually armed with rifles bought from Russian and Czech soldiers operating in Siberia. Some of them observed strict military discipline, probably owing to their being led and trained by veterans of Japanese military service.[4] In occasional forays across the Yalu or the Tumen into Korea they attacked government offices, Japanese officials and residents, and pro-Japanese Koreans, and at times engaged in small-scale skirmishes with Japanese garrison troops.[5]

These nationalists hoped, of course, to regain Korean independence by military action. Although this seems fantastic in restrospect, certain facts indicate that their aspiration was not altogether unrealistic. There was the confusion in eastern Siberia. After the revolution in Russia proper, the Bolsheviks moved eastward and fought White Russians, Czechs, Americans, and Japanese for control of Siberia. The Bolsheviks, alone in this international struggle, appealed to the Koreans for an alliance, promising to support their cause when the revolution had succeeded in Siberia. In the confusion arms were easily accessible to the Koreans from deserters from the various camps, as well as from the Bolsheviks eager for their support. Already a large number of Koreans living in Siberia had joined the Bolshevik forces either individually or in groups.[6] But the hopes of the Korean militarists were soon shattered. First their sanctuary in Manchuria became unsafe after 1920; later it turned out that the Russians were not trustworthy.

Previously the Japanese government had requested the Chang Tso-lin regime in Mukden to subjugate or remove the Korean nationalists in the Sino-Korean border area, but at the time no positive action was taken by the Chinese. Even when the government in Mukden ordered that the Koreans be restrained, local officials ignored the orders and on some occasions when Chinese troops were dispatched from Mukden to subjugate the nationalists, warned them beforehand to evacuate the region.[7]

But this protection was short-lived. Between May and August, 1920, under strong pressure from the Japanese, the Chang regime sent two subjugation forces into the Chientao area. Since these forces were accompanied by Japanese advisers, the local people dared not protect the Koreans, of whom more than six hundred were arrested. During the autumn of 1920 two Japanese regiments stationed in central Manchuria were allowed to patrol the border area; they also arrested about six hundred Koreans, of whom eighty-one were killed immediately.[8]

In June, 1920 a contingent of the Japanese 19th Division was sent to northern Chientao and suffered 120 casualties at the hands of the Koreans, who hailed this encounter as a great victory.[9] Its long-run effect was rather that of increasing the irritation of the Japanese, for in October they sent parts of their 19th and 21st divisions from Korea, together with a brigade from the Siberian Expeditionary Force, to eliminate the "Korean recalcitrants." The Chinese government in Peking refused to grant permission for the entry of these troops into Manchuria, but, according to a Japanese report, "since the situation in Chientao required immediate action, the original plan was carried out." [10]

This large-scale attack, accompanied by extraordinary atrocities, forced the nationalist border groups to retreat from their Manchurian sanctuaries to Siberia.[11] Before abandoning their hideouts they tasted on a few occasions glories of victory over superior forces, the most celebrated being the battle at Ch'ingshan-li, where the Japanese troops, surprised in a narrow valley and attacked from three directions, suffered a thousand or more casualties and Korean casualties were less than two hundred. Here, from October 19 to 22, 1920, three brigades of Japanese were engaged by about 1,800 Koreans.[12]

But prolonged combat against superior forces was definitely to the disadvantage of the nationalists. After a few major encounters, therefore, they began to retreat to Siberia through the town of Mishan. Japanese forces then occupied all of southeastern Manchuria with little resistance.

At Mishan most of the Korean bands from North Chientao united in late 1920 as the Greater Korean Independence Army (*Taehan Tongnip Kundan*), numbering about 3,500 men and divided into three battalions under the general command of Sŏ Il. Those in the West Chientao area, however, were not included. The united army then retreated en masse to Siberia. Late in March, 1921, several of the leaders met at Iman and formed what became known as the

Greater Korean Independence Corps (*Taehan Tongnipdan*) to which some small groups operating in Siberia were added.[13] The army was organized into two brigades, one stationed at Iman (later at Irkutsk), the other at Ningan-hsien in Manchuria. A military academy was established within the second brigade under the direction of a soldier hero, Kim Chwa-jin. After the Japanese troops withdrew from Chientao, armed bands of Koreans went back into the area to recruit.

Meanwhile negotiations were carried on with the Bolsheviks at Chita, the capital of the Far Eastern Republic. An agreement was reached whereby the Koreans were to assist the Bolsheviks in the warfare against the White Russians and other enemies of the revolution and in return were to receive assistance in their struggle for independence.[14] As a consequence of this agreement about two thousand Korean soldiers moved to the vicinity of Alekseyevsk (now Svobodny) and a military academy for Koreans was established at Irkutsk.

Conflicts with Korean Communists in Siberia, however, soon brought about a disaster for the nationalist militarists. The Korean Communists in Siberia, Manchuria, and China proper were divided between two major factions—the Irkutsk faction and the Shanghai-Chita faction.[15] The militarist nationalists from Manchuria had close ties with the Shanghai-Chita faction led by Yi Tong-hwi, who had recently resigned as premier of the Provisional Government. Yi had been a military leader in Manchuria and had sought to maintain close connections with the Korean forces there. The Irkutsk faction had a close relationship with the Far Eastern secretariat of the Comintern in Irkutsk, headed by Boris Shumiatsky. They did not have a comparable military group under their influence. Evidently the leaders of this faction decided to bring the Korean military groups under its control. In June, 1921, they established the Korean Revolutionary Military Congress (*Koryŏ Hyŏngmyŏng Kunjŏng Uihoe*) with the support of Shumiatsky and, asserting that the Korean groups in Siberia were beset with internal dissension, claimed authority to unite them under one command.[16]

This claim was rejected by the Greater Korean Independence Army, which charged that the Irkutsk group was seeking to integrate the Korean forces with the Bolshevik army instead of carrying on the struggle for independence.[17] The Irkutsk group then accused the

Independence Army of being antirevolutionary and adhering solely to nationalism. On June 27, the Irkutsk faction and Russian troops surrounded the Independence forces at Alekseyevsk and demanded their immediate disarmament. Fighting broke out, and hundreds of Koreans were killed or wounded. Nearly a thousand Independence soldiers were captured and were taken to Irkutsk, where some of the leaders were imprisoned and the enlisted men were mustered into the Bolshevik army. This occurrence became known as the "Free City incident." Thereafter the Bolsheviks ruled that only those Koreans could have arms who were enrolled with Soviet troops or were members of an accepted Communist party.[18]

The disarming of their troops and the Free City incident ended the activities of the Korean nationalists in Siberia. Some of the leaders reappeared in North Chientao and organized the remaining Koreans in that area to continue operations against the Japanese, but the tie with the Bolsheviks was severed. While the situation in Siberia was still chaotic, the Bolsheviks had solicited their help; when order was finally restored in 1922, the nationalists were discarded as a nuisance, and even their infiltration of the Korean border along Siberia was forbidden. The Bolsheviks thenceforth concentrated on spreading Communist propaganda among Koreans in and out of the homeland.

Although the Russians and Chinese initially seemed sympathetic, this attitude was only temporary. Whenever their own interest was likely to be hampered by the presence of the Korean nationalists, the Russian and Chinese governments and people did not hesitate to turn against them. The Japanese did not have to press very hard to persuade the Bolsheviks to eliminate the Korean nationalists from Siberia. In Manchuria after 1925, when the Japanese offered rewards for the capture of Korean nationalists, many Chinese were willing to take part in the hunt.

The Korean nationalists were alone. Reliance upon others' assistance, or even sympathy, was proving to be futile and often damaging. There was no one but their own people to rely upon. But the Free City incident displayed another facet of the problem: differences among the compatriots because of ideology and the place of residence. Some Koreans in Siberia were more Russianized than others; some were second- or third-generation residents, and their outlook was no longer thoroughly Korean. Some regarded themselves either as Russians or as members of the International Communist movement rather than as mere nationals of a particular country.

The Korean troops disarmed, scattered, or Bolshevized in the Free City incident were from North Chientao. The situation of those in West Chientao was not much better. They had accomplished nothing spectacular and were chiefly significant, by reason of their endurance and existence, as an expression of Korean resistance and nationalism. Although more military groups sprang up in West Chientao than in North Chientao, their strength was less, owing to the smaller Korean population in the mountainous hinterland of Huatien, Kuantien, Hsingching, and other prefectures in the area. There were also groups in Changpai and Linchiang prefectures at the foot of Changpai Mountain. Scarcity of supplies and the difficulty of stationing of troops in such terrain also were responsible for their smaller numbers. Yet this geographical condition enabled them to evade Japanese subjugation longer than their counterparts in North Chientao. These small groups of fifty to five hundred men continued occasional raids across the Yalu River. Between 1923 and 1926 they united in various consolidations.[19]

After 1926 there was a union movement among the Koreans in Manchuria, China proper, and Korea. Associations to promote the organization of the United Korean Independence party were organized in Shanghai, Peking, and various parts of Manchuria. In contrast to failure elsewhere, in Manchuria progress was made in the direction of unity. There the Koreans were hard pressed because of the Chinese government's agreement with the Japanese to subjugate them. They were also variously oppressed and abused by Chinese landlords and local officials. Thus in Manchuria they fully realized that they could protect themselves only if they were united.

In 1927 leaders of the three major groups in West Chientao met at Kirin for negotiations. Before a decision was reached on forming a union, the Japanese forced the Chang Tso-lin government to arrest them. These leaders were subsequently released as a result of much effort on the part of other Koreans and the Chinese in the area, but the union was not accomplished.[20] In May, 1928, another such meeting was held at Kirin, but the Japanese learned of it and again pressed the Chinese police to arrest the Koreans. Most of the leaders escaped, but again unification was prevented.[21]

The nationalists in Manchuria eventually reached an agreement to unite, but they were never able to join their forces. One group was infiltrated by Communists and was split in two.[22] The others were internally sundered by policy disagreements. The result was that dissenters and the Communists formed a group of their own as the "National Center" (*Kungminbu*) in April, 1929. The rest of the nationalists were organized on July 26, 1930 as the Korean Independence party (*Hanguk Tongnip-dang*).[23]

The Kungminbu acted as the self-governing agency of the Korean residents in the hinterland area of Kuantien and Chian prefectures. This group became known also as the Korean Revolutionary party (*Chosŏn Hyŏngmyŏng-dang*).[24] It established branches in Manchuria and sent agents into Korea to establish branches there and propagandize for both communism and nationalism. There was a considerable Communist influence within this party. It had also a so-called army of its own, of undetermined size, which continued the mobilization and training of young Koreans. After the Japanese began open aggression in Manchuria in 1931 this army was a considerable harassment to them. In March, 1932, its troops defeated the Japanese at Hsinpin.

As the news of the victory spread, additional recruits were mobilized, and the number of troops in the Korean Revolutionary Army reached a substantial total.[25] In the initial period of occupation Japanese troops and police severely persecuted the Koreans in Manchuria as recalcitrants; the general population therefore had an added incentive to join the movement. In February, 1933, this Korean "army" joined the Chinese "Liaoning Save-The-Nation-Association" (*Liaoning Chiukuo-hui*) and undertook military intelligence and propaganda work.

Allied Korean and Chinese forces won a major victory at Hsingching in October, 1933, and caused much damage to Japanese and "Manchukuo" troops during the next few months, but their military equipment was too primitive and their supplies were too meager for sustaining an offensive against a modern army. Eventually the Chinese leaders fled to China proper or to the hinterlands and a small Korean unit retreated to China. According to Mun Mu-gyŏng, who headed the remnants, about two hundred soldiers of the Revolutionary Army stayed on in Manchuria.[26] When their party joined the other nationalists in China in the Korean National Revolutionary party (*Minjok Hyŏngmyŏng-dang*) in 1935, their army had about one thousand members and 400 items of weapons.[27] The remnants of the army and the party in Manchuria maintained a close connection with the forces of Yang Tsing-yü, who was the head of the Southern Manchuria Committee of the Chinese Communist party and commander of the First Route Army of the Northeast Anti-Japanese Federated Army.[28]

The Korean Independence Party (*Hanguk Tongnip-dang*), formed in 1930, was led by men who had suffered the bitter experience of the Free City incident. Having their activities concentrated in the more accessible area of central Kirin Province, the members of this party were exposed to greater risks than their compatriots in the hinterlands. The Japanese succeeded in arresting a few of the leaders, but the party's army carried on in concert with Chinese forces and on occasion rendered severe damage to the Japanese and the newly formed Manchukuo troops.[29] After nearly two years of joint operations, internal disputes among the Chinese forces eventually affected the alliance, causing the Koreans to retreat into China proper late in 1933.

Most of the Korean groups in Manchuria were operating independently of the Korean nationalists in China proper and the United States. After some contacts in the early 1920's communications became increasingly difficult; there was, probably, no pressing need for close liaison.

The morale of the Korean nationalists in China was low. Besides the loss of those who returned to Korea or otherwise divorced themselves from the nationalist movement, they suffered also from defections to communism. At least a hundred active nationalists in Shanghai were drawn into the Communist faction by 1921.[30] Money was a crucial concern. Whereas most of the nationalists had to depend upon contributions for their subsistence, the Communist coterie headed by Yi Tong-hwi and Kim Rip enjoyed the use of abundant funds, having at their disposal the money received from Moscow and withheld by Yi and Kim.

The Provisional Government in Shanghai continued, if mostly on paper, but after several of the important leaders withdrew, it never regained its original prestige. It was no longer a government in the sense of being a representative body of the Korean people. Neither was it a headquarters of Korean leadership. Nevertheless, some diehards still believed in the utility of the Provisional Government even though they were no longer confident of the possibilities they had once envisaged for it. These nationalists seem to have developed a feeling of the identity of their government with the struggle for independence. They still hoped that it might be recognized by foreign powers and again become the center for the Korean nationalist movement.

The Provisional Government, while these few tenaciously clung to it, was beset internally by factional struggles. There was difficulty in sustaining even the skeleton of an organization. When Yi Tong-hwi resigned the premiership, President Syngman Rhee attempted to remedy the situation by offering the position to An Ch'ang-ho, who declined it.[31] Rhee then appointed Yi Tong-nyŏng, the Minister of Home Affairs, to the premiership, but he held office for only four months and was succeeded, in May, 1921, by the Minister of Justice, Shin Kyu-sik, who subsequently was given also the post of Foreign Minister. Although there were younger nationalists—Shin Ik-hi, Yun Ki-sŏp, Son Chŏng-do, Kim Ku, and others—and the reins were gradually shifted to the younger men, age was still a requisite in a leader if he was to mobilize the support of the Korean public. The shortage of renowned and revered heroes was a grave problem for the Provisional Government in the early 1920's when its most important task in China was to win out over opposed nationalist factions and the Communists in the struggle for leadership in China.

In this state of peril the Provisional Government could not perform any important function or carry out any significant activities. Its condition can be shown by citing a few exchanges of cablegrams between Shanghai and Washington in 1922. Shin Kyu-sik's premiership was faltering. The Provisional Legislative Assembly notified Rhee on April 17: "Situation of the government is urgent. Please instruct us as to your policy for maintaining the government and correcting the situation." Rhee's response, on April 18, was to appoint No (Ro) Paek-rin as premier and direct that the cabinet be reorganized. Another cablegram from Shanghai, on May 16, reported that the situation was critical: "No Paek-rin is not available for the premiership and there are no officers in the government. It is virtually in a state of anarchy. Please carry out your responsibilities immediately and instruct us within five days." Rhee replied: "If you start confusion there in Shanghai it will affect the collection of funds here (in the United States) and cause financial difficulty. Therefore promptly adjust the situation." [32]

The situation, however, did not improve. No Paek-rin and Yi Tong-nyŏng rotated in the office of the premier merely to keep the government in existence. In August, 1924, the Provisional Legislative Assembly decided that, since Rhee was away from the seat of the government and did not perform his duties, the premier in Shanghai should serve as acting president.[33] Rhee's supporters evidently had lost confidence in his effectiveness. We shall return to this subject.

Although disputes on vain issues continued, the Provisional Government was in fact dormant. Even so its skeleton was held together and new premiers were appointed. Late in 1925 the presidential system of government was replaced by the premier system. On September 2, 1926, the *Tongnip Shinmun* (Shanghai) summarized the successive cabinets as follows:

> Since the late Pak Ŭn-sik resigned on July 7, 1925, when the old constitution lost effect, the Provisional Government has continued on record by a half year of Yi Sang-yong's cabinet and another half year of Ch'oe Ch'ang-sik's proxy government while Ch'oe was president of the Legislative Assembly. But in actuality Yi did not have a cabinet and Ch'oe's government was in name only. The Provisional Government had in truth an empty existence. Revision of the constitution therefore became a meaningless drama, and the prospects of the great enterprise were indeed gloomy.[34]

Rapid turnover occurred not only in the executive department, but in the Legislative Assembly, whose members often resigned, individually or in groups. The government was at a standstill, and the Assembly had no significant business on which to deliberate. In December, 1926, Kim Ku succeeded to the leadership after Yi Sang-yong. He has described the situation as follows:

> Thus the government was again organized. But because of financial difficulties, there was no way to sustain the government. Rent for the government office was thirty yuan, and the salary of the office boy was twenty yuan. Since we were not able to meet even these needs, we were sued several times by the landlord. . . . I slept in the office and ate at the homes of compatriots who were employed, going in turn from one home to another . . . I was a beggar, but a high-class one.[35]

Contacts with the outside world had dwindled:

When Syngman Rhee was president, there were many Chinese visiting the office and even many foreigners with blue eyes and a high nose. But now the only foreigners visiting us were the French policemen accompanied by Japanese policemen to arrest us, or the landlord who demanded rent. Even the number of nationalists, which once numbered more than a thousand, shrank to only a few score.[36]

Amid this disillusionment and somewhat comical hardship, the so-called impeachment of President Rhee took place. Although not a matter of great significance to the independence movement, as a whole, this incident was symptomatic of the problems faced by the nationalists, especially as regards money. Even at the beginning, when it was more affluent, the Provisional Government depended heavily on funds collected in the United States and Hawaii. The jurisdictional dispute over these funds between the Korean National Association, in Los Angeles, and the Korean Commission under Rhee in Washington were settled by a proclamation of the Minister of Finance in February, 1920, which cancelled the collecting of donations and provided for future fund-raising through the sale of bonds issued by the Commission. As the situation in Shanghai went from bad to worse, President Rhee decided that sending money there would be a complete waste. A special newsletter issued by the Korean Commission on July 3, 1924, declared that money sent by the Koreans in the United States was contributing only to factional turmoil, and revealed that it had stopped sending funds to the Provisional Government. Some funds, however, continued to be sent by the Korean Residents Association in Hawaii directly to Shanghai. The newsletter stated that the Commission had till then condoned this irregularity, but had lately reprimanded the chief of the Residents Association, Kim Yong-gi, in order that there should be no repetition. In short, the Commission asserted absolute authority in United States territory on behalf of the Provisional Government.[37]

Minister of Finance Yi Shi-yŏng, who had earlier been a supporter of Rhee, now sent to him a letter of protest emphasizing the fact that the Commission was not a government in itself and was not above the Provisional Government:

. . . The Ministry of Finance had entrusted the financial administration in the United States [to the Commission], but this was only to assist financial administration according to the law and not to invade the administrative authorities of the government.[38]

Yi then gave instructions to the chief of the Korean Residents Association in Hawaii:

The revenue of the state cannot be interfered with except by legally defined agencies. It is impossible to determine what kind of organization the Commission is, but if funds are not sufficient for operation, the government will supply the funds according to law. The Commission will not be permitted to disturb the laws on tax collection. Even if the Commission were above the government, it could not freely change the law by a single sheet of newsletter without any exchange of words with the government. Since its illegality and destructiveness are obvious, an investigation has been ordered.[39]

More letters were exchanged between Shanghai and Washington, but there was no improvement in the relationship. Finally the group in Shanghai, on March 10, 1925, issued an order in the name of Acting President Pak Ŭn-sik and the cabinet, abolishing the Commission. The order was, of course, not expected to be effective, but it served as a declaration of breach of association. The order declared the Commission to be an illegal organization that lacked the endorsement of the government and existed merely by its acquiescence. Further, the order declared, the Commission had collected a poll tax from Koreans in Hawaii, misused the money, and made no accounting to the government. In general, the order charged that the Commission was ineffective in its activities, that it created confusion among the people, and that it obstructed the activities of the government.[40]

On March 13 ten members of the Provisional Legislative Assembly introduced a resolution to impeach Rhee on the grounds that: (*a*) he had violated the Provisional Constitution by issuing orders to stop the payment of taxes without the signatures of the cabinet members; (*b*) he had divided the Korean people into two geographical groups, one of which he professed to rule despite a constitutional provision requiring the chief executive to preside over the entire government; (*c*) his letters attacking the Shanghai government were of a nature befitting the leader of a faction rather than the chief officer of the government as a whole; and (*d*) he had denounced the provisional constitution by proclaiming that he would not resign until a new government was formed in Seoul.[41] The resolution was adopted on

March 18, and on March 25 a five-member board of impeachment found the president guilty as charged. Interestingly enough, the board members were those who had introduced the resolution to impeach Rhee.

The impeachment of Rhee and the order to abolish the Commission did not improve the situation of the Provisional Government. Rhee asserted his title to the presidency under the Seoul constitution and continued the Korean Commission by his authority as head of the government.[42] His followers declared that the Pak Ŭn-sik cabinet was an illegal government and the Provisional Legislature an illegal institution owing to Pak's having been installed as the acting president —any procedure deviating from the system proclaimed in Seoul, i.e., any action to abrogate Rhee's authority as president, was regarded as unconstitutional and illegal.

Anticipating what was to occur, an editorial in *Shinhan Minbo* on January 29, 1925, asserted that as long as there were more than a thousand Koreans in Hawaii supporting Rhee as president, no good would come of impeaching him. The problem of the absentee presidency had plagued the Provisional Government for six years, and there was no solution for it; the editorial advised, rather, that the presidency be either abolished or left alone, and that concern be focused on the independence movement. An editorial on May 21 asserted the Korean Commission had been very successful in collecting funds; that, generally, the Koreans in the United States and Hawaii favored the poll tax and the sale of bonds in order that diplomatic activities, through which independence might be obtained, could be carried on; and that, since the Provisional Government was inactive, sole reliance on the Commission could easily be justified.

Such was, in actuality, the state of affairs. The disruption of the Shanghai government was foreseeable in 1921, and its confused and ineffective condition in 1925 was obvious. To fill in the other side of the picture, we must look back over the activities of the nationalists in the United States and particularly the role of the Korean Commission.

We have noted that Rhee left the United States in the latter part of 1920 to visit the Provisional Legislative Assembly in Shanghai. The chairman of the Commission, Kim Kyu-sik, left for Shanghai in January, 1921. In their absence Hyŏn Sun, who had been the vice-minister of foreign affairs in Shanghai, was appointed acting chairman. Hyŏn had taken part in the nationalist movement in the Far East since 1919, when he was dispatched to Shanghai by the leaders of the March First movement in Seoul. Under Hyŏn the Commission continued propaganda activities as usual. Before Rhee returned to Washington, however, serious disputes developed between Hyŏn and the other members of the Commission, Philip Jaisohn and Henry Chung. According to a communiqué issued later by Hyŏn, he observed that relations between the United States and Japan had become critical after President Harding was inaugurated in 1921, with a likelihood of war, and he thought there was a favorable opportunity to request recognition of Korean independence. When he informed Rhee of the situation and requested appointment as Korean ambassador, Rhee sent credentials to the Commission and instructed the group to act according to need. Establishment of the embassy was confirmed in a cablegram sent to him on April 4. On Hyŏn's authority as ambassador $1,000 was drawn from Commission funds for setting up the embassy, and announcement of the embassy was sent to persons in the American government, including the members of Congress. An official request for recognition of Korean independence was sent to the Secretary of State on May 11.[43]

Hyŏn's ambassadorial role seems to have been resented by Jaisohn and Chung, who, according to a Japanese report, brought suit against him on the charge of embezzling $1,500 of Commission funds.[44] Hyŏn retaliated by suspending Chung and legal counselor Fred A. Dolph from their duties and notifying American officials of this action; he also made a public assertion that Jaisohn as a naturalized American was not qualified to represent Korea. His behavior was soon made known to Rhee, and on April 26 he was relieved from his appointment as ambassador and acting chairman of the Commission.[45]

Jaisohn and his group issued a public letter on May 7 charging that Hyŏn had disclosed state secrets, sent official letters to the United States after being dismissed, usurped funds, stolen important documents, and caused financial losses amounting to $4,000.[46] The letter demanded the return of various articles and documents taken from the Commission and offered $400 for Hyŏn's passage to China. Hyŏn requested a larger sum and, this being refused, lived on in the building originally meant to be the embassy and proclaimed himself minister plenipotentiary. The Jaisohn letter also asserted that since a dismissed official had sent a letter to the United States government an apology was due on the part of the Korean president and government. Rhee may have offered such an apology upon his return, for Hyŏn issued a statement sometime later denouncing Rhee for submitting a petition for a League mandate over Korea in 1919; the statement added that Rhee had prevented Korean independence by officially apologizing to the United States government and thus canceling Hyŏn's request for recognition.[47] We need not pass judgment on the merit or defects of the disputants, but the conclusions reached by a Japanese report are worth noting:

> . . . The discord among them had its origin in the appointment of Hyŏn Sun as the minister and the resulting struggle for power. The problem of embezzlement by Hyŏn was brought about because of these facts. On the other hand, it also indicated that the Korean residents were growing weary of the movement and that resources were becoming scarce.[48]

When Rhee returned in August, the situation of the Commission improved. Rhee served as chairman, Jaisohn was appointed vice-chairman, and in addition to Dolph former Senator Charles S. Thomas, of Colorado, was enlisted as special legal counsel. The name of the body was altered to "Korean Commission to the Conference on Limitation of Armament" and all efforts were concentrated on the disarmament conference to be held in Washington between November 12, 1921, and February 6, 1922. The Commission is reported to have spent about $12,000 during the conference.[49]

Before the opening of the conference Dolph prepared a 44-page "Brief for Korea" and presented it to Secretary Hughes. It was an appeal for Korean independence similar to those offered on other occasions, but the argument was from the legal point of view. It pointed to the treaties concluded by various nations with Korea before the annexation and argued that "the nations of the world who made treaties with Korea, including the United States, must still regard Korea as a separate entity and the treaties in force, irrespective of any assertion or claims of Japan . . ." [50] On October 1, 1921, a letter of appeal was sent by the Commission to the United States delegation, followed by a letter to the conference on December 1.[51] The League of the Friends of Korea was also enlisted, and a letter from this body was sent to Secretary Hughes; a supplementary appeal was addressed to the conference on January 25, 1922, repeating similar demands.[52] The Commission also produced a petition for independence signed by 108 leaders in various fields within Korea which denounced the annexation, proclaimed the Provisional Government as the true government of Korea, and requested opposition to the military policy of Japan.[53]

Before the Washington Conference, moreover, and even before Harding was inaugurated, the nationalists had a link with the president-to-be through Senator George W. Norris. Jaisohn had provided Norris with a summary history of Korea, and with this information Norris discussed on the Senate floor the problem of assisting Korea. Harding was present and thus came to know of the Korean problem. Later, through an introduction by Norris, Jaisohn called on Harding, who in turn referred him to Hughes, then a member of the Supreme Court.[54]

Jaisohn evidently made a favorable impression. When Hughes became Secretary of State, Jaisohn requested that the atrocities committed by the Japanese be made known and emergency measures be taken by the Conference. Hughes promised that, although no official action would be taken at the Conference, he would give an unofficial warning to the Japanese that the Koreans must not be treated unjustly. Describing an unofficial meeting between Hughes and the Japanese chief delegates, Admiral Katō Tomozaburō and Prince Tokugawa Iesato, Jaisohn's autobiography relates that Tokugawa asserted that Syngman Rhee and others who had signed the appeal to the conference were not qualified to be representatives of the Korean people—they had left Korea several decades ago and no one in Korea knew anything about them. Hughes then showed to Tokugawa the petition signed by representatives within Korea and said:

> This is not a forged document. I advise privately from the humanistic point of view that innocent Korean people must not be cruelly treated. Japan is a first-class nation. And she must have the magnanimity and generosity befitting first-class status. . . . I advise you now privately, but if Japan does not change her policy toward Korea, the United States will be forced to take official action because of the pressure of the churches and other public opinion in this country.

Tokugawa promised a change in policy toward Korea within four months. Jaisohn asserted, therefore, that he was somewhat responsible for the institution of the so-called culture polity in Korea.[55]

Nothing else came of the efforts put forth at the Disarmament Conference, but the Korean Commission was maintained until 1928.[56]

During 1921 the nationalists in Shanghai formed an association to support the efforts of the Korean Commission at the Disarmament Conference. On August 13, two days after invitations were sent by President Harding to various powers, the Association to Support the Diplomatic Work at the Pacific Conference (*Tae-T'aepy'ŏngyang Hoei Oegyo Huwonhoe*) was organized in Shanghai, headed by Hong Chin. The name was derived from a statement in the invitation that, in connection with the limitation of national armament, "Pacific and Far Eastern questions" could also be discussed. The association held meetings where speeches were made to arouse the interest of Koreans, published a weekly news magazine, *Sŏnjŏn* ("Propaganda"), and collected donations to be sent to Washington.[57] The Provisional Government also sent an appeal to the conference and appointed Rhee and Jaisohn as its delegates. Hopes subsided when no action in behalf of Korea was taken by the conference.

An association of different character, the Korean Labor-Soldier Association (*Hanguk Nobyŏnghoe*) emerged in Shanghai about this time. Its purpose was to train more than ten thousand soldiers within the next ten years and raise a million or more yuan to contribute to the liberation of the homeland. Kim Ku was selected to be president of the board of directors of the association.

The Labor-Soldier Association had a grandiose goal and hardly anyone to draw money from. The membership remained at less than fifty, and little money was collected. At a second general meeting on April 1, 1924, only thirteen members were present, the funds accumulated were reported to be about 370 yuan, and the number of young men supported by the association at Chinese military and technical institutions was thirteen. Two years later, funds accumulated were reported as 420 yuan. Members were continually being dropped for delinquency in paying dues. In 1929 Kim Ku and sixteen others were expelled on this account.[58]

A remaining manifestation of the Korean nationalist movement abroad between 1921 and 1931 was the Korean National Representatives Conference (*Kungmin Taep'yohoe*), held in Shanghai in 1923. The conference ended in disagreement, but it provides a focal point from which various nationalist organizations can be examined. We have already noted that the Koreans active in Shanghai were divided between the Communist and the Provisional Government groups, with some persons on the periphery of one or the other. At the same time there were various military groups in Manchuria both in and out of the Communist camp. All of these played some part in the conference, revealing their characteristics and beliefs.

The first attempt to assemble national representatives dated back to February, 1921, when Won Se-hun, Pak Ŭn-sik, and others issued a proclamation calling for a meeting to discuss the future of the nationalist movement. They argued that united action of all the groups was mandatory, "either as the will of Heaven or as the will of the people." Various groups in the past had not been able to unite, and the Provisional Government had failed in the task of consolidating the movement because of internal conflicts. The Provisional Legislative Assembly had been designed to supervise the government and correct the mistakes, but it was no longer in a condition to perform its duties. The proclamation asserted that unification must therefore be brought about through a fundamental reform, in order to open up a new phase of the movement, and that since the decisions must be made by the people, a conference of national representatives was necessary.[59] A few of the signers of the proclamation were already members of the Koryŏ Communist party; some others were still members of the Provisional Legislative Assembly.

This proclamation in Shanghai was soon echoed in North China. In the Peking-Tientsin area a number of Korean leaders advocated military action. One of the more prominent was Pak Yong-man. Pak, a graduate of the University of Nebraska, had trained Koreans in Hawaii. According to some sources, he went to the Far East in May, 1919, as an intelligence officer in the United States Siberian Expeditionary Forces.[60] The Provisional Government elected him Minister of Foreign Affairs in September, 1919, as he had also been designated by the Seoul government, but he does not seem to have been pleased with the position. He arrived in Shanghai in March, 1920, and by July another person was being relieved from the position of acting minister, indicating that Pak had not served in this office long, if at all.[61] Years before, Pak was a close friend of Syngman Rhee in Hawaii, but the two had clashed over the policy for the nationalist movement, Pak advocating military tactics and Rhee diplomatic propaganda. It is very likely that Pak's animosity toward Rhee kept him apart from the Provisional Government.

Japanese police recorded Pak's activities in Siberia. As early as December, 1919, he was in Vladivostok as deputy chief of the Sino-Russian Joint Propaganda Department, headed by a Russian, Wurin (M. I. Yurin ?). A 1921 report mentions the connections established by Pak Yong-man and Wurin, officially a delegate of the Far Eastern Republic, but also an agent of the Comintern: "Wurin's group arrived in Peking in the summer of 1920, and had been disseminating propaganda. Although their activities were primarily aimed at the Chinese, it is clear that the Koreans also were influenced. In particular, Pak Yong-man is still in the area and has joined hands with Wurin's group." [62]

The group in Peking also included such well-known figures as Shin Ch'ae-ho, a historian, and Kim Ch'ang-suk, a Confucian scholar who had been engaged in anti-Japanese propaganda work among the Chinese in Peking along with Pak Ŭn-sik.[63] Shin had been a member of the Provisional Legislative Assembly. Another leader in this group was Nam Kong-sŏn, who had organized the Mutual Assistance Association (*Tongjehoe*) in Chientao and attempted to carry out a military operation.

These elements met in Peking on April 17, 1921, in a so-called Military Unification Conference and denounced the Provisional Government. They made the familiar charge, somewhat altered, that it was "headed by a national traitor who petitioned the United States to place Korea under a mandate in order to make Korea a colony of the United States," and simultaneously issued a declaration stressing the need for a solution of the fundamental problem of the supreme organization in order that the military activities might be united and an effective operation be carried out against the Japanese. In order to come to an agreement on the supreme organization, the public opinion of the entire Korean nation was to be determined by holding a conference of national representatives.[64] The points advanced by the Peking group were of course identical with those advocated by Pak Ŭn-sik and others in Shanghai. Although this might seem to indicate that the two groups were reaching an implicit agreement, the fact remained that each group desired to build the supreme organization round itself. Thus the site of the conference constituted a subject of dispute; eventually the gathering took place in Shanghai.

The call for a conference advanced by the Shanghai and Peking groups was echoed by An Ch'ang-ho on May 12, 1921. In a speech at Shanghai immediately after his resignation from the Provisional Government, An Ch'ang-ho reviewed the independence movement of the past and outlined policies to be followed in the future. In the past, he asserted, Koreans in forces of only a few dozen or few hundred persons had risen in revolt; they had fought with the conviction that shedding their blood would leave to posterity the spirit of independence; but deep inside their minds they were hoping to obtain aid from outside, and their desperate actions were motivated by lack of conviction that the independence movement could succeed. This, said An, was a mistake—future military activities would have to be carried out with the conviction that the enemy finally would be driven out and totally subjugated, and to this end a large army should be prepared over a long period of time.

The task of unifying the Korean nationalists, An asserted, was the supreme and immediate problem. The nationalists must gather together and decide on methods to be followed, but in order to establish national policies the opinion of the majority of the entire people must be heard. He concluded that a conference should be held, at which representatives of all Korean groups everywhere would be present. He still recognized the Provisional Government and Legislative Assembly although their work in the past had been inadequate. Because the Provisional Government was not perfectly representative, the compatriots in Russia and North Chientao did not coöperate with it. Therefore, An held, all those opposing the Provisional Government as well as those supporting it must gather together to iron out their differences.[65]

After the second meeting, on May 19, a preparation committee was established with the support of the more than three hundred persons attending. Most of those on this committee were former members of the Provisional Government. Steps were taken immediately to assemble leaders from various areas. A Japanese source indicates that delegates were sent to West and North Chientao, Peking, Tientsin, Tokyo, Korea, the United States, and Siberia.[66]

The National Representatives Conference finally met on January 3, 1923, in Shanghai, with 61 groups and 113 delegates participating. Kim Tong-sam, a leader from Chientao, was elected president of the conference and An Ch'ang-ho vice-president. After three months and ninety-two meetings, the nationalists were still unable to come to a unifying agreement. The discussion on military affairs centered round such issues as the Free City incident (or Alekseyevsk incident) and other conflicts among the guerrilla groups in Manchuria. The discussion on financial affairs led to the case of the funds from Russia. The discussion on diplomacy led to the case of the petition for a mandate. These thorny issues that had split the nationalists before came up again at the conference and prevented conciliation.[67]

The Provisional Government itself was frequently mentioned as a cause of disruption, according to both An Ch'ang-ho and Yŏ Un-hyŏng, who were the prominent figures at the conference.[68] A moderate group, including An, Yŏ, and others previously connected with the government, advocated retaining the Provisional Government provided reforms were made. A radical group, including Won Se-hun, Kim Tu-bong, Chang Kŏn-sang, and Shin Ch'ae-ho, advocated forming a new government as the center of the nationalist movement.[69] Since the groups in Peking and Chientao had already emphatically denounced the Provisional Government, and since some of their objections arose from deep-seated personal beliefs, there was no room for conciliation on this issue. Besides, military groups in Manchuria and Siberia were also divided over the Provisional Government, some of them being adamantly indifferent to it.[70] Thus the efforts to bring about over-all unity of the Korean revolutionaries at the National Representatives Conference failed.

The Korean nationalists of this period were men made nearly desperate by the lack of means; the only common factors they shared were their misery and their aspiration for independence. They were, also, aware that their aspiration would not be accomplished within the near future. Misery and aspiration were hardly factors that could bring about unity. The negative forces working against it were too numerous and too strong.

Similar efforts for unity were made in the late 1920's under the initiative of Communists in Shanghai, Peking, and Manchuria who organized the Associations for Promotion of the United Korean Independence Party. The association in Shanghai was formed March 21, 1927. Its declaration, stressing the need for unity, bears the names of twenty-five persons, including such prominent figures as Yi Tong-nyŏng, Kim Ku, and Cho So-ang. It also bore the names of known Communists or proto-Communists such as Kim Tu-bong and Chŏng T'ae-hi.[71] An Ch'ang-ho declined to join because the association included Communists and the Peking branch had been organized by Chang Kŏn-sang and Won Se-hun, both known Communists.[72]

An had lost faith in the unification efforts. "I believed," he said, "that this would cause internal discord and would eventually collapse. I believed that the idea of unification must be propagated among the people for a long period to make them fully understand it." An also expressed his fear that in an alliance the nationalists of the traditional type would be dominated by the Communists: "Since the Communists are carrying out their movement with a considerable degree of theory behind their movement, we nationalists must also establish political principles to counter them. Otherwise, we will be absorbed by the Communists." [73]

Thus the decade of the nineteen-twenties ended pessimistically for the Korean nationalism. There were a few glorious moments for the nationalist militarists in Manchuria, but they always had to pay a high price for their brief successes. The odds against them were monumental, and only devotion and stubbornness kept their movement active. Nationalists in other areas spent most of their time disputing among themselves or waiting for the world situation to become more favorable.[74]

Meanwhile the world political scene was relatively peaceful, the might of Japan was increasing, and there was general disillusionment among the Korean people. By 1930, twenty years had passed since the kingdom was annexed. Japan was beginning to turn to a dangerous course in this decade, and the rise of the military clique in Japanese politics darkened the outlook for the Korean nationalists.

Another significant environmental factor was the impact of the Russian Revolution in 1917, which reached the Koreans by way of Siberia within a matter of a year. The Communist movement soon flourished among Koreans in Siberia, Manchuria, Japan, and Korea itself. Communism became the vogue for many of the Korean students in Korea and Japan. It also became an effective tool for some of the more passionate and radical nationalists, for it promised liberation of the politically and economically oppressed nations as well as individuals.

The inroads of communism into the traditional nationalist camp shaped, in large measure, the future course of the Korean nationalist movement and, indeed, the future of Korea. Like the Chinese nationalists, the Korean nationalists not only had the Japanese to contend with, but the Communists as well. Rivalry between the traditional or "right" nationalists and the Communists became more obvious and intense after 1931 when the Korean nationalist movement regained its vitality.

10

The Manchurian Incident and the Resurgence of the Korean Nationalist Movement

THE YEAR 1931 saw the beginning of the end of the Japanese Empire. Japan had been laden with relatively serious problems since the end of World War I. She had suffered in the postwar economic slump and then in the great earthquake of 1923. The government's attempt to avert financial disaster through a subsidy system for industry led to the financial crisis of 1927. Before Japan had recovered from this shock, it was swept into the world-wide depression of 1929, which began to affect the Japanese economy in the spring of 1930.

Although the monopolies and major industries were protected by the government and hence weathered the economic storms of the postwar period without too great a strain, protection was not extended to the shopkeepers, small businessmen, farmers, and workers. Significantly, many of the new officers who joined the army after 1920 were from families which suffered the consequences of economic depression and destitution without mitigation. Close connections between the government and big business, as evidenced by recurrent reports of scandals in the late 1920's, left unfavorable impressions of so-called parliamentary democracy upon the masses and the military officers. These factors partly explain the rise of ultrarightist groups among the military men and some of the coups attempted by them against the party governments.

Furthermore, the government's effort to balance the budget through contraction of the army and navy brought strong resentment from younger officers of junior rank. According to Shidehara Kijūrō, Minister of Foreign Affairs after 1924, the prestige of the army was at its lowest in the late 1920's, and the effort to restore this prestige was largely responsible for the "Manchurian incident" of 1931.[1]

The army officers' frustration, however, was not owing solely to domestic conditions. They had also been exasperated by the vacillating policies of the government with regard to Manchuria. When it became clear that the government was not ready to let the Kwantung (Kantō) Army take Manchuria by force, younger officers in that army became restless. Recurrent boycotts of Japanese goods were revived in China after July, 1931, when the Wanpaoshan incident exploded in Korea.

The Kwantung Army finally attacked Chinese troops in Mukden on September 18, 1931, under the pretext that they had offered a challenge by destroying the Japanese-controlled railroad. This was the beginning of the so-called Manchurian incident, the first of a series of aggressive wars.

The Japanese occupation of Manchuria affected the Korean nationalists both favorably and adversely. The situation was bad for them because the occupation and the establishment of the puppet regime of "Manchukuo" meant the complete loss of their base for operations in the contiguous border areas of Manchuria, Siberia, and China proper. This region had provided a sanctuary for Korean military groups escaping from the Japanese attacks, and its Korean residents were their only reliable source of subsistence.

The Provisional Government, not with complete success, had proclaimed its jurisdiction over these residents. Military leaders enlisted young men from the region and collected funds and provisions there. Even after the Mukden agreement in 1925, whereby Chang Tso-lin agreed to subdue the Koreans in Manchuria, the nationalists could appeal for and get their support. Indiscriminate persecution by the Chinese authorities and rampant banditry caused them to turn to the militarist nationalists for protection. Further, Korean schools and various religious institutions in Manchuria and Siberia propagated nationalism, and southeastern Manchuria, especially, resembled a Korean nation-in-exile.

The Japanese occupation and the establishment of Manchukuo in 1932 completely altered this picture. All the nationalist movements in Manchuria became objects of persistent Japanese attack. Since in Siberia the nationalist movement in its traditional form had already been stifled by the consolidation of Bolshevik power in the early 1920's, the absorption of Manchuria by Japan was a deadly blow, for the Korean population in China proper was very small in comparison with that in Siberia and Manchuria.

Yet Japanese expansionist policy had a favorable side. It provoked strong antagonism among the Chinese—or, rather, intensified feelings already aroused by such Japanese actions as the Twenty-one Demands and the occupation of Kiaochow Bay during the First World War. More recently the Japanese Army had been blocking the northward advance of Chinese nationalist forces, and there had been frequent Chinese boycotts of Japanese goods.[2] The Wanpaoshan and Manchurian incidents of 1931 and the "Shanghai incident" in 1932 climaxed anti-Japanese sentiment among the Chinese.

When Japanese Marines attacked troops of the Nineteenth Route Army in Shanghai in January, 1932, workers, students, and other citizens flocked to its aid. The Japanese needed three and a half additional divisions to win a nominal victory:

> With only rifles and machine guns [the Nineteenth Route Army] withstood the Japanese assaults from land, sea, and air, receiving the wholehearted cooperation of the population of Shanghai—a kind of public support rarely given in China, where common soldiers were generally depreciated.[3]

Thus the Korean nationalists had a potential ally. They could appeal to anti-Japanese sentiment among the Chinese people and solicit assistance in their endeavor for Korean independence. The relationship was strained, however, because of a horrifying occurrence in 1931.

Inflamed by exaggerated reports of a dispute between some Korean and Chinese farmers at Wanpaoshan in southeastern Manchuria, in July, 1931, Koreans in various parts of Korea massacred many Chinese residents and destroyed their property.[4] To the agitated Chinese masses, therefore, the Koreans appeared not as being oppressed by the Japanese, but rather as participating with them or their agents in aggression against China. The Korean nationalists had to prove that their people were actually friends of China and enemies of Japan. Mere propaganda would not serve.

In these circumstances the Korean nationalists turned to terrorist practices. They had tried to build up an army of their own and had failed. Although propaganda activities were continued, no effect was evident. With limited personnel and funds, terrorism seemed the only feasible activity left. It gained world-wide publicity at little or no cost to themselves. Until 1937, when they joined the anti-Japanese warfare of the Chinese, their efforts in China were largely given to terrorism.

Two such acts in 1932 brought a complete change in the future of the Korean nationalist movement. These were masterminded by Kim Ku. Behind him were the Korean Independence party (*Hanguk Tongnip-dang*) and the Provisional Government, then in only nominal existence.

The new party was the result of a regrouping of the Koreans in Shanghai in 1930. While Chinese sentiment was rapidly turning against the Japanese in the late 1920's, the Korean nationalists were slowly preparing for future activities. In January, 1930, a number of the leaders formed the Korean Independence party for the purpose of rallying in one group and reviving the Provisional Government. The party membership included Yi Tong-nyŏng, An Ch'ang-ho, Kim Ku, Yi Shi-yŏng, Yi T'ak, and others previously connected with the government. It was decided, contrary to precedent, that the party was not to be made known publicly until considerable forces were gathered within it, and a vigorous campaign for membership in the Shanghai area ensued. Until April, 1931, when a party communiqué was sent to the Chinese National Congress in Nanking, its name was not openly used.[5]

These leaders, representing the rightist wing of the nationalists, decided upon terrorist activities against the Japanese as the only solution to their predicament. Kim Ku, long chief of the police bureau, was then the head of the Provisional Government and was entrusted with carrying out the program. He staged the Sakurada Gate and Hungk'ou Park incidents, and is reported to have received $1,000 from his supporters in Hawaii in November, 1931, for the expenses.[6]

Although only one person was involved in each, the effect of these two incidents was far greater in winning Chinese support than the activities of hundreds of Korean guerrilla troops in Manchuria.

On January 8, 1932, a Korean, Yi Pong-ch'ang, threw a hand grenade at the state procession of the Japanese emperor outside the Sakurada Gate of the palace in Tokyo. Exploding near the second carriage, in which the Minister of the Royal Household was riding, the grenade destroyed a part of the carriage and wounded two horses; the emperor's carriage was about a hundred feet away. Yi Pong-ch'ang was arrested and sentenced to death.

As far as his intention to kill the emperor was concerned, Yi's mission was a failure, but in China at this time anti-Japanese feeling was intense. The occurrence at Sakurada Gate was reported January 9 in the *Minkuo Jihpao* ("Republic Daily"), the organ of the Shanghai branch of the Kuomintang, under the headline "A Korean, Yi Pong-ch'ang, sniped at the Japanese emperor, but unfortunately missed." The same headline was carried in Tsingtao and Changsha. Japanese troops and police raided the newspaper office in Shanghai and destroyed its plant, and when the Japanese government formally instituted a protest, the other newspapers carrying the headline were shut down.[7]

On January 18, in Shanghai, five Japanese monks were attacked and killed by some Chinese. Two days later, Japanese residents held a public meeting and demanded that their government send troops to suppress anti-Japanese acts, citing the newspaper headlines and the murder of the monks.[8] On January 28 Japanese and Chinese troops exchanged fire, beginning a battle—the Shanghai incident—that lasted until March 3. The Sakurada Gate incident was in some degree responsible for this; in any event, the work of Yi Pong-ch'ang was well publicized round the world, and the nationalist leaders reaped the desired end of propaganda.

While the fighting was going on, Kim Ku had planned to destroy the Japanese military depots and airplane hangers, using Korean workers within the Japanese Army, but the combat was over before this could be done. He also sent two agents to Korea to assassinate the governor-general, without success.[9]

An incident staged by Kim Ku in Shanghai on April 29 brought immediate results. The victorious Japanese were planning to celebrate their success on the emperor's birthday. Japanese residents were instructed to bring lunch boxes and water canteens to Hungk'ou Park. Kim Ku had the chief of a Chinese ordnance works produce bombs shaped like lunch boxes and canteens—the effect of the Sakurada Gate incident was already evident in Chinese coöperativeness. These bombs were of high capacity because, according to Kim Ku, the Chinese regretted the low-capacity grenade used in Tokyo. Twenty such bombs were delivered.[10]

On April 29 a large-scale military parade was held in Hungk'ou Park and was reviewed by the senior Japanese military and naval officers who had led their forces against the Chinese in Shanghai. After the parade the Japanese anthem was played and was to be followed by speeches. Just before the anthem was finished, Yun Pong-gil threw a bomb at the dais where the dignitaries were standing. The explosion seriously injured the following: Shigemitsu Mamoru, the Japanese minister plenipotentiary to China; General Shirakawa Yoshinori, commander of the Japanese forces in Shanghai; Admiral Nomura Kichisaburō, commander of the Third Fleet; Major General Ueda Kenkichi, commander of the Ninth Division, who had headed the Japanese forces before Shirakawa; Kawabata Teiji, chairman of the Japanese Residents Association, which had called the troops into Shanghai; and Murai Kuramatsu, the consul general. Kawabata died the next day; Shigemitsu lost his right leg; and Nomura lost his right eye. Shirakawa died later as a result of his wounds.[11]

The Chinese government did express—perfunctorily—its regret, but the true feelings of the populace can be surmised. The Japanese could not accuse the government, since Chinese were barred from the celebration; Koreans were technically subjects of the Japanese emperor; hence the Japanese had no one to blame but themselves. After Kim Ku let it be known that the two bombing incidents were carried out on his orders, various Chinese leaders made contact with him, and small amounts of material aid began to reach him.[12] Meanwhile, Japanese consulate police, and military personnel made mass arrests of Koreans, and an extremely large reward (at first 200,000 yuan, later 600,000) was offered for the arrest of Kim Ku. As a prominent nationalist, An Ch'ang-ho was arrested and sent to Korea. Through the assistance of sympathetic Chinese, Kim Ku escaped, and though he and other leaders were forced into hiding, new channels for help hitherto unavailable to the Korean nationalists were opened up.

Kim Ku describes an interview with Chiang Kai-shek in Nanking sometime between late 1932 and early 1933. A Korean, Pak Ch'an-ik, was a member of the Kuomintang and was acquainted with a right-hand man to Chiang, Ch'en Kuo-fu, who arranged the meeting. Chiang told Kim that the people of the Far East ought to adopt democracy according to the Three People's Principles of Sun Yat-sen. Kim stated that if a million yuan were provided, he could incite riots in Japan, Korea, and Manchuria. Chiang asked for a written plan, which was provided later. Kim was then invited to Ch'en Kuo-fu's residence and an alternative long-range plan was presented by the Chinese. Ch'en told Kim that assassinations would be ineffective because emperors or military commanders could always be replaced; he suggested instead that the Koreans ought to train officers for the independence movement. The officers could be trained at the Loyang branch of the Chinese Military Academy.[13]

According to a Japanese report, Kim was to be allowed 2,500 yuan a month for living expenses and additional amounts as occasions arose. The trained Korean officers were to be placed in the Chinese Army and Air Force to facilitate their safety and convenience for operations in China. A five-man committee to supervise the affairs of the Koreans was established, the members including Ch'en Kuo-fu, Ch'en Li-fu, and An Kong-gŭn. An was the only Korean member.[14]

This was the beginning of a long and close relationship between Kim Ku and the Chinese nationalist government, and for the first time in many years the future of the Korean nationalist movement showed some hope. About one hundred young Koreans were mobilized under Kim Ku and enrolled in the Loyang Military Academy.

In May, 1933, while Kim Ku was still mobilizing trainees, Yi Kyu-ch'ae of the Korean Independence party of Manchuria came to Nanking and met with him. As we have seen in the preceding chapter, this party had considerable forces and had been very active in Manchuria. Large-scale operations had been carried out against Japanese and Manchukuo forces in coöperation with Chinese groups. But the Japanese forces were too strong and numerous for the Koreans, and the Chinese allies were dwindling. The party and its troops, therefore, wished to evacuate to China proper.

Kim Ku immediately issued 1,800 yuan for the transport of Yi Kyu-ch'ae's troops and concluded an agreement to place qualified members of the Independence Army (under the party) in the Loyang

Military Academy. Late in 1933 Yi Ch'ŏng-ch'ŏn (alias Chi Tae-hyŏng), the commander of the Independence Army, and Yi Pŏm-sŏk, one of the leaders, became instructors at Loyang and about a hundred followers were enrolled in the academy.[15]

Although the future of the Korean nationalist movement under the leadership of Kim Ku seemed promising, this favorable condition did not last. Early in 1934, because of disagreements with Yi Ch'ŏng-ch'ŏn, Kim withdrew seventeen of his followers from the Loyang academy, placing them in the Chinese Central Military Academy at Nanking. Many of his recruits, however, sided with Yi and stayed at Loyang.[16]

The split between Kim Ku and Yi Ch'ŏng-ch'ŏn was symptomatic of many problems to be faced by the Korean nationalists afterward. Kim had the confidence of the Chinese government; he had a long record as a patriot; and by steadfast determination he had become an important leader. Yet he was unable to consolidate the other nationalists under his leadership. The stresses that brought about his breach with Yi exemplify the general problems of the nationalists.

First, there was the constant problem of Japanese vigilance. Practically every move of the Koreans was watched. The Japanese used every means available to pressure the French authorities in Shanghai to restrict the movements of the Koreans in the French Concession and later applied similar pressures to the Chinese government. The Korean Independence party of Shanghai, the backbone of Kim Ku's initial activities, disintegrated as a result. In March, 1933, Yi Yu-p'il, the secretary-general of the party, was arrested by the Japanese, and in October Kim Ch'ŏl, another right-hand man of Kim Ku. Other members fled the city, and the party lost cohesion.

Another problem seems to have been the personal weaknesses of the leader. O Myŏn-jik, who had been a close follower, told his Japanese interrogator in 1936:

> [Kim's] spirit of perseverance and courage to overcome all difficulties were remarkable . . . It is an undeniable fact that throughout the forty years since the Tonghak rebellion, he had worked for the nation and did not care for his personal interest if it [conflicted with] the interest of the public. He has been respected by all in this regard and even the opponents of Kim Ku would not deny this fact. What is then the reason that he, once so loved, was rejected? I think it is because although he is honest he lacks discernment, and he is

> easily manipulated by ambitious politicians. He also lacks the penetrative insight to judge people; therefore, he is not effective in using people. Consequently there are discrepancies between plans and the actual results, and activities end in failure.
>
> Also, because of a lack of education, he does not have a good understanding of the current situation, cannot establish firm policies, and has set up no fundamental policy for the training of the masses . . . So the passionate students decided that following Kim Ku, who wastes time meaninglessly, was not advantageous for the Korean independence movement, and finally they revolted against him.[17]

Judging from the desertion of the new recruits, Kim's deficiencies seem to have been such as O Myŏn-jik alleged. Further, he lost the support of many of the former members of the Independence party of Shanghai.[18] Some of them joined with the Manchurian group early in 1934 to establish the New Korean Independence party (*Shinhan Tongnip-dang*).[19]

That same year Kim Ku gathered about eighty followers into a military group, the Korean Independence Army Special Duty Unit (*Hanguk Tongnipkun T'ŭngmudae*). One of the objects of this unit was "to arm every Korean for the Korean revolution and destroy the Japanese imperialism." Kim also established a training center in Nanking to prepare new recruits for the Chinese Central Military Academy, but when their training was completed he negotiated for their enrolment, he was faced with another setback. The Japanese government, well aware of his activities and connections, had made a strong protest to the Chinese government, which at this time was attempting to appease Japan, whereupon the academy was compelled to refuse to admit Kim's followers. Late in 1935, with only nine followers remaining under him, Kim disbanded the Special Unit. Evidently he was not very well supplied by the Chinese, for he had difficulty paying the rent for the training compounds; according to O Myŏn-jik, he received only his living expenses after the Special Unit program was dissolved.[20]

While Kim Ku was having these difficulties, a united-front movement led by left-wing groups among the nationalists was looming in China. Although the initial terrorist activities of Kim Ku won the sympathy and later the support of the Chinese, and much of the revival of Korean nationalist activities in China was owing to his efforts, his opponents reaped more of the benefit.

As early as June, 1927, nationalists and Communists had formed the Shanghai Association for the Promotion of the United Korean Independence Party, which accomplished very little and was officially dissolved in October, 1929. Most of the nationalists then withdrew from united-front efforts, while the Korean Communists in Shanghai immediately set up the League of Korean Independence Movement Workers (*Yu-Ho Hanguk Tongnip Undongja Tongmaeng*).[21] This group published an organ *Ap-p'u-ro* ("Forward") and occasionally secured the assistance of the rightist nationalists in street demonstrations and public ceremonies on anniversaries, but their efforts to absorb them were not successful.

After 1932 leadership in the movement for unity was taken not by Comintern-oriented Koreans but by Kim Won-bong, who might be called a national-communist. In order to understand the union movement and the left-wing nationalist movement of this period, it is necessary to retrace some of the activities of Kim Won-bong.

Kim Won-bong's activities went back to the year of the March First movement. In November, 1919, Kim, then in his early twenties, gathered twelve followers in Chilin, Manchuria. They swore to each other to fight the Japanese and took the name of Uiyŏldan—the "Righteous Fighters Corps." The principal aim of this small group was to kill Japanese—also pro-Japanese Koreans—and to destroy their property. It is remarkable that the sworn brothers remained united in their activities until 1945 without a traitor among them.[22]

Considering their small number, Kim Won-bong and his group carried on an impressive amount of terrorism. By 1921 they had already thrown bombs into the Pusan police station, the Milyang police station, and the Korean Government-General Building. Until 1925 the Uiyŏldan sporadically sent agents into Korea. Although none of these succeeded in assassinating any major Japanese political figure or destroying anything significant, their attempts were reported in newspapers in Korea and thus were known to the populace. On March 28, 1933, three of the group attempted to assassinate General Tanaka Giichi in Shanghai, but instead killed an Englishwoman who stepped into the way of the pistol shot intended for him.

Kim Won-bong's early status in the Communist movement is not clear. He had contacts with Communists in 1919, but since the nationalists and Communists freely intermingled before 1921, this does not prove that Kim was a member of the party at the time. Nor is it certain whether he was involved with Korean Communist activities in China between 1921 and 1927. He is, however, reported to have taken a major role as a Communist in 1928 when he conferred in Shanghai with a Korean Communist, An Kwang-ch'ŏn, about the reconstruction of the Korean Communist party and went on to Peking to organize the Reconstruction League of the Korean Communist Party with a few Communists there, at the same time establishing the Leninist Political School. Between April, 1929, and February, 1931, the school trained nineteen students and sent them to Korea; most of them were arrested in 1934 for connections with the preparation committee of the Communist Youth League in Seoul and the Kangnŭng Red Farmers Union.[23]

When the Chinese became more violently anti-Japanese after the seizure of Manchuria, Kim Won-bong moved to Nanking and, according to the Japanese police, made contact with high officials of the Chinese Nationalist government in May, 1932, and proposed a Sino-Korean alliance to counter Japanese aggression. Chiang Kai-shek therefore assigned Chiang To, who was simultaneously the head of the secret Lan-I-Shê (the intelligence group under the Chen brothers), publisher of the *Chungkuo Jihpao* ("China Daily"), and president of the alumni association of Whampoa Military Academy, to guide Kim's activities.[24]

Kim Won-bong was granted 3,000 yuan a month (some sources say 2,500 yuan) for his activities and given the use of the officers training center outside Nanking, under the control of the Chinese Military Commission, as a training compound for Koreans. For concealment from the Japanese police, the Korean unit was designated as the Sixth Branch Unit of the training center. The six-month program, in which the Korean students lived apart from the Chinese and had a separate curriculum, covered both military training and an education in Communist-oriented revolutionary doctrines which Kim Ku's trainees did not receive. Whereas Kim Ku entrusted the entire training program to the Chinese academy, Kim Won-bong saw to it that his followers emerged not merely as qualified military officers, but also as indoctrinated revolutionaries.[25]

The number of trainees under Kim Won-bong was not very large, only twenty-six in the first class and fifty-five in the second; but they were intended to be agitators and organizers, not simply soldiers. Among the twenty instructors were three Chinese military officers; in addition, there were lectures by original members of the Uiyŏldan and such veteran leftist nationalists as Kim Tu-bong and Kim Kyu-sik. Although the original agreement with the Chinese government seems to have been that the graduates would be used in military or terrorist activities in Manchuria, most of them were sent into Korea on missions to organize workers, students, and farmers and to establish branches of the Uiyŏldan or branches of the Korean Communist party. They were also instructed to form "vanguard units" which would be headed by Communists and converted to guerrilla units in the event of a world war.[26] The graduates sent by Kim Won-bong contributed substantially to the Communist movement in Korea in this period. It is reasonable to assume that the Chinese government was not aware of the true intentions of Kim Won-bong and his associates, because the alliance between the Kuomintang and the Chinese Communists had already been broken off in 1927.

The launching of the union or united-front movement of Korean nationalists in the summer of 1932 coincided with the arrival of Kim Won-bong in Nanking. Although his name is not associated with this endeavor, the three leaders who initiated it had family or other connections with him. These three, all of moderately leftist leanings, were Kim Kyu-sik, Ch'oe Tong-o, and Kim Tu-bong. Kim Kyu-sik had been Minister of Foreign Affairs and afterward Minister of Education in the Provisional Government during its early period. At this time he was not affiliated with any group. He had, however, lectured at the training center and according to a Japanese report was a member of the central executive committee of the Uiyŏldan.[27] Ch'oe was a leader of the Korean Revolutionary party of Manchuria, which was infiltrated by Communists, but his ideological position is not known. Kim Tu-bong, at the time a member of the Korean Independence party of Shanghai, had associated with Communists as early as 1919.[28]

On July 12 a preparation committee met in Shanghai, and on November 10 the Korean Anti-Japanese Front Unification League (*Hanguk Tae-il Chŏnsŏn T'ongil Tongmaeng*) was formed.[29] Until 1934 the League solicited various Korean groups to form a united front against the Japanese, but in effect served merely as a liaison organ without bringing about any unity. On March 1, 1934, a second plenary conference of the League was held in Nanking, and on April 12 a letter was sent out, calling for a conference of various groups.[30] The letter requested replies by September 1, but there were none. A second letter, sent on September 2, announced a conference to be held on February 20, 1935, but only a few groups responded. The League then postponed the conference to June 20.

The reason for the postponement was the rejection of the unification movement by the Provisional Government and the Shanghai Korean Independence party. Joining the union movement would have meant dissolving the Provisional Government, as well as turning over the followers of the party to the new alliance. Although the party existed in little more than name at this time, its leaders were unwilling to see it disappear. When the Unification League sent out its call for the conference, therefore, the party leaders resorted to evasive tactics. A plenary conference of the party, scheduled for January 15, 1935, was put off to February 15 so that the members might not attend the conference of the unification movement. There was some opposition within the party to these moves, but nevertheless resolutions were carried that (1) the Provisional Government must be positively supported, (2) the party may not be dissolved, and (3) the proposal to join the united front must be declined.

Abstention of the Korean Independence party of Shanghai would have defeated the intent of the Unification League, which was to establish a single, united Korean party. On May 25, in an emergency session, the party reversed its stand and resolved to dissolve itself and join the alliance. A dissenting minority then withdrew from the party.[31]

Kim Ku, of course, occupied a prominent position among the Korean nationalists, and his participation would have strengthened the alliance. Attempts to persuade him to join were refused for three reasons: first, movements of this kind in the past had never lasted very long, and the factors causing their failure still existed; second, he did not wish to associate with Kim Won-bong and the other Communists; third, the Provisional Government must not be dissolved. Kim's staunch defense of the Provisional Government gave encouragement to the minority group in the Korean Independence party of Shanghai and led to a counteralliance, to which we will turn presently.[32]

As we have seen, the unification movement among the Korean nationalists and Communists was, on the one hand, courting the Chinese Nationalist government; on the other, its leaders were ready to bargain with any power that might offer assistance. Early in June, 1935, when prospects for the alliance were favorable, the Unification League informed the Chinese Nationalist government that "the activities of the new alliance movement of the Korean nationalists are not mere splinter-group activities as in the past, but propose to unify the entire movement under one organization," and that, "since this is not only for the interest of the Korean people, but would also contribute to the happiness of the entire Chinese people, considerable assistance must be provided to the movement by the Chinese government." Yet at the same time the officers of the League resolved that in the event the Chinese government did not recognize the unified organization, all the Korean pilots and engineers working in the Chinese Nationalist army would be simultaneously withdrawn and attached to the Canton army.[33] This bold attitude was possible because of the confused situation in China, immediately before the "long march" northward of the Chinese Communist forces led by Mao Tse-tung. Whether this resolution was transmitted to the Chinese Nationalists is not known, however, and it must be regarded as primarily a show of strength to rally scattered Korean groups.

After three years of preparation the conference of the Korean organizations was finally convened in Nanking. At a preliminary session, June 20–29, 1935, the Uiyŏldan delegates, the Korean Revolutionary party of Manchuria, the Shanghai Korean Independence party, the New Korean Independence party, and the Greater Korean Independence party of Hawaii [34] were prepared to dissolve their parties and immediately amalgamate them into the new alliance and were granted voting privileges. Other delegates, who needed the approval of their headquarters, were allowed to participate in discussions without voting—these represented the New York Korean Residents Association, the Korean National Association in North America (Los Angeles and Honolulu), and the Comrades Society (*Dongjihoe*) (Honolulu).

The official conference, from June 29 to July 3, was taken up with the naming of the new party and the drafting of party platforms, constitution, and policies. Then on July 4 a conference of the new party was convened and the items agreed upon at the previous conference were passed with some revisions. The "party principle" (*tang kang*) or platform adopted by the new Korean National Revolutionary party (*Minjok Hyŏnmyŏng-dang*) shows some leftist tendencies. Its seventeen points were as follows:[35]

Destroy the exploiting forces of the enemy Japan and complete the independence of our people
Purge all feudal and other antirevolutionary forces and establish a democratic regime
Eliminate the economic system under which the minority exploits the majority, and establish a system in which all citizens may maintain equal livelihood
Execute local autonomy based on prefectures
Arm the entire nation
Institute an equal suffrage for all and the right to be elected
Grant the people freedom of speech, assembly, publication, organization, and faith
Grant equal rights to women
Institute nationalization of land and distribute the land to the farmers
Nationalize large-scale industries and monopoly enterprises
Institute economic national planning
Protect free movement of labor
Institute a progressive tax system
Operate national compulsory education and professional education
Establish old people's homes, nurseries, and relief organizations as public institutions
Confiscate all properties of the national traitors and public and private properties of the Japanese in Korea
Maintain close liaison with and support the liberation movement of the world's oppressed peoples according to the principles of freedom, equality and mutual assistance

The central committee of the new party decided that all members, properties, and activities of the various groups should come under its jurisdiction before July 25. The Uiyŏldan, under Kim Won-bong, was the strongest of the groups, and this may explain both his possession of the leadership of the newly established party and the fact that its political platform was in essence the same as that of the Uiyŏldan.[36] In every practical sense the Korean National Revolutionary party was a continuation of the Uiyŏldan with the power of the other groups added. Most of the important positions in the party fell to members of the Uiyŏldan or those who had previous connections with it. The power of Kim Won-bong was based not only on the number of his followers, but also on his having the largest income. He was drawing up to 3,000 yuan a month from the Kuomintang, and the livelihood of some members depended on this.[37]

Although Kim Ku and a few other prominent nationalists declined to join the new party and a minority from the Korean Independence party of Shanghai withdrew from it, the unification movement was an undeniable success. It included the Uiyŏldan, two major military groups from Manchuria, and some elements from the Shanghai party. Even some of the nationalist groups in the United States rendered support. Although Kim Ku was still regarded as its foremost rival, he was not in a very strong position in this period to offer much opposition. The party could boast itself to be the strongest Korean nationalist group, and its claim had material justification. Although it had its share of internal struggles, as will be seen, and its activities were essentially the same as those carried on by the separate groups, it had the strength of a united command and hence more vitality. By the middle of 1936 the Korean National Revolutionary party had, aside from the headquarters at Nanking in central China, branches in East China (Shanghai), South China (Canton), West China (Nanchang), and North China (Peking) and special branches in Korea (Seoul) and Manchuria (Changchun).[38] These were, however, established by reorganizing in each area various elements which had been under one or another of the original groups, and in some of them the problem of loyalty developed later; the headquarters in Nanking was not always successful in winning the primary loyalty of the branches.

As has been mentioned, the training of followers was begun by Kim Won-bong and Yi Ch'ŏng-ch'ŏn before the amalgamation. Kim finished the training of his second class at Nanking in April, 1934, and Yi's followers were graduated at Loyang in April, 1935. After March, 1935, both started the training of additional recruits. When the parties were united in July, the trainees were brought together; in October thirty-six were graduated from the joint training center.[39]

At the end of the year, while the Korean National Revolutionary party was training potential agitators and organizers, the Chinese government sent instructions which necessitated a change in the program: "Owing to the protests of the Japanese, active assistance hereafter will not be possible. Training of the students must be discontinued as soon as possible, and preparations must be made so that even if the assistance is entirely stopped this may not hinder the activities." [40] Under strong pressure from the Japanese, who now had full control over North China, the Chinese Nationalists since the beginning of 1933 had yielded to one demand after another, and one of the terms of the Ho-Umetsu agreement of July, 1935, called for the removal of objectionable troops and officials.[41]

The party therefore decided to discontinue training and move into the so-called second stage—the dispatch of trained agents to Korea, Manchuria, and North China to engage in espionage against the Japanese, assassination of the Japanese officials, and destruction of installations. In March, 1936, fifteen agents were sent into Manchuria. Later in the year, as the international situation became more ominous in the Far East, the party predicted a world war and dispatched forty to fifty agents into North China, Manchuria, and Korea. Their mission was to create confusion in occupied areas through assassination and destruction, thus aiding the cause of the enemies of Japan.

From its establishment until April, 1937, when the Yi Ch'ŏng-ch'ŏn group withdrew,[42] the party seemed on the surface to be operating smoothly, but there were undercurrents of friction between the two principal leaders, Kim Won-bong and Yi Ch'ŏng-ch'ŏn. Since the party officers were periodically elected by plenary conferences in Nanking, the number of members of each group remaining in the Nanking area became important. Agents to be dispatched were carefully selected so that no imbalance would result. According to a Japanese source, however, Kim Won-bong manipulated the situation to his advantage.[43] Yi Ch'ŏng-ch'ŏn, on the other hand, seems to have maintained closer contacts with Manchuria. He was himself from Manchuria, and he was the head of the party's military department. Reportedly, the group in Manchuria reverted to their original name of the Korean Revolutionary party (*Chosŏn Hyŏngmyŏng-dang*) soon after the united party was established; when a representative of the group was reprimanded for this splinter action, he replied that it was necessary to use the old designation in order to solicit funds in the area of operation—if the headquarters was going to insist on the new name, it would have to provide complete financial support and necessary supplies.[44] Another indication of distrust cropped up in the soliciting of funds from the Chinese. During a campaign in 1936 to raise five thousand dollars Yi Ch'ŏng-ch'ŏn approached Chang Hsüeh-liang, the war lord in Sian, and obtained substantial aid. Yi may have intended using the contact with Chang to build up his own standing and secure a source of support in the event of a disruption of the united party.[45]

In August, 1936, Kim Won-bong personally made an agreement with the Chinese group at Sian and planned a series of bomb incidents. Bombs produced by his followers were to be used against both the Japanese and the Kuomintang government. Because of an explosion during the making of the bombs, the plot was discovered. The Yi group vehemently attacked Kim Won-bong for carrying out activities of grave significance without the consent of the party as a whole, and attempted to expel him. Only through the intervention of more neutral elements within the party was disruption avoided.[46] Still another threat to unity was the printing of the Uiyŏldan emblem in the third issue of the party organ *Minjok Hyŏngmyŏng* ("National Revolution"). Other elements of the party protested and eventually the organ was discontinued. This sensitivity showed the instability of the alliance.

Aside from ideological and personal differences among the leaders within the organization, there is another important factor to be considered. Kim Ku and Yi Ch'ŏng-ch'ŏn were far closer in their ideologies or beliefs than Yi and Kim Won-bong. There are indications that Kim Ku utilized this situation to the maximum to disrupt the Korean National Revolutionary party.

A resurgence of opposition was begun by the minority in the Korean Independence party of Shanghai who had refused to join the united front. The first efforts of this group, headed by Song Pyŏng-jo and Ch'a Ri-sŏk, were directed toward reconstruction of the Provisional Government; the title no doubt had some prestige and weight in dealings with the Chinese. Song and Ch'a made contacts with nationalists around Nanking who were not enrolled in the Korean National Revolutionary party. There were twenty to thirty followers in Kim Ku's group, and there were several former members of the dissolved Korean Independence party. Cho So-ang's group defected from the united party by September, 1935, and nineteen leaders from various groups met from October 19 to November 2, calling their meetings the "Temporary Session of the Legislative Assembly of the Provisional Government" and reviving the council of ministers, which decided upon portfolios and appointments to the cabinet.[47]

The proclamation issued by the new cabinet reflected the circumstances which had brought about the revival of the Provisional Government and was in essence an attack upon the Korean National Revolutionary party. Alluding to intrigues carried on by some elements for destroying the Provisional Government, it asserted that they had discarded obligations and major principles in order to display their own thoughts or garner private advantages, employed double standards, deceived their own consciences, displayed opportunism under the flowery name of so-called union, and attempted to eliminate the Provisional Government, an act which had not been accomplished even by the strenuous efforts of the enemy. "Only through the torment of the sense of duties," the proclamation concluded, "did we rally ourselves to save the Provisional Government." [48] In opposition to the united front, the Provisional Government group formed a political party of its own, the Korean National party (*Hanguk Kungmin-dang*). Kim Ku was elected head of the party's board of trustees, with leaders of the Provisional Government as members of the board. The party declaration reiterated the cabinet's proclamation, citing the unprincipled nature of the opposition, and appealed to the national spirit and historical tradition of Korea. As positive principles of its own, however, the party merely affirmed its goal of complete liberation of Korea and its support of the principles of "equality of all in politics, economy, and education." [49]

Although the opponents of the united-front group were thus rallied under the Provisional Government and the Korean National party, they accomplished very little until 1937. An effort to mobilize new members in Canton and Shanghai was unavailing; most of the nationalists in those areas were already in the other camp. The Provisional Government and its party were top-heavy organizations with no citizens to govern and few members to direct. The only exception was the party's Youth Corps, the reorganized body of Kim Ku's followers, with a membership of about twenty.[50] Party and corps both published magazines, whose contents were largely directed against the Korean National Revolutionary party.[51]

The Korean nationalist movement between 1931 and 1936 can be summarized as follows: Kim Ku's terrorist activities won initial recognition of the nationalists by the Chinese; the Chinese government began to provide the Koreans the financial and spiritual support they needed; then most of the nationalists were divided into two camps, with the majority on the side of the leftists. These developments revealed two important problems attending the Korean nationalist movement: the characteristics of the leadership and the nature of the so-called united front. Indeed these are the crucial problems in any modern nationalist movement.

Evidence of weakness in leadership is clear. Kim Ku had the greatest initial advantages. He was a hero in the eyes of the Chinese, recognized by the government and civilian leaders as a potential ally, and he received considerable financial and other support; he had also the backing of a majority of the Korean leaders, at least in the beginning. Chinese support put him in an advantageous position for uniting his compatriots. But Kim failed to utilize these advantages, and most of his followers went over to Kim Won-bong. Kim Ku lacked an educational background adequate for a proper understanding of the situation and the formulation of a long-range policy to guide the movement. His pride in his exploits alienated some of his colleagues and revealed insensitivity in his perception of human nature. Yet, these were only superficial reasons for his failure. A better explanation would take into consideration the facts that the movement required a ruthless leader capable of planning and executing terrorist activities—for it was obvious that the Korean nationalists could not obtain the support of the antagonized Chinese without some violent action—while at the same time it required one capable of long-range thinking in terms of unity of the movement and future policies. This latter function demanded a person of intellectual depth and understanding. In short, the movement required a leader with the qualities of two different persons. Such a leader as An Ch'ang-ho might have been able to fill the requirements of the second category. For the task of activating the movement, however, a leader like Kim was more suitable. This was clearly recognized when the Independence party in Shanghai selected Kim Ku to carry out its terrorist missions. Once a person appears in the limelight, however, it is difficult for a leader of another type and disposition to replace him. Hence the movement may have been revitalized, but the other and perhaps more important need could not be filled.

The problems of leadership were directly related to the problem of a united front. The deficiencies of Kim Ku eventually alienated a majority of the nationalists and enhanced the possibilities for a united front, which came about when the left-wing elements were able to find common ground with those whom we may call the rightists and achieved an alliance. In terms of formal structure, of course, the united front was more than an alliance. The previously existing political groups were dissolved, and a single party was established. In actuality, however, the united party was still no more than an alliance. Personal ties of leader-follower groups do not disappear in a short period, especially when the groups joining in a united front have differing geographical origins and social backgrounds. When ideological differences are added, the unity of the larger entity becomes precarious. Suspicions and doubts cannot be eliminated by the stroke of a pen, no matter how urgent the need for unity may be. The officers of the Korean National Revolutionary party amounted to a coalition cabinet. By its nature a coalition cabinet cannot long survive external and internal pressures, being merely a means to an end. The end in this coalition seems to have been the fortification of their own power by individuals or, at the most, groups.

Fortification of the power of each group among the Korean Nationalists in 1936 was possible only through a major war in the Far East. Thus every Korean group in China anticipated further assistance from the Chinese government in the event of a full-scale war between China and Japan. Therefore all the nationalists, regardless of ideologies or beliefs, eagerly awaited such a war, which they believed would eventually demolish the Japanese Empire and enhance their own power.

11

The Road to Chungking

On July 7, 1937, Japanese and Chinese troops exchanged fire at the Marco Polo Bridge, nine miles southwest of Peking. This small incident eventually led to an undeclared major war between the two Great Powers of the Far East. The reckless aggression of the Japanese military clique, which eventually joined the warfare in China with that of the Second World War, was not to be crushed until 1945. The years after 1937 brought incalculable tragedy to the Far East, but the war in China, which the Chiang Kai-shek government so strenuously avoided, was what the Korean nationalists had been waiting for.

The exasperated nationalists could see no real hope for their cause except in a major war. Korean students had speculated on the result of a Sino-Japanese war as early as 1916. The students in Japan reasoned during the First World War that if China and Japan went to war the United States would come to the aid of China; they hoped that the United States would then be attentive to the Korean aspiration for independence.[1] This reasoning prevailed among the Korean nationalists of later years, and thus the developments in Manchuria after 1931 reanimated their hopes; but in 1931 their expectations were premature. The consequences of the incident at the Marco Polo

Bridge, however, were unmistakable. The Chinese government could no longer vacillate. A final showdown was inevitable, and the war was on.

Immediately after the incident the Chinese government seems to have taken the initiative to form an alliance with the Koreans. According to a Japanese report, the Chinese government on July 10 invited Kim Ku, Kim Won-bong, and other leaders to a joint conference at Lushan, near Nanking, where the Chinese representatives urged the necessity of developing a united front against Japan and offered the Koreans a large sum of money for "important missions." The proposal of course was accepted.[2]

In September the Chinese government summoned the Korean leaders again and instructed them to mobilize young Koreans to receive training for special—that is, intelligence—duties. Kim Won-bong and Kim Ku thereupon sent urgent notices to their followers, and as a result eighty-three young men gathered at Nanking and on December 1 were enrolled into the Shengtze Military Academy's special training unit. The distribution of trainees according to groups is not known, but the majority belonged to the leftist camp of the Korean National Revolutionary party. Some of the followers of Kim Ku had already joined the Chinese Army individually; only a few, if any, followers of Kim Ku went to Shengtze.[3]

Japanese reports during 1937 are very revealing of increased activity among the Koreans in China:[4]

1. Financial assistance to Kim Ku continues as before, but Kim Won-bong is receiving more funds from Chang Hsüeh-liang . . . [The] assistance is several times as much as the amount provided before, and the Koreans have ample financial resources.

2. Both Kim Ku and Kim Won-bong have their own automobiles and are leading comfortable lives. They seem to be looking for personnel to carry out activities to disturb the area behind the [Japanese] war front.

3. Korean anarchists of the Chŏng Hwa-am group are coöperating with their Chinese counterparts recently released from prison [and] are planning terrorist activities. They have already obtained considerable funds.

4. A Chinese magazine, *Hanhsüeh* ("Sweat and Blood"), of September, 1937, published an article "Concerning the United Front of the Sino-Korean people and Anti-Japanese Koreans." It praised the Koreans who have already joined the anti-Japanese front and advocated that the Chinese coöperate with the Koreans and form a powerful unit . . .

5. A "Declaration of the Korean Liberation Movement Group Regarding

the Sino-Japanese War" was issued in August, 1937, in the name of the Patriotic Corps (*Aegukdan,* headed by Kim Ku) and six other organizations, emphasizing the need for joint operations by the Koreans and the Chinese.

6. Sŏk Chŏng of the Korean National Revolutionary party is in Shanghai attempting to obtain military information about the Japanese Army.

7. Kim Ku sent Yu Cha-myŏng to Chŏng Hwa-am, an anarchist leader, with a personal letter saying: "Let us forget all the things of the past, transcend our theoretical differences, and unite. I have funds as well as machinery. All nationalists except a few in Kim Won-bong's group are united. Let us work together on good terms as in the past. Please come to me immediately because I would like to confer with you." Chŏng left for Chenchiang to see Kim Ku.

8. Sŏk Chŏng, an officer of the Korean National Revolutionary party, and Pae Ch'ŏn-t'aek, an employee of the Chinese police, are broadcasting in Korean from the Shanghai broadcasting station for fifteen minutes nightly from 0045 A.M. Their anti-Japanese broadcast immediately follows the Japanese-language broadcast by the Chinese.

9. [The Korean National party] has its headquarters in Nanking . . . A branch is established in Shanghai within the French Concession [and] is maintaining connections with Tai Li, the head of the Special Unit of the Nanking Military Committee . . . The Investigation Section of the party is collecting information on the Japanese military arrangements and the locations of military depots . . . It is said that the results of the night action of the Chinese airplanes are largely owing to these reports.

Many more reports of a similar nature testify to the reanimation of the Korean nationalist movement. The nationalists as a whole were forming alliances with the Chinese groups, those with military training were joining the Chinese forces, espionage activities were being carried out, and attempts were being made by both the Korean National Revolutionary party and the Korean National party to bring the Korean anarchists into their ranks. The general policy of the nationalists followed these lines until 1945.

Although the movement became highly active after July, 1937, the nationalists were soon compelled to retreat from the Shanghai-Nanking area. The Chinese abandoned Shanghai on November 8 and Nanking on December 13. A few Korean underground agents remained in Shanghai, but the majority moved to safer areas, following the trial of the Kuomintang government.

Before retreating inland, however, the right-wing nationalists underwent some organizational shuffling. They were steadily moving toward the establishment of a unified party. The formation of a federation in 1937 was the first step in this move.

Cho So-ang had been rejected by the Provisional Government and by the Korean National party headed by Kim Ku, but he and his followers kept the name of the Korean Independence party.[5] Yi Ch'ŏng-ch'ŏn and his followers, separated from the Korean National Revolutionary party, revived the name of the Korean Revolutionary party (*Chosŏn Hyŏngmyŏng-dang*) in May, 1937. These two splinter groups joined with the Korean National party and six organizations in the United States and Hawaii to issue a "Joint Declaration of the Korean Restoration Movement Organizations" (*Hanguk Kwangbok Undong Tanch'e Yŏnhap Sŏnŏn*) in August, 1937.[6] Because of controversies within the Korean community in each area, the Korean National Associations in North America and Hawaii had been largely inactive since the early 1920's. When the situation in the Far East began to favor the nationalists in early 1930's, however, these overseas Koreans reactivated their old organizations and engaged in propagandizing and fund raising. They supported the Provisional Government.[7]

One of the overseas groups, the Comrades Society (*Dongjihoe*) was guided by Syngman Rhee. This organization, from its inception in 1921 in Honolulu, supported Rhee and was the major source of his political strength. The animosity between Rhee's followers and the others in the United States and Hawaii was never quite reconciled, and the appearance of the Comrades Society among the groups that endorsed the declaration seems strange. There was, however, correspondence between Rhee and Kim Ku around 1937.[8] We may note in passing that Rhee went to Geneva in 1933 and presented to the League of Nations two petitions for Korean independence.[9] Rhee during these years was isolated from most of the nationalists, and except for some of the speaking tours on behalf of the nationalists, he concentrated on educational activities for the Koreans in Hawaii.

The joint declaration was a propaganda document; no factual information appears in the text. The points stressed are the urgent need for unity and the legitimacy of the Provisional Government. The leaders admitted the weaknesses of the movement in the past: "Our blood and strength have not been adequate to repel the enemy." This weakness, they intimated, was owing in part to previous lack of unity and to incorrect strategies; adverse conditions were also blamed; but another, and more abominable, obstacle was the emergence of "antinational and antirevolutionary forces of various kinds" which hindered and confused the nationalist movement:

> The Provisional Government is the orthodox heritage of the March First movement, accomplished by the blood of our people, and it is a public weapon of our people defended with our blood. It is the absolute duty of the nationalists to support it. The Provisional Government has the sanctity and important mission of countering the enemy nation. The core of our nationalist front is, of course, the party organization. But it is inconvenient for a party to lead the general public directly. It has to act through various partial, functional groups. But the government by nature has the characteristics of totality through which the entire people can be led directly. Also, the existence of the government solemnly signifies the existence of our nation, and it contributes to our movement invisibly by inspiring our people. . . . The party is the brain of the government; the government the body of the party. Only through this kind of intertwined relationship will the spirit and the flesh of our front be consolidated and our movement powerfully and actively develop.[10]

With this declaration, the right-wing nationalists opened up a new phase of activity, which was interrupted by their having to retreat from the Shanghai-Nanking area. The leaders assembled at Changsha, Hunan Province, in May, 1938, and tried to restore the movement. At that time an attempt was made to assassinate Kim Ku. A young Korean, Yi Un-hwan, broke into a meeting of the Korean Restoration Movement Federation and fired several pistol shots. Kim Ku and Hyŏn Ik-ch'ŏl, a military leader from Manchuria, were seriously wounded. Hyŏn died upon arrival at a hospital; Kim's wound was so critical that doctors left him unattended for a few hours believing the case to be hopeless. The would-be assassin was from the same rightist group as Kim and was a man he had helped.[11]

The cause of this attempt cannot be determined. Kim Ku believed that Yi's attempt was spurred by slander spread against him by Pak Ch'ang-se and Kang Ch'ang-je, members of the Korean Independence party. A Japanese estimation implicated the same two persons and adduced a motive:

> When the Federation was formed, Kim Ku promised Yi Ch'ŏng-ch'ŏn, Kang Ch'ang-je, Pak Ch'ang-se, and others that there would be no discrimination in the treatment of the members. But there has been considerable material and spiritual discrimination. In addition, Kim Ku always acted in a dictatorial manner, and those mentioned above came to have resentment against Kim.[12]

Another Japanese report quotes a statement attributed to the leaders of the Korean National Revolutionary party:

> The attempt of Yi Un-hwan at the instigation of Pak Ch'ang-se and Kang Ch'ang-je looks as though it were a consequence of struggle for leadership. But deducing from the fact that Pak had been walking around the streets in Shanghai without fear during the Shanghai incident as well as his hiding at his own home, Pak had a secret agreement with the Japanese police to kill Kim Ku.[13]

If the latter explanation is true, Kim was a victim of the Japanese; if the other, Kim was a poor leader. Judging from his loss of many followers, he was not an effective coördinator. The quoted statement must be taken with reservations since Pak, along with Cho So-ang, was a hated renegade from the party. It seems clear in either case that internal harmony in the nationalist camp was imperfect and that the leaders did not quite abide by the hortatory remarks they put into the declaration.[14]

Whether this incident had a bearing on the activities of the right-wing nationalist groups is not clear, but their power declined thereafter until 1940. They were also again compelled to retreat, this time to Chungking, the last wartime capital of the Chinese Nationalist government.

There are indications that the Chinese government cultivated both the right and left groups of the Korean nationalists and brought the leaders together on occasion. The groups, however, carried on their activities apart, and while in the midst of retreat the right-wing nationalists were making some halting progress in their attempt for unity, the leftists also were engaged in consolidating their forces.

During the months when young Koreans were being trained at the Shengtze Academy, the Korean National Revolutionary party of Kim Won-bong does not seem to have accomplished any major activity. In December, 1937, the party made an alliance in Hankow with a handful of anarchists (the Korean Revolutionary Federation) and about a dozen Koreans from Nanking (the Korean National Liberation Workers League) and formed the Korean National Front Federation (*Chosŏn Minjok Chŏnsŏn Yŏnmaeng*). This was done mainly as a countermove against the union movement of the rightists.[15]

But when the graduation of the trainees from their six-month training period drew near—graduation was set for May 24, 1938—

members of the central committee of the Korean National Revolutionary party went to Chiangling, to which the academy had been evacuated, and began to prepare for future activities. A message to the trainees on May 17 announced that a central committee meeting would be held on May 19 to discuss the future direction of activities of the graduates and the problem of party unification. There were, so the message said, some extremists within the party who had to be dealt with at the meeting. The trainees were requested to select ten representatives to attend. On the night of May 17 the trainees met and decided on their policy. A minority advocated activities within China; the majority advocated advancing into Manchuria to join or act in liaison with a Chinese force, the Northeastern Anti-Japanese Volunteer Army (*Tungpei K'angjih Iyung-chün*). The majority opinion was adopted. On unification of the party the trainees decided that consolidation must be brought about gradually.[16]

The Korean National Revolutionary party thereupon held an all-party plenary conference from May 19 to May 22 at Chiangling and adopted nine resolutions, some of which, excerpted, are significant of developments that were to involve this party:

> Since the party is separated from the movement within Korea and confined to China proper, there has been no active expansion in the party enterprise and the entire membership is feeling privation. Therefore, the party must make a firm link with the entire movement in Korea and it must develop the movement as a part of the total Korean movement.
>
> . . . the main units of the party must advance to Manchuria, and the activities of the party members must be developed on the foundation of the masses. Because of geographical conditions and the character of the party, the advancement of the main units to Manchuria must take the form of armed collective operations.
>
> In the event that direct advance into Manchuria is impossible within a short period, the party must directly join in the anti-Japanese war. By meritorious acts it must win the recognition of the Chinese revolutionary world . . . By this means the connection with the movements in Korea and advancement to Manchuria will be made possible.
>
> Regardless of the form of activity to be taken by the armed units . . . the primary requirement is to maintain the special designation of Korea. Therefore, the members must not be dispersed to join various forces as individuals.
>
> Even if the members join in the anti-Japanese war in China, they must be sent to Manchuria as soon as it is possible, so that connections may be made with the masses in Korea.

Activities to mobilize the Korean masses living in the enemy-occupied area in China and intelligence activities in the same area are essential. But these are only accessory to the entire work . . .[17]

The plenary conference also drafted a policy to be followed in dealing with the Chinese government:

It must be realized that the most important mission of the unit is to advance to Manchuria, arm the Koreans in that area, and destroy the Japanese imperialism in Korea.

The present designation, the "Chinese Military Committee Special Mobile Unit, Korean Unit," must be altered to the "Korean National Revolutionary Party Army." Even if the designation cannot be altered, it must be recognized that this unit is in essence the army of the Korean National Revolutionary party.

Since the basic principle is to advance to the Manchurian area, we must be located in areas from which the advance toward Manchuria is most convenient.[18]

Despite this display of determination at the Chiangling conference, later developments revealed conflicts within the party. The academy graduates were in favor of marching north; Kim Won-bong, the party leader, opposed this. Kim wished to confine the activities of party to Kuomintang-occupied areas and thereby strengthen his hand in dealing with the Chinese government. The graduates, however, were fully aware of their predominant position within the party—in that they were its only assets—and were not willing to bend to the leader's wishes. This was the first sign of Kim's failing leadership.

Upon graduation all the former trainees were moved to Wuchang. There Kim Won-bong attempted to enforce his opinion against the decision of the plenary conference. The graduates discovered that he was secretly making arrangements with the Chinese government to confine their activities to Kuomintang-occupied areas, and a major split of the party occurred.[19]

On June 10 forty-nine party members, including six members of the central committee, issued a statement declaring their withdrawal from the party. This group crossed the Yangtze River to Hankow, where they organized the Korean Youth Wartime Service Corps (*Chosŏn Ch'ŏngnyŏn Chŏnsi Pongmu-dan*).[20] The corps is reported to have made some contact with the Chinese Communists' Eighth Route Army in North China and to have appealed for financial assistance.[21] The corps leader, Ch'oe Ch'ang-sŏk (Yi Kŏn-u), is reported to have held an extremely leftist ideology and to have regarded Kim Won-bong's policies and ideology as straggling.[22] Ch'oe's leadership might account for the group's making an approach to the Chinese Communists.

Kim Won-bong, being about to lose a large part of his following, proposed to the Chinese Military Council in July that young Koreans be organized into a Korean volunteer army, to be sent to various war areas to assist Chinese forces. The council agreed to this, on the condition that the Koreans of all groups would support it. Kim Won-bong immediately notified the Service Corps and Kim Ku's group and urged their coöperation. Kim Ku's group rejected the proposal, but the Service Corps, which was already feeling financial difficulty, immediately accepted, renaming itself the Korean Youth Vanguard League (*Chosŏn Ch'ŏngnyŏn Chŏnwi Tongmaeng*), and joind the Korean National Front Federation. This seems to have satisfied the council, which then approved the creation of the volunteer unit. On October 10 a ceremony formalizing the establishment of the Korean Volunteer Corps (*Chosŏn Ulyong-dae*) was held in Hankow. The corps was placed under a guidance committee composed of five members of the Political Department of the Chinese Military Council and four directors of the Korean National Front Federation. Kim Won-bong was selected as commander.[23]

The Korean Volunteer Corps consisted of two companies and a headquarters unit. In the composition of the two companies, party alignment was maintained. Thus the first company consisted of forty-four members of the Korean National Revolutionary party under the leadership of Pak Hyo-sam, the second of thirty members of the Vanguard League under Yi Ik-sŏng. The personnel of the headquarters unit consisted of thirteen members of both groups and was located in Kweilin, Kwangsi Province. The party character of the companies became important when the assignment of areas was made: Vanguard League members wished to move into Manchuria, and Kim Won-bong wished the Korean Revolutionary party members to remain within China proper. Therefore, twenty-four members of the second company, with two members of the headquarters unit, were sent to the military command covering Honan and Shansi provinces, and their commander and the remaining fifteen men of the company were sent to the command covering the area north of the Yangtze River. The entire first company was assigned to the command covering the area south of the Yangtze.[24]

The Korean Volunteer Corps was used mainly for directing political propaganda toward Japanese troops and the Chinese people:

> Members went to various front lines, spread leaflets among the enemy, posted slogans, and broadcasted to the enemy troops at the front lines (through megaphones) . . . Besides these activities, the Koreans helped various headquarters translate enemy documents, train political personnel, and interrogate and educate prisoners. They also participated in several battles.[25]

Meanwhile the Korean National Revolutionary party worked to enlarge its membership by sending out secret agents. The number of Koreans in China, especially in the Japanese-occupied areas, was rapidly increasing, and both the party and the Volunteer Corps propagandized among the newcomers. Although results were not spectacular, by 1940 the corps was able to establish a third branch unit composed mostly of recruits from Japanese-occupied areas.

Late in 1938 a united front of the Korean revolutionaries was proposed again, this time by the Chinese Nationalist government, which was fighting against the Japanese in a united front with the Chinese Communists. In November, Ch'ên Kuo-fu consulted Kim Ku in Changsha, where he was recovering from his wound, and got his consent to the idea. In January, 1939, Kim Won-bong was called to Chungking, where he was met by Ch'ên Ch'êng, a famous leader and member of the Military Council; he also agreed to the Chinese advice. In May the two Korean leaders issued an "Open Letter to Comrades and Compatriots." In this they confessed to past mistakes in being unable to unite for the common cause, reviewed the favorable international climate, elaborated on the weakness of Japan, expounded their political principles, and urged all Koreans to unite. The formula advocated in the letter was to dissolve all the existing organizations and establish a new united organization.[26]

Unity, however, was not attained. The two leaders seem to have been willing to accept the advice of the Chinese; their followers were not. In the leftist camp of Kim Won-bong were some extremists who denounced any sort of alliance with Kim Ku; some others, less extreme, would accept unity in a party alliance or federation, but were not willing to liquidate their organizations. Kim Ku faced a similar problem. Some of his supporters were opposed to any alliance with leftists or Communists, whatever the circumstances might be. Especially strong opposition came from Kim's supporters in the United States and Hawaii who were providing him with financial support. When the project collapsed, Kim Ku offered an apology to his supporters and followers for his misjudgment.[27]

The Japanese police duly recorded these developments:

> [Despite the declaration,] the two groups are still working separately. Kim Won-bong is relying on the Korean Volunteer Corps. In order to counter this, Kim Ku organized the Revolutionary Front Combat Area Maneuvering Unit (*Kwangbok Chinsŏn Chŏnji Kongjaktae*) in Liuchou, Kwangsi Province, in early February, 1939.[28]

Although its name was long and impressive, the new unit under Kim Ku had only about thirty members. Presumably this group did not accomplish much, for Kim's account of the years between 1938 and 1940 is largely concerned, aside from his efforts to unify the Korean nationalists, with the retreat of his colleagues and their families from Nanking to Changsha and then to Chungking.

Proposals for an alliance of the nationalists—the left and the right—had been recurrent ever since the Provisional Government was established in Shanghai. After the disruption, efforts were continued by both the leftists and the rightists. Under multiple pressures not quite confined to the ideological issues, all these efforts failed. But the failure in 1939 was more significant than those before, for the Korean revolutionaries then had a good environment and incentive to unite, factors absent in the past. This was the first time the Chinese Nationalists had exerted any kind of pressure upon them to unite. It is true that the Chinese united front was brought about only after the Sian incident, when Chiang Kai-shek was kidnapped by subordinates who exerted pressure for a united front; nonetheless, the Chinese Nationalists in 1939 were eager for the Koreans to unite similarly.

Further, the principal leaders were desirous of forming a united front. As they declared in the "Open Letter," it was a necessity, regardless of Chinese pressure. There is no doubt that Kim Ku was anti-Communist or that Kim Won-bong was a Communist sympathizer; yet they were willing to join for a greater cause.

Analysis of the opposition illuminates some important factors. In 1935 the leftists under Kim Won-bong had been willing to establish the Korean National Revolutionary party, which bore some semblance to a united front; but at that time they were sure that the leadership would be held by the old members of the Uiyŏldan. Kim Ku, the dominating figure among the rightists, was absent from the alliance. In the proposed united front of 1939 Kim Ku was the central figure and the leftists, no longer sure of their position, were unwilling to gamble with their power.

Within the leftist camp the strongest opposition came from the groups in North China. Already Kim Won-bong's party had split, in 1938, because some of the members thought him "straggling" in his ideology and policies. The split came over the choice of areas of operation for the graduates of the Shengtze Academy, but the seceders had other apprehensions: a united front against the Japanese was a desirable thing, but at no point were they willing to sacrifice the integrity of the Communist organizations for it. Since even the united front of the Chinese was precarious—three hundred Chinese Communist guerrillas were alleged to have been massacred in Shantung in the spring of 1939—there was some justification for the Korean Communists' rejection of the proposal to dissolve parties for the sake of a new united party.

The uncoöperative attitude of the Korean rightists in China toward communism has been noted. Kim Ku relates in his autobiography that the members of his party strongly objected to his proposal for complete unity with the leftists although they did not object to the idea of an alliance.[29] There remained also the objections from the nationalists in the United States and Hawaii, who in the 1920's had been largely passive but began to participate actively after 1931. Since these nationalists gave financial and moral support to the Provisional Government, their sentiment had to be considered. Since the nationalists in Siberia had suffered greatly from the advent of the Bolsheviks, and in view of the general unpopularity of communism in the United States, the apprehensive attitude of the Korean nationalists in the United States and Hawaii is understandable.

The separation of the Korean revolutionaries into two large blocs had become more and more apparent as the years went by. Was Korea doomed to be divided into two camps when liberation came? Before reaching a conclusion on this question we must explore the developments after 1940.

12

Finale of the Exiled Movement

THE half-decade between 1940 and 1945 opened a new era in world history. Atomic weapons were created, and the United States emerged for the first time as an active world leader. Perhaps even more significantly, the embryonic developments of the so-called cold war were forming rapidly during this period.

In China, the Kuomintang and the Chinese Communist party were still maintaining their precarious alliance to repel their common enemy, Japan, but the Communist party was ever increasing in size and power and was beginning to challenge the Kuomintang more strongly than before. The increase of its forces in North China had a direct impact upon the Korean nationalist movement, and indeed upon the future of Korea. It was in this period that the Chinese Communists began to develop their Korea policy.

One effect of their policy was to perpetuate the bipolarization of the Korean revolutionaries, whose divided condition they exploited to the maximum in order to foster the power of the extreme left faction. In so doing they repulsed the moderate left elements who were in favor of forming a united front with the right-wing nationalists.

It has been noted in the previous chapter that left-wing Korean revolutionaries in China were reunited in the Korean Volunteer Corps in October, 1938. This resulted from a desperate move by Kim Won-bong to prevent the disintegration of the left. Some of his allies and followers had opposed him on the grounds of ideological purity: Kim was a Communist, but not a doctrinaire. Others raised objections over the area of operation: Kim favored the Kuomintang-occupied areas, the extremists the northern front occupied by the Chinese Communists.

The Korean Volunteer Corps proved to be no more than a stopgap measure. The action taken by Kim Won-bong, with the aid of the Kuomintang, was to place the dissidents under his nominal command, but to send them off to North China where they could operate independently. All of this, including the northward movement of the dissidents, was financed by Kuomintang funds and conducted under Kuomintang protection. Once they were in North China, these few dozen youths, the second company of the Korean Volunteer Corps, quickly found a new ally.

Between 1939 and 1940 a new Korean leader was emerging in North China with Chinese Communist backing. The limited information available on Mu Chŏng indicates that he had been very active in the Chinese Communist movement and had attained positions of importance in the Communist army.[1]

Whether the initiative to organize a special unit within the Chinese Communist army composed solely of the Koreans was taken by the Chinese or Mu Chŏng himself cannot be determined. According to Sŏ Pyŏng-gon, Mu was relieved of the post of chief of operations of the Eighth Route Army because of a stomach ailment and was obliged to rest for a year. When he had regained his health, he gathered about three hundred young Koreans from Shanghai, Nanking, Peking, and the Wuhan area and established a Korean unit. A number of these were graduates of the Anti-Japanese Military-Political College in Yenan, and some were graduates of military schools in Moscow. The latter were youths who had fought the Japanese in Manchuria and then been sent to Moscow to study military science. Mu Chŏng's Korean unit began to engage in battles in 1939.[2]

Quite naturally, the second company under Yi Ik-sŏng and other members of the Korean Volunteer Corps who were dissatisfied with the leadership of Kim Won-bong and had been seeking ties with the Chinese Communists rallied around Mu Chŏng:

Immediately after the establishment of the Korean Volunteer Corps . . . the leader of the Vanguard Unit, which had previously seceded from Korean National Revolutionary party of Kim Won-bong, went to Yenan, made contacts with an extreme-left Korean Communist, Mu Chŏng, and established in 1939 a preparatory committee of the North China Korean Youth Federation (*Hwabuk Chosŏn Ch'ŏngnyŏn Yŏnhaphoe*) . . . The main purpose of the Federation was to advance the Volunteer Corps to the north.[3]

On January 10, 1941, the North China Korean Youth Federation was formally launched in the Chintungnan T'aihang mountain region. Mu Chŏng became its president. How many persons participated at the beginning is not known, but the membership increased rapidly as numbers of young Koreans came in from Chungking and Loyang. Three branches were established during 1941, with about twenty members in each. The first branch had at least fifty members by August, 1942.[4]

The immediate goal of the Federation was to absorb the Koreans arriving in North China. An initial declaration strongly urged both men and women to join the Federation. It appealed to patriotism for Korea and stressed the possibilities for the liberation of Korea presented by the Sino-Japanese conflict. All revolutionary individuals and groups, regardless of ideology or religion, were to be welcomed.[5]

Although in its declaration and platforms the Federation did not mention a Communist society as a final goal, there is little room for doubt regarding its ideology. The first issue of the Federation's *Chosŏn Ch'ŏngnyŏn* ("Korean Youth") referred to the United States and Great Britain as imperialistic nations which were about to be destroyed by imperialistic wars and presented the Soviet Union as a nation rapidly moving toward the liberation of oppressed peoples.[6] Later developments suggest that Communist leaders, Korean and Chinese, had already reached a basic agreement on the future policies toward Korea which were to guide immediate policies toward the Korean nationalist movement.

Establishment of the Federation was a step. The Communist, or rather the Chinese Communist, design on Korea can be reconstructed as follows: The Sino-Korean relationship is of great significance for the national interest of China; it is necessary that the future Korea be in friendly hands; it is most logical, therefore, to build up a Korean army under the guidance of Chinese Communists and see to it that the members of the army be indebted to and share a common ideology with them; all Korean troops now under the Kuomintang must be brought under the Chinese Communist party so that the Kuomintang-sponsored troops shall not offer any rivalry in the future.

This fantastic yet far-sighted policy was immediately put into execution. By July, 1941, most of the Korean Volunteer Corps members under the Kuomintang were transferred to North China undetected by the Chinese Nationalists. The new arrivals, in combination with Korean forces already present, were reorganized as the North China Branch Unit of the Volunteer Corps. The new force was, of course, under the command of Chinese Communists. Pak Hyo-sam, commander of the third company of the Volunteer Corps, established in Chungking in January, 1940, was put over the North China Branch Unit. Yi Ik-sŏng, commander of the second company, and Wang Cha-in, commander of the first company, were put over companies in the new force.[7]

Some contacts still existed between the North China Branch Unit and Chungking.[8] But the establishment of the new force made a major change in the balance of power. Kim Won-bong still was officially commander of the Korean Volunteer Corps, and the North China Branch Unit was officially part of the older organization, but Kim's source of support was the Kuomintang, whereas the North China Korean Youth Federation under Mu Chŏng and the North China Branch Unit were controlled by the Chinese Communist party and no longer needed financial support from Kim or the Kuomintang. Thus Kim lost control of the troops in the north.

How was this seemingly impossible task of stealing the Korean troops from the Kuomintang accomplished? Or was this merely a voluntary action on the part of the Koreans? Korean Communist sources are very vague with regard to these questions. The answers, however, have been provided by a Chinese author, Ssu Ma-lu, who was able to speak with unquestionable authority. Ssu, a graduate of the Communist party school in Yenan and at the time a party member, was private secretary to Kim Won-bong in Chungking. He was also the head of the Chinese Editorial Committee of the Korean Volunteer Corps. In his autobiography Ssu first deals with his observation of the general condition of the Korean Volunteer Corps and its relationship with the Chinese Communist party:

The Korean Volunteer Corps had approximately 300 members. . . . Although the number of personnel was not very large, their quality was extremely good. All were around twenty-five years of age. During thirty years of Korea's loss of sovereignty, most of them grew up in revolutionary families. They had wandered about with their fathers since the downfall of Korea and were ceaselessly instilled with revolutionary sentiment. Their bodies were strong; they went through difficulties in living, were not afraid of sacrificing themselves, and were firm in determination, pure in thoughts, simple in social relations. Also every one understood at least the Chinese, Korean, and Japanese languages. These Korean youths who had all these qualifications did not know that they were already noticed by Chou En-lai (who was then in Chungking) and were targets hunted by the Chinese Communist party. At this time (September, 1940) the Chinese Communists were studying ways of maneuvering the situation.[9]

Ssu Ma-lu published several articles in Chungking on the Korean problem. Since Chinese writers familiar with this subject were few, Ssu came to be recognized as a Korean expert. When the Chinese Communist party noted that his writings were from the Marx-Leninist viewpoint, their leaders in Chungking gave him many bonuses.

Hsü Ping, an old acquaintance and superior of Ssu, was ordered to cultivate him and then invite him to a dinner at the Chou En-lai mansion. Ssu, still a plain party member, had the glory of dining with such persons as Chou En-lai, Tung Pi-wu (later vice-president of the Peking regime), Yeh Chien-ying (chief of staff of the Eighteenth Group Army and later the head of Kwangtung Province), Mrs. Hsü (Chang Hsiao-mei, the leader of the women's movement in Chungking), Ch'en Chia-k'ang (confidential secretary of the Chinese Communist party delegation) and Hsü Ping (later the head of the Newspaper Office of the Peking government). Hsü praised him in front of these party leaders, at the same time assuring him that he was trusted by the party and regarded as very important.[10]

After the dinner Ssu had a private talk with Chou En-lai for a few minutes. Chou told him: "The Sino-Korean relations will be of great importance in the future. At the time of the first Sino-Japanese war, China failed in Korea and this was the signal for the collapse of the Ch'ing dynasty." Chou perhaps intimated that Ssu was in a crucial position to influence these relations. Ssu, "exalted and glorified" by this treatment, was conquered by vanity, at least temporarily. Presently he was being consulted frequently by Hsü Ping, who

> gradually demanded that I let him know everything about the Korean Volunteer Corps, factions among the Koreans in China, their relationship with the Chinese [Nationalist] government, internal organizations of the Korean Volunteer Corps, individual analysis of the Korean revolutionaries, etc. I told him everything I knew and searched for new information when I did not already know.

Later Ssu Ma-lu was put in touch with Ch'en Chia-k'ang, given the assignment of persuading Kim Won-bong to send the Korean Volunteer Corps troops to North China, the region occupied by the Chinese Communists. Of course, this transfer went counter to Kim's policies. His desire to keep the troops in the Kuomintang area had precipitated a rupture of the Korean Volunteer Corps. But, according to Ssu, persuading him was an easy task, for the following reasons: Ssu had provided Kim with much information; Kim trusted him and valued his opinions; and Kim's uncle (Kim Tu-bong) and wife both supported Ssu's opinion. Ssu told Kim that the Japanese were sending great numbers of Korean immigrants into North China, and that expansion and development of the Volunteer Corps would be possible only if it were sent there, behind the enemy lines.[11]

Although Kim Won-bong was easily persuaded, there were obstacles. According to Ssu, the Chinese Nationalist government paid close attention to any movements of the Volunteer Corps, and this attention was very difficult to evade. Nothing, however, was impossible for the Communist leaders:

> Therefore, the party sent me an assistant. Through another friend of Kim Won-bong, he was introduced to the Korean Volunteer Corps and became the secretary. He assisted me in giving false reports to the government. After that, we sent out 80 per cent of the Korean Volunteer Corps troops to North China, and while the government was still asleep we sent out twenty to thirty troops to the Third, Fifth, and the Sixth war areas, shuffling them back and forth. Our secret was never discovered, and we even obtained commendations [from the Kuomintang]. Kim Won-bong received funds from both the Kuomintang and the Chinese Communist party.[12]

The Chinese Communist leaders thus accomplished their initial goal through the aid of Ssu Ma-lu and by cunning strategies of their own, and Kim Won-bong was cast aside. Ssu writes that when all the Korean Volunteer Corps troops reached North China, the Chinese Communist party suddenly changed their attitude. Ch'en Chia-K'ang told me in an authoritative tone of voice, "We Communists depend on trust; we must never take over comrades for money. The Corps wanted to go to North China. This was their own wish, a voluntary one. We have already helped them. The Korean revolution is their own business.

Ssu pleaded that Kim was suffering because he was in disfavor with the Kuomintang and in great financial distress. Evidently the Kuomintang had discovered the intrigues and Kim had suffered the consequences, being in no position to explain the situation. After a long argument Ch'en Chia-k'ang agreed to talk with Chou En-lai and lend Kim Won-bong 10,000 yuan. After a few days, however, Ch'en gave Ssu only 5,000 yuan. Kim was very displeased and wanted to return the money. Ssu had to placate him with improvised explanations.[13]

Since, as we have related, the second company of the Korean Volunteer Corps had wished for various reasons to go to North China, the transfer was not totally owing to the Communist trickery. But the second company had no more than seventy or eighty members; therefore, Ssu's account explains the shifting of the rest of the Corps to the north.

Ssu relates further miseries of Kim Won-bong. Kim wished to go to North China when the officers of the Korean Volunteer Corps were taken there by airplane. But Chou En-lai refused him. Ch'en Chia-k'ang's official explanation was that "Comrade En-lai wishes to have Mr. Kim stay in Chungking. Activities here are becoming more important than ever. Revolutionary activities are the same anywhere." But, Ssu says, the real reason was that the party feared that if Kim went to North China, the leadership of the Volunteer Corps would fall to him again. He was finally branded by the party as a "petty-bourgeois, opportunist, and individual heroist," although he was not publicly condemned.[14]

In the meantime the Korean Volunteer Corps–North China Branch Unit set out to realize its objectives and by August, 1942, according to the Japanese police, had sent about twenty agents into various occupied areas, including Shanghai, Hankow, and Peking, to work among the Koreans coming into North China.[15]

In September, 1941, the North China Korean Youth School was established with the support of the Chinese Communists, and in

January, 1942, its classes were begun, with Mu Chŏng as the principal.[16] It was subsequently renamed the North China Korean Revolution School (*Hwabuk Chosŏn Hyŏngmyŏng Hakkyo*). According to a Japanese account in 1944, the school was "designed to educate and train surrendered and kidnapped Koreans." Any Korean man or woman above sixteen years of age was qualified for enrollment. The school offered the attractions of free tuition and living expenses along with possibilities for enrollment later in higher educational institutions.[17]

In August, 1942, the North China Korean Youth Federation was renamed the North China Korean Independence League (*Hwabak Chosŏn Tongnip Tongmaeng*), and the Korean Volunteer Corps–North China Branch Unit was renamed the Korean Volunteers Army, North China Branch Unit. Kim Tu-bong, a noted scholar, came to Yenan from Chungking and was placed as the chairman of the Korean Independence League's executive committee. Mu Chŏng replaced Pak Hyo-sam as the commander of the Korean Volunteers Army. Declarations and platforms issued at this time mention such objectives as "long-term and continuous anti-enemy activities," and "the establishment of a revolutionary base behind the enemy-occupied area." The declaration of the Independence League asserted: "We shall firmly and steadily continue our struggle against the Japanese and complete the emancipation of the Korean people through enlarging the political influence, increasing the revolutionary strength, tempering ourselves, strengthening internal unity, and uniting the compatriots in North China, the revolutionists within Korea, the revolutionary organizations, and the armed units." [18]

As the war progressed in the Far East and the Japanese began to lose ground, the Chinese Communist forces increased in strength and the Korean organizations associated with them in North China also gained momentum. Thus the Korean Communists and proto-Communists assisted the cause of the Chinese Communist warfare against Japan and at the same time built up their own strength. There is every indication that these activities were continued without substantial change up to V-J Day. After the Japanese surrender, the Korean Volunteers Army moved to Manchuria, fortified by a significant number of Korean youths who had deserted from the Japanese Army, and there aided the Chinese Communists in warfare against the Chinese Nationalists.[19] They eventually returned to Korea and became an important part of the North Korean forces.

The intrusion of the Chinese Communist party into Korean politics in China moved most of the Korean left-wing nationalists to North China. There, under the Communists, they carried on their activities independently of the rest of the nationalists, who were congregated in the Chungking-Kweilin region.

Kim Ku's account of the years from 1938 to 1940 probably is typical for all the right-wing nationalists. They and their families were occupied with moving from Nanking to Changsha and then on southwestwardly, mostly to Chungking, the Chinese capital. Efforts to increase their political effectiveness by consolidation were continued, however, and in April, 1940, three parties—the Korean Independence party, Korean National party, and Korean Revolutionary party—dissolved themselves and joined in a new Korean Independence party (*Hanguk Tongnip-dang*). Some of the supporters in Hawaii—the United Society (*Tanhaphoe*) and the Patriotic Corps (*Aegukdan*)—dissolved and united in the Hawaiian branch of the new party.[20]

The declaration and several other pronouncements of the Korean Independence party maintained the policy of support for the Provisional Government and its objectives.[21] Since the leadership of the party and the government was held by the same persons, there was virtually no difference between the two entities. Kim Ku was the head of both. The only new policy was that "officers and troops shall be trained in unity, and the Revolutionary Army shall be established." (This was a policy established in 1937 when a military committee was created within the Provisional Government, but the committee had not performed any function in the interval.) In an interview reported in the *Hsiangkang Lipao* ("Hong Kong Independence"), June 23–24, 1940, Kim Ku stated: "In order that the people who lost sovereignty over their country should recover their land, it is necessary to cultivate power. Where does this power come from? It comes from unity and consolidation." The article went on to comment:

> The greatest contribution toward China of the Korean revolutionaries after the rise of the Sino-Japanese war is the united army of the Chinese and the Koreans in Manchuria. . . . At present the main activities of the Koreans

in the deep inland of China is to prepare and organize the Restoration Army. On this matter Mr. Kim, representing the Provisional Government and the various parties, has appealed to President Chiang and has received his approval.[22]

The point stressed in the interview was the forming of the Revolutionary Army, or as it came to be designated, the Korean Restoration Army (*Hanguk Kwangbok-kun*). In making the "greatest contribution," the Koreans of the leftist bloc were already doing their share, and it was natural that the rightists should be eager to equal or surpass them. Further, although the Chinese government was sympathetic to Kim Ku and the Provisional Government, continuing support could not be expected without their contributing materially to the Chinese cause. Kim Ku expressed the situation bluntly: "The Chinese government built a house for our big family [of all the nationalists] and also bought another house in Chungking for our use, but it was indifferent to our request for assistance toward the independence movement." [23] Considering the difficulties the Chinese faced during the years after 1937, their attitude is understandable.

Kim Ku let it be known that he could no longer keep on asking for help and hence wished to go to the United States, where he might appeal to the American government. When he applied to the Chinese government for a passport, an official remarked, "You have been in China for a long time. Would it not be better to leave a record of some achievement?" Kim states that he then offered his plan for the Restoration Army and obtained immediate approval.[24] Perhaps he dramatizes the story for effect, but the preparations were made in any case, and on September 17, 1940, the creation of the army was formally marked by ceremonies in Chungking attended by Chinese officials and other guests.

According to the *Takungpao* ("The Impartial," Chungking), about two hundred officers took part in the ceremonies.[25] The Restoration Army was given widespread publicity by the Chinese press in greatly exaggerated form. Actually it was a modest venture, for although the Chinese government was willing to provide support, there were in the area very few young Koreans available for enlistment. It is doubtful whether the total manpower of the army, let alone its officers, reached the figure of two hundred. A Japanese report on four of the five units of the army put their strength as, respectively, fifty,

fifty, five, and "a handful." [26] A summary account of the army by a Korean author, covering its activities up to August, 1943, indicates that its numbers were increased in the meanwhile; even with allowance for some exaggeration, the record is not ignoble: "newly mobilized troops and officers, 3,600; those receiving training, 2,900; enemy facilities destroyed, 17; guerrilla operations, 14; propaganda materials distributed, 8 kinds; underground organizations, 27; members of the army killed in action or died of illness, 175." [27]

In July, 1942, the Restoration Army was reorganized into three branch units, with about forty troops of the Korean Volunteer Corps forming the First Branch Unit. These were troops still under the direction of Kim Won-bong, who at this time also became vice-commander of the Restoration Army, thus signaling the amalgamation of the Volunteer Corps forces with those under the Provisional Government. The Volunteer Corps troops in North China, however, ignored the reorganization and kept their old name. The inclusion of the leftist Kim Won-bong in the leadership was significant of pressures the Provisional Government and the Korean Independence party were experiencing. The episode of the secret transfer of most of the Volunteer Corps troops to the north must have compromised all Koreans in the eyes of the Chinese government, especially if we assume that the true situation of Kim's involvement with the Chinese Communists had not yet been revealed, wherefore the Kuomintang government would be demanding more than token evidences of coöperation between the Korean right and left groups. The reorganization of the Restoration Army in July, 1942, was part of negotiations between Chungking and the Provisional Government which postulated that the supreme command of the army rested in Chiang Kai-shek, that the Restoration Army should not occupy Chinese territory without permission or appoint administrative officials at will, and that it should continue its coöperation with the Kuomintang forces until it reached the Korean border. Thus the Chungking government was tightening its control over the Koreans. The sought-for unity of all Korean elements led to the acceptance of leftist, probably Communist, elements into the Provisional Government.

As early as December, 1941, the Provisional Legislative Assembly had forced the resignation of its president, Kim Pung-jun, who had received Communists as members of the Assembly without going through established procedures for admitting them.[28] But in October, 1942, leftists were admitted, and two of them, Kim Kyu-sik and Chang Kŏn-sang, were elected to the National Council, the decision-making body of the Provisional Government. Because of conflicts of opinion, the leftists obstructed proceedings of the Assembly for three months between October and December, 1943, and deadlocked the proposed constitutional revision onward until April, 1944.[29] It should be understood, however, that the rightists were tenacious in their viewpoints and that the exiled leaders did not have a great deal of business at hand except that of building and rebuilding the government. Kim Ku says: "My life in Chungking consisted in taking shelter [from the Japanese air raids] with the members of the Provisional Government and eating and sleeping once in a while." [30]

The constitutional revision, when passed, increased the membership of the National Council from eight to fourteen. In the ensuing elections the council posts went to eight members of the Korean Independence party, four of the Korean National Revolutionary party, one Korean People's Liberation League leader, and one anarchist. This distribution was probably according to the proportional strength of each group in Chungking. In the cabinet Kim Ku remained as president, the new post of vice-president went to the moderate leftist Kim Kyu-sik, and Kim Won-bong was Minister of Military Affairs.[31]

Thus the nationalists in Chungking, right and left, in early 1944 again presented a united front under the Provisional Government—the first since the disruption of the government in 1921. But the alliance in 1944 was much the weaker, and we detect something unholy in it. Chinese pressure has been indicated as impelling the Koreans to this semblance of unity. But if we consider that the leaders took months to decide on somewhat trivial matters, it is reasonable to look for other motives.

In the forming of the coalition cabinet, in the late summer or early autumn of 1944, timing seems to have been a factor. The admission of leftists to the Assembly occurred in October, 1942. In November of that year the Japanese fleet was defeated in the Solomon Islands. In November of 1943 the leaders of the Allies declared at Cairo that "in due course" Korea should become free and independent. By February, 1944, the invasion of the Marshall Islands had begun, and by June the invasion of France. It gradually had become clear that Japan and her allies would be defeated, and presently it was clear that the end of the war was approaching. The Korean nationalist leaders could, by 1944, contemplate the future of the Korean nation and, more particularly, their possible future roles in the homeland. This was a position quite different from that of 1919, when the leaders could only contemplate and quarrel over the means to win independence.

This is not to say, however, that the leaders in 1944 were merely selfish individuals whose primary interest was in promoting their own advantage. The nationalists' nearly half a century of bitter struggles had not been fought for personal well-being, internal feuds and factional struggles notwithstanding. As the end of the Second World War approached, they had, regardless of their political views, reason to be more patriotic than ever before. But patriotism and the contemplation of the future of Korea did not diminish the importance of the immediate problems. What if the Provisional Government were recognized by the Allies and allowed to return to Korea as a legitimate government? Obviously the leftist leaders, who had been aloof from the Provisional Government in the past, wanted to share the spoils. The rightists, on their part, did not wish to yield disproportionately to the leftists, whom they did not consider to be a part of the nationalist movement.

In 1945, in the midst of this right and left tension, some fifty young Koreans arrived in Chungking. All were deserters from the Japanese Army and most were so-called student volunteers enlisted by the Japanese in 1938 or afterwards.[32] First reaching the Chinese forces in Shantung, they had insisted that they be transferred to Chungking.[33] Korean and Chinese leaders were impressed, and the band of young Koreans indeed did offer new hope for the Korean nationalist leaders.[34]

Initially the feeling of the leaders was reciprocated. The new arrivals held deep respect for the nationalist leaders for their long dedication to the cause of liberation of the homeland. They were filled with determination to follow in the footsteps of the leaders and willing to sacrifice their lives, as some of their friends had already done in escaping from the Japanese Army. Within a matter of weeks, however, they discovered the deep current of factionalism. According to Chang Chun-ha:

> . . . members of the cabinet took turns to give us a talk every morning. We were not aware at first, but we soon realized that every talk was filled with propaganda about the member's own party and criticism of the others'. Frankly, we were bewildered. We were enraged by this betrayal. This was too far from what we had anticipated.[35]

Receptions for the new arrival were also used to win them into factions. The "student troops," as they were called, then refused to attend the receptions, including the one given by the Korean Independence party:

> So the tactics of reception parties failed completely. But they did not cease their attempt to win us into their own political parties. They seem to have realized that winning us in a group could not be accomplished. Now they changed their tactics to win us individually. They pursued their tactics tenaciously. Thus they invited a few of us for drinks. The Kim Won-bong group even used women to lure us. Their struggle was exactly like that of a roaring beast fighting for a piece of meat. This ugly scene went from bad to worse as days went by.[36]

Finally Chang Chun-ha announced at a public meeting that he would rather volunteer for the Japanese Air Force so that he might bomb the Provisional Government Building in Chungking. The student troops eventually were moved to Sian, where Yi Pŏm-sok, the head of the Second Branch Unit of the Korean Restoration Army, had made an agreement with an American intelligence unit to train young Koreans for missions behind the enemy lines.[37]

But the factional struggles did not cease, having become embittered men's habit, acquired through decades of harsh experience, a pattern of behavior, a means for survival, a way of life. The aggrieved and exasperated revolutionary leaders were the men who, returning to Korea, were to hold the foremost positions in postwar Korean politics.

The training of the student troops at Sian offered new hope for the rightist group, but suddenly the end of the war came, too soon for the Korean nationalists. Kim Ku received the news of the Japanese surrender with a feeling of disappointment and deflation while he was inspecting the trainees at Sian. This emotion did not stem solely from Kim's egocentricity, but from the Provisional Government's being deprived of the opportunity of establishing acknowledged claims over Korea. Kim Ku had failed to become another De Gaulle, whose provisional government was recognized by the Allies in October, 1944.

Kim relates that he went to Sian in a military airplane, but had to return in a civilian airplane. In Chungking the whole populace was in confusion, including the Korean nationalists. The Legislative Assembly was torn between two groups, one advocating immediate dissolution and return to Korea, the other the advancement of the Provisional Government into Korea as an entity. Kim Ku sided with the latter group, and the Korean Restoration Army started to enlist all the former Korean members of the Japanese Army in China.[38] But the United States occupation forces in Korea rejected the Provisional Government as a legitimate government; the nationalists, therefore, were obliged to return to Korea as individuals. Although the revolutionaries were given a celebratory reception honoring their record, they failed to execute the dream of transplanting the Provisional Government as the government of Korea.

Before closing this chapter we must look briefly into the developments among the supporters of the Provisional Government in the United States and Hawaii. These Koreans were important in the nationalist movement not only for their steady financial contributions to the Provisional Government, but also for their own activities toward liberation.

As has been indicated from time to time, Korean communities in the United States and Hawaii were torn by factional struggles caused by personal and ideological differences; however, intensification of war in the Far East had served as a stimulus for unity. In September, 1940, a union movement was launched, and on April 20, 1941, delegates from nine organizations met in Honolulu in the "Korean Conference Abroad." The delegates pledged the support of the Provisional Government and the yearly collection of fifteen dollars per person as an "independence fund." Two thirds of this fund was to be sent to the Provisional Government, the remainder being allocated to so-called diplomatic activities. Syngman Rhee was nominated to the post of a diplomatic agent, pending the decision of the Provisional Government in Chungking.[39]

The Conference also created the United Korean Committee in America, which continued propaganda for the cause of Korean independence, particularly urging the recognition of the Provisional Government by the United States, and provided some financial support for the Provisional Government, secured the exemption of Koreans in United States territory from the Alien Registration Act of 1940, and organized Korean units in the California National Guard.[40] But unity was disrupted in 1943, when Syngman Rhee's group (the *Dongjihoe*) seceded from the committee.[41]

Some mention must be made of the activities of Syngman Rhee on behalf of the long-established Korean Committee and the Provisional Government. Rhee had been relentlessly carrying on pseudo-diplomatic work aimed at the recognition of the Provisional Government by Western powers. In some periods, as in the years from 1919 to 1923 and from 1941 to 1943, his efforts were aided by the Korean community in the United States, but in some years he had only the support of his party in Hawaii. According to his official biographer,

> The late thirties were dark days for Syngman Rhee. His policy of seeking to revive his lost nation through appeals to the self-interest and good sense of the West was seemingly bankrupt. His leadership never made any deep impression on the American officials to whom he tried to appeal, and as decade piled upon decade with his program barren of results, his own following began to disintegrate. Damaging divisions developed among the expatriate Koreans, and the Korean National Association in Hawaii came into the control of men who opposed Rhee with great bitterness. . . . Rhee was denounced as stubborn, uncompromising and ambitious, and was charged with clinging to the shreds of a discredited program in the vain hope of salvaging some kind of personal advantage. His most loyal friends and supporters were weary from years of fruitless struggle and sacrifice. In those days Rhee had little but his religious faith to sustain him.[42]

Between 1941 and 1945 Rhee sent a series of letters to the Department of State appealing for American recognition, but the Department largely ignored Rhee's claims, even questioning his qualification as the representative of Korea.[43] Except for the Cairo Declaration in November, 1943, the dark days for Rhee did not brighten much until 1945.

In April, 1945, when the United Nations Conference was held in San Francisco, Korean leaders from different groups in the United States and Hawaii again assembled together—only temporarily—to present the case of Korea, but the "Korean representatives" were not admitted to the conference. An appeal from the Provisional Government to the United Nations Conference did not receive any response.[44] The nationalists approached various delegations at the conference and lobbied for the inclusion of Korea as a charter member of the United Nations, but no one was willing to recognize the exiles' government.[45] It should be remembered that the host nation, the United States, gave no encouragement to the Korean nationalists. They were at best met with pity, at worst with contempt.

Thus the movement abroad drew to a close in 1945 with the nationalists disunited, frustrated, and exasperated. The opening of the Sino-Japanese war in 1937 and the entrance of the United States into the Second World War in 1941 had aroused high hopes. The nationalists had assumed that Chinese national interests coincided with the aspirations of the Koreans and that therefore a grand army of the Korean people might be established with Chinese aid. They had also assumed that the United States, when it was finally at war with Japan, would quickly grant recognition to their provisional government and render all the support demanded. If we use the anticipations of the nationalists as a standard for judgment, the Korean nationalist movement was a failure. Kim Ku's deflated reaction to the Japanese surrender attests to this interpretation.

The failure to establish the grand army of the Korean people was not owing to a lack of sympathy of the Chinese government. The Chinese would have welcomed a large army of Koreans who could contribute substantially to the war against the Japanese. All the young Korean men living within the Chinese jurisdiction were enlisted, but the number was not sufficient for even a battalion. A much larger number of young men of Korean origin could be found in the United States and Hawaii, but they were American citizens and subject to other obligations.

Still, the Provisional Government could have assembled a larger unit had not the Chinese Communists laid their plans for utilizing Koreans. If the Korean soldiers in North China had remained under its control, the Provisional Government could have kept more prestige and status with the Chinese and, indeed, could have asserted more rights in postwar Korean politics. The Chinese Communists, however, were more astute in assaying the future of the Korean question than the Koreans themselves.

The weakness of the nationalist movement was not confined to its inability to establish an army. The exiles were completely cut off from Korea for a considerable period. Only through the student troops who arrived in 1945 were they able to hear directly how Korea had changed since the 1920's. Enlisting the support of the Korean people within the homeland would have been impossible to undertake.

It is understandable, then, that the United States and other foreign powers at war against Japan should not have been willing to recognize the Provisional Government. The Chinese government did conclude agreements with the Provisional Government on military matters, but this was not tantamount to recognizing it as the legitimate government representing the Korean people. Other foreign powers had no basis for treating the exiles as the representatives of a nation. Even the government of the United States, if it had been willing to recognize a Korean government-in-exile, lacked a basis for deciding which of the rival claimants truly represented Korea.

Factionalism among the nationalists not only did not subside after 1940: it became intensified. The measure of power among the nationalists in China was the number of followers each leader had under him. This explains the harsh competition for the student troops at Chungking in 1945.

The problem of factionalism among the exiled politicians is closely related to the question of leadership. The lack of a dominant leader perpetuated the factional struggles. But how could a dominant leader have emerged among the exiled nationalists? The two essential qualifications for a strong leader under the circumstances prevalent in China were that he should have the ability to obtain substantial foreign aid and that his personality should attract and retain followers. To obtain foreign aid, however, it would be necessary for him to show his power. Without a large following to carry out whatever he proposed, he could not show his power. Thus he would have to compromise with different factions to present a picture of strength. But when such a centrifugal group was so formed, how could he exercise any discipline to maintain control? When particularly harsh rivalry exists, as it did among the nationalists, no one leader can become dominant. The problem can be seen to be extremely acute when we consider the fact that the number of Koreans available for recruitment as followers was extremely small.

Finally, we must also take cognizance of the problem of ideology.

The inroads made by communism into Korean politics in China accelerated the serious centrifugal forces already present. The stress of division according to ideological lines became particularly acute after 1940, when the Chinese Communists began to take an active interest in the Koreans. The relationship between the traditional, pure, or rightist nationalist camp and the leftist camp had been strained, but there had been frequent attempts at coalition. The Chinese Communists, however, removed the extreme left group to North China and separated them geographically from the other nationalists.

This brings us to the question presented at the end of the preceding chapter. Assuming that the United States and the Soviet Union had not divided Korea into two parts for military occupation purposes, would the leaders in postwar Korea have been capable of working together without destroying each other? Since there are many contingent factors to be considered, this question cannot be answered adequately. But the evidence of prewar Korean politics in China leads us to answer in the negative.

The failure to achieve a truly united front during the prewar and wartime period considerably weakened the nationalist movement, but for the time being there were no other consequences. If the rightists and the Communists could not agree, they could operate separately. What would have happened, then, if these rival camps had been confronted suddenly with the responsibilities of governing a nation? Each group would have competed for more power and influence among the masses, and, had the balance of power tilted too unfavorably to one side, the weaker camp would inevitably have resorted to violence to restore the balance. The revolutionaries demonstrated throughout four decades of struggles that they were not prone to compromise. Nor would they concede defeat gracefully. The extreme and closed character of the legacy of the past fostered no tradition of compromise among the Koreans.

A final factor to be considered is foreign influence. The Chinese Communists made it clear by 1940 that they considered the Korean question to be of utmost importance. They were not willing to let Korea slip into unfriendly hands. It is true that the Chinese Communists did not take a major role in postwar Korean affairs until 1950. They were too engrossed with their own problem of unifying China. But it was unlikely that they would long abstain from Korean politics if and when their interests were impaired and when they had the means to manipulate the situation. Chou En-lai's statement of September, 1940, that "The Sino-Korean relations will be of great importance in the future," echoed sharply over the world a decade later.

V

Nationalism within Korea

13

Japanese Rule: The Middle Phase

THE MARCH FIRST movement brought about a number of significant changes in Korea. The Japanese government under Premier Hara Takashi made comparatively drastic adjustments in its policy toward the annexed country. The rigid military dictatorship of Governors-General Terauchi and Hasegawa was replaced by the appeasement policy of Admiral Saitō Minoru. Gendarmes were replaced by civilian police, although many gendarmes merely changed their titles and uniforms. The publishing of Korean newspapers and magazines was permitted. Organizations could be formed and could hold meetings. Short of allowing direct appeals for independence or the overthrow of the *status quo*, the new regime exhibited political leniency. The line between legitimate and illegitimate activities was very flexibly drawn, however, and the always efficient police were ever at hand to suppress any trend toward subversiveness.

In the intellectual sphere, a period of disillusionment set in. Many Korean intellectuals had aspired to Western liberalism as their ideal. But the West had failed them in 1919 by not showing any intention of practising what, in Wilson's Fourteen Points, it had seemed to preach. Perhaps the West showed a course for the Korean people to take, but they were too feeble to follow it, and they had no outside help. Disillusionment with Western liberalism led most intellectuals to reexamine their past and contemplate the future, a soul-searching experience. As a result, some of them turned to the purely nationalistic theme of "strength for Korea" and others to the more attractive ideology of Marxism. To some of these disillusioned intellectuals in Korea, Marxism seemed to explain the cause of their misery and point the way out.

Although the economy of the peninsula was improving and the Japanese government even called Korea "thriving Chōsen," the prosperity was not shared by the Korean population. The number of emigrants increased year after year in almost the same proportion as the influx of the Japanese immigrants, and more and more land was taken up by the Japanese. Economic exploitation, backed by the regime, sustained the hatred of the Koreans for the Japanese and furthered the cause of Korean nationalism.

The nationalist movement within Korea lacked cohesion. The fact that many important nationalist leaders were in exile and many others were imprisoned by the Japanese partly explains this phenomenon, but omniscient and omnipotent police, intellectual chaos, and economic deterioration were far more significant factors. For several years after 1919 there were sporadic mass movements, some instances of unity among different groups, and some uprisings. The nationalist movement as a whole, however, needed much more cohesion if it was to be effective. In 1936 Minami Jirō was inaugurated as governor-general. Minami, an army general, turned Korea into a gigantic military depot and pursued a stringent assimilation policy. Under his rule the movement came to a halt. Because the pressure of the government upon Korean nationalist leaders was especially strong, many of them eventually yielded to it and became collaborators with the Japanese. As Tocqueville acutely observed a century ago, patriotism is not durable in a conquered nation.

It is easy to understand why, alternatively, many leaders turned to the idea of strengthening the nation. One obvious lesson of the March First movement was that independence could not be attained through emotional appeals alone. Large-scale uprisings did arouse sympathies abroad and even bring about some reforms in government, but this was far from independence, or even from autonomy within the Japanese Empire. In order to acquire independence, it seemed that the Korean people would have to rely on their own strength in terms of economy, education, and politics.

Of course, a movement of this kind—a movement to strengthen the nation—was not new to Korea. There had been the reform movement of the Independence Club in the 1890's and the movement of the New People's Society (*Shinminhoe*) immediately before the annexation. There were numerous attempts by various leaders to awaken the Korean people. But the leaders of past movements had lacked sufficient time to accomplish their aims. They were, also, fighting against the reactionary native regime, which had the staunch support of the self-aggrandizing elite. The public was ignorant and could not comprehend what the progressives were frantically asserting.

The situation in 1920 was considerably different from that of the years before 1910. Korea was now under an alien rule. The xenophobic sentiment deeply ingrained in the populace, and particularly their hatred of the Japanese, might be mobilized for the positive goal of strengthening Korea. The people were now more attentive to the voices of the leaders. The increasing literacy of the people after the vernacular language was popularized in writing made propaganda more effective, and the Japanese government had finally relaxed its tight control over the media of propaganda.

One of those who stressed the need for a stronger Korea was Yi Kwang-su. Yi had been an active leader while still a student in Japan. Going to Shanghai in 1919, he held office in the Provisional Government, but, disillusioned by developments there, he returned to Korea in 1921. In many ways, Yi Kwang-su symbolizes a large segment of the Korean nationalists. He was a radical idealist until 1920. He had believed in obtaining Korean independence through demonstrations and movements in exile. But soon he became a realist, although an optimistic one. His actions were no longer based on emotions and hopes alone. He became a calculator of what was feasible in the immediate future in order to attain the long-range goal. In his autobiography he offers an explanation for his change of mind:

> I think it was in the autumn of 1919 when I heard about the Corps for the Advancement of Individuals (*Hŭngsadan*) from An Ch'ang-ho. The principles of the Corps for the Advancement of Individuals and the behavior of An Ch'ang-ho impressed me very deeply. After hearing about the principles . . . I was convinced that the independence of our nation could not be attained

through a [radical] movement, but only through cultivating the strength of the nation. The only way to cultivate the strength of the nation was through strengthening individuals and organizing them. Without this kind of collective strength, it would not be possible to realize independence. Even if independence were attained through the assistance of other nations, this could not be sustained for long. When I realized this, there was no choice for me but to return to Korea, where most of the Korean people were living. I concluded that a revolutionary movement in a sovereign nation is easier abroad, but a similar movement for a people without sovereignty is easier within the country. I saw actual examples from India and China. Most of the Korean nationalists, however, were abroad. This was exactly the thing that would throw Korea into the hands of the Japanese. . . . Korea looked as though it were empty of nationalist leaders.[1]

Sometime after his return from Shanghai and amid the charges of treason from some radical Koreans, Yi Kwang-su published a series of essays in *Kaebyŏk* ("Creation") magazine in 1921, reviewing the reform movement of the past and suggesting future policies.[2] Yi found three major defects in the movements of the past: political overtones, lack of selectivity of membership in organizations, and general lack of trained personnel. For the future he suggested that the Korean people must foster morality, acquire modern knowledge, improve individual and social life, and accumulate wealth. There would be no outside help for the Korean people:

> Independence cannot be attained by outside help or by pure luck. . . . Even if the happiness of the Korean people should depend solely upon political independence, this will not be mailed in a package either by the League of Nations or by the disarmament conference.

Thus critical of movements in which he had been active, Yi was also skeptical of the leftist movements that were growing popular among the younger generation:

> Only when the Korean people, individually or as a nation, have the ability to carry out a civilized life, will they be able to determine their own fate. Only then will they be able to decide whether they should be assimilated, be autonomous, become independent, or carry out a movement of great historical significance.[3]

One of the fields in which the nationalists made a concerted effort was education. In a long-range plan of national reform and national re-creation, the importance of education is obvious. After the 1890's many Korean leaders were acutely aware that Japan had become a world power because of her rapid absorption of Western knowledge. It followed that the way for Korea to improve her fate and eventually acquire independence was to educate the masses and train new leaders. Up to 1919, however, modern education was largely confined to the cities. In the countryside, conservative and reactionary forces were dominant; many rural yangbans clung to the view that Western knowledge was heretical. But the active participation of students in the March First movement shocked the reactionaries into opening their minds. The fact that the Korean students in Japan actually led the movement surprised them even more. After 1919, therefore, the urgings of the leaders that the younger generation should be educated in modern schools was accepted with enthusiasm even by conservative elements. Soon schools of every level were filled and the number of applicants exceeded the capacity many times.

The surge for education reached a climax in the effort to establish a university. In November, 1922, forty-seven prominent Koreans formed a "Preparation Committee for the Establishment of the People's University" (*Minrip Taehak Kisŏng Chunbihoe*).[4] Their argument was that Korea's foremost need was to educate the people at the highest level. The "statement of purport" of the committee appealed to the national pride and suggested that the establishment of a university was a prerequisite to independence.[5] The term "independence," was carefully avoided, but the intent of the leaders was clearly understood by the people and by the police.

The first goal of the preparation committee was the raising of ten million yen. They envisaged a university consisting of a liberal arts college, a medical school, and an engineering school. Their aspiration was noble, and the response to their appeal for money was enthusiastic. The project, however, was moribund by 1925. An editorial in *Tonga Ilbo* ("East Asian Daily," Seoul), the foremost nationalist paper in Korea, attributed the failure to basic shortcomings in the Korean people: stinginess, lack of group consciousness, lack of understanding of the power of a congregated group, and lack of mutual trust.[6] But the impetus for a people's university had also been considerably weakened by the founding of a government-sponsored university. The plan for Keijo Imperial University was made known in 1922, and the university was opened in 1926.

Although the people's university was not established, the drive for education continued. Korean students in increasing numbers applied for secondary and higher education. The Japanese government-general also accelerated its school program; the number of elementary schools was increased from one in every three districts (*myŏn*) in 1922 to one in nearly every district in 1933 (from 518 in 1919 to 2,221 in 1934).[7] Yet the government admitted, however, that in 1933 fewer than twenty per cent of the children of elementary-school age were enrolled.[8] The number of secondary schools for Koreans slightly more than doubled from 18 (with 3,843 students) in 1919 to 43 (with 19,531 students) in 1934.[9] Since there were not enough schools to meet the demand, particularly at the college level, the number of Korean students studying in secondary and higher institutions in Japan increased annually, reaching 6,000 in 1936.[10]

Connected with education were the circuit lectures conducted by students. After 1922 many Korean students in Japan came home every summer vacation and delivered lectures and instruction courses to enlighten the people and reduce illiteracy. Newspaper companies often were sponsors, contributing financial and propaganda support. Youth associations also conducted speech tours. In 1933 there were 546 students from nineteen secondary schools and colleges taking part, and attracting the attention of the police. "They traveled to almost every corner of Korea, earnestly carrying out edification and propaganda work. Many of them talked in nationalistic and insurgent tones, which resulted in severe suppression. Thirteen meetings were suspended by the order of the police." [11] Such programs were continued until the late 1930's, when the government prohibited all activities distinctly Korean in content.

In another direction, the national reform movement was concerned with the encouragement of native industries. This arose out of dire necessity, and it was markedly influenced by a similar movement in India. Some newspapers, notably *Tonga Ilbo* and *Chosŏn Ilbo* ("Korea Daily," Seoul), were miniature nationalist movements in themselves, often providing leadership and boldly criticizing the government. An editorial of November 13, 1922, in *Tonga Ilbo* was one of the earliest writings to encourage native industries:

> It is well known that the Indian revolutionary leader Gandhi preached national unity and encouragement of cotton spinning, the greatest industry in India, as the only way to attain complete independence for India. . . .

Although Gandhi's advocating the revival of primitive industry may seem unmodern, we admire him for his sagacity in pointing out the way toward the eternal welfare and happiness of the Indian people. . . . When we reflect upon ourselves and think about the future, we desperately feel the necessity of devising means for self-protection. What is our economic strength, and how has foreign economy trampled upon our economic foundation? . . . It is obvious that under the present capitalistic economic policy, we cannot resist the major trend, no matter how self-conscious and aroused the Korean people become. There is a world of divergence between Japan and Korea in the size of capital, quality of techniques, maturity of economic organizations, and government protection. . . . It is the unsympathetic who ridicule the Koreans as lacking earnestness. Our only means of survival is to restrict foreign commodities and encourage national (native) products.

Soon the Korean Youth Federation opened a contest for the best slogans on the subject.[12] Those selected by the Federation were "Our life with our products" and "Korean products for Korean people." Taking the hint from India, the Koreans decided to boycott Japanese goods as much as possible and thereby increase their own productivity. This movement advanced a step farther when some fifty students and others organized the "Self-Production Society" (*Chajakhoe*) in December, 1922. The means suggested by this society for the survival of the nation were:

The Korean people must unite and use Korean commodities only, excluding all imported goods.

The Korean people must urgently produce all necessary goods for themselves.

The Korean people must not mortgage or sell land, but must strive to purchase it.[13]

Many groups—youth, women's, labor, farmer, student, and religious—then resolved that their members must wear Korean products only, imposing fines for violations. These organizations carried out vigorous campaigns through lectures and street demonstrations, and for a few months newspapers in Korea were cluttered with the reports of their activities. Some boycott leagues against Japanese and Chinese stores were formed. In addition, the Society for the Encouragement of Native Products (*Mulsan Changnyŏhoe*) was organized as a national association in February, 1923, and had branches in almost every village.[14]

The intensity of the native industries movement was reflected in a statement made in 1937 by Matsumura Matsumori, head of the Bureau of Industry of the Korean Government-General:

Immediately after the "manse" disturbance [the uprising of March 1, 1919], every corner of Korea was filled with anti-Japanese thought. Japanese residents in Korea engaged in various industries felt the pressure directly or indirectly and were ill at ease. Especially in remote areas without adequate security forces many Japanese closed their farms, mines, fisheries, and stores either to return to Japan or to move to Japanese sectors in Korea. Because of the anti-Japanese barrier, administration for the promotion of industries could not be carried out: we had to wait for the madness to calm down. It was at this time that the Korean newspapers wielded their spiteful pens to drive out Japanese industrialists, Japanese capital, and Japanese commodities. This created a most repugnant atmosphere. The sudden rise of a desire for education could also be seen as the result of a desire to build up Korean industry.

Matsumura further reported the complaints of Japanese residents that they could not engage in their enterprises at ease unless the stringent and tenacious anti-Japanese attitude was destroyed.[15]

Although ardor subsided within a few years, it was revived again in the 1930's after the inauguration of General Ugaki Issei as governor-general. The depressed economic situation of that time was felt especially in agriculture and caused many disturbances in farm villages, where tenants went on strike against the landlords with alarming frequency and the number of families "without an adequate supply of food"—starving in the spring season—was appalling.[16] A government survey gave the following report on the situation of the farm population:

Approximately 80 per cent of these farmers are of the indigent class. Most of these are people of no means, generally without benefit of education, lacking in concern about their environment, and unable to improve farming conditions. They are engrossed in old habits, content with a low standard of living. They annually complain of lack of food. Most of them earn 50 to 200 yen a year. When confronted with necessity, they cannot afford to consider the consequences; they merely accumulate high-interest debts. Their year's effort in the crops is mostly for payment for borrowed food or interest; they do not have any surplus. In extreme cases, considerable numbers of them rely on wild plants and trees for food during the spring. These are the results of long years of exploitation which have deprived of them the spirit of diligence, frugality, and saving. They neither have hope for improvement nor make any effort toward it.[17]

The Ugaki administration therefore carried on a vigorous campaign to instruct the farmers in raising enough food to feed themselves, budgeting their expenses, and reducing their debts. Since the effort to regenerate the farmers coincided with announced aims of the Korean nationalists, some nationalists took part in the government program, at the same time seeking to strengthen their own cause and utilize the opportunity to further the boycott of Japanese goods and propagate the idea of Korean self-sufficiency.[18]

The government's farm program was also accepted by religious groups. Nationalists in Christian and Ch'ŏndogyo groups turned their attention with growing intensity to the farmers. Among others, the Presbyterian and Methodist churches conducted lectures on topics ranging from the modern methods of agriculture to side-line jobs for farmers. The Ch'ŏndogyo had already established the Korean Farmers Association in 1925. By 1930 it had a membership of 22,000. There were some socialists among its leaders. This group set up coöperatives, including a rubber-products factory in Pyongyang and a farmers' school in Seoul; they also started the joint sale of silkworms and a movement for lowering the cost of irrigation and the amelioration of tenant contracts. In 1931 they organized debt-adjustment unions to win the support of farmers.[19]

Having noted some of the attempts to advance the welfare and win the support of the farmers, we must add that the ideological impact was slight. The crucial problem for most farmers was subsistence, and the intellectual and romantic lines of approach used by nationalist leaders were sometimes beyond their comprehension. Further, the movement to regenerate the farmers and the entire movement to strengthen Korea faced a fundamental problem. All such efforts were operating against a formidable foe, the political superstructure. Although details varied from period to period, depending on the character of the governors-general, the fixed policy of the government was that the Korean economy should be integrated with the total economic structure of the Japanese Empire. Thus it was somewhat absurd to conceive of developing the backward industries of the Koreans in competition with the advanced and well-financed Japanese industries in the home islands and in Korea, and it was nearly impossible for the landless farmers of Korea to escape the cycle of debts and starvation. For the improvement of Korean industry and the general welfare of the Korean people, fundamental changes were needed rather than piecemeal improvements. Without fundamental changes, the room for improvement was very limited.

Aside from the political factor limiting the extent of potential success, leaders of the "stronger Korea" movement had a serious internal problem. Parochialism or provincialism among the Korean people prevented unification of the movement. Groups in each area of effort strove to gain followings for their own cliques, and the loyalty of the followers was focused on the group rather than the movement, accompanied by contests for power among leaders. The movement also suffered considerable damage from the constant charge by Marxist intellectuals that its gradualist policy was necessarily a bourgeois tactic designed to enrich a small number of industrialists by exploiting the masses. This kind of movement, the Marxists asserted, would only deviate the class consciousness of the indigent masses; it should therefore be countered by all possible means. Since these leftist leaders were influential in farmer and labor organizations throughout Korea, their opposition was by no means a negligible force.

To stress the meager results of the movement in terms of improvement of the Korean economy, however, is to present only one side of the picture. Although the professed purpose was to cultivate the strength of Korea so as to improve the welfare of the people, by implication the movement stressed the distinctiveness of the Korean people from the Japanese and sought to nurture national consciousness among the masses. This was the reason why the Japanese authorities watched it closely and frequently suppressed lectures, publications, and street demonstrations. The active participation of nationalist leaders in the government-sponsored movement for the regeneration of the farmers was correctly seen as partly an attempt to win hegemony of the movement from the Japanese government and thereby strengthen national consciousness among the farming masses.

Compared with the "stronger Korea" movement, the nonconciliation movement was more popular. Its guiding principle was to censure Japanese policy, so as to keep the consciousness of the Korean people alive. Except for a brief period between 1927 and 1931, the nonconciliation movement was not organized. It was in essence negative, in that it opposed the regime without proposing a distinct program of its own.

The nationalists in this category shared the anti-Japanese sentiment of their compatriots abroad, but they made no attempt to use violence, which was not only unfeasible within Korea, but also undesirable: any attempt to form a large-scale violent group would be forestalled by the police, and the sacrifices demanded of the participants would be too great. The people in Korea also lacked the means to engage in this kind of activity. The nonconciliatory nationalists within Korea therefore had to content themselves with sporadic and spontaneous demonstrations, verbal attacks on the government, and the exposing of atrocities. Newspapers assisted them by outright or veiled criticism of Japanese policy. The *Tonga Ilbo, Chosŏn Ilbo,* and others also appealed to Korean national consciousness by engaging in verbal battles against the pro-Japanese home-rule group, which had the support of the government.

After 1920 small groups of pro-Japanese Koreans tried to obtain suffrage for the Koreans. They asserted that since independence was totally out of the realm of possibility, the Koreans ought to integrate with the Japanese as soon as possible and enjoy equal status with them. The National Society (*Kungmin Hyŏphoe*), headed by Min Won-sik, was one of the leading groups of this land. Min's group occasionally submitted petitions to the Japanese Diet appealing for the grant of suffrage to the Koreans. When it became apparent that suffrage was not very likely to be granted, the pro-Japanese groups turned to a campaign for home rule. But their movement was unpopular with other leaders and the masses, and strong attacks were launched every time they took some action.[20]

Eleven pro-Japanese groups united in March, 1924, establishing the Federation of Interested Persons of Various Groups (*Kakp'a Yuji Yŏnmaeng*). The Federation issued a declaration that Japanese-Korean amalgamation was the result of the demand of the time; it was to join the two peoples, promoting the people's welfare and accelerating the national prosperity. It sought nothing but "to maintain peace in the Far East and to follow the trend of advancement of the world." The declaration also accused the independence movement of fancifulness, resulting in a hundred harms, but no gain. This was exactly what the government had been preaching constantly, and this pro-Japanese group had the strong support of the government.[21]

Nationalist groups countered this pro-Japanese pronouncement with a bitter verbal blow. The newspaper *Tonga Ilbo* accused the pro-Japanese groups of begging for the favor of the government by using pro-Japanese slogans about fusion of the two peoples and harmony of capital and labor in order to promote individual interests.[22] Enraged pro-Japanese groups resorted to physical violence, battering the publisher and a director of *Tonga Ilbo*. The members of Labor Fraternal Association (*Nodong Sangaehoe*) were particularly active in intimidating prominent nationalists. The newspaper thereby retaliated with a headline exposé about the violence and printed a series of editorials labeling the pro-Japanese groups as national traitors. Because the police quietly ignored the violence, the newspaper accused the governor-general of not living up to the announced goals of his cultural policy.[23]

As the disputes continued, more nationalists rallied round *Tonga Ilbo*, and plans were made for a mass meeting on April 22. When the police suppressed the meeting as instigatory to violence, a committee having the support of thirty-one nationalist groups decided to hold a conference on June 20 to denounce the government's action. The police immediately prohibited the meeting and arrested five members of the preparatory committee.[24] Because of this, more than a hundred leaders met June 23 and adopted resolutions denouncing the highhandedness of the government and declaring their determination to continue the speech meetings and demonstrations against oppression.[25] As the situation turned from bad to worse for the government, there was frequent suppression of newspapers and magazines. Between January and June, 1924, thirty-eight issues of daily papers, three issues of monthly magazines, and seven out of eleven issues of a leftist magazine, *Shinsaenghwal* ("New Life"), were suppressed.[26]

Nonviolent resistance movements took many forms. Because of the frequent suppression of publications, Korean intellectuals criticized the government's policy as a denial of freedom of the press. Their piecemeal approach was consolidated in 1925 when about seven hundred publishers and reporters met at Seoul in a conference which adopted resolutions denouncing, among other things, the restriction of freedom of assembly and freedom of the press.[27]

Labor, farmer, and youth groups also joined in the resistance movements. Professing to promote fraternity and the welfare of their members, they had also a common denominator in Korean nationalism, evidenced by the frequent suppression of their meetings. A national gathering of about five hundred representatives of labor, farmer, youth, and other groups assembled in Seoul on April 20, 1925, in a "Conference of Workers in the Mass Movement" which the police suppressed in its second day, prohibiting further meetings. Although this conference was led by a Communist group, the so-called Tuesday Society, it had wide support among non-Communists.[28]

Religious groups also were active in the resistance movement. Ch'ŏndogyo believers and Christians had led the March First movement, and this legacy was not easily eliminated. As late as 1934 religious groups were "encouraging a national spirit for resistance behind the shelter of preaching." This was a particularly strong tendency among Ch'ŏndogyo members:

> Although they always act calmly, they take themselves to be the leaders of the nationalist movement in Korea. They point to the Tonghak rebellion and the March First movement, and secretly talk of carrying out a great event. They have organized the Youth party, Youth League, Farmers group (*Nongminsa*), Labor group (*Nodongsa*), Married Women's Corps (*Naesŏngdan*), Women's League (*Yŏsŏng Tongmaeng*), Youth Association, Juniors' Society, Student Society, etc., to penetrate into every class and prepare for the future event. Although the highest officers pretend to be moderate and calm and occasionally advocate a home-rule movement or collaborate with government officials, the middle-echelon officers and teachers travel around and instigate a national spirit for resistance through cant, irony, or satire.[29]

Thus most of the organized groups in Korea—economic, professional, and religious—maintained a hostile attitude toward Japanese rule. Even so, most of the activities were local in scale and not systematically united. Each group followed policies of its own choosing and usually attempted to organize only one particular social class in each locality. Korean society was fragmented into multi-groups, each without much communication with the others. In most instances the leadership of a group was confined to a particular community, instead of being extended to a larger area. Only the religious groups maintained organizations on a national scale. But the religious leaders had experienced hardship in 1919 and were reluctant to join any overt nonreligious movement for fear that the government might make reprisals against their purely religious activities. More than anything else, however, the great obstacle to unity of the nationalist movement was the division into Communist and non-Communist camps. Despite many shared goals and aspirations, they were mostly hostile toward each other. The Communists labeled the non-Communist nationalists as bourgeois and reactionary. The traditional, pure, or right-wing nationalists charged the Communists with being foreign-dominated and pathetic individuals. Yet from 1927 to 1931 nationalists and Communists were united under the banner of "Shinganhoe," and the strength of the coalition was phenomenal.[30]

In preceding chapters we have seen that many of the nationalists abroad turned to communism in search of assistance for their nationalist aims. After 1921, partly in an effort to establish credit with the Comintern and partly to foster the power of their own warring groups, the proto-Communists abroad sent funds and agents into Korea. Also, some Korean students in Japan were affected by the tide of Marxism there and helped introduce communism. In 1925 the Korean Communist party was organized in Seoul, and thereafter Communist-oriented intellectuals infiltrated many farmer, labor, youth, and women's organizations; the press also had a considerable share of young Marxists. Although Communists within Korea were dispersed in many rival factions, they posed a formidable opposition to the established but disorganized traditional nationalist camp.[31]

Communist initiative was largely responsible for the alliance of nationalists and Communists in 1927 and its breakup in 1931. Since the alliance also suited the purpose of the traditional or right-wing nationalists, they readily accepted the invitation and reaped whatever gains were possible from the union. In 1931 they resisted the move for dissolution, but were outmaneuvered by the Communists.

The formation of Shinganhoe was directly influenced by the current of theoretical struggles among the Japanese Marxists. After the mass arrests of Communists in Japan in 1923, the Japanese Communist party dissolved itself. Soon a movement for reëstablishment was started, and the so-called second Japanese Communist party was formed in 1926. Fukumoto Kazuo, a member of the party's central executive committee and a major theoretician, argued in a number of tracts published in 1926 that the ideology of the Labor-Farmer faction (*Rōnōha*) of Yamakawa Hitoshi contained impure elements which ought to be eliminated. Purification meant discarding ambivalent elements and establishing a party of disciplined and completely indoctrinated revolutionaries. Fukumotoism was characterized by an organizational theory of "splits and unity," insisting upon the necessity of ideological purification before seeking the support of the masses. The rival faction of Yamakawa had advocated a mass party, maintaining that the consciousness of the masses would advance in time and that gradually they would be prepared to accept Marxism: it was only then that the party should be organized as a disciplined party of the proletariat. Eventually the Comintern took an intermediate position, denouncing Fukumotoism as left-wing extremism and Yamakawaism as right-wing opportunism. According to Comintern instructions, a functioning Communist party was necessary in Japan in order that the masses should have access to correct leadership, but the party was simultaneously to work for a broad coalition of "progressive, multi-class forces" on behalf of democracy and to struggle vigorously to obtain the leadership and directional authority.[32] Some of the young Korean Marxists in Tokyo, who had mostly been engrossed in abstract theoretical studies, were suddenly awakened by this turn of events. They began to mimic the current slogans of their Japanese counterparts, and presently were urging that the purely intellectual study groups be abolished, factional differences be eliminated, and a broad united front of the Korean people be established. Some of them returned home in late 1926 and took part in the campaign for a united front.

The movement to form a united party was already in progress in Korea by the spring of 1926. Kang Tal-yŏng, the secretary of the Korean Communist party, conferred with nationalist leaders on March 10 concerning coöperation between nonconciliatory nationalists and Communists. The meeting was held at the home of Kwŏn Tong-jin, a leader of Ch'ŏndogyo, and the decision as to strategy was that the unified party should be based upon the foundation of Ch'ŏndogyo.[33] In April, Kang wrote to a Korean Communist in Shanghai about an investigation of the attitude of Ch'oe Rin, the leader of what was called the "new faction" in Ch'ŏndogyo. Kang's letter spells out some of the intentions of the Communists:

> We are planning to organize the Korean National party (*Chosŏn Kungmindang*) in coöperation with nonconciliatory nationalists. We plan to become the core of the party and maintain a double organization system. . . . As soon as this investigation [of Ch'oe's group] is finished, we shall carry out the plan immediately.[34]

The Ch'oe group, however, was leaning toward home rule and did not show any interest; nor did other gradualists. But the more radical nonconciliatory nationalists saw the feasibility of uniting in an anti-Japanese movement. Indeed, even before the establishment of the Shinganhoe coalition in 1927 there seems to have been coöperation between the "old faction" in Ch'ŏndogyo (the Kwŏn Tong-jin group) and the Communists. An instance can be seen in the attempt at nationwide demonstrations on June 10, 1926.

The June 10 incident was intended to be a replica of that of March 1, 1919. The last emperor of Korea, Sunjong, died on April 25, and general social unrest ensued, as when his father died in 1919. There were some gatherings to mourn his death, merchants closed their shops, students carried out strikes in a number of schools, the number of labor strikes increased, and there was a rumor in Seoul that a riot was planned for the day of the national funeral ceremonies, scheduled for June 10. Horrified by the prospect of a national uprising, the police banned all meetings and conducted searches. One Korean suspect was discovered to have a printed copy of a nationalist leaflet. This clue led to a search of the Ch'ŏndogyo buildings. Four kinds of leaflets intended for distribution on the funeral day, about 50,000 copies altogether, were discovered and confiscated.[35] Documents linking Communists in Korea with others abroad and with Comintern were also discovered, and mass arrests followed.

Some Communists escaped arrest and on June 10 distributed leaflets reading "Twenty million compatriots—Drive out the enemy! The price of freedom is blood—Long live Korea!" Riotous demonstrations took place in Seoul and were joined by mourners shouting "manse." Similar attempts elsewhere were forestalled by arrests of Communists. No direct evidence of collaboration in the demonstration exists, but it is clear that some understanding had been reached between the Communists and some Ch'ŏndogyo elements.

Preparation for the united party progressed steadily. A Japanese source indicates that the Communists, particularly the Seoul faction, made an all-out effort for unity. They established the People's Prosperity Society (*Minhŭnghoe*) for propaganda tasks and set up a nationalist party preparation committee in Vladivostok to enlist the support of comrades abroad. This Committee sent agents into Korea to persuade nationalists of both the right and the left.[36] Eventually, on February 15, 1927, Shinganhoe emerged as a national organization of the Korean people.

Because of the very nature of Shinganhoe, in that it was to represent the people as a whole, the leadership went to a traditional nationalist, Yi Sang-jae. Although the leftists held considerable strength in local organizations, they were not able to offer so popular a national leader as the rightists. Yi had a long record in nationalist movements dating back to the Independence Club of 1896. He had been active in the Christian education and people's university movements and was the publisher of the *Chosŏn Ilbo*.[37] Kwŏn Tong-jin, a leader of Ch'ŏndogyo, became the vice-president.

Organizational activities progressed rapidly. The headquarters of labor, farmer, and youth organizations, with branches throughout Korea, announced their change of direction and pledged their support. Since the leadership included prominent persons in strong religious groups (Christian, Ch'ŏndogyo, and Buddhist) as well as in the fields of publishing, law, and education, Shinganhoe had no difficulty in mustering strength. Women were mobilized in Sharon Friend Society (*Kun-u-hoe*). In each area Shinganhoe became the central organization, serving as the coördinator of different activities. Branches were also established in Japan and Manchuria. For once, the Korean people seemed to have joined together under one banner. These varied groups, a police report stated, "strove for the mobilization of unorganized masses, cried for reform in the social system, attacked and criticized [Japanese] rule over Korea, analyzed various incidents with nationalist prejudice, and brought in their viewpoints on every local problem." [38]

In effect, Shinganhoe served as the opposition party to the government. But since it was not an opposition party in the ordinary political sense, not a party with the probability or even possibility of taking over governmental power, its sentiments and activities tended toward violence. For instance, it intervened in and helped further the student strikes and demonstrations, commonly known as the Kwangju student incident, that agitated Korea for five months in late 1929 and early 1930 and extended all over the country, eventually involving 194 schools and about 54,000 students.[39] Although few adults took part openly in these disturbances, various nationalist and Communist groups associated with Shinganhoe were working in the background to instigate the students. The main grievance voiced by the students and the press was the attitude of superiority displayed by Japanese students and teachers. The Korean people as a whole had been humiliated by this attitude and deeply hurt in their national pride. In this respect the uprisings by the students against the discriminatory policies of the government represented a success for the nationalists, for the goal of the Shinganhoe groups in these years was to enhance national consciousness.

The students' reaction against contemptuous and condescending attitudes of the Japanese, combined with the desire to promote the lot of the Korean people, is characteristic of all the nationalist movements in this period.[40] It is true that there were at least three major groupings—the moderates, the non-Communist radicals, and the Communists—each advocating different tactics and professing different ideologies, but the distinction among them was more apparent than real.

Such ultraradical groups as the Communists declared the overthrow of the Japanese Empire and the establishment of a Communist Korea to be their ultimate goal. They utilized every opportunity to make their views known, attacking both the Japanese government and the moderate Koreans as enemies of the people. The actual strength of the Communists, however, was weak, and police vigilance against them was especially severe. Communists themselves were divided into minute factions which impeded the progress of their programs and favored the chances of police discovery. This weakness within the Communist camp necessitated the alliance in Shinganhoe with the nationalists, whose influence extended to broader segments of the population. The Communists found it more convenient to manipulate the leadership of a larger and stronger group than to build their own organization. But the alliance required a compromise. Thus they found themselves advocating much the same tactics and slogans as the other nationalists.

The non-Communist radical groups also found themselves in an ambivalent position. While they were strongly opposed to the government-sponsored home-rule movement of their more conservative compatriots, they were well aware of the dangers of violent action and therefore chose to maneuver cautiously within the confines established by the Japanese police in order to sustain the national consciousness and at the same time propagate stronger anti-Japanese feelings among the masses. Except for the Communists, who often resorted to violent and illegal means of operation, as a whole the nationalists in Korea strove to maintain the legal sanction of the government, although most of their activities were at the periphery of the maximum legal limits. They reasoned that being moderate was better than being totally suppressed.

Whereas the nationalists abroad, as well as some Communists in Korea, were operating with little or no popular support and could abrogate their responsibilities to the populace on the pretext that the end justified the means, the other nationalists in the homeland had large followings subject to police reprisals in the event of any violent action on the part of the leaders. It is also possible that the leaders within Korea had a stronger sense of responsibilities toward their families. Whereas the nationalists abroad were separated from all but their immediate relatives, and sometimes from these, and were completely dedicating themselves to the cause of independence, the nationalists within Korea could not act so freely: any action that endangered a leader automatically threatened the livelihood and very existence of his entire family.

This rationality of the moderate groups, however, was accompanied by strong emotionalism that showed up in the chronic frustration of their efforts by various internal no less than external factors. That is to say, the conceiving and planning of activities were based not so much upon meticulous calculation of possibilities and the obstacles to be surmounted as upon wishes and desires. To note the emotional aspect of the nationalist movement, of course, is not to castigate it. Being totally realistic, given the situation in Korea, would have meant the total elimination of the nationalist movements.

Emotionalism was particularly strong in the more radical groups. The platforms of Shinganhoe show that the radical nationalists and the Communists did not propose any positive formula except that of the consolidation of the people. No articulate social, political, and economic programs were proposed. The activities of Shinganhoe suggest that the radical nationalists were mainly interested in attacking the Japanese and enhancing the national consciousness of the people.

The student disturbances in 1929 and 1930 particularly showed the altered emotional aspect of the period, compared to 1919. Unlike the March First movement, these demonstrations were motivated not by hopes for Korean independence, but by resentment against the Japanese. It is undeniable that there was a strong sense of patriotism for Korea. But this was manifested in a negative, anti-Japanese or anti-Chinese form with little intellectual and ideological content. Some intellectuals proposed programs to strengthen Korea and some others introduced the Marxist formula; both schools attracted followings, but neither was able to sustain enthusiasm for long. The Japanese government, acutely aware of the dangers presented by any kind of strong Korean movement in opposition to their rule, made every effort to obstruct sustained unity. Further, the government was able to manipulate this unorganized and highly emotional sense of patriotism into diversional outlets, as in the anti-Chinese riots and killings following the Wanpaoshan incident of July, 1931.

The establishment of Shinganhoe offered a ray of hope to the confused nationalist movement. It brought together two rival groups, Communists and non-Communists. It offered a forum where Koreans could develop policies and voice their sentiments and aspirations in unison. But these hopes were soon shattered, when Communist strategy demanded its dissolution.

14

Japanese Rule: The Last Phase

THE ALLIANCE in 1927 of radical elements of the nationalists and Communists in a "single party of the Korean people," Shinganhoe, was precarious. It was brought about because of mutual agreement on one, and probably only one, issue—their opposition to the Japanese government. The radicals of the right joined the alliance because it would further the cause of the nationalist movement as a whole. The Communist bloc joined because their strategy at the time so dictated. As Kang Tal-Yŏng, the chief secretary of the Korean Communist party, confided to his comrade in Shanghai, the intention of the Communists was to hold the hegemony of the coalition in order to lead the entire Korean movement into class warfare while maintaining their own party's organizational structure.

But after three years the Communists discovered that instead of their being able to manipulate the entire movement as they had hoped, the alliance was undermining the position of the Communist bloc:

Although many social groups existed in form, Shinganhoe and its branches tended to take over the functions of various social groups. This resulted in advocacy in some circles that labor, farmer, youth, and women's departments be established within Shinganhoe, recognizing it as the sole party of the Korean people. Some advocated that the labor and farmer unions be dissolved and the entire working masses be consolidated under Shinganhoe. Some others advocated that the class movement be removed, concentrating only on the nationalist movement. Still others asserted that, since Korea was at the stage of bourgeois revolution, the hegemony of revolution must be held by the bourgeoisie.

Varying theories, all undermining the initial idea of the Communist leaders, were advocated not only by rightist nationalists, but within the Communist ranks as well. Communist collaborators with the rightists produced "sectarian movements" which "pushed the Korean Communist party behind the Shinganhoe" and "prevented various social organizations under the Communist party from carrying out their original functions." [1]

Obviously, this was not what the Communists had intended. The Comintern theses of 1926 to the Japanese Communist party had directed the winning of leadership of the mass movement along with a strong build-up of the party core. The program did not include the liquidation of labor, farmer, and other organizations for the sake of a bourgeois revolution. Neither was it "correct policy" to dismantle the party.

Because of the frequent arrests of Communists, furthermore, the left wing within Shinganhoe was waning in power. At the third central executive meeting of Shinganhoe, in November, 1930, elections of officers turned the leadership markedly to the right.[2] Kim Pyŏng-no, the new chairman, was concerned lest the radical and extreme leftist tendencies displayed by some branches of Shinganhoe might endanger its existence as a legal organization. While serving as acting chairman after the arrest of his predecessor, he had been striving to lead the organization in a moderate direction. The election of Kim and other rightists immediately brought from some branches the accusation that they were opportunistic renegades who would make the organization a subsidiary of the home-rule movement. When a Communist leader in Tokyo, Ko Kyŏng-gŭn, began to advocate dissolution of Shinganhoe, left-wing members in various branches took up the cry. Leftist leaders within and outside Shinganhoe charged that it was a petty bourgeois organization, undermining the revolutionary cause.

Arguments for the dissolution of Shinganhoe had their source in Comintern directives. Although the view of the Marxist-Leninist faction of An Kwang-ch'ŏn that Korea was in the state of bourgeois revolution would seem to have been in perfect agreement with the Marxist tenet of two-stage revolution, this did not meet the current strategy of the Comintern. At Moscow in September, 1928, the sixth congress of the Comintern in effect repudiated the position taken by the Marxist-Leninists. The theme of the "Colonial Theses" issued by the congress were repeated in the famous "December Theses" (1928) of the Executive Committee of the Communist International:

> In all their work and action the Communists of Korea must strictly preserve the full independence of the revolutionary labour movement which must be definitely dissociated from all of the revolutionary struggle demands, temporary collaboration, and under some conditions even a temporary alliance of the Communist Party and national-revolutionary movement inasmuch as that movement . . . is revolutionary, is possible. This collaboration, however, must by no means "find expression in a fusion of the Communist movement with the bourgeois-revolutionary movement." With regard to the bourgeois opposition the Communists may conclude agreements with them "if the action of the bourgeois opposition can be utilized for the development of a mass movement and, if such agreement will in no way restrict the freedom of the Communist Party in its agitation among the masses and in their organizations. In this connection, Communists must not only fully preserve their political independence and reveal their own position, but on the basis of action they must open the eyes of the toiling masses under the influence of the bourgeois opposition so that they may see the unreliability of that opposition and the danger of the bourgeois-democratic illusions disseminated by it." [3]

But obviously the developments within Shinganhoe were not meeting the requirements of the Comintern theses. The "revolutionary labor movement" was about to be engulfed into the "bourgeois" nationalist movement: the collaboration in Shinganhoe was approaching a fusion of the Communist movement with that of the bourgeois elements, the Communist agitation desired by the Comintern was being minimized, and the bourgeois nationalist movement was getting the upper hand.

Agitation among local leaders resulted in a second national conference of Shinganhoe, at Seoul in May, 1931. The headquarters group, determinedly opposed to the leftist policy, attempted to soothe the situation, but to no avail. The leftists outvoted them by 43 to 3, and the "coalition party of the Korean people" was formally dissolved. The government-general, which had been troubled by the existence of such a powerful Korean group, prevented the opponents of the dissolution from even issuing a statement of their views.[4]

According to the Comintern theses, the Communists were to reinvigorate the labor and farmer unions along revolutionary lines. They made some progress in this direction, but the police were too well informed about Communist strategies to leave them free to pursue the Comintern policy. The always efficient "thought police" tightened its control as fast as the Communists made headway, making impossible their continuing any front organization activities. As a consequence, the Communists went underground.

The dissolution of Shinganhoe proved to be almost fatal to the rightist elements insofar as a wide organizational movement was concerned. There were some attempts at the reconstruction of a national organization, but none of these progressed very far. In January of 1932 a number of the leaders established the National Organization Control Conference (*Minjok Tanch'e T'ongje Hyŏpuihoe*), but the attempt failed because of obstructions by leftists. In July Christian nationalists in Pyongyang formed the Construction Middle Association (*Kŏnjunghoe*), but, according to the police, those who joined this organization were different in character from what was desired by the leaders, who therefore withdrew from it; presumably there was an attempt at leftist infiltration.[5] Although many social and religious groups remained in the nationalist category, the enthusiasm for a national organization markedly declined after 1931, owing in large part to the obstructive tactics of the left and the suppressive hands of the government.

During the decade of the 1920's the government had leaned toward appeasement rather than outright oppression. This is not to say that its policy was liberal—the number of newspapers suppressed would defy such an assertion, but there was some degree of tolerance. After 1931 the ascendancy of the military clique in Japanese politics altered the situation in Korea. The government put pressure on Korean leaders to support the Japanese cause in Manchuria and elsewhere, and noncoöperation was regarded as a hostile action. The control of the thought police was tightened, and even the utterance of a complaint became a punishable crime. On the other hand, the government successfully diverted the resentment of the Korean masses by exaggerated reports of the Wanpaoshan incident. Japan was presented as the protector of the suffering Koreans in Manchuria against the Chinese. Since there had been frequent occurrences of maltreatment of

Koreans in Manchuria by petty officials, it was a relatively easy task for the government to inflame the Korean masses against the Chinese. The Wanpaoshan incident produced an abrupt change in mass opinion, and thereafter the nationalist leaders found it considerably more difficult to continue their anti-Japanese movement. After 1931, also, there was a rising tendency of acquiescence and complacency toward the Japanese government. After the First World War, Japan advanced rapidly in international standing. Her hegemony in the Far East was uncontested, and even the overt aggression by her armies in Manchuria and North China was not effectively opposed. The League of Nations seemed powerless in the face of Japanese might. To many of the Koreans, the wisest thing seemed to be to adjust themselves to the situation rather than try to defy an unchallengeable world power.

The years after 1933 were a period of difficulty for the Korean Communists as well as the traditional nationalists. In June, 1933, the foremost Japanese Communists, Sano Manabu and Nabeyama Sadahiko, announced their abandonment of communism and pledged their loyalty to the emperor, whom they declared to be the symbol of national unity. They saw the operations of the Japanese Army on the continent as a step toward the liberation of Asia. Within two months about a third of arrested Japanese Communists followed suit, and within a few years nearly 90 per cent of those arrested pledged their loyalty.[6] Some Japanese Communists who attempted to reconstruct the declining party were murdered by the police. The current of conversion swept the Korean Communist camp as well, and many Korean Communists followed the example of the Japanese leaders.

Thus the situation became more and more difficult for the nationalist and Communist leaders in Korea. But hope was not totally abandoned. Die-hards in both camps saw some signs of weakening in the Japanese Empire. The Japanese political scene in the first half of the 1930's was not at all stable. In 1932 a financial magnate and a former minister of finance—Baron Dan Takuma and Inoue Junnosuke—were assassinated by the Blood Oath Group (*Ketsumeidan*) and Premier Inukai Tsuyoshi was murdered by some naval officers who spread terror in government offices in Tokyo before submitting to the gendarmes. The year 1932 was also marked by extreme famine and numerous riots. In March, 1933, Japan was isolated internationally by her withdrawal from the League of Nations. The country was harassed by internal and external problems, and the existence of the empire seemed imperiled.

While the international and domestic situation of Japan was changing rapidly, the nationalists in Korea generally played the role of indifferent spectators. Organizational movement went into a stalemate, and there was not much freedom for either the right or the left to exploit. The Communists scored a success in organizing a few anti-imperial associations among students and Communist farmer and labor unions, but these were quickly detected and dissolved by the police. The normally nationalistic press also was toned down by sensitive police officials.

In the summer of 1936, however, there was jubilation among the Korean people because of the winning of the international marathon race by a Korean champion. At the eleventh Olympic Games, in Berlin, the first and third places in the marathon were won by Korean students, Son Ki-jŏng and Nam Sŭng-yong. This victory was celebrated in Japan as well as Korea, since the champions appeared in the games as members of the Japanese team. But the Korean public and newspapers specially noted the fact that both champions were Koreans rather than Japanese. The newspapers devoted long columns to the event and used the occasion to boost the pride and praise the superiority of the Korean people.

When the news reached Japan, Korean students and others held lantern parades in Tokyo for two nights. While the champions were returning home, celebrations were prepared. Korean students, newspapermen, and Y.M.C.A. members in Tokyo planned to hold an autumn exercise match of the students in their honor, and in Korea there was a plan for constructing a national athletic hall to commemorate the event. But both the exercise match and the hall were prohibited by the police.[7]

The victory of the Korean athletes produced a few nationalist martyrs. Because the Osaka newspaper *Asahi* brought in a newsreel film of the marathon race to show in Japan, the *Tonga Ilbo* sponsored a program to show the newsreel in Korea also. In a photograph reproduced in advertisements of the program, however, the *Tonga Ilbo* and the *Chosŏn Chungang Ilbo* ("Korean Central Daily") deleted the Japanese flag emblem from the uniform of Son Ki-jŏng.[8] The deletion of the emblem became a major issue, and several staff members of

Tonga Ilbo were arrested. They were released after forty days of questioning, but were forever barred from the press. The newspaper itself was suspended from publication for nine months. The similar deletion by *Chosŏn Chungang Ilbo* was not immediately detected, but the newspaper voluntarily suspended publication.[9] (It might be added here that Yŏ Un-hyŏng, the left-wing nationalist leader in China before his arrest in 1929, was the president of the latter paper.) Although the marathon victory and the incident involving the deletion of the Japanese emblem elated nationalist sentiment in Korea, large-scale exploitation by nationalist leaders would have been inconceivable. The police in Korea were increasingly suspicious of those who had ever held prominent positions in nationalist and Communist movements, and not only was their detection system efficient, but the individual detectives, some Koreans in particular, were hysterically concerned with setting records for themselves, seeking pretexts for arrest and prosecution upon the least suspicion of anti-Japanese or antigovernment attitudes. The arrest and prosecution of thirty-five members of the Korean Linguistic Association in 1942 was typical.[10]

In 1937 the opening of the Sino-Japanese war brought great changes. Because of its strategic position, Korea was quickly converted into a military depot, and more sacrifice than ever was demanded from the people. The ultranationalist Japanese leaders who launched the reckless drive for expansion were well aware of the risks involved in attacking China, and nothing was to be spared in the cause of the war. From the end of 1937 to early in 1938 all the economic life of the empire was frozen and labor, materials, funds, and prices were placed under government control. The switch to wartime regulations crushed all middle-sized and small industries owned by Koreans. Lack of materials forced small merchants to suspend their businesses. Laborers and office employees in civilian industries were thrown out of work. Rapid inflation forced most of the Korean people into indigence. A severe drought in 1938, said to be the worst in eighty years, worsened the situation of the farmers, from whom meanwhile more and more rice tax was demanded.

The government of course anticipated that the economic difficulties would brew discontent. Therefore the police force was augmented. The existing laws were freely interpreted to suppress all possible sources of disturbance. The newspapers were virtually turned into propaganda organs of the government through strict censorship and intimidation. For the cause of victory in war, no private opinions contradictory to the government policy were to be tolerated. At the end of 1939 the government urged the Korean newspapers to shut down, so as to "meet the demand of the time." When the publishers did not voluntarily comply, the newspapers were abolished by forced sale.[11]

In an effort to secure total support for the war the Japanese government initiated the "Movement for the General Mobilization of the National Spirit." This was begun in Japan in September, 1937, and transplanted to Korea in July, 1938. By means of the so-called Korean Federation of the movement, the "patriotic group" system (*aikokuhan*) was established throughout the country, each group consisting of several households. This elaborate network of *han* ("squads"), *kumi* ("teams"), and *chŏ* ("streets") in each administrative unit served both as a controlling mechanism over the people and a rapid and sure system of communication. As a means of attaining spiritual unity, all the population was coerced into marching to Shinto shrines periodically to pray for the victory of the Japanese armed forces. Since food rationing was administered through the "patriotic groups," the system operated with maximum efficiency.

The most urgent problem for the government in Korea after the beginning of the Sino-Japanese war was the assimilation of the Korean people. Although the policy of Japanization had been pursued ever since the annexation in 1910, the Koreans were still far from being assimilated. The international and domestic situation of Japan after the outbreak of the war demanded an intensification of the policy. Japan needed not only the material resources and strategic position of the Korean peninsula, but also the native manpower. Casualties mounted as the war front expanded, and there was an acute shortage of troops. Koreans had not been subject to conscription, but they now constituted a significant reserve for the Japanese military.

The government had, of course, a choice of more than one way of conscripting Koreans. There was the precedent of the British in India during the First World War, when independence was promised as a reward for submitting to conscription. But this alternative was not very attractive. The promise of independence would only enliven the nationalist movement, as it had done in India, and complete independence of Korea after the Japanese victory would weaken the empire.

The only practicable alternative was to accelerate the assimilation process. In 1938, therefore, the government abolished Korean-language instruction in all secondary schools. Soon the elementary schools ceased to teach Korean, and the use of Japanese became mandatory. Students were disciplined for their usage of Korean in or out of school. All instruction was geared to "clarity of national polity" (*kokutai meichō*) and loyalty to the emperor. School instruction began with "worship toward the east," reciting the "oath of the Imperial subject," and veneration of the shelf for Shinto tablets installed in every classroom. Students were taught to believe in the "spirit of Yamato" and the superiority of the Japanese race, of which the Korean people were to be deemed a part. Of course, these daily programs were not confined to the schools. All government agencies, factories, "patriotic groups" and public gatherings of any kind had to begin their activities with the same standard procedures.[12]

An essential part of the stepped-up program for assimilation was the permission granted to the Korean people to change their monosyllabic surnames to multisyllabic Japanese forms. They were free to choose whatever surnames they preferred, so long as these were not distinctly Korean. Strong pressures were applied against persons who were adamant toward this special grace of the emperor. Police and other agencies were mobilized to enforce the program; in some cases the food ration was cut off or children were barred from schools if families did not comply within a given time. Some Koreans welcomed the opportunity and selected the most Japanese-sounding names they could find. The more nationalistic families reported a change in the pronunciation of their names, keeping the same Chinese character for the written form. Some merely added one more character to their original surnames, distinctly preserving the original name.

The final step in the assimilation program was the recruitment of Korean young men for military service. The process of recruitment began soon after the outbreak of the war. Before adopting actual conscription, however, the government announced in February, 1938, a euphemistic program, the "Korean Army Special Volunteer Troops

System." The government and the government-inspired press played up the theme of the "grace of the emperor," proclaiming it a great and distinct privilege to serve in the Imperial Army. Administration of the program was entrusted to the police. Since more volunteers from a jurisdiction meant a better record to show to their superiors, police officials exerted pressures to bring in as many recruits as possible. There were 2,946 volunteers in 1938 and 12,348 in 1939.[13] In August, 1943, when the war had become world-wide, full-scale conscription was put into effect and the façade of the volunteer system was abandoned.

Thus, Korea went into another "dark age" after 1937. Restriction of freedom and the imposition of totalitarian rule were not confined to Korea, for all political parties and liberals in Japan suffered the same fate; but it is important to note that such expansionist generals as Minami Jirō and Koiso Kuniaki were governors-general of Korea after 1936. What, then, was the attitude of the general public in Korea toward the expansionist policy of the government after 1937?

The nationalist leaders of the earlier period showed varied reactions. There were some who chose or were persuaded to collaborate with the regime. Some of these were genuinely impressed by Japanese strength and wished the Korean people to share the fruits of expansion; some others merely paid lip service because of police pressure. Owing to the prestige of the veteran nationalist leaders among the Korean masses, the government resorted to all possible means to get their support. Those who participated in the government's campaign for closer ties between the Japanese and the Koreans urged young men to enlist in the Imperial Army and their elders to donate money to the government, to help bring about Japanese victory. A police report in 1938 stated that about half of the formerly nationalistic or socialistic organizations still existing at that time—youth, athletic, labor, farmer, etc.—either collaborated with or paid lip service to the government policy.[14]

A large proportion of the formerly active nationalists and Communists, however, remained indifferent to government pressures. They accurately predicted the outcome of the war and decided to wait for time to pass by. Their attitude was summed up in a report of the police department in Kyonggi Province in 1939:

When the China incident occurred in July, 1937, they saw it as the precursor of a world war and asserted that Japan would be economically ruined and eventually defeated. This kind of propaganda is evident from frequent arrests . . . Because of the epoch-making revision of the Education Ordinance in 1938 and the institution of the voluntary troop system, there are those who assert that the government policy is merely to uproot the traditional Korean civilization and that Korean youths who do not have any relation to the war are sent to the war front for the imperialist cause. . . . Since attempts by subversives are conceivable, a thorough vigilance network is at work to prevent any disturbance. But it is wrong to interpret the tranquility as an indication of their trust in the Imperial government or intention to become loyal subjects . . .[15]

The same report commented on the uncertain loyalty of farmers and laborers in the province:

Because of new [wartime] industries, the number of laborers is increasing rapidly, reaching about 200,000. Among the farmers, who represent 51 per cent of the total population in the province, about 60 per cent are of the pure tenant and indigent class. Because of their environment the lower-class laborers and farmers are very apt to become the prey of the Communists.[16]

The students were hardly a source of content for the police, either. Among the 42,490 students in the 37 secondary and higher-level schools in Kyonggi Province as of May, 1939 (including 23,900 students in 53 private schools), the report stated:

Although the number of those implicated in ideological cases is decreasing and they are turning from the once-held vogue of socialism, the national revolutionary consciousness deeply held in their hearts is not removed. With the slightest excuses, they promote opposition between Japanese and Koreans, or plan and carry out school strikes. . . . The cases of arrests and punishments are not disappearing at all, and lately the students have been resorting to the most cunning and skillful methods.[17]

The police expressed more confidence in the general public, which we may take to mean the more or less well-to-do bourgeois class and the white-collar workers:

Most of the general public in the province are pleased with the government policy and praise the benefits of Imperial rule. Public opinion became noticeably better after the Manchurian incident. . . . In particular, the quick victory of the Imperial Army in China in July, 1937, the ensuing conquests of Nanking, Canton, and Wuhan, and the alliance of the Axis powers displayed the strength of the empire, and trust in the government became stronger.[18]

The confidence was qualified, however, by a notice of effects of inflation:

> . . . at present, not to mention the commoners' class, even the upper-class families [are] feeling threatened. . . . The rapid rise in the price of commodities, the lack of materials, the discontinuation of peacetime industry, and the lagging military-supply industry have affected many employees and the public. Farm villages are suffering from drought and in some areas cannot obtain food. The lack of rice and staples gave an extraordinary shock to public opinion, and society is in a precarious condition, easily manipulable by the recalcitrants.[19]

Some rumors rampant since the beginning of the Sino-Japanese war were also recorded:

> It is doubtful that Japan will win, because the Chinese also have good training and military preparedness.
>
> Old reserve troops are recruited, and this indicates the weakness and eventual defeat of Japan.
>
> If Chinese troops come into Korea, all Koreans will be massacred.
>
> There are Russia, Britain, and America behind China, and they will not tolerate the defeat of China. No matter how strong the Japanese military forces, Japan will eventually lose as Germany did in the World War.[20]

Clearly, the Japanese position in Korea, despite the accelerated assimilation program and the "movement to mobilize the national spirit," largely depended on the course of the war. As the war went on and the likelihood of Japanese victory waned, those Koreans who had deeply involved themselves in pro-Japanese activities became panicky. The entire population, regardless of attitude or status, was painfully experiencing the economic destitution of the Japanese Empire, and belief in the might of Japan declined in the same proportion as the difficulties mounted.

As has been mentioned, worshiping in Shinto shrines was one of the essential parts of the "mobilization of the national spirit" enforced by the government. The members of every organization within Korea—economic, social, or religious—were required to go to shrines at least once a month. This program obviously conflicted with Christian beliefs and tenets. At the end of 1938 there were 5,185 Christian churches in Korea, and the church members numbered about a half million.[21] Christians, always a thorn in the side of the government, had taken a large part in nationalist movements. Now the fact that their churches had to use the Korean language (because most of the older people, particularly women, were unable either to speak or to read Japanese) was an affront to official policy. The requirement of worship in Shinto shrines and bowing to the east effectively alienated the Christians. According to a Government-General history:

> Touched off by the Pyongyang Sungsil school's refusal to worship in Shinto shrines on November 14, 1935, the example of the Northern Presbyterians was extended to the Southern Presbyterians. By February, 1938, the Northern Presbyterian group had decided to close eight secondary schools operated by it, and the Southern Presbyterians had closed ten schools (one secondary and nine elementary). Approximately 273,000 [Christians] expressed their agreement with the decision of the Presbyterians. . . . This kind of attitude not only contradicted the fundamentals of our national polity, but greatly affected the general mobilization of the national spirit, and could not be ignored . . .[22]

A report of the Thought Section stated:

> . . . Of course there are some Christians who voluntarily joined in every kind of patriotic movement, as did other Koreans. . . . But most of them have an inclination to loathe joining the patriotic movement. In some areas, not only the Christians, but also the students of Christian schools totally abstained from such events as seeing-off the soldiers. Those belonging to the Presbyterian sect and the Salvation Army tend to be very cool and indifferent toward current developments. Rather, they take antiwar or antistate attitudes. There is a considerable number who have been warned or punished for these actions. Also there are many who refuse to bow to the direction of the Imperial palace or to worship in shrines. There are also many who refuse to make church buildings available for the round-table meetings held by the police.[23]

Some actions held to be antiwar or antistate and subject to punishment as crimes were: objecting to war as sinful and cruel; telling church members not to sew *senninbari* (the thousand-stitch cloth belts given to soldiers for good luck); opposing the China incident; failing to pray for the victory of Japan and praying instead for an end to war; refusing to participate in public events held on Sundays; slipping out of public parades in order to avoid worshiping at Shinto shrines. The thought report concluded that:

It is also very doubtful that those who go to worship in Shinto shrines and pray for the victory of the Imperial Army are doing it from their own hearts. These actions are done because of stern instructions from the authorities or coercion by public opinion . . .[24]

The social and economic unrest in Korea after 1937 indicated that the nationalist movement still had a strong potential, despite or because of the Japanese programs of political suppression and territorial expansion. The added misery brought about by the war, or wars, furthered the awakening of the masses, who had largely been indifferent to political events. The marked discontent and high degree of national consciousness can stand also as a tribute to the work of the nationalist leaders, rightist and Communist, and especially so with regard to the younger generation of Koreans born after the annexation, who had been indoctrinated by the Japanese formula for education. For example, most of the thirty-eight students of Chunchon Higher Common School arrested in 1939 for having organized a reading group for Korean independence confessed to the police that they acquired strong national consciousness by reading such literature as Yi Kwang-su's *Chosŏn ui hyŏnjae wa changnae.*[25]

Although the Communists had the ulterior motive of communizing Korea, they always advocated independence. The combination of nationalism and communism had a potent appeal, and the relatively strong Communist movement in Korea between 1927 and 1932 owed much to its use of nationalist ideas. Many young Koreans became Communists by way of the nationalist camp, joining the Communists when they were convinced that the moderate nationalist movement could not accomplish what it intended and that only class warfare on a mass scale would bring results. Of course, the adventure offered by an underground movement may also have been attractive.

In summary, probably the most significant characteristic of the nationalist movement within Korea between 1920 and 1945 was the lack of ideological unity. This was an unavoidable consequence of historical developments. Western liberalism did not bring any answer to the immediate problems of Korea, and at the same time it engendered such iconoclastic tendencies among the leading intellectuals that the young Koreans could not fall back to the old concepts of Confucianism. Also, the modernization of education distinctly had an effect. The young intellectuals, unable to agree on a new ideology to replace the old, could not agree on the future prospects of Korea. Some romantic hopes, nurtured by liberal currents in Japan and the outside world and combined with the conviction of the uniqueness of the Korean people, kept the nationalist sentiment alive, but no single formula for the movement was found. Therefore the intellectuals directed their efforts to whatever they considered best or expedient at the moment under the strong influence of domestic and international stimuli.

Another characteristic of the nationalist movement within Korea was its being generally a frustrated endeavor. Its leaders—if we may use the term loosely—were frustrated persons, dissatisfied with what they saw in the present and unable to direct the course of the future. Because the leaders had no voice in decision making, the Korean people as a whole suffered—as, for instance, in the movement for a "stronger Korea." If the formulas suggested by the leaders of this particular movement were to be successful, there was needed a strong power to direct or even coerce the people. Not all Koreans—or for that matter, not even a majority—were enlightened enough to understand what these leaders were preaching; most were fully occupied finding means to avoid starvation. This movement needed a regulatory force which only a government could have, and the nongovernmental means of control possible under the old social system had all but disappeared.

Within Korea, as abroad, the nationalist movement adhered to parochialism. This characteristic was a legacy of the primitive economic system of the country. It was, also, fostered by the policies followed by the rulers of Korea before 1910. Korea had not known any stimuli powerful enough to eliminate this residue of the past—even the demise of the kingdom seems to have been too weak a stimulus to affect it much. Thus the progressive students in Tokyo often formed groups according to their provincial origins: the same was largely true of other organizations. The Korean people were able to unite beyond parochial boundaries when they were spontaneously and emotionally opposing a common enemy, but any constructive organizational work was based on the participants' provincial origin or other personal ties. Although there was a development away from desiring the gains of one small group and toward desiring gain for the Korean nation, the Koreans were not yet able to abandon the habits of the past in forming groups and factions.

Another noteworthy characteristic was the influence of the students who attended Japanese universities. Because of the fact that the nationalist movement within Korea was of a reformist nature, the number of leaders from the older generations was not very significant. As time passed, the older leaders gradually ceased activity and surrendered leadership to younger men. The most active elements in the nationalist and Communist movements after the 1920's were, therefore, from the generation that attended secondary and higher institutions in the decade beginning in 1910. Since Korea did not have modern colleges and universities until much later, it was only natural that students who attended universities in Japan and other countries between 1910 and 1919 came to positions of leadership, having had the benefit of the best available modern education. Since Korea was seeking new knowledge and the culture of the West, these students came to hold more prestige than any other element in Korean society.

Intellectual currents and the direction of various movements in Korea after 1920, therefore, were largely akin to the situation in Japan. Japanese universities were in a sense a hotbed for radical movements in Korea. They produced the humanitarian and liberal leaders of Korea up to the March First movement and, later, in the early 1920's, a sizable number of socialists, anarchists, and Communists. The striking difference between the Korean students and the Japanese was that the radically affected Japanese students, upon finding respectable positions in society, eventually turned to conservatism after their graduation. The Korean students did not have any normal employment to suit their education and, therefore, turned to the nationalist and Communist movements among their compatriots.

The Korean students in this period, like those in China, were in no sense the subservient class of the society. Students in a country undergoing modernization, especially where iconoclastic tendencies are strong, are not mere followers, but leaders. They have less traditionalism in themselves to battle against, and they are not yet hardened into timidity and caution as are their elders. Because of their inexperience and immature age, however, they tend to drift into radical and sometimes irresponsible movements. They lack the prudence in which their elders sometimes overindulge. Students in subject nations are often well trained in the art of opposition without proportionate training in the art of "positive thinking."

Finally, and probably as the consequence of the characteristics already noted, the movement in Korea was unfavorable to the emergence of any charismatic leader. The alignments were too minutely divided. Differences in ideology, policy orientation, and personal background were disruptive. Parochialism was never eliminated. Differences between young iconoclastic leaders and old traditional leaders were hardly to be reconciled. Heads of the old monarchical house never emerged as national leaders. The Japanese government maneuvered effectively to prevent the overcoming of divisiveness.

It can be said that the nationalist and Communist movement after 1920 produced a strongly nationally conscious Korean people without an effective leader. It produced many leaders of diverse temperament and influence. It also produced an ideologically fragmented nation. This was the Korea of 1945 which welcomed the liberation and along with it the rival leaders and groups from abroad who had fought for the cause of independence for nearly half a century. The returnees added to the ferment within Korea and only intensified the struggle for national leadership. The battle that was renewed in 1945 has not yet been concluded.

Conclusions

JAPAN, through her conquest and rule of Korea, awakened and sustained Korean nationalism. Japan provided the negative and yet the most powerful symbol for Korean nationalism, a national enemy.

In this early resistance movement we find the beginnings of the Korean nationalist movement. The Tonghak rebellion of 1894 was in part a xenophobic movement. Later the Tonghaks overtly used anti-Japanese slogans, as did the "Righteous Armies" in 1895 and again in 1907.

To a great extent, the Korean militaristic nationalists abroad after the annexation inherited the pattern of action from the earlier resistance movement. To be sure, after the annexation they were no longer striving to maintain the *status quo.* They instead sought means to overthrow the alien regime in Korea. Yet most of these nationalists had the same background and motive as the earlier resistance fighters, particularly the nationalists in Manchuria and Siberia.

But the Korean nationalist movement was not homogeneous and, moreover, it underwent a series of complex changes during a period of sixty years. The transition from simple defense of the old order to what may be called "positive nationalism" took at least three decades. Compared with similar developments in some other parts of Asia and in most of Africa, the transition was accomplished in Korea in a relatively short period.

It is impossible, however, to determine exactly what proportion of the Korean people had national consciousness before the capitulation of the kingdom. All the indications are that members of the yangban class were highly aware and proud of their nationality. The cultural achievements of old Korea justified this attitude. The Confucians during the Yi dynasty also displayed great national pride in the belief that their application of Confucian principles was surpassed only in China. The special treatment accorded to the Korean kingdom by the Son of Heaven among his many tributary states buttressed this attitude. And yet it is hardly possible to speak of national consciousness among the Korean masses under the old regime. Social divisions were too rigid, suppression of the lowly masses was too severe, and provincial and regional discriminations were too stringent for the masses to identify themselves with the elite. National consciousness among the masses could grow only when the ruling classes were discredited and the class boundaries weakened. In this connection, the Tonghak rebellion performed an important function. The Japanese conquest of Korea in 1910 and the absolute rule thereafter imposed popularized national consciousness.

We can trace this "positive nationalism" in Korea back to the progressive scholars who were active between the late seventeenth and early nineteenth century and to the progressives of 1884 and 1896. But it is only after the annexation, and more specifically, after the March First movement of 1919, that positive nationalism took a firm hold. Its modern development can be attributed to three factors: increasing contact with Japan and the West, the emergence of a new elite, and the continuing presence of the Japanese in Korea.

The first two factors are closely intertwined. At first, outside contacts were limited to small numbers of government officials and those selected by the government to be sent abroad. But the masses began to have contacts with the Western civilization, initially through the missionaries in churches and schools and later through translated literature and news reports. Also the number of Korean students attending Japanese colleges and universities increased, especially after the annexation.

Through the colleges and universities the Japanese intellectual world contributed greatly to the process of modernizing Korea and arousing Korean nationalism. When the students returned home, they slowly but steadily replaced the old-generation elite as the leaders of Korea. By observing the economic, technological, and intellectual advancement in Japan, they recognized the backwardness of their own nation, and because the Japanese intellectuals were liberally oriented, the Korean students were quick to discover the inner contradiction of Japanese policy. After 1919, when restrictions on journalism was relaxed, the young Korean leaders did not hesitate to imitate the Japanese intellectuals in taking the role of social critics.

Although it is true that the Japanese-educated young Koreans gradually replaced the old elite, we must not ignore other processes of transformation in leadership. One of these was provided by the Christian churches. A significant number of older-generation leaders were transformed in their thought pattern and behavior through close contacts with the missionaries. Along with Christian ideas, the missionaries brought liberal Western thoughts upon which much of Korean nationalism was nurtured. The churches produced not only spiritual leaders, but also reformers and educators.

Western influence cannot be exaggerated. The very existence of the Western nations was a strong inspiration to the Korean nationalists. Although many of the Western powers were colonialist, the Korean intellectuals identified the West as the source of progressive liberalism and anticolonialism. Korean nationalists abroad attached great importance to all international conferences, even though Japan was a participant in those conferences. Many Korean nationalists, especially after 1930, were convinced of the inevitability of the Western powers' fighting Japan in a Pacific war which they hoped would bring about Korean independence. Without this hope, the nationalist movement probably would not have endured.

The peculiar fact that Korea had become the colony of a non-Western power differentiates Korean nationalism from any other colonial nationalism. Whereas most of the colonial nationalists around the world looked upon the Western powers, or the white race as a whole, with at best suspicion and at worst hatred, the Korean nationalists looked upon the Western world as the pioneer of liberalism and a new civilization. Liberalism in the West preached equality of mankind and liberty and welfare of individuals. Koreans therefore accepted Woodrow Wilson's doctrine of self-determination at face value.

And yet the West was indifferent to Korean aspirations. Despite the liberal tradition, Western diplomacy and political actions in the international arena seemed to be dictated by the power politics of the authoritarian empires of the past. This contradiction within the Western civilization must have exasperated many a Korean nationalist. Reinhold Niebuhr's explanation of this contradiction appeared in 1932, but probably none of the Korean intellectuals had opportunity to understand him.[1] Furthermore, an understanding of the cause of this contradiction probably would not have eliminated their frustration.

Disillusionment with the West, therefore, led many young intellectuals and other nationalists in Korea to look to Soviet Russia. Marxism seemed to many of these to be truly liberal. Perhaps the immediate tactics of Communism, i.e., the tactic of liberation of the oppressed peoples, appealed more to the Korean intellectuals than the long-range ideal of the liberation of man. They tended to think in terms of the nation first, then the individual. Despite the strong egocentricity manifested by Korean nationalists and Communists in action, the position of the individual had not been justified intellectually.

These various factors explained the strong current of liberalism and radicalism in the Korean nationalist movement. There was, however, something lacking in Korean liberalism. Intellectual and nonintellectual nationalists alike borrowed the liberal slogans of the West and shouted demands for self-determination, the equality of man, and democracy in politics, but these were imported ideas. Korea had been a deeply conservative nation. Ideals may change, but deep-rooted habits and behavior do not change so rapidly. Reform-oriented nationalists were greatly hindered by this fact.

The third factor, the continuing presence of the Japanese in Korea, had both positive and negative impacts upon Korean nationalism. The large number of Japanese officials and prosperous Japanese immigrants constantly reminded the people that Korea was an enforced dependent. The attitude of the Japanese wounded Korean pride. The strong competition offered by the Japanese in the fields of industry, commerce, and agriculture under government protection may not have damaged the economy as a whole, but it disturbed settled practices and was seen by Koreans as a hindrance to their getting a livelihood. In these ways antagonism toward Japan was sustained and Korean nationalism was intensified.

But it is also possible to see the presence of the Japanese as enlightening. Although not many Koreans were benefiting from the rise of new industries and enterprises, the people could observe the ways in which the Japanese approached certain tasks and also their materially more advanced mode of living. In technology they offered a model for the Korean population to follow. It is certainly possible that the better standard of living enjoyed by the Japanese made the Koreans envious and inspired them to desire independence so as to seek the same advantages.

Depending upon one's criteria of judgment, the Korean nationalist movement may be regarded as either a failure or a success. If the success depends upon the winning of independence, the movement was a failure. Korean independence was not accomplished by the Koreans themselves. Their activities contributed toward the decision at the Cairo conference that in due course Korea should be free, but the factors involved in the Cairo decision were too complicated for much emphasis to be given to the efforts of the Korean nationalists.

If, however, judgment should be reached on more modest levels —as, for instance, the fostering of national consciousness or sustaining of resistance, the Korean nationalist movement can be regarded a success. It must not be forgotten that by 1945 Japan had ruled Korea for nearly four decades. It is not a commonplace of history that an independence movement should last as long as that of the Koreans. The nationalists' determination and continuance are worthy to be admired despite all the human weaknesses manifested.

Perhaps it is wrong to attempt to render a judgment upon such a movement. Rather, it must be understood.

Notes

NOTES TO CHAPTER 1
Legacy of the Past

[1] The teachings of Chu Hsi probably were imported during the reign of Ch'ungyŏl (1275–1308) or of Ch'ungsŏn (1309–1313). Yi Pyŏng-do, *Kuksa Taegwan* [General Survey of National History] (4th ed.; Seoul: Pomungak, 1956), p. 271. See also Takahashi Tōru, "Chōsen ni okeru shushigaku" [Teachings of Chu Hsi in Korea], *Shibun*, XIII, No. 11 (Oct., 1931), 1–18.

[2] *Chu-tzu Yu-lei* [Classified Conversations of Chu Hsi], XII, 8, cited in Fung Yu-lan, *A History of Chinese Philosophy*, trans. Derk Bodde (Princeton, N.J.: Princeton University Press, 1953), II, 559–560.

[3] Cf. Ch'oe Ik-han *et al.*, *Progressive Scholars at the Close of the Feudal Age in Korea* (Pyongyang, 1955), p. 28.

[4] R. M. MacIver, *The Web of Government* (New York: Macmillan, 1947), p. 98.

[5] Quoted in H. H. Gerth and C. Wright Mills (eds.), *From Max Weber; Essays in Sociology* (London: Routledge and Kegan Paul, 1948), p. 417.

[6] *Ibid.*

[7] Exceptions developed at a later period, and there were nobles by adoption. "These are rich individuals who use their money to buy titles of nobility, not from the king or the ministers, but from some powerful family. They thus gain the right to be inscribed on the genealogical registers as descendants of so-and-so, and from that time on all the members of the family recognize them as relatives before the government and public, and sustain and protect them as such . . . This practice is contrary to the letter of the law, but it has nowadays passed into the *mores*, and both the ministers and the king himself are obliged to tolerate it." Charles Dallet, *Histoire de l'Eglise de Corée* (Paris, 1874), I, 111, cited and translated in Human Relations Area Files, *Traditional Korea* (New Haven, Conn., 1954), p. 111.

[8] Gerth and Mills (eds.), *From Max Weber*, pp. 444, 418.

[9] An American observer commented on the tradition-bound education of the Koreans: "We aim at the development and preparation of the student in a practical way for life before him: the Korean has no such thought. He aims to fix or asphyxiate the mind, in order that he may shut the present out and live only in the past. . . . With us education is an exercise of the

faculties, in order that the mind may grow; in Korea it is like a foot bandage or plaster of Paris jacket for the mind; once fairly put on, and all growth and development is at an end." James S. Gale, *Korean Sketches* (New York, 1898), pp. 176–177.

[10] Gerth and Mills (eds.), *From Max Weber*, p. 428.

[11] The yangbans were confronted with a serious problem of unemployment. On the occasion of a civil service examination conducted in the royal presence (the highest grade of examinations) in 1739, for example, about 16,000 literati competed for only a score of positions; in 1769 about 12,000 competed for a similarly small number. The size of the yangban population was estimated in 1750 to be about half that of the commoners. Ishii Toshio, "Kōki Richō tōsōshi ni tsuite no ichi kōsatsu" [Party Squabbles in the Later Yi Dynasty], *Shakai keizai shigaku*, X, No. 7 (Oct., 1940), 77. Ishii's data are from the *Yŏngjong sillok* [Annals of King Yŏngjong].

In 1900 the yangban population in Seoul was estimated as one twentieth of the total of about 200,000. Shinobe Junpei, *Kanhantō* [Korean Peninsula] (Tokyo, 1901), p. 111.

[12] "Anything that interferes with the rigid fulfillment of *yei* (Confucian propriety) is of course to be avoided, for which reason no gentleman indulges in manual labor, or in fact in labor of any kind. His life consists in one supreme command of coolie service, while the coolie responds to every order. The lighting of his pipe or the rubbing of ink on the inkstone, must be done for him. Down to the simplest requirement of life he does nothing." Gale, *Korean Sketches*, pp. 183–184.

[13] As reported by a Catholic priest in 1855 to his superior in Peking. Dallet, *Histoire de l'Eglise de Corée*, II, 387.

[14] *Ibid.*, I, 25, 27, as cited in *Traditional Korea*, pp. 24–25.

[15] There are numerous Japanese and Korean studies of the factional struggles during the three hundred years preceding the annexation. A recent essay is Ōtani Morishige, "Tōzai buntō ni okeru senpai kōhai no tairitsu ni tsuite" [On the Confrontation between Young and Elder in the East-West Party Strife], *Chōsen gakuhō*, No. 14 (Oct., 1959), pp. 463–476. In English, Edward W. Wagner, "The Literati Purges; Case Studies in the Factionalism of the Early Yi Dynasty" (unpublished doctoral dissertation, Harvard University, 1959), utilizes primary sources in treating the period from 1498 to 1519.

[16] Gregory Henderson discusses one of the scholars in "Chong Ta-san; A Study in Korea's Intellectual History," *Journal of Asian Studies*, XVI, No. 3 (May, 1957), 377–386. See also Hyŏn Sang-yun, *Chosŏn yuhaksa* [History of Korean Confucianism] (Seoul: Minjung Sogwan, 1954), pp. 320–365; Takahashi Tōru, "Tei Chazan no daigaku keisetsu" [A Study of Chŏng Ta-san's Philosophical Theory of Confucianism], *Tenri daigaku gakuhō*, VII, No. 1 (Oct., 1955), 1–19; and Hong Yi-sup, *Chŏng Yakyong ui chŏngch'i kyŏngje sasang yŏngu* [The Politico-Economic Thought of Yakyong Chŏng, 1762–1836] (Seoul, 1959).

[17] From "Yŏnjol-ji-jo," an article on the training of soldiers, in his *Mongmin simsŏ* [Maxims of Government], Vol. XXVII.

[18] *Ibid.*, Vol. II, chap. i.

[19] *The Four Books; The Works of Mencius,* trans. James Legge (Shanghai: Chinese Book Co., 1930), chap. iv, sec. 6.
[20] See Mary C. Wright, "Adaptability of Ch'ing Diplomacy; The Case of Korea," *Journal of Asian Studies,* XVII, No. 3 (May, 1958), 363–381.
[21] Ch'oe Ik-han *et al., Progressive Scholars . . . ,* p. 29.
[22] *Sunjong sillok* [Annals of King Sunjong], Jan. 10, 1801, II, 4.
[23] Cf. Oda Shōgo, *Shinmi Kōkeirairan no kenkyū* [A Study of the Hong Kyŏngnae Rebellion of 1811] (Seoul, 1934).
[24] Dallet, *Histoire de l'Eglise de Corée,* II, 160–162, as cited in *Traditional Korea,* pp. 158–159.

NOTES TO CHAPTER 2
The Tonghak Rebellion

[1] See quotations from Choe's *Kyohunga* [Song of Edification] in Ishii Toshio, "Kyōso Sai Saigū ni okeru Tōgaku shisō no rekishiteki tenkai" [The Historical Development of Tonghak Thoughts by Founder Ch'oe Che-u], *Rekishigaku kenkyū,* II, No. 1 (Jan., 1941), 17–60.
[2] Summarized from Ishii, *op. cit.* See also William M. Junkin, "The Tong Hak," *Korean Repository,* II (Feb., 1895), 56–61.
[3] For the rules and rituals of Tonghak see Murakami Chijun, *Chōsen no ruiji shūkyō* [Pseudo Religions in Korea], Korean Government-General, Investigation Series, No. 42 (Seoul, 1935).
[4] Tabohashi Kiyoshi, *Kindai Nissen kankei no kenkyū* [A Study of Modern Japanese-Korean Relations] (Seoul: Korean Government-General, 1940), II, 213.
[5] Cited by Ishii, *op. cit.,* p. 47. Also in Kim Sang-gi, *Tonghak kwa Tonghak-nan* [Tonghak and the Tonghak Rebellion] (Seoul: Taesŏng Ch'ulp'ansa, 1947), p. 22, and in the petition presented to the king in 1893. For the petition see Tabohashi, *Kindai Nissen kankei no kenkyū,* II, 220–222.
[6] Ishii, *op. cit.,* pp. 47–48.
[7] *Paekbŏm ilji; Kim Ku chasŏjŏn* [Memoirs of Paekbŏm: Autobiography of Kim Ku] (Seoul: Koryŏ Sŏnbongsa, 1947), pp. 26–33.
[8] Writings of Ch'oe Che-u, the basic documents of Tonghak.
[9] Kim's childhood name.
[10] Kim Sang-gi, *Tonghak kwa Tonghaknan,* pp. 65–67. Ch'oe did not clearly define the purpose of the gathering. His statement deplores the actions of officials, alludes to the persecutions, and stresses the need for amelioration.
[11] Tabohashi, *Kindai Nissen kankei no kenkyū,* II, 230–237; National History Editorial Committee, *Tonghaknan kirok* [Records of the Tonghak Rebellion], (Seoul, 1959), I, 109–122.
[12] *Ibid.,* I, 108–109.
[13] A widespread revolt in 1862 and other, sporadic revolts. See National

History Editorial Committee, *Imsullok* [Records of the Year Imsul] (Seoul, 1958).

[14] See the interrogation of Chŏn Pong-jun in National History Editorial Committee, *Tonghaknan kirok,* II, 522.

[15] For the personal background of Chŏn Pong-jun and his possible connections with the Taewongun (the former regent of Korea) see Kim Sang-gi, *Tonghak kwa Tonghaknan,* pp. 78–81.

[16] *Ibid.,* pp. 82–83.

[17] Mar. 25 by the lunar calendar.

[18] Tabohashi, *Kindai Nissen kankei no kenkyū,* II, 246–247.

[19] *Ibid.,* p. 251. Tabohashi quotes the proclamation in full.

[20] Kim Sang-gi, *Tonghak kwa Tonghaknan,* pp. 101–102. Kim Ku recalled seeing many yangbans dragged to open roads and forced to weave straw shoes. *Op. cit.,* p. 35.

[21] For details of the Tonghak campaign see Kim Sang-gi, *Tonghak kwa Tonghaknan,* pp. 77–114, and Tabohashi, *Kindai Nissen kankei no kenkyū,* II.

[22] Kim Sang-gi, *Tonghak kwa Tonghaknan,* p. 104.

[23] *Ibid.,* pp. 105–108.

[24] *Ibid.,* pp. 109–113. See also Hwang Hyŏn, *Maech'ŏn yarok* [Unofficial Record of Maech'ŏn], National History Material Series, No. 1 (Seoul, 1955), p. 164.

[25] *Ibid.,* p. 167.

[26] *Korean Repository,* II (June, 1895), 201–208. The author is not identified.

[27] Kim Sang-gi, *Tonghak kwa Tonghaknan,* pp. 113–114.

NOTES TO CHAPTER 3

The First Sino-Japanese War and the Genesis of Korean Nationalism

[1] Yüan was a dominant figure in Korea until 1894, when he fled to Peking. In 1913 he was elected the first president of the Republic of China and in 1916 briefly assumed the imperial title.

[2] The following monographs are available on the attempted *coup d'état* of 1884: Min T'ae-wŏn, *Kapsin Chŏngbyŏn kwa Kim Ok Kyun* [The Kapsin Revolution and Kim Ok-kyun] (Seoul: Kukche Munhwa Hyŏphoe, 1947); Kim To-t'ae (ed.), *Sŏ Chae P'il paksa chasŏjŏn* [Autobiography of Dr. Sŏ Chae-p'il] (Seoul: Susonsa, 1948); Kokin Kinenkai (ed.), *Kin Gyokkin den* [Biography of Kim Ok-kyun] (Tokyo: Keiō Shuppansha, 1944); Inoue Kakugorō, *Koshi yōzon* [Old Papers] (Tokyo, 1907–1911), vols. I–II, VI. Events following the 1884 incident are presented in detail in Tabohashi Kiyoshi, *Kindai Nisshisen kankei no kenkyū—Tenshin jōyaku yori nisshi kaisen ni itaru* [A Study of Modern Japanese-Chinese-Korean Relations—

From the Tientsin Treaty to the Opening of the Sino-Japanese War], *Bulletin of the Faculty of Law and Letters* (Seoul), Misc. Ser. No. 3 (1930).

[3] Sin Ki-sŏk, "Taewongun ui kuch'i sŏkhoe—Chungguk ui taehan kansŏp ui ilchŏl" [A Study on the Kidnaping and Release of the Taewongun by China —An Aspect of China's Intervention in Korea], *Chŏngch'ihak,* I, No. 1 (Apr., 1959), 28–51.

[4] The issue divided the leaders of the new regime in Japan in 1873, resulting in the "Southwestern war" [*Sainan sensō*].

[5] Interesting analyses of the causes of the Chinese defeat in the Sino-Japanese War are available in Li Fang-ch'ên, *Chungkuo chintai-shih* [History of Modern China] (Taipei: Wuchou Publishing Co., 1946), I, 453–468, and Li Chien-nung, *The Political History of Modern China, 1840–1928,* ed. and trans. Ssu-yu Teng and Jeremy Ingalls (New York: Van Nostrand, 1956), pp. 140–143.

[6] Li Chien-nung says the number was 1,500 (*op. cit.,* p. 135); Li Fang-ch'ên says 4,000 (*op. cit.,* I, 439). The Japanese general staff estimate was about 5,000. (See n. 13, below.)

[7] Li Hung-chang, *Tien-kao* (Telegram correspondence), p. 15, quoted in Li Chien-nung, *op. cit.,* p. 134.

[8] *Ibid.* This conversation is also recorded in Sugimura Fukashi (Shun), "*Meiji nijū shichi-hachi nen zaikan kushinroku*" [Record of Difficulties in Korea, 1894–1895], MS in Archives of the Japanese Ministry of Foreign Affairs, consulted in Library of Congress microfilm copy, Reel P–11, pp. 291–296 (original does not have pagination—page numbers cited are those of the copy); hereinafter cited as AJMFA.

[9] *Ibid.,* pp. 296–298.

[10] Mutsu Munemitsu, *Kenkenroku* [Record of Afflictions] (n.p., 1895), p. 3. Mutsu was Minister of Foreign Affairs at this time.

[11] Yamazaki Yūshin, *Ōtori Keisuke-den* [Biography of Ōtori Keisuke], pp. 334–335, quoted in Shinobu Seizaburō, *Mutsu gaikō* [Mutsu Diplomacy] (Tokyo, 1935), p. 172.

[12] Hayashi Tadasu, *Atowa mukashi no ki* [Recollections], pp. 210–211, quoted in Shinobu, *Mutsu gaikō,* p. 169.

[13] *Ibid.,* pp. 210–211. Tokutomi Sohō, a close friend of Kawakami, related that in order to provoke the war Mutsu and Kawakami hid from Premier Itō all the telegraphic reports leading to peaceful solutions. Later the facts became known, and Itō was furious and threatened to resign. *Sohō jijoden* [Autobiography of Sohō], pp. 297–298, quoted in Shinobu, pp. 170–171. General Kawakami is said to have boasted of his trickery in sending 8,000 or more troops into Korea as a brigade. *Ibid.,* pp. 173–174. For more on the part played by the army, see *ibid.,* pp. 164–175.

[14] Tabohashi Kiyoshi, *Kindai Nissen kankei no kenkyū* [Study of Modern Japanese-Korean Relations] (Seoul: Korean Government-General, 1940), II, 304.

[15] "Nisshin kaisen shōshi" [Short History of Sino-Japanese Sea Battles], *Umi to sora,* IV, No. 13, 18–19, quoted in Tabohashi, *Kindai Nissen kankei no kenkyū,* II, 312–314.

[16] *Nisshinkan kōshō jiken kiji* [Record of Negotiations Between Japan, China, and Korea], Oct., 1894, in AJMFA, Reel P–11, p.v.m., pp. 105–106.

This annotated documentary collection was prepared by Katō Takaaki, chief of the Bureau of Political Affairs, Ministry of Foreign Affairs. The quoted excerpts were dated June 11–12.

[17] Sugimura, *op. cit.*, pp. 320–322. Ōtori also sent a telegram on June 13 to the Foreign Minister requesting evacuation of the Japanese troops to Tsushima. *Nisshinkan kōshō jiken kiji*, pp. 107–109.

[18] *Ibid.*, p. 109. According to Mutsu, Ōtori reported the condition in Korea accurately, but the situation within Japan at the time did not allow the policy to be reversed. *Kenkenroku*, p. 17.

[19] *Nisshinkan kōshō jiken kiji*, p. 112.

[20] *Ibid.*, p. 113.

[21] *Ibid.*, p. 109. The telegram was sent on June 14 and received in Tokyo on June 16.

[22] A cousin of the queen and leader of Min clan.

[23] This was a rumor at the time.

[24] Sugimura, *op. cit.*, pp. 315–318. Sugimura's proposals are particularly important because he had stayed on and carried out his designs, whereas Ōtori was replaced as minister to Korea by Miura Gorō.

[25] As the Japanese government had expected, the Chinese government rejected the offer of joint efforts. Tabohashi, *Kindai Nissen kankei no kenkyū*, II, 343–346.

[26] The telegram Mutsu sent to Ōtori on June 15 reads as follows: "The reasons you stated in your telegram of June 14 noon are well understood. However, even though the rebels are subjugated and peace has been restored at the moment, disputes between Japan and China in the future cannot be avoided. In these circumstances the cabinet decided to take firm action to carry out the reform of the Korean government and to demand of the Chinese government that a joint committee be appointed for this purpose. This will be submitted by me to the Chinese Minister in Japan tomorrow. This must be kept entirely secret, and no one, including Yüan Shih-kai, must know of it. During the period of negotiation on this subject it is necessary that our troops be retained in Seoul upon whatever excuse may be available. This secrecy is required because Li Hung-chang is very anxious for evacuation of the Japanese troops and seems to be willing to attain his desire even if it may require evacuation of the Chinese troops. As a reason for delaying the evacuation of our troops, you are to follow a most open method and send the members of the legation or the consulate to the immediate area of rebellion to investigate. This investigation is to be conducted as slowly as possible, and it is desirable that the report relate conditions opposite to peaceful conditions. If it is necessary, policemen may be sent with the investigators for their protection. Regarding the fear of dispatch of Russian troops, that is not likely to happen in the near future, judging from my conversation with the Russian Minister [in Japan] and telegrams from the Japanese Minister in Britain . . ." *Nisshinkan kōshō jiken kiji*, pp. 114–115.

[27] Tabohashi, *Kindai Nissen kankei no kenkyū*, II, 348–349.

[28] Mutsu, *Kenkenroku*, p. 24; Sugimura, *op. cit.*, pp. 345–346.

[29] *Nisshinkan kōshō jiken kiji*, pp. 117–121.

[30] The five points were: (1) Reform the central government and the local government system and select personnel from all classes and families. (2) Re-

form the financial system and cultivate the resources in the country. (3) Readjust the laws, reform the judicial system, and bring about impartial trials. (4) Suppress the insurrections within the country and establish necessary military preparations for the maintenance of order. (5) Firmly establish the educational system. For the entire memorandum, see *ibid.*, pp. 135–136.

[31] Mutsu, *Kenkenroku*, pp. 79–80.

[32] Tabohashi, *Kindai Nissen kankei no kenkyū*, II, 434.

[33] Reform of the cabinet organization, construction of railroads between Seoul and the major ports, establishment of a communications network between the major cities, etc.

[34] Ten articles were to be carried out within six months and another ten within two years. *Nisshinkan kōshō jiken kiji*, pp. 140–146.

[35] *Ibid.*, pp. 156–157.

[36] *Ibid.*, pp. 159–174.

[37] *Ibid.* See also *Chūnichi kōshō shiryō* [Historical Material on Sino-Japanese Negotiations], II, 1207, quoted in Tabohashi, *Kindai Nissen kankei no kenkyū*, II, 424–425.

[38] Article 1 of the Japanese-Korean treaty of amity (1876) said that Korea was a "self-determining state." The ambiguity of the term could be interpreted either as independent (for which there is another term, *dokuritsu* or *tongnip*, vis-à-vis *jishu* or *chaju* used in the text) or as self-governing under a suzerain power.

[39] *Nisshinkan kōshō jiken kiji*, pp. 175–176.

[40] The ex-regent agreed to take power only after Sugimura Fukashi (Shun), the first secretary of the Japanese mission in Korea, put into writing that the Japanese did not intend to take any Korean territory and were acting solely out of righteousness. For the difficulties of the Japanese in persuading him see Sugimura, *op. cit.*, pp. 405–425.

[41] A detailed account is given in Hwang Hyŏn, *Maech'ŏn yarok* [Unofficial Record of Maech'ŏn], National History Material Series, No. 1 (Seoul, 1955), pp. 145–146. See also Sugimura, *op. cit.*, pp. 402–437.

[42] For the reorganization of the cabinet and reforms instituted between 1894 and 1895 see Tabohashi Kiyoshi, "Kindai Chōsen ni okeru seijiteki kaikaku" [Political Reforms in Modern Korea], in *Kindai Chōsen-shi kenkyū* [A Study of Modern Korean History], Korean History Editorial Society Series, No. 1 (Seoul: Korean Government-General, 1944), pp. 1–302.

[43] Particularly Pak Yŏng-hyo and Sŏ Kwang-bŏm, the leaders of the 1884 *émeute*.

[44] Hwang Hyŏn, *op. cit.*, p. 179.

[45] Inoue Kaoru Kō Denki Hensankai, *Segai Inoue kō den* [Biography of Marquis Segai Inoue] (Tokyo: Naigai Shoseki Co., 1933), IV, 512.

[46] The Japanese statement is quoted in Sugimura, *op. cit.*, pp. 758–798; English translation in *Korean Repository*, III (1896), 122–125.

[47] English translation, *ibid.*, pp. 120–142. A copy of the report prepared by Kwŏn Chae-hyŏng, Vice-Minister of Justice and a judge of the Higher Court under the pro-Russian cabinet, *Kaeguk obaek sanyŏn p'alwŏl sabyŏn pokosŏ* [Report on the August, 1895, Incident] (n.d.), is in the Library of Congress. See also Chŏng Kyo, *Hanguk kenyŏnsa* [History of Later Years of Korea], National History Material Series, No. 5 (Seoul, 1957), I, 111–118.

It seems that the queen was aware of the danger to her life. Both the report of the Higher Court and that of Hwang Hyŏn (*Maech'ŏn yarok*, pp. 183–184) state that she considered leaving the palace and on the night of the assassination had confided her fears and her intention to Chŏng Pyŏng-ha, then the Minister of Agriculture, Commerce, and Industry, who assured her that she was safe and caused her to remain at the palace.

[48] For excerpts from the Japanese press see *Korean Repository*, II (1895), 431–435.

[49] Chŏng Kyo, *op. cit.*, I, 128.

[50] *Korean Repository*, II, 390–391, referring to conditions on the morning of Oct. 8.

[51] Yi Chae-sŏn, a cousin of the king, stated in court later that Im called upon him and showed him two edicts purporting to come from the king. Prince Yi induced Im to leave the edicts with him and later showed them to the king, who pronounced them false. Im Ch'oe-su stated in court that he forged the edicts. "He received the edicts, but he said he forged them fearing that the King may be ill-affected." Chŏng Kyo, *op. cit.*, I, 125.

[52] *Ibid.*, pp. 123–124.

[53] *Ibid.*, p. 133.

[54] The trial court had maintained close contacts with the cabinet. Chang Pak, who sat as the chief justice at the trial, soon became the Minister of Justice of the last pro-Japanese cabinet, which ordered the cutting-off of topknots. *Ibid.*, p. 135.

[55] *Ibid.*, p. 128.

[56] He was on a wandering trip in Korea and Manchuria to "broaden his perspective and to obtain Chinese friends." *Paekbŏm ilji: Kim Ku chasŏjŏn*, [Memoirs of Paekbom: Autobiography of Kim Ku] (Seoul: Koryŏ Sŏnbongsa, 1947), pp. 52–67.

[57] *Ibid.*, pp. 60–67.

[58] *Ibid.*, pp. 77–86.

[59] In 1882, because she had been reported to have been killed by the rioters, the people had been ordered to wear mourning.

[60] Chŏng Kyo, *op. cit.*, I, 134. See also Hwang Hyŏn, *op. cit.*, p. 191.

[61] Homer Hulbert, *The Passing of Korea* (New York: Doubleday, Page and Co., 1906), pp. 148–149.

[62] *Op. cit.*, p. 71. Hwang Hyŏn says that An Pyŏng-ch'an, a Confucian scholar, wrote this phrase in his own blood when he was ordered to cut his hair. *Maech'ŏn yarok*, p. 196.

[63] *Ibid.*, p. 198; Chŏng Kyo, *op. cit.*, I, 136.

[64] The authors of the biography of Komura Jutarō assert that the revolt in Chunchon was enlarged by participants in the Nov. 28 incident to draw the Royal Guards and assist a political revolution in Seoul. Although this theory is very plausible, the authors do not offer any substantial evidence. Japanese Ministry of Foreign Affairs, *Komura gaikōshi* [History of Komura Diplomacy] (Tokyo: Akatani Shoten, 1953), I, 80–81. This biography is based on the notes of Shibuo Junpei.

[65] *Ibid.*, p. 81.

[66] Letter to Jennie Everett, Feb. 14, 1896, and address to the Naval War College, in Allen's manuscript papers, quoted in Fred H. Harrington, *God, Mam-*

mon, and the Japanese (Madison: University of Wisconsin Press, 1944), pp. 288–289.

[67] Hwang Hyŏn, *op. cit.*, pp. 193–194.

[68] Hugh Borton, *Japan's Modern Century* (New York: Ronald Press, 1955), p. 208.

[69] On the thesis that "the tripartite intervention was the most important single event in recent times which diverted Japan toward a policy of nationalist aggression," see *ibid.*, pp. 210–212.

[70] Hayashi Gonsuke, *Waga shichijūnen o kataru* [My Seventy Years], ed. Iwai Sonjin (Tokyo: Daiichi Shobō, 1935), pp. 198–199. Hayashi was Minister to Korea from 1899 to 1905.

[71] The statement was made in connection with a proposal to control Japanese migration into Korea. The entire proposal, which covered other aspects of the Japanese policy toward Korea also, is available in Inoue, *Segai Inoue kō den*, IV, 483–491.

[72] For an unfavorable critical diagnosis of the queen see Shakuo Shunjō, *Chōsen heigōshi* [History of the Korean Annexation] (Tokyo, 1926), pp. 149–166. A more sympathetic view is expressed in *Korean Review*, IV (1904), 6–7.

[73] Biographical accounts of many of the leaders are available in An Sang-do, *Kiro sup'il* [Stray Notes on Horseback], National History Material Series, No. 2 (Seoul, 1955), pp. 27–55.

[74] Hwang Hyŏn, *op. cit.*, p. 198.

[75] *Ibid.*, p. 194.

NOTES TO CHAPTER 4
The Reformist Movement

[1] The king immediately ordered that all the pro-Japanese cabinet members should be arrested and killed. Premier Kim Hong-jip, who was actually a conscientious and loyal patriot, defied warnings to escape and became the first victim. Chŏng Pyŏng-ha, who had prevented the escape of the queen from her assassins (see chap. iii, n. 47), was likewise taken and killed. The bodies of the two were dragged into the streets, where an agitated mob was allowed to stone and otherwise humiliate them. The other pro-Japanese cabinet members, except Ŏ Yun-jung, who was killed by a mob on the outskirts of Seoul, escaped to the Japanese legation and were escorted to Japan. For details see Chŏng Kyo, *Hanguk kenyŏnsa* [History of Later Years of Korea], National History Material Series, No. 5 (Seoul, 1957), I, 137–138; Hwang Hyŏn, *Maech'ŏn yarok* [Unofficial Record of Maech'ŏn], National History Material Series, No. 1 (Seoul, 1955), pp. 193–195.

The new cabinet included Pak Chŏng-yang, premier; Yi Wan-yong, foreign minister (with two other acting posts); Yi Pŏm-jin, minister of Justice; Yi

Yun-yong, minister of the army. In April, Yun Yong-sŏn became premier and Sim Sang-hun became minister of finance.

[2] According to Roman R. Rosen, the Russian ambassador to Japan (1897–1900, 1903–1904), the king requested the new tsar, Nicholas II, to place Korea under Russian protection. The tsar granted this request, but his Minister of Foreign Affairs, Lobanov-Rostovsky, intervened and revoked the decision. *Forty Years of Diplomacy* (New York: Knopf, 1922), I, 125–126, 140–141.

[3] *Hwang Hyŏn, op. cit.*, p. 209.

[4] *Ibid.*, pp. 219–220. The value of the *won* at this period cannot be exactly determined. Hwang states, however, that the newly established salary scale for a provincial governor was 2,000 *won* a year (p. 204).

". . . the emperor wished to construct a grandiose monument. He therefore sent a man to Nanking, China, to produce a copy of the tomb of Empress Kao of Ming [although] the annual income of our treasury would not cover one tenth of the expenditure. This was finally done [but] many features had to be omitted . . ." (p. 220).

The funeral is described also in the *Korean Repository*, IV (1897), 433–434.

[5] Japanese Ministry of Foreign Affairs, *Komura gaikōshi* [History of Komura Diplomacy] (Tokyo: Akatani Shoten, 1953), I, 82.

[6] *Ibid.*, p. 83.

[7] Article II of the Memorandum. See Carnegie Endowment for International Peace, *Korea: Treaties and Agreements* (Washington, 1921), pp. 21–22.

[8] *Ibid.*, pp. 23–24.

[9] Chŏng Kyo, *op. cit.*, I, 41. Hwang Hyŏn reports the same. *Maech'ŏn yarok*, p. 209.

[10] *Ibid.*

[11] *Op. cit.*, I, 151–152. See also Hwang Hyŏn, *op. cit.*, pp. 223–224. Nam resigned from his post after the concubine exposed the scheme.

[12] The reason given for his dismissal was that his incompetence in interpreting led to unfriendly relationships between Korea and Russia. Later Kim attempted to assassinate the monarch by poisoning, but the plot was discovered and he was executed. *Ibid.*, pp. 226, 228. See also Chŏng Kyo, *op. cit.*, I, 223–224.

[13] Hwang Hyŏn says that throngs of people came to the king every day with presents, seeking special privileges in mining, fishing, business, and other affairs, and expecting to attain sudden riches. *Maech'ŏn yarok*, pp. 247–248.

[14] *Ibid.*, pp. 293, 297. The appointment, which was limited to sixteen months, was worth 20,000 to 60,000 *ryang*. (One *ryang* was equal to 45 *won*.) The governors recovered their money during their incumbency.

[15] On revolts from 1898 to 1903, see *ibid.*, pp. 223, 249, 260, 263, 282, 291; on banditry, pp. 250–252, 259–260, 265, 274; on the Tonghaks, pp. 250, 255, 261, 267.

[16] For the reform movement of the Independence Club see Clarence N. Weems, Jr., "The Korean Reform and Independence Movement, 1881–1898" (unpublished doctoral dissertation, Columbia University, 1954).

[17] He states in his autobiography that he and Kim Ok-kyun were remotely related. Through Kim Ok-kyun he met Pak Yŏng-hyo and Sŏ Kwang-bŏm, the

leaders of the 1884 *émuete*. These young men met a Buddhist monk who had a book called *Manguk sagi* ("History of Nations") which he had obtained from Japan. When the monk revealed that he traveled to Japan often, Kim Ok-kyun asked him to bring back more books. These Kim and the group ravenously read, risking the danger of being detected and imprisoned, and came to have revolutionary ideas. Kim To-t'ae (ed.), *Sŏ Chae P'il paksa chasŏjŏn* [Autobiography of Dr. Sŏ Chae-p'il] (Seoul: Susonsa, 1948), pp. 62–65. A short biography is available in Channing Liem (Yim Ch'ang-yŏng), *America's Finest Gift to Korea: The Life of Philip Jaisohn* (New York: William Frederick Press, 1952).

[18] *Sŏ Chae P'il paksa chasŏjŏn,* pp. 149–167. The comrade was Pak Yŏng-hyo. They met in Washington, D.C.

[19] *Ibid.*, pp. 167–168.

[20] *Ibid.*, p. 198.

[21] Komura, a graduate of Harvard, was in control of the government of Premier Kim Hong-jip. He told Jaisohn that, since the standards of public life were low in Korea, the American idea of democracy must not be propagated. *Ibid.*

[22] *Ibid.*, pp. 199–205.

[23] A complete collection (vols. I–IV, 1896–1899), is in the Honnold Library, Claremont, Calif. The New York Public Library has vols. I–III, the part published by Jaisohn himself, but lacks the Korean editions in vols. II and III. A reprinting is in progress in Korea; the first volume appeared in 1959 (Seoul: Sege Ilbo-sa).

[24] *Sŏ Chae P'il paksa chasŏjŏn*, p. 213.

[25] For a content analysis of Jaisohn's editorials see Weems, *op. cit.*

[26] *Korea and Her Neighbors* (New York: Fleming H. Revell Co., 1898), pp. 439–440.

After Jaisohn was forced to leave Korea in May, 1898, his beliefs were carried on by his followers; but the attitude of the newspaper became pessimistic. An editorial of July 26, 1898, lamenting the backwardness of the people and their lack of interest in public affairs, made a plea for a representative legislature, but observed that this was not possible in the existing situation. An editorial the next day added that because of the people's ignorance it did not matter now whether Korea was ruled by one or by many: the only road for survival was that of furthering education. The editorial estimated that at least forty to fifty years would pass before a representative body could function in Korea.

[27] Among them were Yi Wan-yong, the Minister of Foreign Affairs; An Kyŏng-su, the Minister of Police Affairs; Yi Yun-yong, the Minister of Finance; Yi Ch'ae-yŏn, the mayor of Seoul; and such well-known civilian leaders as Yi Sang-jae, O Se-ch'ang, Namgung Ŏk, and Yun Ch'i-ho. An was president; Yi Wan-yong, chairman. *Tongnip Shinmun,* July 4, 1896.

[28] *Sŏ Chae P'il paksa chasŏjŏn*, p. 216.

[29] *Ibid.*, p. 217.

[30] IV (1897), 437.

[31] For a text of the letter and description of the meetings see Chŏng Kyo, *op. cit.*, I, 176–179. See *Korean Repository*, V (1898), 109–113, for the background of the Deer Island incident.

Chŏng was one of the radical group within the Independence Club. His book is the best source on the club's activities.

[32] *Ibid.;* Chŏng Kyo, *op. cit.*, I, 176–177; Japanese Ministry of Foreign Affairs, *Komura gaikōshi*, I, 96–97.

[33] The Japanese Ministry of Foreign Affairs noted that "The indignation and anger of Spayer at this time can be seen in the fact that when Spayer met Minister Katō he told him that the Korean royal court could not be saved without resorting to some radical measure. Also, in his opinion, Korea could never be independent and hence it was necessary for Japan and Russia to divide Korea and protect it." *Ibid.*, p. 97.

[34] An English translation of the letter is in *Korean Repository*, V, 113.

[35] *Op. cit.*, I, 182.

[36] *Korean Repository*, V, 114. There are differences among sources as to the date.

Chŏng Kyo states that Yi Sŭng-man (Syngman Rhee) was named as one of the orators. *Op. cit.*, I, 182–183. Rhee was one of the younger members of the Independence Club who joined it through the Mutual Assistance Society (Hyŏpsŏnghoe) organized in Paejae Haktang, a Methodist mission school. Jaisohn occasionally delivered lectures on politics at this school, where he also served as a part-time instructor in geography.

[37] Hayashi Gonsuke says that the king sent to the Japanese Minister, Katō Masuo, for advice. Katō advised the Korean government to thank the Russians for their past assistance and graciously refuse further assistance. Hayashi adds that the king became annoyed by Russian dominance while still in the legation and occasionally sent messengers to the Japanese legation with information on Russian plans. *Waga shichijūnen o kataru* [My Seventy Years], ed. Iwai Sonjin (Tokyo: Daiichi Shobo, 1935), p. 202. Hayashi was Japanese Minister to Korea from 1899 to 1905. See also Japanese Ministry of Foreign Affairs, *Komura gaikōshi*, I, 97.

[38] Jaisohn's friend Homer Hulbert says in his *History of Korea* (Seoul, 1905): "Dr. Jaisohn [was] blunt and outspoken in his advice to His Majesty, and it was apparent that the latter listened with growing impatience" (II, 310). Lillias H. Underwood, in *Underwood of Korea* (New York: Fleming H. Revell Co., 1918), says that he was "gifted, brilliant and eloquent," but also "impatient, precipitate, and lacking in diplomatic tact and soon made many bitter enemies" (p. 184).

[39] Hwang Hyŏn noted that after 1884 "rebels escaped abroad, were naturalized there, and returned to Korea at their convenience. Relying on the foreigners' power, [they] ridiculed His Majesty and constrained the Ministers. Sŏ Chae-p'il did not call himself a subject even when meeting His Majesty." *Op. cit.*, p. 303.

[40] *Ibid.*, p. 298. Chŏng Kyo says that the American consul general, Dr. Allen, had been flattering the royal family members and was specially favored by the king. Hence he accepted the king's view and urged Jaisohn to leave. *Op. cit.*, I, 190.

[41] *Ibid.*, pp. 236–239. But see n. 26, above, for a premonitory pessimistic tone that was appearing in the *Independent*'s editorials at this time.

[42] The memorials submitted on this occasion accused the cabinet ministers of "not abiding by the laws, aggrandising themselves, levying miscellaneous

taxes to properties from the people, and not correcting irregularities in government." *Ibid.*, pp. 247–259.

[43] The translation is from T. H. Yun, "Popular Movements in Korea," *Korean Repository*, V (1898), 465–469. Since Mar. 11, 1898, Yun had been the acting president and was later president of the Independence Club. See also Chŏng Kyo, *op. cit.*, I, 278–285, and *The Independent*, Nov. 1, 1898.

[44] Chŏng Kyo, *op. cit.*, I, 289–290.

[45] *Ibid.*, pp. 293–312.

[46] T. H. Yun, *op. cit.*, p. 468.

[47] *Ibid.*, pp. 468–469. Italics added. For further details see Chŏng Kyo, *op. cit.*, I, 312–407. Pak Yŏng-hyo (cited as Yonghio) attempted to overthrow the government in 1895 and had been exiled in Japan. While seventeen leaders of the club were detained, Pak sent funds to assist the arrested. Because of this action, the king inquired about a possible connection between the club and Pak. *Ibid.*, pp. 308, 328.

[48] *The Independent*, Dec. 31, 1898.

[49] On the Christian missionary activities, including educational works, see Lark-June G. Paik, *The History of the Protestant Mission in Korea*, 1832–1910 (Pyongyang: Union Christian College Press, 1929).

NOTES TO CHAPTER 5
Demise of the Korean Kingdom

[1] The Rosen-Nishi agreement of Apr. 25, 1898. Japan acquiesced to Russia's lease of Kwantung (Port Arthur and Dairen). Article III of the agreement read: "In view of the wide development taken by the commercial and industrial enterprise of Japan in Korea, as well as the large number of Japanese subjects residing in that country, the Russian Government will not hinder the development of commercial and industrial relations between Japan and Korea." Japanese Ministry of Foreign Affairs, *Komura gaikōshi* [History of Komura Diplomacy] (Tokyo: Akatani Shoten, 1953), I, 100.

[2] David J. Dallin, *The Rise of Russia in Asia* (New Haven: Yale University Press, 1949), chaps. i–iii. See also Andrew Malozemoff, *Russian Far Eastern Policy, 1881–1904; With Special Emphasis on the Causes of the Russo-Japanese War* (Berkeley and Los Angeles: University of California Press, 1958), *passim.*

[3] Full text of the protocol is in Carnegie Endowment for International Peace, *Korea: Treaties and Agreements* (Washington, 1921), pp. 36–37.

[4] Assassinated in San Francisco by a Korean, Chang In-hwan, Mar. 23, 1908.

[5] *Waga shichijūnen o kataru* [My Seventy Years], ed. Iwai Sonjin (Tokyo: Daiichi Shobō, 1935), pp. 213–214.

[6] *Ibid.*, pp. 214–215, 219–222.

[7] George T. Ladd, *In Korea with Marquis Ito* (London: Longmans, Green, 1908). The author was a professor of religion at Yale University.

[8] *Ibid.*, p. 260.

[9] Hasegawa Yoshimichi, in command of the Japanese Army in Korea and, by the agreement of Aug. 22, 1904, the adviser on security.

[10] *Ibid.*, pp. 261–262. Italics in the original.

[11] Issue of Nov. 20, 1905.

[12] Ch'oe Chun, *Hanguk shinmunsa* [History of Korean Newspapers] (Seoul: Iljogak, 1960), pp. 123–126; Hwang Hyŏn, *Maech'ŏn yarok* [Unofficial Record of Maech'ŏn], National History Material Series, No. 1 (Seoul, 1955), pp. 349–351. Ladd agrees in substance except that he denies any coercion. *Op. cit.*, p. 266. Another Korean account is available in Chŏng Kyo, *Hanguk kenyŏnsa* [History of Later Years of Korea], National History Material Series, No. 5 (Seoul, 1957), II, 173.

[13] Hayashi, *op. cit.*, pp. 224–225.

[14] F. A. McKenzie, *The Tragedy of Korea* (London: Hodder and Stoughton, 1908), p. 134.

[15] Hayashi, *op. cit.*, pp. 231–232.

[16] Ch'oe Chun, *op. cit.*, pp. 121–132; Hwang Hyŏn, *op. cit.*, pp. 351–363; Chŏng Kyo, *op. cit.*, II, 176–206.

[17] Headquarters, Japanese Garrison Army in Korea, *Bōto tōbatsushi* [Record of Subjugation of Insurgents] (Seoul, 1913), p. 23.

[18] Hwang Hyŏn, *op. cit.*, pp. 326–328, 331–333, 359–363, 376–383.

[19] *Ibid.*, pp. 402–403.

[20] Headquarters, Japanese Garrison Army in Korea, *Bōto tōbatsushi,* table following p. 10 and Appendix table II.

[21] Allen, letter, Apr. 14, 1904, reprinted in *Congressional Record,* 66th Cong., 1st sess. (1919), p. 6611; Hulbert, address at the Korean Liberty Conference, Mar. 1, 1942, in United Korean Committee in America, *Korean Liberty Conference* (Los Angeles and Honolulu, 1942), Appendix.

[22] The emperor's letter to Roosevelt is reprinted in *Congressional Record,* 66th Cong., 1st sess. (1919), pp. 6814–6815, and 67th Cong., 2d sess. (1922), p. 4183; also in *Korea Review,* I, No. 7 (Sept., 1919), 1–2, and McKenzie, *op. cit.*, pp. 102–103.

See also "Kankoku ni oite dai ni-kai bankoku heiwa kaigi e misshi haken narabi ni dō-koku kōtei no jōi oyobi Nikkan kyōyaku teiketsu ikken" [Documents Relating to the Dispatch of the Secret Korean Mission to the Second International Peace Conference, the Abdication of the Korean Emperor, and the Conclusion of the Japanese-Korean Agreement]; in AJMFA, M.T. 2.4.1.9., Reels 382–384, pp. 700–701.

[23] According to Yu Cha-hu, *Hae-a Milsa* [The Hague Emissaries] (Seoul: Yugil Sŏjŏm, 1948). Yu is the son-in-law of Yi Chun. Although Yu does not cite sources, most of his information can be checked in documents. See also Yu's *Yi Chun sŏnsaeng-jŏn* [Biography of Master Yi Chun] (Seoul: Tongbang Munhwasa, 1947). One most impressive collection of pertinent documents is that of the Japanese Ministry of Foreign Affairs mentioned in n. 22.

The petition (in French) submitted to the conference on June 27, 1907, is printed in Japanese Ministry of Foreign Affairs, Asia Bureau, *Chōsen dokuritsu undō mondai* [Problems of Korean Independence], Reference Material Series, No. 24 (no date), pp. 46–72; in AJMFA, Reel SP 4, Special Study No. 8. A copy of this publication is at the Hoover Institution, Stanford, Calif.

[24] Yu Cha-hu, *Hae-a Milsa*, pp. 64–78.

[25] Komatsu Midori, *Chōsen heigō no rimen* [Inside Story of the Korean Annexation] (Tokyo: Chūgai Hyōronsha, 1920), p. 27. Komatsu was a confidant of Itō.

[26] *Ibid.*, pp. 30–31. The church where the draft of the letter was found was attended by both Yi Chun and Yi Sang-sŏl.

[27] Song ("Noda Heijirō") was a man of lower-class origin and had lived in Japan for several years. He returned to Korea in 1905 as an interpreter and showed his allegiance to Japan by requisitioning labor and supplies for the Japanese Army. Recognized by Itō as promising, he was given the post of minister in the Yi Wan-yong cabinet. Komatsu Midori, who gives this background of Song, says that "Sometimes he was mischievous and surprised policemen and was arrested on suspicion of being a political criminal. . . . the formal post of a minister did not suit him very well." *Op. cit.*, pp. 47–49. Song was dismissed in Feb., 1909. Chŏng Kyo, *op. cit.*, II, 309.

According to Kuzuo Yoshihisa, the head of the Black Dragon Society (*Kokuryūkai*), Uchida Ryōhei instructed Song to use the cabinet to bring about the abdication. *Nikkan gappō hishi* [Secret History of the Japanese-Korean Amalgamation] (Tokyo: Kokuryūkai, 1930), I, 281–282. Since the Black Dragon Society had been an important tool of the Japanese expansionists, Kuzuo's account can be taken at face value. For communications between Itō and the Tokyo government and Itō and Uchida see, *ibid.*, pp. 282 ff.

[28] Komatsu, *op. cit.*, p. 33. Komatsu, admittedly a close friend of Song, says that he heard this denunciation of the emperor later directly from Song. For Korean accounts, similar in content, see Chŏng Kyo, *op. cit.*, II, 266–269.

[29] According to a letter of Kurachi Tetsukichi, head of the Bureau of Political Affairs of the Japanese Foreign Ministry, the decision to annex Korea was reached on Apr. 10, 1909, between Premier Katsura Tarō, Foreign Minister Komura Jutarō, and Regent-General Itō. The Japanese cabinet and emperor sanctioned the decision on July 6. Itō was assassinated by An Chung-gŭn in Harbin on Oct. 26. Komatsu, *op. cit.*, p. 15. This refutes the argument that the Korean annexation was prompted by Itō's assassination.

For detailed treatments of the final years of the Korean kingdom see Komatsu, *op. cit.;* Chong-ik Kim, "Japan in Korea (1905–1910): The Techniques of Political Power" (unpublished doctoral dissertation, Stanford University, 1959); and Chon Dong, "Japanese Annexation of Korea: A Study of Korean-Japanese Relations to 1910" (unpublished doctoral dissertation, University of Colorado, 1955). For a study of the Japanese politics leading to Korean annexation, see Hilary Conroy, *The Japanese Seizure of Korea: 1868–1910* (Philadelphia: University of Pennsylvania Press, 1960).

For the text of the treaty of annexation see Carnegie Endowment for International Peace, *op. cit.*, pp. 64–67.

[30] Chŏng Kyo, *op. cit.*, II, 267–269.

[31] *Ibid.*, pp. 272–273. For a strongly pro-Japanese account of these crowds see Ladd, *op. cit.*, pp. 423–427. Ladd estimated the crowd near Yi Wan-yong's residence at the time of setting the fire was about 1,000.

[32] See Chŏng Kyo, *op. cit.*, II, 274–281.

[33] Headquarters, Japanese Garrison Army in Korea, *Bōto tōbatsushi*, Appendix. A military deployment map indicates the size and location of both Japanese and Korean units.

[34] Chŏng Kyo, *op. cit.*, II, 284–285.

[35] *Bōto tōbatsushi*, table following p. 10.

[36] *Ibid.*, p. 7.

[37] *Ibid.*, table following p. 10.

[38] *Ibid.*, pp. 8–9.

[39] *Ibid.*, pp. 7–8; summarized.

[40] The report was entitled "Bōto Jōsei" [Condition of the Rebels]. Quoted in Komori Tokuji, *Akashi Motojirō* (Taipei: Taiwan Nichinichi Shinpō-sha, 1928), I, 419–421.

[41] *Op. cit.*, p. 151.

[42] Akashi's report, in Komori, *op. cit.*, I, 421.

[43] *Bōto tōbatsu-shi*, table following p. 10.

[44] Komori, *op. cit.*, I, 428–429.

[45] *Ibid.*, p. 430.

[46] The quoted phrases apply in the sense defined by James S. Coleman in his *Nigeria: Background to Nationalism* (Berkeley and Los Angeles: University of California Press, 1958). Coleman sees traditional nationalism as characterized by "resistance to (initial) penetration and occupation, early revolts provoked by the imposition or operation of alien political or economic coercions, and nativistic or messianic movements which provided psychological or emotional outlets for the tensions and frustrations produced by rapid cultural change." Modern nationalism "includes sentiments, activities, and organizational developments aimed explicitly at the self-government and independence of . . . a nation-state existing on a basis of equality in an international state system. Its distinguishing features are (*a*) the explicit goal of . . . self-government; (*b*) the concept of . . . unity; (*c*) the predominance of westernized elements in leadership groups; (*d*) the development of permanent political associations to pursue nationalist objectives; and (*e*) the predominance of modern political values and ideals" (pp. 169–170).

[47] See Ch'oe Chun, *op. cit.*, pp. 146–150.

NOTES TO CHAPTER 6
Japanese Rule: The First Phase

[1] Or *Nikkan gappō*.

[2] The biographer of Akashi tells that he was reprimanded by his superior for devoting so much time to the study and is said to have answered, "A soldier must rule a colony when he conquers a country." Komori Tokuji, *Akashi Motojirō* (Taipei: Taiwan Nichinichi Shinpō-sha, 1928), I, 86.

[3] These harsh remarks are quoted from Shakuo Shunjō, *Chōsen heigō-shi*

[History of Korean Annexation], (Tokyo, 1926), pp. 825–826. For similar remarks see Komori, *op. cit.*, I, 501–505. Akashi left Korea in 1914 and became the governor-general of Taiwan in 1919.

[4] Shakuo, *op. cit.*, pp. 815, 825.

[5] See Korean Government-General, *Annual Report of Reforms and Progress in Chosen, 1911–1912* (Seoul, 1912), p. 54; hereinafter cited as *Annual Report.* The title of this series varies.

[6] Shakuo, *op. cit.*, p. 875. In Korea during the three-year period from Aug. 31, 1910, to Aug. 31, 1913, 427 Japanese publications and 182 foreign publications were suppressed. Komori, *op. cit.*, I, 492.

[7] Ch'oe Chun, *Hanguk shinmunsa* [History of Korean Newspapers] (Seoul: Iljogak, 1960), pp. 184–187.

[8] Shakuo, *op. cit.*, pp. 816–817.

[9] Komori, *op. cit.*, I, 491–492.

[10] Quoted in Shakuo, *op. cit.*, p. 818.

[11] *Ibid.*, quoted, p. 822.

[12] In Oct., 1916, Terauchi became premier. Because all members of the Constitutional Association [*Kenseikai*] opposed the Terauchi cabinet, he had to dissolve the 38th Diet on Jan. 23, 1917.

[13] Komori, *op. cit.*, I, 458–459.

[14] *Ibid.*, p. 838.

[15] For the New People's Association see Yi Kwang-su, *Tosan An Ch'ang-ho* (Seoul, 1956), a biography of An Ch'ang-ho (Tosan), one of the founders.

[16] For details of the tortures and the final trials see Sŏnu Hun, *Minjok ui sunan: Paek-o in sakŏn* [Suffering of the Nation: The 105 Men Incident] (Seoul, 1955). The author, then nineteen years old, was acquitted by the court, but was subjected to all the tortures for more than a year. For the proceedings of the trials which reveal the fabrication see D. J. Evans (ed.), *The Korean Conspiracy Trial: Full Proceedings* (Kobe, 1913). The Japanese text of the judgment is available in Korean Government-General, Bureau of Justice, *Chōsen dokuritsu shisō undō no hensen* [Changes in the Korean Independence Thought Movement] (Seoul, 1931), pp. 95–116.

[17] *Ibid.*, pp. 7–9.

[18] Of 16,916,078 Koreans in Korea at the end of 1920, there were 14,366,589 (84.9 per cent) classified under agriculture, forestry, and stock farming. *Annual Report, 1918–1921* (Seoul, 1921), p. 15.

[19] My description of the old form of landownership and the new form of land administration adopted by the Japanese relies upon a study by Pak Mungyu, "Nōson shakai bunka jigyō no kiten to shiteno tochi chōsa jigyō ni tsuite" [On the Land Survey Enterprise as the Basis of the Differentiation of Farm Villages] in Keijō Teikoku Daigaku Hōbungakkai, *Chōsen shakai keizaishi kenkyū* [Study on the History of the Korean Social Economy] (Tokyo: Tōkō Shoin, 1933), pp. 525–567.

[20] The Japanese government carried out a similar program in Manchuria during the 1930's and confiscated a great area of Chinese land in Manchuria. In northeastern Manchuria the farmers rose in revolt. New York *Times*, July 2, 1934. See also Tōyama Shigeki, Imai Seiichi, and Fujiwara Akira, *Shōwashi* [History of Shōwa Era] (Tokyo: Iwanami, 1959), pp. 114–115. The similarities are striking.

[21] About five per cent of the total cultivated area had been under the direct jurisdiction of the Korean government. The government-general decreed that these lands should be nationally owned, including the houses and other fixed property upon them. The farmers who had been tilling the lands, and had enjoyed perpetual tenure and other privileges, were granted tenant contracts limited to ten years or less. Pak Mun-gyu, *op. cit.*, pp. 551–552.

[22] *Ibid.*, p. 558.

[23] *Ibid.*, p. 556.

[24] Korean Government-General, *Chōsen ni okeru Naichijin* [Japanese in Korea], Chōsa shiryō [Investigation Material Series], No. 2 (1923), p. 4.

[25] Pak Mun-gyu, *op. cit.*, p. 11. One *chōbu* equals 2.45 acres.

[26] Korean Government-General, *Chōsen ni okeru Naichijin*, pp. 47–48. This figure includes the holding of the Tōyō Takushoku (Oriental Colonial Company), a government-enterprise corporation. The total cultivated area in 1918 was 4,342,091 *chōbu* and in 1921 was 4,322,035 *chōbu*. Pak Mun-gyu, *op. cit.*, p. 34.

[27] Cf. Katō Fusakura, *Chōsen sōjō no shinsō* [True Picture of the Korean Disturbance] (Seoul: Keijō Nippō-sha, 1920), pp. 5–16.

[28] Headquarters of the Japanese Korean Gendarmerie, *Taishō hachinen Chōsen sojō jiken jōkyō* [The Condition of the 1919 Uprisings in Korea] (Seoul, 1919), pp. 383–384.

[29] An example in point is the textbook for elementary schools, *Kukmin sohak tokpon* [National Elementary Reader], published by the government in 1896. Subjects treated in this textbook are Great Korea; The Extension of Learning; Hanyang (the capital); Our Home; the Story of His Majesty Sejong; Time; The Treaty Powers; London; Wind; Beehives; History of Ulchi Mundok; Garfield and the Independence of America. For a discussion of this textbook see "The Kukmin Sohak Tokpon," *Korean Repository*, IV (1897), 356–357.

[30] For education work by protestant missions see Lark-June G. Paik, *The History of Protestant Missions in Korea, 1832–1910* (Pyongyang: Union Christian College Press, 1929).

[31] Instructions of the governor-general to the provincial governors, Oct. 5, 1910, in Shakuo, *op. cit.*, pp. 719–734.

[32] *Ibid.*, pp. 726–728.

[33] Quoted in Paek Ch'ŏl, *Shinmunhak sajosa* [History of New Literary Current] (2d ed.; Seoul: Minjung Sŏgwan, 1953), p. 64. The novel was published in 1918. The title means "Heartless."

[34] According to Korean Government-General, Bureau of Education, *Sōjō to gakkō* [The Uprisings and the Schools] (Seoul, 1921), pp. 9–13.

[35] At the end of 1917 there were 659 Korean students in Japan. *Annual Report, 1917–1918*, p. 12.

[36] A Japanese report in 1920 listed the names of 21 Korean nationalists who had attended Japanese schools and universities and later taken an active part in the Korean Provisional Government in Shanghai. Ministry of Home Affairs (?), *Chōsenjin jōkyō* [Conditions of the Koreans], No. 3 (June, 1920), pp. 34 ff.; in AJMFA, Reel SP 44, Special Study No. 129.

[37] *Chōsenjin jōkyō*, No. 1 (1916), p. 14.

[38] *Chōsenjin jōkyō*, No. 3 (June, 1920).

[39] Yoshino Sakuzō (1878–1933). Yosino Junjō, his son, noted in the epi-

logue to *Yoshino Sakuzō hakase minshu shugi ronshū* [Collected Essays of Dr. Yoshino Sakuzō on Democracy] (Tokyo: Shinkigensha, 1946) that the number of Korean and Chinese students influenced by Yoshino was considerable (I, 319).

[40] For an excellent analysis of this society see Uchida Yoshihiko and Shiota Shōbee, "Various Types of Young Intellectuals," in *Kindai Nihon shisōshi kōza* [Symposium on the History of Modern Japanese Thought] (Tokyo: Chikuma Shobō, 1959), IV, 271–282. Most of the theoreticians of the labor, socialist, and Communist movements in Japan emerged from this organization.

[41] According to a Korean student in the group, Kim U-yong. *Minjok kongdong saenghwal gwa to-ui* [Community Life of the People, and Morality] (Pusan: Shinsaeng Kongronsa, 1957), pp. 210–217.

[42] For example, *Kungminbo* [National News], published in Honolulu. In April, 1916, copies of two issues in the possession of Korean students were confiscated. There were many similar incidents. *Chōsenjin jōkyō*, No. 1, p. 16.

[43] Three hundred copies of Pak Ŭn-sik's *Hanguk t'ongsa* [Tragic History of Korea], published in Shanghai, were smuggled into Japan in November, 1915, and distributed by Korean students. *Ibid.*

[44] In 1916 three Korean students at Meiji University were caught writing essays on "The Present Situation in Korea" and "The Spirit of the Students Abroad," intended for publication abroad. *Ibid.*

[45] In March, 1909, *Taehan hŭnghak-po* was published as an organ of the Greater Korean Promotion-of-Education Association (*Taehan Hŭnghak-hoe*) in Tokyo; it included articles denouncing the contemplated annexation. The Student Fraternal Association (*Hakuhoe*) published its organ *Hak-ji-kwang* [Light of Study] in Tokyo, beginning in 1914. Four out of the nine issues published up to May, 1916, were suppressed because of anti-Japanese articles. *Kŭndae sajo* [Modern Thought Currents] was published by Hwang Sŏk-u in Tokyo in 1916; some copies taken to Korea were confiscated. *Ibid.*

[46] *Ibid.*, pp. 18–19.

[47] *Ibid.*, p. 19.

[48] *Ibid.*, p. 17.

[49] See Robert A. Scalapino and Harold Schiffrin, "Early Socialist Currents in the Chinese Revolutionary Movement: Sun Yat-sen and Liang Ch'i-ch'ao," *Journal of Asian Studies*, XVIII, No. 3 (May, 1959), 321–342.

[50] The Korean nationalist movement in later years, however, was greatly influenced by Marxism and other types of socialism.

NOTES TO CHAPTER 7
The March First Movement

[1] Anglicized name Shinicky—presidential candidate in 1956.

[2] *Chosejin jōkyō* [Conditions of the Koreans], No. 1 (1916), p. 17; in AJMFA, Reel SP 44, Special Study No. 128.

[3] *Ibid.*

[4] The journey, culminating in the unsuccessful attempt to present the petition to Roosevelt, is described in Robert T. Oliver, *Syngman Rhee: The Man Behind the Myth* (New York: Dodd, Mead, 1954), pp. 84–90. The petition is reprinted in F. A. McKenzie, *The Tragedy of Korea* (London: Hodder and Stoughton, 1908), pp. 311–312.

[5] For a general summary of the nationalist activities in the United States and Hawaii see Warren Y. Kim (Kim Won-yong), *Chae Mi Hanin osimnyŏnsa* [Fifty-Year History of the Koreans in America] (Reedley, Calif., privately published, 1959), pp. 310–352; hereinafter cited as Fifty-Year History of Koreans in America.

[6] Based on "An Shōkō jimmon chōsasho" [Interrogation of An Ch'ang-ho], in Korean Government-General, High Court, Prosecutor's Bureau, Thought Section, *Chōsen shisō undō chōsa shiryō* [Korean Thought Movement Investigation Materials], No. 2 (Seoul, Mar., 1933), p. 123; hereinafter cited as Interrogation of An.

[7] New York *Times,* Mar. 9, 1919.

[8] The text of the petition has not been available to me. Since this petition requested the placement of Korea under the mandate system of the League, some nationalists, particularly in 1921, denounced Rhee as having betrayed the spirit of independence. See p. 149 ff., *infra.*

[9] Yŏ Un-hong, "Life of Lyuh Woon Hyung" (unpublished MS), pp. 31–32. Crane was a member of the Special Diplomatic Commission to Russia in 1917, American Commissioner on Mandates in Turkey in 1919, and American Minister to China from May, 1920 to June, 1921.

[10] From the interrogation of Yŏ Un-hyŏng, in *Chōsen shisō undō chōsa shiryō,* pp. 3–7. For Kim's activities in Paris see chap. 9, above.

[11] *Chōsenjin jōkyō,* No. 3 (1920), p. 20.

[12] *Na ui kobaek* [My Confessions] (Seoul: Ch'unch'usa, 1948), pp. 103–106.

[13] *Ibid.,* p. 102. The role of the people mentioned here will become clear presently.

[14] *Ibid.,* pp. 102–103.

[15] *Chōsenjin jōkyō,* No. 3, p. 21, *op. cit.* The same source prints in Japanese the declaration of independence, petition, and resolution (pp. 23–25, 25–26, 26–27). For a personal account by one of the original committee members see Chŏn Yong-t'aek, "Tonggyŏng yuhaksaeng ui tongnip undong" [Independence Movement of the Students in Tokyo], *Shinch'ŏnji* (Seoul), I, No. 2 (Mar., 1946), 97–99.

[16] "Sam-il undong ui hoe-sang" [Recollection of the March First Movement], *Shich'ŏnji,* I, No. 2, 26–30.

[17] *Ibid.*

[18] *Ibid.,* pp. 28–29.

[19] Headquarters of the (Japanese) Korean Gendarmerie, *Taishō hachinen Chōsen sōjō jiken jōkyō* [The Condition of the 1919 Uprisings in Korea] (Seoul, 1919), pp. 60–61; hereinafter cited as Gendarmerie Report.

Yi Kwang-su states that he had approached McCune in Tokyo, telling him about the plan and asking him to correct the English translation of the declaration, and that McCune asked to be excused on the ground that he was en route from the United States to Korea, but offered to introduce Yi to another American. *Na ui kobaek*, p. 104. McCune, evidently, was aware of the general situation. Whether he had any negotiations with Wilson cannot be determined.

[20] Gendarmerie Report, pp. 13–14.

[21] Korean Government-General, Bureau of Education, *Sōjō to gakkō* [The Uprisings and the Schools] (Seoul, 1921), p. 5. Names and addresses of all the students in middle schools and above, as well as those in Japan, were sent to the police authorities by the Bureau of Education. On Feb. 29, 1919, the police and the Bureau agreed that as a precaution all those students believed to be involved in the movement should be arrested in the early morning of Mar. 1.

[22] Gendarmerie Report, pp. 1, 25.

[23] Korean Government-General, Governor's Office, *Chōsen no dokuritsu shisō oyobi undō* [The Korean Independence Thought and Movement] (Seoul, 1924), p. 68.

[24] Gendarmerie Report, p. 14.

[25] Korean Government-General, Bureau of Justice, *Chōsen dokuritsu shisō undō no hensen* [Changes in the Korean Independence Thought Movement] (Seoul, 1931), pp. 42–44; *Chōsen no dokuritsu shisō oyobi undō*, pp. 42–44.

Negotiations with renowned former officials, such as Pak Yong-hyo, Yun Yong-gu, Han Kyn-sŏl, and Kim Yun-sik, were unsuccessful. The reason these men declined is not known. Late in May the plans of some former official to distribute independence documents were thwarted by the security forces. Archives of the Japanese Army, Navy and Other Agencies, consulted in Library of Congress microfilm copy, Reel 122, frame 35573; hereinafter cited as AJAN.

[26] *Chōsen no dokuritsu shisō oyobi undō*, pp. 45, 47–49.

[27] *Ibid.*, pp. 64–65.

[28] *Ibid.*

[29] *Ibid.*, p. 58.

[30] *Ibid.*, p. 49.

[31] Ch'oe Nam-sŏn has described his experience in "Nae ka ssŭn tongnip sŏnŏnsŏ" [The Declaration of Independence Which I Wrote], *Saebyŏk* [Aurora], Mar., 1955, pp. 8-9.

[32] *Chōsen no dokuritsu shisō oyobi undō*, p. 50.

[33] *Ibid.*, p. 63.

[34] See, for a detailed description of channels of distribution, *ibid.*, pp. 59–60.

[35] *Ibid.*, pp. 60–62. Many additional copies were reprinted or mimeographed locally. Gendarmerie Report, p. 53.

[36] Shakuo Shunjō, *Chōsen heigō-shi* [History of Korean Annexation] (Tokyo, 1926), pp. 876–877.

[37] For the psychological condition of the people see *Chōsen no dokuritsu shisō oyobi undō*, pp. 68–69.

[38] *Ibid.*, pp. 83–84. The date refers to the lunar calendar.

[39] *Ibid.*, pp. 82–85.

[40] *Ibid.*, p. 69.

[41] *Ibid.*, p. 67. The description of scenes provided here is based on official

reports in order to minimize sensationalism, more likely to appear in other sources.

[42] *Ibid.*, p. 71. The planning and the events at the park are described in detail by Chŏng Chae-yong, the man who read the declaration at the park, in "Sasimnyŏnjŏn kŭnalui Pagoda kongwon" [Pagoda Park Forty Years Ago Today], *Sasange,* VIII, No. 3 (Mar., 1960), 234–238.

[43] *Chōsen no dokuritsu shisō oyobi undō,* pp. 72, 74, 76.

[44] *Ibid.*, p. 96.

[45] Pak Ŭn-sik, *Hanguk tongnip undong ji hyŏl-sa* [The History of the Korean Independence Movement] (Shanghai, Wei-Hsin-she, 1920), Part II, p. 42. His statistics include the uprisings in Manchuria, which are estimated to have involved approximately 50,000.

[46] Headquarters of Korean Gendarmerie and Korean Government-General, Office of the Police Director, *Chōsen sōjō jiken ichiranhyō* [Table of the Korean Uprising Incident] (Seoul, Apr., 1919), p. 2.

The report states that the list "includes only those uprisings conducted in areas where the gendarmes and policemen were stationed. Those incidents discovered later or simple uprisings of fifty or fewer persons shouting 'manse' were not counted. These number 242 (additional) incidents."

[47] *Ibid.*

[48] Henry Chung, *The Case for Korea* (New York: Fleming H. Revell Co., 1921), p. 346.

[49] Other monthly totals are: Apr., 5,357; May, 4,763; June, 1,202; July, 569; Aug., 562; Sept., 240; Oct., 258; and Nov., 415. *Chōsen no dokuritsu shisō oyobi undō,* pp. 98–106. The total given for the period is 19,525, but the total by months is 26,343. Perhaps the smaller total omits the repeated arrests of the same persons.

[50] A translation of declaration is readily available through the Office of Information, Republic of Korea. See also F. A. McKenzie, *Korea's Fight for Freedom* (New York: Fleming H. Revell Co., 1920), pp. 247–250.

[51] "Sam-il undong ui hoe-sang," *op. cit.*

[52] Gendarmerie Report, pp. 33–34.

[53] *Ibid.*, p. 66.

[54] Korean Government-General, Bureau of Education, *Sōjō to gakkō,* pp. 8–13. The statistics provided in this report are divided into provinces. The Gendarmerie Report lists a larger number in several provinces, but the statistics are incomplete (pp. 463–513).

[55] *Ibid.*, p. 453.

[56] *Chōsen no dokuritsu shisō oyobi undō,* p. 80.

[57] *Ibid.* It was reported that anonymous donations were thrown into small shops that would have been unable to continue the strike without extreme financial strain.

[58] Gendarmerie Report, p. 79.

[59] *Ibid.*, p. 199.

[60] *Ibid.*, p. 79.

[61] Federal Council of the Churches of Christ in America, Commission on Relations with the Orient, *The Korean Situation: Authentic Accounts of Recent Events by Eye Witnesses* (New York, 1919), pp. 16–17. This 125-page book is full of similar accounts. For more see Chung, *The Case of Korea,* and McKenzie, *Korea's Fight for Freedom, passim.*

[62] Quoted in a mimeographed document of the Japanese Army, "Eikoku taishikan tsuki bukan yori daijin ni naihō no kiroku jikō oyobi kore ni taisuru setsumei" [A Record Submitted by the British Embassy Military Attaché to the Minister, and Explanations] (n.d.); in AJAN, Reel 122, frames 35838–35839.

[63] *Ibid.*, frames 35840–35841.

[64] Gendarmerie Report, p. 259.

[65] Jaisohn and his Independence Club provided a theme for Ku Yon-hak's novel *Sŏl-chung-mae* [Plum in the Snow], published in 1908 and later adapted into a play by Yi In-jik.

[66] See Paek Ch'ŏl, *Shinmunhak sajosa* [History of New Literary Current] (2d ed.; Seoul: Minjung Sŏgwan, 1953), pp. 31–32.

NOTES TO CHAPTER 8
The Korean Provisional Government

[1] For Korean nationalist activities in Manchuria and Siberia before 1919 see Robert A. Scalapino and Chong-Sik Lee, "Origins of the Korean Communist Movement, I," *Journal of Asian Studies*, XX, No. 1 (Nov., 1960), pp. 13–14. For activities in Hawaii see Bernice B. H. Kim, "The Koreans in Hawaii" (unpublished Master's thesis, University of Hawaii, 1937).

[2] Yi Kwang-su, *Na ui kobaek* [My Confessions] (Seoul: Ch'unch'usa, 1948), pp. 107–114. See also, in Korean Government-General, High Court, Prosecutor's Bureau, *Chōsen shisō undō chōsa shiryō* [Korean Thought Movement Investigation Materials], No. 2 (Seoul, Mar., 1933), p. 12, "Ro Unkyō chōsasho [Interrogation of Yŏ Un-hyŏng]; hereinafter cited as Interrogation of Yŏ.

[3] Interrogation of Yŏ, pp. 83–84.

[4] Yi Kwang-su, *op. cit.*, pp. 113–119.

[5] *Ibid.*, p. 119. According to Pak Ŭn-sik, who was president of the Provisional Government in 1925, Yi Pong-su returned from Seoul with a message from the leaders of the Tongnip-dan ["Independence Corps"] suggesting the establishment of the Provisional Government. *Hanguk tongnip undong ji hyŏlsa* [History of the Korean Independence Movement] (Shanghai, 1920), p. 56. But Yi Kwang-su disagrees, and he was directly implicated with the planning, whereas Pak was not.

[6] Japanese Consulate General in Shanghai, Police Department, *Chōsen minzoku undō nenkan* [Yearbook of the Korean National Movement] (Shanghai, 1932), pp. 3–5; hereinafter cited as Yearbook of the Korean National Movement. Based on documents of the Provisional Government and other Korean organizations confiscated by the Police Department at the Korean Residents Association on Apr. 30, 1932, this is one of the most valuable sources.

[7] Yi Kwang-su, *op. cit.*, p. 120.

[8] Yi Shi-yŏng was vice president of the Republic of Korea from 1948 to 1952.

[9] Mun never accepted his post. He was the head of the All-Korean National Congress in the Maritime Province, Siberia, and was interested chiefly in military activities. See Scalapino and Lee, *op. cit.*, pp. 13, 20, 26–27.

[10] Yŏ Un-hyŏng, who was present at the meetings, said that until An Ch'ang-ho arrived in Shanghai the organization of the government was intended to be temporary. Interrogation of Yo, p. 12.

[11] Because the French consul in Shanghai objected to international publicity, the announcement was sent only to Koreans. *Ibid.*, p. 84.

[12] Interrogation of An, pp. 124, 127, 131.

[13] *Ibid.*, p. 124. See also the biography by Yi Kwang-su, *Tosan An Ch'ang-ho* (Seoul: Taesŏng Munhwasa, 1956), pp. 76–77.

[14] Arguments in support of the government presented by this group were that (1) the people in Korea were either being killed or thrown into prison for the sake of independence and the Shanghai group could not sit still and watch these developments, and (2) the task of strengthening the people would be facilitated if it were done in the name of the Provisional Government. An is reported to have been affected by the first argument in particular. *Ibid.*, p. 78.

[15] An feared that the establishment of a government by a handful of leaders might split the nationalists permanently. *Ibid.*, pp. 78–80.

[16] According to Yi Kwang-su, $25,000 was brought from the United States. *Ibid.*, p. 80. Yŏ Un-hyŏng said that Yun Hyŏn-jin brought $20,000 to $30,000 from the United States and that 30,000 to 40,000 yen was received from Korea. "We sent 30,000 yen to Kim Kyu-sik [in Paris] and while we were planning to publish a magazine the Provisional Government was organized. So the remainder of the money was spent for the establishment of the Provisional Government." Interrogation of Yŏ, p. 37.

[17] Proceedings of the Legislative Assembly in Aug.–Sept., 1919, reprinted in *Shinhan Minbo* [New Korea], Oct. 2–Nov. 4, 1919, published in Korean at Los Angeles. Information about the Assembly, unless otherwise indicated, is from this source.

[18] Hayashi Raisaburō, the prosecutor who prepared the Japanese Supreme Court's "Senjin dokuritsu undō ni kansuru chōsa hōkokusho" [Report on the Korean Independence Movement] (Tokyo, 1920; mimeographed), stated that "An Ch'ang-ho has a distinguished intellectual capacity and eloquence [and] is also very able in harmonizing differences and compromising differences of individual points of view" (pp. 14–15); hereinafter cited as Hayashi Report.

[19] Cf. Warren Y. Kim, Fifty-Year History of the Koreans in America, pp. 455–456, and Kim Pyŏng-jo, *Hanguk tongnip undongsa* [History of Korean Independence Movement] (Shanghai, 1921), I, 63.

A Japanese police document dated Apr. 13, 1919, reports the discovery of a declaration and constitution, printed in Seoul and dated Apr. 10, designating Son Pyŏng-hi, a leader of the March First movement, as the president and Rhee as vice-president and premier; it also indicates that a meeting of the National Congress and the Independence Party (*Chajudang*) had been held in Seoul. See Higher Police Report No. 11227; in AJAN, Reel 126, frames 40932–40940.

[20] Proceedings reprinted in *Shinhan Minbo,* Oct. 2, 1919. See also Interrogation of An, pp. 133–134.

[21] Both cablegrams quoted in Warren Y. Kim, *op. cit.*, pp. 459–460.
[22] Yi Kwang-su, *Tosan An Ch'ang-ho*, p. 83.
[23] It is interesting to note the similarities of the system adopted in 1919 to that adopted in 1948.
[24] Yi Man-gyu, *Yŏ Un-hyŏng sŏnsaeng t'ujaeng-sa* [History of Yŏ Un-hyŏng's Struggle] (Seoul, 1946), pp. 23–24.
[25] Hayashi Report, p. 11.
[26] Yŏ Un-hyŏng placed An Ch'ang-ho in this category also. Interrogation of Yŏ, p. 30.
[27] Hayashi Report, pp. 25–26.
[28] Interrogation of An, p. 169. This statement was made in 1932.
[29] The full text is available in Japanese translation in Hayashi Report, pp. 124–144. Premier Yi Tong-hwi's speech of Mar. 3, 1920, expressing similar views appears on pp. 148–151.
[30] Articles 20, 21, and 24. Japanese translation in Hayashi Report, pp. 104–109.
[31] For names of agents sent to Korea and the officers in each area see Yearbook of the Korean National Movement, pp. 59–62, 99–112, 121, 123–124, 159–162. Among numerous references to Shaw see Interrogation of An, p. 147, and Hayashi Report, p. 78. A letter of protest by the British Chamber of Commerce in Shanghai against the treatment of Shaw by the Japanese is reprinted in *La Corée Libre*, I, No. 7 (Nov., 1920), 196–197.
[32] For organizations of various kinds in Korea which came under the influence of the Provisional Government see Yearbook of the Korean National Movement, pp. 46–52.
[33] North Chientao included the Hunch'un, Wangch'ing, Yenchi, and Holung prefectures in the southeastern corner of Manchuria. Koreans populated this area heavily; the Chinese constituted a minority. West Chientao—the T'unghua and Huatien prefectures—was less heavily populated by Koreans.
[34] A complete list of the documents available concerning the Koreans in Manchuria would fill several pages. For a selection see Scalapino and Lee, *op. cit.*
[35] Yi Kwang-su, *Tosan An Ch'ang-ho*, pp. 92–93.
[36] *Ibid.*, pp. 93–94.
[37] Sŏnu Hun, *Minjok ui sunan: Paek o in sakŏn jinsang* [Suffering of the Nation: The Truth of the 105 Men Incident] (Seoul, 1955), pp. 109–117.
[38] Yi Kwang-su, *Tosan An Ch'ang-ho*, p. 94.
[39] Dated Mar., 1920; quoted in Yearbook of the Korean National Movement, p. 76.
[40] Kim is believed to have received 30,000 yen in 1919 from the Association. The amount sent by the Provisional Government is not known. Warren Y. Kim says that the Korean National Association in the United States sent $3,000 (*op. cit.*, pp. 368–369).
[41] The texts are reprinted in Carlton W. Kendall, *The Truth About Korea* (San Francisco: Korean National Association, 1919), pp. 59–70, 71–93.

The arguments in Kim's petition, recalling those presented at The Hague in 1907, are essentially the same as those proclaimed in the declaration of independence at Seoul. In this respect Kim's activities in France were an extension of the March First movement.

Copies of letters submitted in connection with the petition to Georges

Clemenceau, then the president of the peace conference, are available in the Hoover War Collection of the Hoover Institution, Stanford, Calif. The same collection contains copies of letters sent to various delegates, along with the petition and the claims.

[42] Two letters of Kim Kyn-sik requesting the good offices of President Wilson are reprinted in *Korea Review,* I, No. 5 (July, 1919), 9–10. The *Korea Review* was published by the Korean Information Bureau in the United States and edited by Philip Jaisohn.

[43] The Hoover War Collection has copies of the *Circulaire,* Nos. 1, 3, 7–19, 21, 22. The first issue, Apr. 10, 1919, is a reprint of the telegraphic report from Hyŏn Sun in Shanghai. The same collection has a printed pamphlet, *L'Indépendance de La Corée et La Paix* (35 pp.).

[44] Among the guests at a banquet given by him were "General Payeur of the Bureau of Reconstruction; Baron de Gunzburg, Conseilleur d'état de la Russie; M. Frandin, Ministre Plenipotentiarre; and M. Louis Marin, Deputy of Nancy. There were also other prominent men connected with the different delegations of the Peace Conference and a large number of Directors and Redacteurs of the leading Paris papers, as well as many well known correspondents of the leading American, British, Italian and other foreign papers. The Chinese friends were well represented, including M. Lao, the Consul General at Paris. The banquet was presided over by Charles Leboucq, deputy of Paris and vice-president of the Chamber of Deputies. Among those who made speeches were Professor Li Yu Ying, of the University of Peking, Joseph Minor, former president of the Durna in Moscow, and Charles Seldan of the New York *Times*." *Korea Review,* I, No. 7 (Sept., 1919), 9–10; also in *Circulaire,* No. 17.

[45] The work of the Paris bureau was taken over by Hwang Ki-hwan and continued until Sept., 1921.

[46] *Korea Review,* I, No. 1 (Apr., 1919), 90.

[47] Exact figures on attendance are not available, but a photograph taken at Independence Hall shows seventy to eighty persons. *Proceedings of the First Korean Congress* (Philadelphia, 1919), facing p. 40.

[48] For the full text see, *ibid.,* pp. 29–30.

[49] See *Korea Review,* I, No. 1, p. 90. It is apparent that there was more than one "National Congress" meeting in Korea and more than one "Provisional Government."

[50] *Proceedings of the First Korean Congress,* pp. 27–28.

[51] *Ibid.,* pp. 54–55, 71.

[52] By Aug., 1920, the League was said to have 17 branches and more than 10,000 members. Speeches and lectures were delivered by Koreans in churches and at Rotary Club meetings under the sponsorship of League members. *Korea Review,* II, No. 6 (Aug., 1920), back cover. For activities of the League and speeches delivered by the Korean nationalists see vols. I–IV, *passim.*

[53] The exact date is not known. The executive order was published in *Korea Review,* Vol. I, No. 7 (Sept., 1919).

[54] Other members appointed were the Rev. David Lee and Heunju Song. *Ibid.,* p. 11.

[55] Funds for these activities were collected from Korean residents and

sympathizers in the United States and Hawaii. Bonds issued by the Commission in the name of the Provisional Government were sold by agents in the United States, Canada, and Mexico.

[56] *Congressional Record*, Vol. 58, Part II, pp. 2050, 2594–2595.

[57] *Ibid.*, pp. 5595–5608.

[58] *Ibid.*, pp. 6172, 7476.

[59] *Ibid.*, pp. 6812–6826.

[60] On June 14, 1919, Syngman Rhee notified the United States government (and the governments of Great Britain, France, Italy, China, and others) that the Provisional Government of the Republic of Korea had been organized in Seoul. On the basis of the treaty of 1882 Rhee also sent an official communication to the Department of State on June 27 requesting that the United States government "intervene and use [its] good offices." It is not known whether the receipt of these letters was acknowledged. Reprinted in *Korea Review*, I, No. 5 (July, 1919), 8, and No. 6 (Aug., 1919), 8–9.

[61] New York: Fleming H. Revell Co., and London: Simplin, Marshall, 1920. The connection between McKenzie's work and the Commission is indicated in an editorial in *Shinhan Minbo*, Apr. 2, 1925.

[62] New York and London: Fleming H. Revell Co., 1921. Henry Chung received a Ph.D. degree from American University, Washington, on the basis of his book.

[63] No detailed report of its activities in the United Kingdom has been found by me. The *Korea Review*, Vol. II, printed a list of prominent persons who joined the League in No. 8 (Oct., 1920), p. 12, a stenographic record of the meeting in No. 10 (Dec., 1920), pp. 6–9, and the names of the officers and members of the advisory board in No. 11 (Jan., 1921), p. 6.

[64] *Korea Review*, II, No. 10 (Dec., 1920), 8.

[65] The first issue appeared in May, 1920, and contained 32 pages. The Hoover War Collection has Vol. I, Nos. 1–8 (May–Dec., 1920). Whether the magazine was published thereafter is uncertain. It was published by a successor to the bureau organized by Kim Kyu-sik.

[66] No record is available of the amount collected and spent by the Korean Commission in Washington or sent to Shanghai. According to an editorial of *Shinhan Minbo* (Apr. 2, 1925), the Commission may have sent $10,000 to the Provisional Government between 1919 and 1924. The same editorial conjectured that the amount collected during the same period was $50,000 to $60,000.

[67] Kim To-t'ae, ed., *Sŏ Chae P'il paksa chasŏjŏn* [Autobiography of Dr. Sŏ Chae-p'il] (Seoul: Susonsa, 1948), p. 260.

[68] *Hara Takashi nikki* [Diary of Hara Takashi] (Tokyo: Kangensha, 1950), VIII, 267, entry for July 10, 1919.

On Mar. 11, 1919, Hara notified Hasegawa: "The recent incident requires to be treated as an extremely subtle problem in and out of the country. But in actuality, severe action must be taken to prevent the incident from being repeated. But since foreigners are attentive to the problem, adequate care must be taken so that no criticism of cruelty may be invited." *Ibid.*, p. 175.

[69] *Ibid.*, p. 265, entry for July 6, 1919.

[70] According to the Hayashi Report, An Ch'ang-ho frequently visited Sun Yat-sen; no evidence of financial or military support was discovered (p. 41).

Shin Kyu-sik, Minister of Justice of the Provisional Government and a long-time resident of China, is reported to have visited Sun Yat-sen in Canton and had a series of discussions. *Kuangtung Chünpao* [Canton News], Oct. 8, 1920; in AJAN, Reel 123, frames 36845, 36886–36887.

[71] Koryŏ, the title of the dynasty preceding the Yi, here means simply "Korea." For the early Korean Communist movement see Scalapino and Lee, *op. cit.*, pp. 9–16.

[72] Yi's remarks in an intimate conversation, Mar., 1920, according to Hayashi Report, pp. 17–18.

[73] Interrogation of Yŏ, p. 38.

[74] According to Yŏ Un-hyŏng, Yi Tong-hwi sent Han to Moscow secretly and told the others about a month later. *Ibid.*, p. 47.

[75] *Ibid.*, p. 38.

[76] Yearbook of the Korean National Movement, p. 81.

[77] Rhee in his early twenties was active in the Independence Club and was appointed a member of the short-lived Privy Council, a nominal deliberative body of the government. He came to the United States in 1905 after serving a seven-year prison sentence for his speech supporting the pro-Japanese progressive Pak Yŏng-hyo. Rhee received the A.B. degree from George Washington University and the M.A. from Harvard. He received the Ph.D. degree from Princeton in 1910 with a thesis on "The United States and the Neutrality Law." Shin Hung-u, "Ri Shōban o kataru" [Speaking about Syngman Rhee], in Korean Government-General, High Court, Prosecutor's Bureau, Thought Section, *Shisō ihō* [Thought Report Series], No. 16, Sept., 1938, pp. 283–286.

[78] The resolution was passed during the session of Feb. 23–Mar. 30, 1920. Hayashi Report, p. 10. Warren Y. Kim gives the date as Mar. 22 (Fifty-Year History of the Koreans in America, pp. 475–476).

[79] *Ibid.*, pp. 478–480.

[80] *Ibid.*, p. 481. Yi Tong-nyŏng and Yi Shi-yŏng remained in the government.

[81] *Ibid.*, pp. 481–482.

[82] The proclamation is given in Japanese translation in Japanese Ministry of Foreign Affairs, Bureau of Asian Affairs, *Chōsen dokuritsu mondai ni kansuru sankō shiryō,* [Reference Materials on the Problems of the Korean Independence Movement], Reference Material Series, No. 24 (n.d.), pp. 103–135; in AJAN, Reel 122, frames 36751–36754. There is a copy in the Hoover Institution.

[83] *Ibid.*, pp. 125–126. Chŏng-Ku-dan literally means "Righteous-Salvation Corps."

[84] For the Military Unification Conference see Higher Police Report No. 23049, July 20, 1921; in AJAN, Reel 122, frames 36503–36504. The proclamation against the Provisional Government is available in Yearbook of the Korean National Movement, pp. 134, 138–139.

[85] *Ibid.*, pp. 139–140.

[86] *Ibid.*, pp. 130–133.

[87] *Ibid.*, p. 137.

[88] Shin Hŭng-u, *op. cit.*, p. 287.

[89] *Ibid.*, p. 285.

[90] Paek ch'ŏl, *Shinmunhak sajosa* [History of New Literary Current] (Pusan: Minjung Sŏgwan, 1953), p. 118.

[91] See Scalapino and Lee, *op. cit.*, pp. 16 ff. Although another party having the same name had been established by Yi at Khabarovsk in Apr., 1919, and may still have existed, at least on paper, it can be surmised that Yi did not see any contradiction in this. The party was located wherever there were members. Probably Yi regarded himself as the personification of it. Parties such as this were disproportionately top-heavy and their organizations were rudimentary.

[92] "In 1919 the Provisional Government was established, and at that time the Korean people were united at least spiritually. But later it became difficult to maintain unity. My inclinations are not toward political life, and I believe that the Korean independence cannot be achieved in a short period. Therefore, I resigned from the government and intended to strive for the cultivation of strength of the Korean people." Interrogation of An, p. 143.

NOTES TO CHAPTER 9
The Period of Disillusionment

[1] New York: Prentice-Hall, 1938, chap. ii, *passim*.

[2] Some Korean guerrilla activities were continued even after 1931.

[3] Japanese Korean Army Headquarters [Chōsen chūtōgun shireibu], *Chōsen sōjō jiken hōkoku* [Report Concerning the Korean Uprising Incident], No. 22, June 14, 1919; in AJAN, Reel 122, frames 35646–35655.

[4] Hoshino Keigo, "Zai Man Senjin ni tsuite" [Concerning the Koreans in Manchuria], No. 1 (Apr., 1928), pp. 5–7 (MS in Hoover Institution).

[5] Some of these activities are recorded in Japanese Korean Army, Staff Section, *Ōryokkō taigan chihō futei senjin jōkyō, fu futei senjin no sennai shinnyū narabi shuppei ni kansuruken* [Condition of Recalcitrant Koreans in the Area Across the Yalu River; Appendix, Infiltration of Recalcitrant Koreans into Korea and Dispatch of Troops], Aug. 28, 1921; in AJAN, Reel 122, frames 36621–36629. See also, *ibid.*, frames 36409–36411, 36694–36700.

[6] Cf. Robert A. Scalapino and Chong-Sik Lee, "The Origins of the Korean Communist Movement, I," *Journal of Asian Studies*, XX, No. 1 (Nov., 1960), 10–12.

[7] Bureau of Police Affairs, Korean Government-General, *Shina kanken futei Senjin futorishimari jirei* [Examples of Noncontrol of the Recalcitrant Koreans by the Chinese Authorities], June, 1920; in AJMFA, Reel SP 44, Special Study No. 130.

[8] Bureau of Police Affairs, Korean Government-General, *Nishi Kantō ni okeru futei Senjin dantai no jōkyō* [Condition of Recalcitrant Korean Groups in West Chientao], Nov., 1920, pp. 23–24; *ibid.*

[9] *Chōsen minzoku undō nenkan* [Yearbook of the Korean National Move-

ment], Japanese Consulate General in Shanghai, Police Dept. (Shanghai, 1932), p. 83.

[10] Bureau of Police Affairs, Korean Government-General, *Kantō ni okeru futei Senjindan no jōkyō* [Condition of Recalcitrant Korean Groups in Chientao], Oct., 1920, pp. 50–52; in AJMFA, Reel SP 44.

[11] The Japanese Foreign Ministry did not approve their own troops' behavior in Chientao: ". . . the troops did not discriminate between recalcitrant or non-recalcitrant Koreans, and all the Koreans in the area were indiscriminately suppressed. This was just as [was done by] the troops in Siberia who regarded all the Russians in an area as Bolsheviks . . . As a result, the dispatch of the troops in Chientao brought about resentment among the Chinese and also aroused irrevocable enmity among the Koreans." *Kantō shuppei no ken* [Concerning Dispatch of Troops to Chientao]; in AJMFA, Reel SP 45, Special Study No. 135, pp. 2–3.

[12] Sŏ Chŏng-ju puts the Japanese losses at 1,600. *Kim Chwa-jin changgunjŏn* [Biography of General Kim Chwa-jin] (Seoul: Illyu Munhwasa, 1948), p. 160. Ch'ae Kŭn-sik says there were 3,300. *Mujang tongnip undong pisa* [Secret History of Armed Independence Movement] (Seoul, 1947), pp. 98–99. No Japanese report is available.

[13] Korean Government-General, Bureau of Police Affairs, *Taishō jūnen gogatsu chū Kanto chihō jōkyō no gaiyō* [Summary of Conditions in the Chientao Area in May 1921], June, 1921; in AJAN, Reel 122, frames 36418–36437.

[14] Higher Police Report No. 29238, Dec. 5, 1921, in AJAN, Reel 123, frames 36938 ff. See also Ch'ae Kŭn-sik, *op. cit.*, pp. 100–102.

[15] Cf. Scalapino and Lee, *op. cit.*, pp. 9–21.

[16] The proclamation of the Korean Revolutionary Military Congress, dated Sept. 30, 1921, is available in Japanese translation in AJAN, Reel 123, frames 36965–36967.

[17] Statement issued by eleven Korean military groups in Manchuria. *Ibid.*, frames 36959–36964.

[18] Korean Government-General, High Court, Prosecutor's Bureau, *Chōsen shisō undō chōsa shiryō* [Korean Thought Movement Investigation Materials], No. 1 (Seoul, 1932), pp. 26–27.

[19] Reports dealing with the Koreans in Chientao are too numerous to list here. See, however, Hoshino Keigo, *Zai Man Senjin shisō dandai bunpu no gaiyō* [A Summary Report on the Distribution of the Korean Thought Groups in Manchuria] (n.p., 1928; copy in Hoover Institution); Hoshino Keigo, *Zai Man Senjin ni tsuite* [Concerning the Koreans in Manchuria], No. 1 (n.p., Apr., 1928), with an appendix on the Korean thought groups; *Senjin jōkyō* [Condition of the Koreans], June, 1923, in AJMFA, Reel SP 46, Special Study No. 152. The text of the Mitsuya-Yü Chen agreement is available in Japanese Korean Army, *Hizoku torishimari ni kansuru kyōtei* [An Agreement on the Control of the Bandits] (Aug., 1925; mimeographed), in AJAN, Reel 102, frames 8175–8182.

[20] An Ch'ang-ho mentioned some members of the Righteous Group and several other Communists in the vicinity of Chilin as the leaders of this effort. Interrogation of An, pp. 165–166.

[21] Ch'ae Kŭn-sik, *op. cit.*, pp. 146–148.

[22] Sŏ Chŏng-ju, *op. cit.*, p. 166. Connection between the Communists and *Shinminbu* is also indicated in a report of the Korean Government-General, Bureau of Police Affairs, on the "Second Korean Communist Incident," in AJAN, Reel 102, frame 8789.

[23] Ch'ae Kŭn-sik, *op. cit.*, pp. 167 ff.; Korean Government-General, High Court, Prosecutor's Bureau, Thought Section, *Shisō ihō* [Thought Report Series], No. 7 (June, 1936), p. 27.

[24] It may have had as many as 5,500 members. Kim Sŭng-hak, *et. al.*, *Hanguk Tongnip undongsa* [History of Korean Independence Movement] (Seoul, 1956), p. 281.

[25] According to Ch'ae Kŭn-sik, there were more than 2,000 academy-trained officers, and the troops numbered 50,000. *Op. cit.*, p. 168. These figures cannot be checked against other sources.

[26] For details of the fighting see, *ibid.*, pp. 162–171. General Commander Yang Sŏ-bong was killed in action Oct. 12, 1933, and was succeeded by Mun Mu-gyŏng, who finally surrendered to the Japanese on Aug. 27, 1938. Japanese Ministry of Justice, *Shisō geppō* [Thought Monthly Report], Mar., 1939, pp. 293 ff., 307–308.

[27] *Shisō ihō*, No. 5 (Dec., 1935), pp. 93–94.

[28] *Shisō geppō*, Mar., 1939, pp. 309–310.

[29] Ch'ae Kŭn-sik, *op. cit.*, pp. 156 ff.

[30] Higher Police Report No. 18936, June 10, 1921; in AJAN, Reel 122, frames 36337–36338.

[31] Higher Police Report No. 17233, May 27, 1921; in AJAN, Reel 122, frame 36288.

[32] Cited in Warren Y. Kim, Fifty-Year History of the Koreans in America, pp. 483–485.

[33] *Shinhan Minbo* (Los Angeles), Jan. 22, 1925. According to this newspaper, Rhee was infuriated by this decision and contended that the action was unconstitutional. Rhee issued statements accusing the premier and the cabinet members in his magazine, *Pacific Weekly*, saying that he was president by the authority of the government constituted in Seoul which elected him chief executive and hence could not be removed by the Shanghai government.

According to another source, the decision was made in June, 1921. Yearbook of the Korean National Movement, p. 198.

[34] No. 192 (copy consulted in the East Asiatic Library, University of California, Berkeley). See also *Paekbŏm ilji; Kim Ku chasŏjŏn* [Memoirs of Paekbom: Autobiography of Kim Ku] (Seoul: 1947), pp. 288–289.

[35] *Ibid.*, p. 290. Kim Ku established a collegiate form of government, but until 1931 practically no activity was carried out in the name of the Provisional Government.

[36] *Ibid.*, p. 292.

[37] *Shinhan Minbo*, Mar. 5, 1925 (dated Washington, July 3, 1924).

[38] *Ibid.* (dated Nov. 28, 1924). Yi also sent an official communication to the Commission which reiterated the points set forth in his letter to Rhee.

[39] Ministry of Finance, Instruction No. 96, Nov. 28, 1924, *ibid.*

[40] *Ibid.*, Apr. 9, 1925.

[41] *Ibid.*, May 7, 1925; Yearbook of the Korean National Movement, pp. 194–196.

[42] For text of the Seoul constitution see, *ibid.*, p. 11.

[43] For Hyŏn's statement (Republic of Korea Embassy Communiqué No. 2, dated May 12, 1921) and his letter to Secretary Hughes see Japanese Ministry of Foreign Affairs, Bureau of Asiatic Affairs, *Chōsen dokuritsu mondai ni kansuru sankō shiryō* [Reference Materials concerning the Problems of the Korean Independence Movement], pp. 131–132, 137–145; in AJMFA, Reel SP 4. Hyŏn used the title of "Accredited Diplomatic Agent and Representative from the President and Provisional Government of the Republic of Korea to the United States of America."

[44] Higher Police Report No. 23502, "Zai Bei futei Senjin naikō no shinsō" [True Condition of Conflict among the Recalcitrant Koreans in the United States], July 8, 1921; in AJAN, Reel 122, frames 36498–36500.

[45] Yearbook of the Korean National Movement, p. 134.

[46] Issued in the name of acting chairman of the Commission, May 7, 1921. *Chōsen dokuritsu mondai ni kansuru sankō shiryō*, pp. 127–130; in AJMFA, Reel SP 4.

[47] In AJAN, Reel 122, frames 36757–36758. This communiqué is undated.

[48] Higher Police Report No. 23502.

[49] *Shinhan Minbo*, Apr. 2, 1925. According to Warren Y. Kim, Jaisohn organized "Supporters Association of the Great Korean National Representatives Group" (*Taehan Minjok Taep'yodan Huwon-hoe*) and collected $21,219 from Koreans and Americans in various parts of the United States. Fifty-Year History of the Koreans in America, p. 388.

[50] The "Brief" is reprinted in U.S. Congress, Senate, *Korea's Appeal to the Conference on Limitation of Armament*, 67th Cong., 2d sess., 1922, Doc. No. 109, pp. 17–44. Summary in *Korea Review*, III, No. 4 (June, 1921), 7–10.

[51] U.S. Congress, Senate, *op. cit.*, pp. 8–11, 3–7; *Korea Review*, III, No. 8 (Oct., 1921), 6–8, and No. 10 (Dec., 1921), 4–7.

[52] *Korea Review*, III, No. 10, pp. 7–8, and No. 12 (Feb., 1922), pp. 1–2.

[53] Reproduced in Warren Y. Kim, *op. cit.*, pp. 389–393; English translation in *Korea Review*, III, No. 11 (Jan., 1922).

[54] Kim To-t'ae (ed.), *Sŏ Chae-p'il paksa chasŏjŏn* [Autobiography of Dr. Sŏ Chae-p'il] (Seoul: Susonsa, 1948), p. 254.

[55] *Ibid.*, pp. 255–256.

[56] Rhee's activities during these years have been described by Oliver, the American who probably knows him best: "In September, 1922, Rhee returned to Hawaii. But he was far too restless to remain. In January and February, 1924, he sailed from Hawaii to New York, via the Panama Canal, making many stops en route to visit friends and to plant interviews in the newspapers along the way. After several months in Washington, he returned to Honolulu in the late fall of 1924, and settled down uneasily to five more years of work with his school and with the Korean Church. In October, 1929, he set off for San Francisco on another trip across the United States, making stops in Butte, Chicago, New York and Washington, warning all who would listen that the Japanese were engaging in activities inside Korea which indicated plans for

some warlike move beyond the borders. There were few, indeed, who would listen and in January of 1930 Rhee returned once more to Hawaii." *Syngman Rhee: The Man Behind the Myth* (New York: Dodd, Mead, 1954), p. 159.

[57] The amount pledged by Sept. 17 was 955 yuan, of which 159 yuan were collected. See Yearbook of the Korean National Movement, pp. 143–156.

[58] The association was formed in Oct., 1922. The leaders included Kim Ku, then director of the police bureau of the Provisional Government; Son Chŏng-do, long-time president of the Provisional Legislature; Yŏ Un-hyŏng, head of the Korean Residents Association in Shanghai; Yi Yu-p'il, former vice-minister of military affairs; and Yun Ki-sŏp, a prominent militarist in the legislature. Yearbook of the Korean National Movement, pp. 171–172, 187, 207.

[59] Japanese translation in AJAN, Reel 123, frames 37257–37259.

[60] This account is given by Kingsley Lyu, "Korean Nationalist Activities in Hawaii and the United States" (unpublished MS), p. 57. The same source relates that Pak made an agreement with Wu Pei-fu in Peking to set up a military headquarters there. Wu wanted to liquidate Chang Tso-lin with the help of the Koreans. Pak's followers in Hawaii sent him $4,000 for this purpose. The date of Pak's departure is set as May 19, 1919, in Warren Y. Kim, *op. cit.*, p. 189.

[61] Yearbook of the Korean National Movement, pp. 76, 85.

[62] Higher Police Report No. 95, Jan. 8, 1920; in AJAN, Reel 123, frame 36982. Korean Army, Staff Section, *Futei Senjin to Kagekiha to no kankei* [Relationship between the Recalcitrant Koreans and the Bolsheviks]; in AJAN, Reel 122, frames 36367–36368.

[63] About Shin Ch'ae-ho, Kim Ch'ang-suk and Pak Ŭn-sik see An Sang-do, *Kiro sup'il* [Stray Notes on Horseback], National History Material Series, No. 2 (Seoul, 1955), pp. 256–266.

[64] Statement reprinted in *Chōsen dokuritsu mondai ni kansuru sankō shiryō*, pp. 121–125; in AJMFA, Reel SP 4. Declaration summarized in Higher Police Report No. 23049, July 20, 1921; in AJAN, Reel 122, frame 36503.

[65] See Higher Police Report No. 22236, July 16, 1921; in AJAN, Reel 122, frames 36479–36494.

[66] Higher Police Reports No. 22236, in AJAN, Reel 122, frame 36494, and No. 18257, June 6, 1921, *ibid.*, frame 36314. Those elected to the committee included Yŏ Un-hyŏng, president of the Korean Residents Association in Shanghai; Yi T'ak, a military leader in the Chientao area; An Ch'ang-ho; Kim Kyu-sik; To In-gwŏn, former principal of the military academy under the Provisional Government and head of the Military Bureau; and Won Se-hun. Won, originally from Siberia, was a member of the Koryŏ Communist party and one of the chief proponents of the conference.

[67] *Cf.* Warren Y. Kim, *op. cit.*, pp. 489–490.

[68] Interrogation of An, pp. 155–156; Interrogation of Yŏ, p. 31.

[69] In addition to the interrogations of An and Yŏ see also Higher Police Report No. 3943, Feb. 8, 1921; in AJAN, Reel 123, frames 37161–37162.

[70] For example, leaders of six guerrilla groups stated: ". . . our federation purports to attain independence through military power. We cannot join with your government, which does not have any military power and only purports

to attain independence through the sympathy of other nations." Letter quoted in Higher Police Report No. 29135, Nov. 29, 1921; in AJAN, Reel 123, frames 36924–36925.

[71] See *Shisō geppō*, No. 11 (Jan., 1932), pp. 1701–1723. This mimeographed monthly report dealing with the "thought movement" in Korea is available in AJMFA, Reel S 356. (The original report does not have pagination; page numbers used here were added for microfilm.) This publication was succeeded in Dec., 1934, by *Shiso ihō* [Thought Report Series].

[72] Interrogation of An, p. 167.

[73] *Ibid.*, p. 167. Would these remarks not be applicable for the divided Korea of the 1960's?

[74] A report prepared by Prosecutor Hayashi Raisaburō of the Japanese Supreme Court in 1920 suggests some of the strategies used by the Japanese to curb the strength of the Korean nationalists abroad. Hayashi recommended: remove the recalcitrants from the French Concession in Shanghai through diplomatic means; cut their supplies and resources; prevent their propaganda activities; split the unity of the Provisional Government; arrest them through judicial process. See Japanese Supreme Court, "Senjin dokuritsu undō ni kansuru chōsa hōkokusho" [Report on the Korean Independence Movement] (1920; mimeographed), pp. 157–162. There is no doubt that the Japanese followed these recommendations to the letter.

NOTES TO CHAPTER 10
The Manchurian Incident and the Resurgence of the Korean Nationalist Movement

[1] *Gaikō gojūnen* [Fifty Years of Diplomacy] (Tokyo: Yomiuri Shinbun, 1951), pp. 166–167.

[2] Cf. Charles F. Remer, *A Study of Chinese Boycotts* (Baltimore: The Johns Hopkins Press, 1933).

[3] F. F. Liu, *A Military History of Modern China: 1924–1949* (Princeton, N.J.: Princeton University Press, 1956), p. 113.

[4] For a full account see Whitewall Wang, *Wanpaoshan Incident and the Anti-Chinese Riots in Korea* (Nanking: International Relations Committee, n.d.). According to Tōyama Shigeki, Imai Seiichi, and Fujiwara Akira, in *Shōwashi* [History of the Shōwa Era] (Tokyo: Iwanami Shoten, 1959): "This incident was caused by Chinese enmity toward the increasing number of Koreans in Manchuria who immigrated because of depression and poverty in Korea. The Chinese regarded Koreans as the cat's-paw of Japanese imperialism. The Japanese side propagandized this incident in order to divert the [anti-Japanese element of] Korean national consciousness from Japan . . ." (P. 78.)

[5] See Korean Government-General, High Court, Prosecutor's Bureau, Thought Section, *Shisō ihō* [Thought Report Series], No. 7 (June, 1936), pp.

22–25. See also *Shōwa shichinen chū ni okeru shakai undō no jōkyō* [The Situation with Respect to Social Movements in 1932], published by the Security Division (*Keihokyoku*) of the Japanese Home Ministry (Tokyo, 1933), p. 1553; hereinafter cited as *Shakai undō no jōkyō,* followed by the year date.

[6] *Paekbŏm ilji, Kim Ku chasŏjŏn* [Memoirs of Paekbŏm: Autobiography of Kim Ku] (Seoul: 1947), pp. 299–305; Warren Y. Kim, Fifty-Year History of the Koreans in America, p. 215.

[7] Kim Ku, *op. cit.,* pp. 300–301.

[8] Tanaka Ryūkichi, then assistant to the Japanese military attaché in Shanghai, says that the Chinese were hired by him (or his group) to attack the Japanese monks in order to instigate an incident and that he was asked by his colleagues in Manchuria to start an incident in Shanghai in order to divert the attention of the world from the Japanese activities in Manchuria. "Shanghai Incident Was Started This Way," in *Himerareta Shōwashi* [Hidden History of Shōwa Era], special issue of *Chisei* (Tokyo), Dec., 1956, pp. 182–183.

[9] Kim Ku, *op. cit.,* p. 303. Agents Yi Tŏk-ju and Yu Chin-Sik were arrested and sentenced to seven- and six-year terms. See An Sang-do, *Kiro sup'il* [Stray Notes on Horseback], Korean Historical Material Series, No. 2 (Seoul, 1955), pp. 424–425.

[10] *Op. cit.,* pp. 304–305.

[11] The court-martial record of Yun Pong-gil is available in Korean Government-General, High Court, Prosecutor's Bureau, Thought Section, *Shisō geppō* [Thought Monthly Report], II, No. 3 (June, 1932); in AJMFA, Reel S 357, pp. 2074–2080. The London *Times* (Apr. 30) called it an "abominable outrage," and the New York *Times* (Apr. 29) carried a front-page story. See also *Yomiuri Shinbun* (Tokyo), Apr. 30 (evening).

[12] Kim Ku, *op. cit.,* pp. 311–313.

[13] *Ibid.,* pp. 322–324.

[14] *Shisō ihō,* No. 9 (Dec., 1936), pp. 115–116. This information was provided to the Japanese prosecutor by O Myŏn-jik, a follower of Kim Ku, while in Haeju prison. There is no Chinese source available to verify the information. It is certain, however, that Ch'ên Kuo-fu, one of the famous Ch'ên brothers, had close relations with the Koreans. Ch'ên wrote a preface for a Korean translation by Yŏn Su-san of *Shanmin Chui* [Three Principles] and related his intimacy with many Koreans. See *Ch'ên Kuo-fu hsien-sêng ch'üan-chih* [Complete Works of Ch'ên Kuo-fu] (Hong Kong, 1952), IX, 150.

[15] *Shisō ihō,* No. 7 (June, 1936), pp. 29, 37–39.

[16] *Ibid.,* pp. 115–116.

[17] *Ibid.,* pp. 111–114.

[18] At least one of the reasons was his announcement after the Hungk'ou Park incident that it was his own doing. Kim states that he wished to avoid implicating other Koreans, but the others saw it differently. *Op. cit.,* pp. 311–312.

[19] The splinter group of the Shanghai Independence party had named themselves the Korean Revolutionary party (*Hanguk Hyŏngmyŏng-dang*). The Korean Revolutionary party and the Korean Independence party of Manchuria were dissolved simultaneously when the New Korean Independence party was formed. Concerning the formation of the new party, its principles, and its constitution see *Shisō ihō,* No. 7 (June, 1936), pp. 27–29.

[20] *Ibid.*, pp. 34–39.

[21] *Shisō geppō,* No. 11 (Jan., 1932), pp. 1701–1709, available in AJMFA, Reel S 356; page numbers added for microfilm.

[22] Most of the early activities of Kim Won-bong and his group are recorded in Pak T'ae-won, *Yaksan kwa Uiyŏldan* [Yaksan and Uiyŏldan] (Seoul: Paekyang-sa, 1947). "Yaksan" is an alias of Kim Won-bong.

[23] Their trial is reported in *Shisō ihō,* No. 4 (Sept., 1935), pp. 20–32.

[24] *Ibid.*, p. 129. Kim is reported to have attended Whampoa in 1925; thus he may have had support because of school ties. Kim O-sŏng, *Chidoja Kunsang* [An Account of the Leaders] (Seoul: Taesŏng Munhwasa, 1946), I, 62; also *Shisō ihō,* No. 5 (Dec., 1935), p. 85. If these accounts are correct, Kim Won-bong preceded Kim Ku in approaching the Chinese government.

[25] In addition to military training, the trainees were instructed in economics, dialectics, the "Three People's Principles," psychology, the history of the Chinese revolution, the history of the Korean movement, the history of revolutions, the organization of parties, the history of Uiyŏldan, and the current situation in Korea. *Shisō ihō,* No. 4 (Sept., 1935), p. 136.

[26] *Ibid.*, pp. 106–150.

[27] *Ibid.*, p. 135.

[28] He reportedly had a close connection with Yi Tong-hwi and Kim Rip, the leaders of the Koryŏ Communist party. Cf. Robert A. Scalapino and Chong-Sik Lee, "The Origins of the Korean Communist Movement, I," *Journal of Asian Studies,* XX, No. 1 (Nov., 1960), 18.

[29] *Shisō ihō,* No. 5 (Dec., 1935), pp. 85 ff., and No. 7 (June, 1936), pp. 40 ff. The complete text of the League's declaration is printed in both issues.

[30] *Shisō ihō,* No. 5, p. 86.

[31] *Ibid.*, pp. 88–89.

[32] *Ibid.*, p. 89.

[33] *Shisō ihō,* No. 7, p. 43.

[34] This group in Hawaii was composed of the supporters of Pak Yong-man, who had been assassinated by members of Uiyŏldan in Peking. Instead of delegates from Hawaii, Kim Kyu-sik, and Shin Ik-hi represented the group. *Shakai undō no jōkyō,* 1932, p. 1514.

[35] *Shisō ihō,* No. 5, pp. 98–99.

[36] For the political principles of Uiyŏldan, as revised Feb. 12, 1935, see *Shisō ihō,* No. 4 (Sept., 1935), pp. 145–146.

[37] *Shakai undō no jōkyō,* 1936, p. 1590.

[38] *Ibid.*, p. 1572.

[39] *Ibid.*, pp. 1585–1586.

[40] *Ibid.*, p. 1571.

[41] See AJMFA, Reels P 63–P 64, a collection of documents dealing with the problems of North China from May, 1933, to June, 1937.

[42] Yi and his followers revived the name of the Korean Revolutionary party (*Chosŏn Hyŏngmyŏng-dang*) in May, 1937. The East Asiatic Library of the University of California, Berkeley, has a copy of the declaration issued by the party. The declaration blames the failure of the united front on the Uiyŏldan group, which is attacked as "specializing in opportunistic and insidious profiteering, using elegant Communist concepts" (p. 9).

[43] *Shakai undō no jōkyō,* 1936, p. 1578.

[44] *Ibid.*, p. 1573.

[45] *Ibid.*, p. 1578. Yi traveled to Sian in Sept., 1936, received 1,000 dollars as the initial payment, and was promised monthly aid. The unit of currency may have been the Chinese silver dollar. Another source says 1,000 yuan. Criminal Affairs Bureau, Ministry of Justice, Japan, *Shisō jōsei shisatsu hōkokushu* [Collection of Thought-Condition Inspection Tour Reports], No. 3 (May, 1938), p. 6.

[46] *Shakai undō no jōkyō,* 1936, p. 1579.

[47] *Shisō ihō,* No. 7 (June, 1936), pp. 79–95.

[48] *Ibid.*, pp. 97–99; also in *Shakai undō no jōkyō,* 1936, pp. 1558–1559.

[49] *Shisō ihō,* No. 7 (June, 1936), pp. 100–102.

[50] *Ibid.*, pp. 1560–1561; *Shisō ihō,* No. 20 (Sept., 1939), pp. 267–268.

[51] The East Asiatic Library of Columbia University has eight issues of the corps's *Hanch'ŏng* (1936–1937). The East Asiatic Library of the University of California has Nos. 1–2 of the party's *Hanmin* (Mar. 15 and Apr. 29, 1936). A list of the publications of the Korean National party during 1936 is provided in *Shakai undō no jōkyō,* 1936, p. 1567.

NOTES TO CHAPTER 11
The Road to Chungking

[1] Japanese Ministry of Home Affairs (?), *Chōsenjin jōkyō* [Condition of the Koreans], No. 1 (1916), p. 17; in AJMFA, Reel SP 44, Special Study No. 128. This statement is attributed to Song Chin-u.

[2] Korean Government-General, High Court, Prosecutor's Bureau, Thought Section, *Shisō ihō* [Thought Report Series], No. 22 (Mar. 1940), p. 158.

Another source indicates that the Korean leaders held meetings after this conference to decide on future policies. The leaders of the right-wing Provisional Government in a cabinet meeting on July 15 decided that "the opportunity for the Korean people to start an anti-Japanese war and clear the disgrace of our nation has arrived." The cabinet meeting established a military committee with six members under Yu Tong-sŏl to mobilize young Koreans. *Shakai undō no jōkyō,* 1942, p. 949.

[3] *Shisō ihō,* No. 22, pp. 158–159. When Nanking fell to the Japanese later in December, the trainees were moved to Chiangling, Hupei Province.

[4] *Shisō ihō,* No. 14 (Mar., 1938), pp. 219–220, 222. Numbering added.

[5] Cf. *Shakai undō no jōkyō,* 1936, pp. 1569–1570.

[6] The East Asiatic Library, University of California, Berkeley, has a copy of the declaration.

[7] For organizational activities, charters, and other relevant information on these organizations, see Warren Y. Kim (Kim Won-yong), *Chae Mi Hanin osimnyŏnsa* [Fifty-Year History of the Koreans in America] (Reedley, Calif.: privately printed, 1959), pp. 119–133, 164–176.

[8] *Shisō ihō,* No. 14, p. 225.

[9] For Rhee's activities in Geneva see Robert T. Oliver, *Syngman Rhee: The Man Behind the Myth* (New York: Dodd, Mead, 1954), pp. 160–164. The petitions are printed in English in Korean Government-General, High Court, Prosecutor's Bureau, Thought Section, *Shisō geppō* [Thought Monthly Report], III, No. 5 (Aug. 15, 1933) and No. 6 (Sept. 15, 1933); in AJMFA, Reel S 358.

[10] See note 6. Dated Aug. 1, 1937.

[11] *Paekbŏm ilji, Kim Ku chasŏjŏn* [Memoirs of Paekbŏm: Autobiography of Kim Ku] (Seoul, 1947), pp. 335–336; *Shisō ihō*, No. 16 (Sept., 1938), p. 156.

[12] *Ibid.*

[13] Japanese Ministry of Home Affairs, Security Bureau, *Tokkō geppō* [Special High Police Monthly Report], Aug., 1938, pp. 90–91.

[14] In 1949 Kim Ku was assassinated by a young Korean army officer.

[15] *Shakai undō no jōkyō*, 1942, pp. 962–963.

[16] *Shisō ihō*, No. 14, p. 159.

[17] *Shisō ihō*, No. 22, p. 160.

[18] *Ibid.*, p. 161.

[19] *Ibid.*, p. 162.

[20] *Ibid.*

[21] *Tokkō geppō*, Aug., 1938, p. 88. According to this source, the Communists rejected the appeal and advised that the Corps ought to appeal to Kim Wonbong.

[22] *Shakai undō no jōkyō*, 1942, p. 962.

[23] *Shisō ihō*, No. 22, p. 162; *Shakai undō no jōkyō*, 1942, pp. 963–964.

[24] *Ibid.*

[25] Ko Chih-feng, *Ch'ao-hsien ko-ming chi* [The Korean Revolution] (Shanghai: Commercial Press, 1945), pp. 57–58.

[26] Japanese translation in *Shisō ihō*, No. 20 (Sept., 1939), pp. 243–351. The original was in Chinese.

[27] Kim Ku, *op. cit.*, pp. 342–344.

[28] *Shisō geppō*, No. 78 (Dec., 1940), p. 197.

[29] *Op. cit.*, p. 343.

NOTES TO CHAPTER 12
Finale of the Exiled Movement

[1] Sŏ Pyŏng-gon, who wrote a short and yet the most extensive biography available on Mu Chŏng, says that Mu was a graduate of a Chinese Northern Military Academy. He was commissioned captain in the Chinese Nationalist army upon graduation and rapidly rose to lieutenant colonel in 1927, when he was only twenty-two years old. His specialty was artillery. He joined the Chinese Communist party in 1925, and for this reason was arrested by the

Kuomintang government. But the Chinese students in Wuchang (Hupei Province) demanded his release by street demonstrations, and the Kuomintang government released him. For leadership in the Shanghai Communist riots of 1929 he was jailed by the British for two months. He later participated in the construction of the Chinese soviet, rapidly rising in the Communist army from company commander to regiment commander and becoming a member of the Military Committee of the Chinese Communist party. During the "long march" (1934), he was appointed chief of the operations section. In 1936 he studied at the Red Army College in Yenan, after which he was appointed chief of operations of the Eighth Route Army. Later he established an artillery unit, of which he became the commander. He was a close associate of Chu Teh, the noted Communist general. "Mu Chŏng changgun ildae ki" [A Life History of General Mu Chŏng], *Shinch'ŏnji* [New Universe] (Seoul), Mar., 1946, pp. 226, 238–242. Kim O-sŏng says that Mu was a Whampoa Academy graduate. *Chidoja kunsang* [Image of the Leaders] (Seoul: Taesŏng Ch'ulp'ansa, 1946), I, 71. Helen Snow cites him as P'eng Teh-huai's chief of staff. Kim San and Nym Wales, *Song of Ariran* (New York: John Day, 1941), p. 212.

[2] *Ibid.*, 226, 241.

[3] *Shakai undō no jōkyō*, 1942, p. 983.

[4] Japanese Ministry of Home Affairs, Security Division, *Tokkō geppō* [Special High Police Monthly Report], Apr., 1941, p. 96. See also Sŏ Pyŏng-gon, *op. cit.*, p. 226, and *Chōsen minzoku kaihō tōsō-shi* [A History of the Korean People's Struggle for Emancipation] (Kyoto, 1952), a Japanese translation of the Korean original edited by the Korean History Editorial Committee (Pyongyang, 1949), p. 327.

[5] *Tokkō geppō*, Apr., 1941, pp. 97–101.

[6] *Ibid.*, July, 1941, pp. 119–122.

[7] *Shakai undō no jōkyō*, 1942, p. 983.

[8] For example, Chu Yong-in was sent to Chungking for liaison purposes. *Ibid.*

[9] *Tou-cheng shih-pa-nien* [Eighteen Years of Struggle] (Hong Kong: Asia Press, 1952), pp. 173–174.

[10] *Ibid.*, pp. 174–176.

[11] *Ibid.*, pp. 176, 178.

[12] *Ibid.*, pp. 178–179.

[13] *Ibid.*, p. 179.

[14] *Ibid.*, pp. 179–180.

[15] *Shakai undō no jōkyō*, 1942, p. 983.

[16] *Ibid.*

[17] *Tokkō geppō*, Jan., 1944, pp. 80–81.

[18] *Tokkō geppō*, Nov., 1942, pp. 60–62, and *Shakai undō no jōkyō*, 1942, pp. 972, 975. About Kim Tu-bong see Yun Il-mo and Sŏ Pyŏng-gon, "Kim Tu-bong chusŏk ui t'ujaeng-sa" [History of President Kim Tu-bong's Struggles], *Shinch'ŏnji*, Mar., 1946, pp. 205–207. Kim Tu-bong later became vice-chairman of the North Korean People's Committee and then president of the Supreme People's Congress in North Korea. See also the same authors' "Tongnip Tongmaeng ui chŏngch'i nosŏn kwa chujang" [Political Beliefs and the Claims of the Independence League], *ibid.*, pp. 208–209.

[19] According to a Chinese author, the Korean Volunteers Army was ordered

by the Chinese Communists into Manchuria to join with the Soviet Russian army. Li Fang-ch'ên, *Chungkuo chintai-shih* [History of Modern China] (Taipei, Wuchou Publishing Co., 1956), II, 977.

[20] *Paekbŏm ilji: Kim Ku chasŏjŏn* [Memoirs of Paekbŏm: Autobiography of Kim Ku] (Seoul: 1947), p. 344.

[21] *Shakai undō no jōkyō,* 1942, pp. 952–953; *Shisō ihō,* No. 25 (Dec., 1940), pp. 51–54.

[22] *Shisō geppō,* No. 71 (May, 1940), pp. 174–193.

[23] *Op. cit.,* p. 345.

[24] *Ibid.,* pp. 345–346. Kim says that the Chinese Women's Wartime Assistance Society headed by Madame Chiang Kai-shek donated 100,000 yuan for the Restoration Army (p. 347).

[25] Reprinted in *Shisō ihō,* No. 25, pp. 54–55.

[26] *Shakai undō no jōkyō,* 1942, p. 983.

[27] *Mujang tongnip undong pisa* [Secret History of the Armed Independence Movement] (Seoul, 1948 [?]), pp. 205–207.

[28] Paek Kang-un, "Brief History of the Activities of the Provisional Government after the Hungk'ou Incident," in Aeguk Tongji Wonhohoe, *Hanguk tongnip undong-sa* [History of Korean Independence Movement] (Seoul, 1956), pp. 373–374.

[29] *Ibid.,* p. 374; Ko Chih-feng, *Ch'ao-hsien ko-ming-shi* [The Korean Revolution] (Shanghai, Commercial Press, 1945), p. 41.

[30] *Op. cit.,* p. 355.

[31] *Tokkō geppō,* Nov., 1944, pp. 71–72.

[32] The Koreans had not been subject to a draft until 1943. The Japanese government instituted the "student volunteer" system to mobilize Korean students in Feb., 1938. The draft of Koreans began officially in Aug., 1943. "Clearly, among the 250,000 volunteers, there were some solicitations and coercions by the head of prefectures or police chiefs in order to boost their records." Minami Jirō Denki Kankōkai [Editorial Committee of the Biography of Minami Jirō], *Minami Jirō* (Tokyo, 1957), p. 468. Here the implication was that most of the volunteers were true volunteers. Most Koreans agree, however, that the so-called student volunteer system was nothing but a façade. Minami was governor-general of Korea from 1936 to 1942.

[33] The hazardous experience of escaping from a Japanese camp to reaching Chungking is vividly recalled by Chang Chun-ha in a leading Korean magazine, *Sasangae,* VIII, No. 1 (Jan., 1960), 97–105; No. 2 (Feb., 1960), 212–220; No. 3 (Mar., 1960), 216–225; No. 5 (May, 1960), 268–276 (dealing with the experience of receiving "training" at Linch'uan); No. 12 (Dec., 1960), 252–267 (dealing with the bitter experience at Chungking). Chang is now editor of this magazine.

[34] For jubilant remarks about them see Kim Ku, *op. cit.,* p. 347.

[35] *Sasangae,* VIII, No. 12, 258.

[36] *Ibid.*

[37] *Ibid.,* pp. 266–267; Kim Ku, *op. cit.,* pp. 247–350; Paek Kang-un, *op. cit.,* pp. 380–381.

[38] *Op. cit.,* pp. 352–353.

[39] Warren Y. Kim, Fifty-Year History of the Koreans in America, pp. 399–

410. The Provisional Government subsequently appointed Rhee chairman of the Korean Commission in Washington. Kim Ku, *op. cit.*, p. 345.

[40] The funds sent to Chungking seem to have been substantial, but there are no exact data available. The Korean units in the California National Guard had 109 members, ranging from thirty to sixty-five years of age. The unit was officially established Apr. 26, 1942, but its activities seem to have been confined to military drills and reviews. Warren Y. Kim, *op. cit.*, pp. 412–420.

[41] *Ibid.*, pp. 428–432.

[42] Robert T. Oliver, *Syngman Rhee: The Man Behind the Myth* (New York, Dodd, Mead, 1954), p. 171.

[43] For Rhee's activities in the 1940's see, *ibid.*, pp. 171–191. According to Oliver, "In the latter part of 1942, Rhee was flatly informed by Dr. [Stanley] Hornbeck that in the opinion of the State Department he was wholly unknown inside Korea and the Provisional Government was no more than a self-constituted club with limited membership among a group of expatriates" (p. 182).

[44] A five-page "Korean Memorial to the United Nations Conference on International Organization at San Francisco, California" dated Apr. 25, 1945, and signed by Minister of Foreign Affairs of the Provisional Government in Chungking, Tjo Sowang (Cho So-ang), is in the Bureau of International Relations Library, University of California, Berkeley. It is very likely that the copy was drafted (or translated) in San Francisco by the "Korean delegation" and printed in the same city.

[45] Among the Koreans were Syngman Rhee, Charles Ho Kim (of Reedley, Calif.), Kingsley Lyu (now of the Library of Congress), and about a dozen members from various groups. Conversation with Mr. Lyu in Washington, Aug., 1959.

NOTES TO CHAPTER 13
Japanese Rule: The Middle Phase

[1] *Na ui kobaek* [My Confessions] (Seoul: Ch'unch'usa, 1948), pp. 138–139.

[2] Reprinted in his *Chosŏn ui hyŏnjae wa changnae* [Korea's Present and Future] (Seoul: Hungmindang, 1923).

[3] *Op. cit.*, pp. 53–54.

[4] *Tonga Ilbo* (Seoul), Nov. 30, 1922.

[5] Printed in *Tonga Ilbo*, Mar. 30, 1923, p. 7.

[6] Issue of Jan. 1, 1924.

[7] Korean Government-General, *Shisei nijūgonen-shi* [History of Twenty-Five Years' Administration] (Seoul, 1935), p. 904.

[8] Korean Government-General, *Shisei sanjūnen-shi* [History of Thirty Years' Administration] (Seoul, 1940), p. 370.

[9] *Shisei nijūgonen-shi*, p. 904.

[10] Korean Government-General, *Shisei nempō* [Annual Report], 1935–1936, p. 88.

[11] Korean Government-General, Bureau of Police Affairs, "Shōwa kyūnen dai rokujūshichikai teikoku gikai setsumei shiryō" [Explanatory Materials for the 67th Imperial Diet] (1934; mimeographed), p. 54; hereinafter cited as Explanatory Materials. *Tonga Ilbo* issued a reprint series of the circuit lectures.

[12] See *Tonga Ilbo,* Dec. 1, 1922, for an advertisement of the contest.

[13] *Tonga Ilbo,* Dec. 17.

[14] *Ibid.*, Feb. 16, 1923.

[15] Editorial Office of the Korean Administration (*Chōsen Gyōsei Henshū Sōkyoku*), *Chōsen tōchi hiwa* [Secret Stories of the Korean Administration] (Tokyo, 1937), pp. 300–301.

[16] Explanatory Materials, table after p. 92; *Shisei nijūgonen-shi,* p. 722.

[17] *Ibid.*, pp. 716–717.

[18] Explanatory Materials, p. 55.

[19] *Ibid.*, pp. 55–56.

[20] Min Won-sik was assassinated by a Korean student in Tokyo in 1921. Min's family had been granted a title of nobility at the time of the annexation.

[21] *Tonga Ilbo,* Mar. 30, 1924.

[22] Issues of Mar. 30 and Apr. 2, 1924. See also Ch'oe Chun, *Hanguk shinmunsa* [History of Korean Newspapers] (Seoul: Iljogak, 1960).

[23] *Tonga Ilbo,* issues of Apr. 11–12, 1924.

[24] Ch'oe Chun, *op. cit.*, pp. 238–239.

[25] *Ibid.*, p. 240.

[26] *Ibid.*

[27] *Ibid.*, pp. 246–248. It was on this day, Apr. 25, 1925, that the Korean Communist party was organized in Seoul.

[28] *Ibid.*, pp. 249–250.

[29] Explanatory Materials, p. 62.

[30] Literally, "Shinganhoe" means "New Trunk Society" ("trunk" as of a tree). Cho Pyŏng-ok says that the intention was to call the organization Shinhanhoe [New Korean Society], but it was decided that "*han*" [Korea] would be too obvious. *Na ui hoegorok* [My Memoirs] (Seoul: Mingyosa, 1959), p. 95. Shinganhoe and Shinhanhoe are pronounced the same way in Japanese, "Shinkankai."

[31] Cf. Robert A. Scalapino and Chong-Sik Lee, "The Origins of the Korean Communist Movement," *Journal of Asian Studies,* XX, No. 1 (Nov., 1960), 9–31, and No. 2 (Feb., 1961), 149–167. The Communists in Korea would have been much stronger had they not been obsessed with factional struggles.

[32] See the Comintern theses on Japan, July 15, 1927, in *The Communist International, 1919–1943: Documents,* ed. Jane Degras (London: Oxford University Press,), II, 399–400. Complete text in *International Press Correspondence,* VIII, No. 1 (Jan. 3, 1928), 15, and No. 2 (Jan. 6), 37.

[33] Korean Government-General, Bureau of Police Affairs, *Dainiji Chōsen kyōsantō jiken* [The Second Korean Communist Party Incident]; in AJAN, Reel 102, frame 8777. Korean Government-General, High Court, Prosecutor's Bureau, Thought Section, *Chōsen shisō undō chōsa shiryō* [Korean Thought Movement Investigation Materials], No. 1 (Seoul, 1932), pp. 7–8.

[34] Korean Government-General, High Court, Prosecutor's Bureau, Thought Section, *Shisō geppō,* II, No. 9 (Dec. 15, 1932); in AJMFA, Reel S 357, p. 2762.

[35] Keijo District Court, Prosecutors' Bureau, *Chōsen kyōsantō jiken* [Korean Communist Party Incident] (Seoul, n.d.).

[36] *Dainiji Chōsen kyōsantō jiken;* in AJAN, Reel 102, frames 8788–8789.

[37] Cf. Kal Hong-gi (Karl Hong Kee) *Wolnam Yi Sangjae sŏnsaeng yakjŏn* [A Short Biography of Wolnam, Yi Sang-jae] (Seoul: Republic of Korea Public Information Office, 1956).

[38] Explanatory Materials, p. 7.

[39] *Ibid.,* p. 74. Affected were 54 elementary schools, 136 middle schools, and 4 colleges.

[40] Sherwood Eddy, whose general sympathy lies with Japan, noted three indictments by the Koreans: the Japanese policy of assimilation or absorption of the Korean people; dictatorship and autocratic rule by an alien power; and the policy of economic discrimination against the Koreans in favor of the Japanese. After examining these charges in detail, Eddy concluded: "It is undoubtedly true that there has been a highly creditable material advance in the Japanese administration of the country, but there seems to be some truth in the threefold Korean contention that the policy of forcible assimilation and absorption has neither been wholly wise nor successful, but has increased the resentment of the people; that the Japanese rule has been too autocratic and dictatorial, and that there has been at least some economic discrimination with the loss of lands by Koreans which might have been prevented." *The Challenge of the East* (New York: Farrar and Rinehart, 1931), p. 157.

NOTES TO CHAPTER 14
Japanese Rule: The Last Phase

[1] Ch'oe Ch'ang-ik, "Chōsen proretaria kaikyū undō" [Korean Proletarian Class Movement] in Korean History Editorial Committee (ed.), *Chōsen minzoku kaihō tōsōshi* [A History of the Korean People's Struggle for Emancipation] (Kyoto, 1952), a Japanese translation of the Korean original (Pyongyang, 1949), pp. 270–273.

[2] Ministry of Home Affairs, Bureau of Security, *Shōwa rokunenjū ni okeru shakai undō no jōkyō* [Condition of Social Movement during 1931] (Tokyo, 1932), p. 1120.

[3] *International Press Correspondence,* IX, No. 8 (Feb. 15, 1929), 132. The entire December Theses (officially, "Resolution of the E.C.C.I. on the Korean Question") are on pp. 130–133. The Colonial Theses are available in Jane Degras (ed.), *The Communist International, 1919–1943: Documents,* ed. Jane Degras (London: Oxford University Press,), II, 526–548.

[4] See *Shakai undō no jōkyō,* 1931, p. 1122.

[5] Explanatory Materials, pp. 60-61.

[6] The Ministry of Justice reported the conversion of 2,403 out of 2,888 "thought criminals" by Mar., 1943.

[7] *Shakai undō no jōkyō,* 1936, pp. 1485–1486; Keikidō Police Department, *Chian jōkyō* [Security Condition], 1939, p. 7.

[8] Since the champion himself was highly nationalistic, this probably was not against his wish. "Champion Son Ki-jŏng was said to have given autographs to foreigners in Germany signing his name 'Son Ki-jŏng, Korea.' The two champions . . . acted as though they were receptive to the ideas of some nationalists." *Shakai undō no jōkyō,* 1936, pp. 1484–1485.

[9] Ch'oe Chun, *Hanguk shinmunsa* [History of Korean Newspapers] (Seoul: Iljogak, 1960), pp. 318–321. *Shakai undō no jōkyō,* 1936, p. 1484; *Chian jōkyō,* p. 7.

[10] The incident is described in detail by Yi Hi-sŭng, one of those who suffered torture and mistreatment by the police. "Chosŏn ŏhakhoe sakŏn," *Sasangge,* July, 1959 to Jan., 1960 (eight monthly installments).

[11] Ch'oe Chun, *op. cit.,* pp. 308–310, 326–329. The government bought the *Tonga Ilbo* and the *Chosŏn Ilbo* for 500,000 yen and 800,000 yen, respectively.

[12] Korean Government-General, *Shisei sanjūnen-shi* [History of Thirty Years' Administration] (Seoul, 1940), pp. 808–811, 827–833.

[13] *Ibid.,* pp. 801–806.

[14] Korean Government-General, High Court, Prosecutor's Bureau, Thought Section, *Shisō ihō* [Thought Monthly Report], No. 15 (July, 1938), pp. 15–38.

[15] *Chian jōkyō,* 1939, p. 8.

[16] *Ibid.,* p. 2.

[17] *Ibid.,* pp. 2–3. There is an implication that students were strongly influenced by cell groups established on the campuses by Communists and socialists.

[18] *Ibid.,* pp. 8–9.

[19] *Ibid.,* p. 86. The price index of commodities rose steadily from a base of 100 in 1933 to 191.37 in 1939 (p. 85).

[20] *Ibid.,* pp. 39–41. In order to eradicate the rumors, police stations and police detachments held numerous round-table meetings on current affairs to indoctrinate the masses as to the might of Japan. In Kyŏnggi Province alone, in the period Sept. 1–15, 1939, according to the police report, 19,050 meetings were held and were attended by 1,614,329 persons (pp. 52–58). See also reports on "crimes concerning wild rumors" and "investigation of scribblings and posters" in *Shisō ihō,* No. 14 (Mar., 1938), pp. 78–96, and No. 15 (July, 1938), pp. 62–71.

[21] *Shisei sanjūnen-shi,* p. 844.

[22] *Ibid.,* p. 850. The same source refers to efforts meant to reform the Christians and stops there, but in fact many ministers, elders, and ordinary Christians were imprisoned for several years because of their refusal to obey the government's instructions.

[23] *Shisō ihō,* No. 16 (Sept., 1938), p. 10.

[24] *Ibid.,* p. 13.

[25] See *Shisō ihō,* No. 22 (Mar., 1940), pp. 214–229. Yi's book on "Korea's

Present and Future" was published in Seoul in 1923. The students were given prison sentences up to two and a half years.

NOTES TO CONCLUSIONS

[1] *Moral Man and Immoral Society: A Study in Ethics and Politics* (New York, Scribner, 1932).

Index

Index